CONSUMER LAW IN SCOTLAND

THIRD EDITION

By

W.C.H. Ervine

Senior Lecturer in Law, University of Dundee

THOMSON

W. GREEN

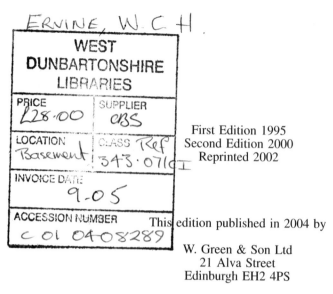
First Edition 1995
Second Edition 2000
Reprinted 2002

This edition published in 2004 by

W. Green & Son Ltd
21 Alva Street
Edinburgh EH2 4PS

www.wgreen.thomson.com

Typeset by Interactive Sciences Limited, Gloucester

Printed in Great Britain by Creative Print and Design

No natural forests were destroyed to make this product;
Only farmed timber was used and replanted

A CIP catalogue record for this book is available from the British Library

ISBN 0414 015576

© W. Green & Son Ltd 2004

The moral rights of the authors have been asserted.

For
Carol and Jonathan

PREFACE TO THE THIRD EDITION

This edition appears after a shorter interval than that which divided the first and second editions. The rapidity of developments in the last four years has been such that the previous edition was becoming seriously outdated. Having remained dormant for several years after its enactment, Pt I of the Consumer Protection Act 1987 has produced a number of interesting decisions of which *A v National Blood Authority* seems to be the most significant. The Sale and Supply of Goods to Consumers Regulations 2002 have made important additions to the remedies available to purchasers of goods while *Clegg v Anderson* has given guidance on the meaning of satisfactory quality and underlined the primacy of rejection as a remedy for consumers who choose to avail themselves of the original Sale of Goods Act remedies. The House of Lords have had their first opportunity to consider the Unfair Terms in Consumer Contracts Regulations in *Director General of Fair Trading v First National Bank plc*. The Enterprise Act 2002 has introduced super complaints and replaced the creaking procedure under Pt III of the Fair Trading Act 1973 with enforcement orders which have the potential to be much more effective. A white paper on the reform of consumer credit law appeared in December 2003 and to its credit the DTI has already begun to implement some of the changes foreshadowed though the details of these were announced too late to allow more than brief reference in the text. Just as final corrections were being made to the text of this edition the DTI published *Extending Competitive Markets: Empowered Consumers, Successful Business*, an important consultation paper on its consumer strategy for the next five years. No comment can be made on that document at this stage other than to encourage readers to study it and to note that it seems likely to ensure that a further edition will be necessary sooner rather than later.

Once again it is a pleasure to thank all those who have helped me. They include officials at government departments and many trading standards officers as well as colleagues in the Department of Law at the University of Dundee. I am also grateful to the staff at W. Green, notably Valerie Malloch, and Rachel Cryer who efficiently saw the book through the production process.

I have tried to state the law as May 7, 2004 though it has been possible to refer to some later developments.

W.C.H. Ervine
Dundee
July 2004

PREFACE TO THE SECOND EDITION

In the five years since the first edition there have been a number of developments in the field of consumer protection which have made it worth producing a new edition. Inevitably there have been more judicial decisions and legislation. In the latter area probably the most significant has been the revised Unfair Terms in Consumer Contracts Regulations 1999 which widen the range of organisations which can seek interdicts to prevent the use of unfair terms. Local government has been reorganised thereby altering the organisation of enforcement. Potentially the most significant development is the White Paper, *Modern markets: Confident consumers* published in 1999. This is the first White Paper to deal with consumer protection and to find any other official document of similar importance in this field one must go back to the Molony Report of 1962. The White Paper promises much, how much will be delivered remains to be seen.

Once again it is a pleasure to thank all those who have helped me. These include officials at various government departments, especially the Office of Fair Trading, and many trading standards officers. I am also indebted to colleagues in the Department of Law at the University of Dundee and the staff of the Law Library who have been unfailingly helpful. I am also grateful for the help and encouragement of the staff at W. Green.

I have tried to state the law as at April 6, 2000 though it has been possible to add some references to developments after that date.

W.C.H. Ervine
Dundee
June 2000

PREFACE TO THE FIRST EDITION

This book attempts to set out the law relating to consumer protection in Scotland. Consumer protection is a recent development and much of the law originates in statutes having application throughout the United Kingdom. While there are a number of good books on the subject they approach the area from the point of view of English practitioners. It seemed to me that there was scope for a book which stated the law in Scotland. Where the law is statutory there are often Scottish decisions interpreting it; and the common law still has an important role to play. In addition, the separateness of the Scottish legal system also has an impact.

The term consumer protection is not a precise one and there can be legitimate difference of opinion as to what material should be covered in such a work. My approach has been to deal with the protection afforded to private consumers of goods and services. It could be objected that even within that definition of the subject there are gaps. This is particularly true when considering the area of services where very little is said, for example, about the important topic of financial services. The answer to this criticism is purely pragmatic: space does not allow everything to be covered; and, in any event, there are excellent specialist works in this area.

Consumer principles are increasingly being applied to areas not normally associated with consumer protection such as the provision of services by the State. Consumer organisations have for some time been dealing with the operation of the courts, the social security system and education. A tentative look at this new aspect of consumer protection has been taken but once again constraints of space have dictated that it should be brief.

I am indebted to numerous people for their help. Over many years staff at the National and Scottish Consumer Councils and trading standards officers have been ready to answer my queries as have officials in various government departments, notably the Office of Fair Trading. My colleagues in the Department of Law at the University of Dundee, and in other departments, have been extremely helpful. Although, with the passage of time, there have been many changes in relation to advertising, trade practices and the institutions of consumer protection, it would not be right to omit mention of my debt to the editors of the *Stair Memorial Encyclopaedia of the Laws of Scotland,* especially Mr Hamish McN. Henderson. Their assistance with my articles on consumer protection and advertising made work in those areas for this book much easier. Judith Pearson of the University of

Aberdeen was good enough to read a draft of Chapter 9, and saved me from a number of errors. Needless to say, the errors in the work are solely my responsibility.

I have endeavoured to state the law as at January 5, 1995, though I have anticipated the coming into force on July 1, of the Unfair Terms in Consumer Contracts Regulations 1994, and it has been possible to incorporate some changes which took place after that date.

W.C.H. Ervine
Dundee
July 1995

CONTENTS

TABLE OF CASES

TABLE OF STATUTES

TABLE OF STATUTORY INSTRUMENTS

SCOTTISH STATUTORY INSTRUMENTS

EUROPEAN LEGISLATION

CHAPTER 1

BACKGROUND AND INSTITUTIONS OF CONSUMER PROTECTION

Consumer protection is essentially a modern topic. Indeed it is tempting **1–01** to say that it is a topic that dates only from the 1960s. Even in 1968 it was not sufficiently well developed to merit a chapter in one of the leading Scottish legal textbooks.[1] As in many other countries in Europe, North America and elsewhere, the 1960s were certainly the beginning of a period of substantial development in Britain in the field of consumer protection.[2]

It would be misleading, however, to give the impression that **1–02** consumer protection does not have a lengthy history. One of the oldest forms of consumer protection is what would now be described as weights and measures legislation. There are numerous examples of such legislation by the Scottish Parliament dating from the Middle Ages. The Weights Act 1425 defined the standard stone at 15 lb. Troy, 16 lb. Scots, and under the Weights Act 1540 burghs were required to keep one set of weights for buying and selling, implying that there was a widespread practice of using one set of weights when buying and another when selling. In the same year standard measures for barrels of salmon and herring were instituted by the Measures Act 1540. The Measures and Weights Act 1587 appointed a commission to prepare a universal standard of weights and measures. The results of its efforts appear as the second Measures and Weights Act 1587 which set out the "Mesuris and wechtis and the just quantitie thereof", while in the Justices of the Peace Act 1661 it was laid down that all measures were to conform with the measure of Linlithgow.

The Measures Act 1685 defined three barleycorns set length-ways as **1–03** an inch, 12 inches as a foot, 36 inches as a yard, 37 inches as a Scots eln and 1760 yards as a mile. The purpose of this Act is stated as being "that there should be a fixed standard for measuring and computation of Myles [*sic*] and that the whole Isle of Britain should be under one certain kind of commensuration". The foot so calculated was to be "the only foot by which all workmen, especially Masons, Wrights, Glasiers,

---

[1] See Gloag and Henderson, *Introduction to the Law of Scotland* (7th ed., 1968). Succeeding editions have had such a chapter.
[2] Borrie, *The Development of Consumer Law and Policy—Bold Spirits and Timorous Souls* (Stevens, 1984), p.2.

and others are ordained to measure their work in all time coming, under the pain of ane hundreth pounds *toties quoties*".[3] The importance of weights and measures was demonstrated by reference to them in the Act of Union, which provided that English weights and measures were to be used throughout the United Kingdom.[4]

1–04   The purity of goods is of cardinal importance to the consumer, and since the nineteenth century, legislation on this topic has continued to expand. In 1860 the "Act for Preventing the Adulteration of Articles of Food or Drink" was a mere 14 sections long.[5] This has gradually grown into a vast corpus of law of which the Food Safety Act 1990 is but the tip of a veritable iceberg of legislation, mostly to be found in statutory instruments.

1–05   The merchandise marks legislation, dating originally from 1862,[6] was the ancestor of the Trade Descriptions Act 1968, and was intended to control misleading claims about goods.

1–06   The legislation mentioned above has in common the fact that it invokes the criminal law as a means of consumer protection. Civil law had a much more limited role to play in protecting the consumer. It is sometimes said that the Sale of Goods Act 1893[7] was the first consumer protection statute of this type. Leaving aside the argument that in Scotland it may actually have weakened the consumer's position by importing alien concepts, it is difficult to see it in this light. True, it could be said to have benefited consumers in the sense that it clarified the law and made it more accessible, but, as one might expect in the age of laissez-faire, it left much scope to the parties to a contract to make their own bargain.

1–07   The role of the courts must not be forgotten. Theirs has not, on the whole, been a prominent role in protecting the consumer. However, *Donoghue v Stevenson*[8] has had immense importance for consumers, as for many other groups, and its reverberations continue to be felt. One might also regret that consumers or their advisers have not been more adventurous in invoking the principles of Scots law. On occasion clear invitations to do seem to have been thoughtlessly ignored. For example in *McKay v Scottish Airways Ltd*[9] Lord President Cooper seemed clearly to be pointing to the adoption of a reasonableness test for exclusion

---

[3] I am indebted to Mr H. McN. Henderson, Deputy General Editor of the Stair Memorial Encyclopaedia, for drawing my attention to this material. For a comprehensive list of old statutes, see the General Index to the Act of the Parliaments of Scotland, Weights and Measures, APS xii 1232, 1233.

[4] See the Treaty of Union between Scotland and England 1707, art.XVII.

[5] *i.e.* the Adulteration of Food and Drink Act 1860 (repealed).

[6] See the Merchandise Marks Act 1862 (repealed).

[7] Although the Sale of Goods Act 1893 was passed in 1894 it describes itself as the Sale of Goods Act 1893: see s.64 (repealed).

[8] 1932 S.C. (H.L.) 31; 1932 S.L.T. 317.

[9] 1948 S.C. 254; 1948 S.L.T. 402.

clauses, but this never seems to have been taken up by counsel in any later case.

While one must not ignore the ancient origins of some aspects of **1–08** consumer protection, it was only in the 1960s that it came to have such prominence. If one were seeking an arbitrary point to use as the beginning of the modern era for consumer protection, July 1962, the date of publication of the Molony Report,[10] would be appropriate. This report reviewed a wide range of consumer issues and advocated reform in many areas. The Trade Descriptions Act 1968 can be traced directly to its recommendations and many other legislative reforms were given an initial impetus by its conclusions.

In the four decades since the publication of the Molony Report much **1–09** has been achieved. Legislation on consumer safety, exclusion clauses, consumer credit and various marketing practices has been enacted. Perhaps of more importance, an institutional structure has been erected with the creation by the Fair Trading Act 1973 of the Office of Fair Trading, and the formation of the National Consumer Council which has a vigorous committee, the Scottish Consumer Council.[11]

In the same four decades the voluntary organisations which play such **1–10** an important role have increased in importance and effectiveness. The Consumers' Association was barely eight years old when the Molony Report was published. It has developed into a dynamic organisation not only providing valuable information on products and services but also effectively lobbying for changes in the law. The Citizens' Advice Bureaux have expanded their network; and in a number of cities consumer groups have been set up under the aegis of the National Federation of Consumer Groups now merged in the National Consumer Federation.

The last two decades have seen important changes in the techniques **1–11** employed to achieve the ends of consumer protection. Administrative control has become more prominent and, perhaps somewhat paradoxically, self-regulation has expanded. The advertising industry is the most striking example of control by self-regulation, but self-regulation has come to play a significant part in other areas such as package holidays, servicing and repair of electrical goods and the car trade. In the consumer white paper *Modern Markets: Confident Consumers* published in July 1999, the Government indicated that they intend to place more emphasis on codes of practice as a way of improving trading standards.[12] There are still many reforms that are necessary as the following pages will, at least, imply. At present the prospects for reform are good following the publication of the white paper. This is the first

---

[10] Final Report of the Committee on Consumer Protection (the Molony Report) Cmnd. 1781 (1962).
[11] See paras 1–35—1–41.
[12] *Modern markets: confident consumers*, Cm. 4410 (1999), Ch.4.

thorough review of consumer protection since the *Molony Report* over 30 years ago and promises a number of reforms.

1–12   As pointed out above, one of the most important developments in the protection of the consumer in recent years has been the creation of a structure of organisations dealing with the subject. To properly understand the operation of consumer protection requires some knowledge of this structure and the next section of this chapter therefore deals with this.

INSTITUTIONS OF CONSUMER PROTECTION

CENTRAL GOVERNMENT AND THE SCOTTISH EXECUTIVE

1–13 On May 12, 1999 for the first time for almost three hundred years a Scottish Parliament met in Edinburgh. This devolved Parliament was created by the Scotland Act 1998 and has wide legislative competence. It can legislate within Scotland on all matters except those that have been reserved to the Westminster Parliament. However, many areas of consumer protection are among these reserved matters. The precise list is set out in Schedule 5, ss.C7 to C9. Most of these are topics which have been the subject of UK-wide legislation. Section C7 is entitled "Consumer Protection" and covers the regulation of the sale and supply of goods and services and fair trading. Section C8 covers product safety and liability as well as product labelling except in relation to food, agricultural and horticultural produce and fish. Section C9 covers weights and measures, units and standards of weight and measurement. Important as these issues are it should be noted that there are several important areas related to consumer protection which are within the competence of the Edinburgh Parliament. The exclusion of food, agricultural and horticultural produce and fish from the reserved matters in C8 has just been noted. It must also be remembered that the Scottish Parliament can legislate concerning the courts, and civil and criminal procedure. These areas impinge directly upon consumer protection. One has only to think of the importance of small claims procedure and the legislation on compensation orders for victims of crime in relation to consumer redress. Also, as we shall see later in this chapter, local government is a devolved matter. As much important enforcement work is carried out by local authorities, the Scottish Parliament and Executive could have an important, if indirect, influence on consumer protection.

1–14   While the role of the Scottish Parliament and Executive in consumer protection should not be overlooked, the government department with the greatest responsibility for consumer protection is the Westminster Department of Trade and Industry (DTI) many of whose functions are carried out on a United Kingdom basis. The DTI is responsible for policy and legislation on trading standards, weights and measures, consumer credit and consumer safety. It is also the sponsoring department for the National Consumer Council, including the Scottish Consumer Council, the Nationalised Industry Consumer Councils, and the British Standards Institution. Competition policy, which is also relevant to consumer protection, is the responsibility of this department. These issues are dealt with by the Department's Consumer and Competition Policy Division which is headed by a junior minister. Where Scottish issues are involved the DTI will liaise with the Scottish Executive.

THE OFFICE OF FAIR TRADING

One of the most important organisations with consumer protection **1–15** functions is the Office of Fair Trading (OFT). The Fair Trading Act 1973 created the post of Director-General of Fair Trading and the administrative structure created to support that post was known as the Office of Fair Trading although, strictly speaking, it had no statutory basis. The various functions set out in the Fair Trading Act were given to the holder of the office of Director General although it was common to refer interchangeably to the Director-General and the Office of Fair Trading. With effect from April 1, 2003, the Office of Fair Trading came into existence as a corporate body and took over the functions of the Director-General of Fair Trading. The creation of the OFT was the result of s.1 of the Enterprise Act 2002, s.2 of which abolished the office of Director-General of Fair Trading.

While the Enterprise Act makes important organisational changes the **1–16** role of the OFT is essentially the same as that of the Director-General of Fair Trading under the Fair Trading Act. As the OFT's leaflet, *A Guide to the Office of Fair Trading* puts it: "Our goal is to make markets work well for consumers. Markets work well when fair-dealing businesses are in open and vigorous competition with each other for custom." This is not dissimilar to the rationale given for the creation of the post of Director General of Fair Trading during the second reading of the Fair Trading Bill when the minister observed:

> "Consumer sovereignty requires that the consumer should be adequately and accurately informed and adequately protected against unfair or misleading marketing techniques, and adequately protected, finally, against abuse of market power, monopoly or aspects of imperfect competition".[13]

In both cases the importance of combining consumer protection and competition law functions in the same organisation was stressed. The current approach gives greater emphasis to the significance of properly

---

[13] 848 HC official Report (5th series), col.454.

functioning markets not just for consumers but also for business and the wider economy.

1–17   The OFT is run by a board which Sch.1 of the Enterprise Act provides shall consist of a chairman and no fewer than four other members appointed by the Secretary of State. One of these may be the chief executive of the OFT and that is the case at present as one of the members is Ms Penny Boys, the current chief executive. Members are appointed for terms of up to five years and may be reappointed. The current chairman is John Vickers, an academic economist, who was the last Director-General of Fair Trading. In addition to the chairman and chief executive there are five non-executive directors with backgrounds in law, business and consumer affairs. The role of the board is to decide the strategy of the OFT: it sets its priorities and plans and is responsible for its performance. It is directly involved in decisions on individual market studies but would take enforcement decisions only on cases of strategic importance.

1–18   The day to day operation of the OFT is carried out by the permanent staff who are civil servants. At March 31, 2003, there were 631 permanent staff compared with 493 at the end of 2001.[14] The annual budget was £51 million in 2002–03 and that for 2003–04 is £55 million. The office is organised into six divisions. Of the three main divisions that on Markets and Policy Initiatives carries out studies to explore how markets and market practices operate. The Consumer Regulation Enforcement division enforces consumer law by taking action against traders who breach legislation, by collaborating with other regulators and by encouraging improved standards through codes of conduct. The Competition Enforcement division investigates possible cartels, seeks to deter abuse of dominant positions in particular markets and assesses the impact of proposed mergers. These divisions are supported by three other divisions. The Communications division keeps consumers, business and professional advisers informed of the work of the office. The Legal division advises not only on the use of the Office's powers but on legislative proposals both domestic and European. The Resources and Services division deals with staffing, training and finance.

1–19   The general functions of the OFT are broadly similar to those of the Director General of Fair Trading though they have been enhanced in important respects by the Enterprise Act. Section 5 of that Act directs it to obtain and keep under review the information needed to carry out its functions effectively. Section 6 makes clear in a way that earlier legislation did not that the OFT may not only inform the public of the benefits of competition and give them information and advice about any of its functions but may also publish educational materials and carry out other educational activities. The Office also advises government and public authorities on possible changes to the law relating to their

---

[14] Office of Fair Trading: Annual Report and Resource Accounts 2002–03 HC 906 p.89.

functions.[15] It is also a general function of the OFT to promote good practice in carrying out economic activities which may affect the economic interests of consumers and, in particular, to approve codes of practice.[16] This reflects an important aspect of the OFT's approach which is currently being given increased emphasis and which is discussed in more detail in Ch.11.

In addition to these general functions the OFT has various specific **1–20** functions. While this chapter concentrates on the consumer protection functions on the OFT and it is not appropriate to give detailed consideration to its competition functions, it is important to note that a major part of its resources are devoted to the investigation of cartels, abuse of dominant market positions and mergers. As the OFT points out, this work is of the utmost importance for consumers. A recent practical example was total fines of £18.6 million imposed on 10 companies for fixing the price of Umbro replica football kit in breach of the Competition Act 1998. The uncovering this cartel has led to direct benefits for consumers in the form of considerable reductions in the cost of these kits.

An innovation of the Enterprise Act is the procedure in s.11 for a **1–21** "designated consumer body" to make a "super-complaint" to the OFT.[17] This creates a formal procedure by which consumer organisations can bring what they see as some failure in a market for goods and services which is significantly harming the interests of consumers to the attention of the appropriate regulator. It does not prevent anyone else complaining to the OFT but the advantage of being able to use this procedure is that it lays down a timetable for dealing with the complaint. Section 11(2) provides that the OFT must within 90 days of receiving the complaint respond stating how it proposes to deal with it. Only "designated" consumer bodies can make super-complaints and to achieve this status an organisation must "represent the interests of consumers of any description" and the other criteria set out in the *Guidance For Prospective Designated Super Complaints Bodies* published by the Secretary of State for Trade and Industry and available on the DTI's website. This guidance stresses the need for organisations to be independent, experienced and capable of drafting a formal super-complaint. The Consumers' Association, the National Association of Citizens' Advice Bureaux and the National Consumer Council have been designated.[18]

---

[15] Enterprise Act 2002 s.7.
[16] *ibid.*, s.8.
[17] Using powers in s.205 of the Enterprise Act 2002 the procedure has been extended to allow super-complaints to other regulators by the The Enterprise Act (Super-complaints to Regulators) Order 2003 SI 1368.
[18] The Enterprise Act 2002 (Bodies Designated to make Super-complaints) Order 2004 SI 2004/1517

1-22   Before these organisations were formally designated to make super-complaints the system had been operating informally for some time and the OFT has considered four super-complaints. The first about private dentistry was submitted by the Consumers' Association and resulted in a formal study of that market by the OFT's Markets and Policy Initiatives Division. Its report[19] advocated various reform measures such as the provision of better information for patients and the relaxation of certain regulations relating to who could provide dental services. The National Association of Citizens' Advice Bureaux submitted a complaint about doorstep selling which has resulted in a full-scale investigation[20] and in December 2003 the Consumers' Association submitted a complaint about care homes. A complaint about problems experienced in the mail consolidation market which deals with mass mailings was made by the industry watchdog Postwatch. After consulting Postcomm, the industry regulator, the OFT took the matter no further as it was satisfied that Postcomm could deal with the problems through its licensing controls.

1-23   Under Pt 8 of the Enterprise Act 2002 the OFT has important powers to discipline traders who infringe certain domestic or European Community consumer protection legislation. These powers replace the powers under Pt III of the Fair Trading Act and the Stop Now Orders introduced by the Stop Now Orders (EC Directive) Regulations 2001.[21] These powers which are shared with other enforcers are discussed in Ch.11 on the control of trading practices.[22] The Consumer Credit Act 1974 introduced a general licensing system for the credit industry and the OFT operates it.[23]

1-24   The Director-General has acquired further functions under the Estate Agents Act 1979 which gives him wide powers to control the activities of estate agents. The keystone of this is what may be termed negative licensing. Unlike the credit industry where entry is conditional on having a licence, anyone may set up in business as an estate agent. The Director-General, however, has power to prevent a person continuing to carry on such a business in certain circumstances. Section 4 of the Act provides that he may issue warning notices where an estate agent has failed to comply with his obligations under the Act. These included compliance with the rules relating to interest on clients' accounts, informing clients of his charging methods and observing the prohibition on taking pre-contractual deposits or having a personal interest in a transaction. A warning notice states that failure to comply with the

---

[19] *The private dentistry market in the UK*, Office of Fair Trading, March 2003 OFT630.

[20] *Doorstep selling: A report on the market study*, May 2004, OFT716

[21] SI 2001/1422.

[22] Most of Pt II of the Fair Trading Act 1973 which created the Consumer Protection Advisory Committee, defunct these many years, has been repealed. Only those sections necessary to enforce the two remaining orders made under this legislation remain.

[23] For details see Ch.9.

statutory requirements will render the agent unfit to carry on estate agency work and further failure to observe these requirements may result in a banning order being made under s.23. Such an order may also be made by the Director-General where an estate agent has been convicted of offences involving fraud, dishonesty or breaches of the Estate Agents Act or has committed discrimination in the course of estate agency work.

In addition to regulating the consumer credit market the OFT also **1–25** enforces a wide range of other consumer protection legislation which is discussed in other parts of this book. As we shall see it has important powers under the Control of Misleading Advertising Regulations 1988 to stop deceptive or misleading advertising and under the Distance Selling Regulations to protect the interests of home shoppers. One of its greatest successes has been in the exercise of its powers to control unfair contract terms under the Unfair Terms in Consumer Contracts Regulations 1999.[24]

Public Utility Schemes[25]

Public utilities, many of which have recently been privatised, create **1–26** special problems of regulation. The solution adopted has been to create a statutory regulator who in the original privatisation statutes was usually given the title of Director-General. More recently as these arrangements have been revised the model of an office with a corporate identity has been adopted. In the field of communications the Office of Communications Act 2002 set up Ofcom. The Office of Gas Supply (OFGAS) are and the Office of Electricity Regulation (OFFER) were amalgamated in June 1999 to form the Office of Gas and Electricity Markets (OFGEM). These industries have also had consumer organisations such as the Gas Consumers' Council and the regional Electricity Consumer Councils. Consumer interests in the field of communications are now dealt with by an independent consumer council and the gas and electricity bodies have been replaced by a single energy consumer council.[26] One of the functions of the utility regulators is, in conjunction with other bodies, to protect the interests of consumers.

When the Scottish water authorities were originally set up following **1–27** local government reorganisation it was not thought appropriate to have a regulator for what was still a public service. The interests of consumers were looked after by the Scottish Water and Sewerage Customers Council. A regulator, the Office of the Water Industry Commissioner for Scotland, was created by Pt II of the 1999 Water Industry Act whose primary role is to promote the interests of customers of Scottish Water (the body which was formed by the amalgamation of

---

[24] For more detail see Ch.10.
[25] For further details see Ch.8.
[26] See Ch.8.

the three regional water authorities) and he has taken over the functions of the Council.

Local Government

1–28 Much of the day-to-day enforcement of consumer protection measures is carried out by local government. The reorganisation of local government carried out by the Local Government (Scotland) Act 1994 created 29 single purpose district councils in place of the two-tier structure of regions and district councils. The three island authorities also remain in existence. As the weights and measures authorities for their areas, these new councils have statutory responsibility for the enforcement of much consumer protection legislation. They are responsible for the enforcement of weights and measures legislation, labelling and standards requirements of food and drugs, the Trade Descriptions Act 1968 and the Consumer Credit Act 1974. This list includes only the better known pieces of consumer legislation which contain provisions impinging directly on everyday concerns. The enforcement of weights and measures legislation, for example, helps to ensure that the customer receives a kilogramme when he or she requests that amount, or a pint of beer or a quarter gill as appropriate. They also enforce many other pieces of legislation as diverse as the Agriculture Act 1970, dealing with fertilisers and animal feeding stuffs, the Poisons Act 1972 and the Video Recordings Act 1984, to say nothing of many pieces of subordinate legislation often made under the European Communities Act 1972. One advantage of reorganisation has been that it has resulted in all the consumer protection functions of local government being carried out by one council. Previously, the regions were the weights and measures authorities and carried out the bulk of consumer protection work, while the former district councils had responsibilities in the field of food hygiene and the licensing of dealers in second-hand goods under the Civic Government (Scotland) Act 1982.

1–29 To carry out these duties the district councils have set up trading standards or consumer protection services. These are almost invariably located in larger departments often termed environmental health and consumer protection departments, or even protective services departments. The use of the term trading standards service indicates the modern approach to the task which is seen as being neutral between traders and consumers. It recognises that the function of a trading standards department in ensuring fair trading is important not only to consumers but also to those traders who meet their legal obligations. Those who do not trade fairly harm not only consumers but also those traders who act honestly.

1–30 The size of the larger Scottish regions meant that a service of considerable sophistication could often be provided. Strathclyde Region was probably the largest regional consumer protection department in Europe. It was able to build up an impressive unit dealing with unlicensed moneylending. Lothian Region's department had considerable success with specialist task forces such as the Vehicle Enquiry Team. As many authorities are now much smaller than the old regional authorities there must be concern about their ability to deal as effectively with some aspects of their functions as the regions were able to do. However, s.58 of the Local Government (Scotland) Act 1994 permits two or more councils to combine in providing services and it may be that trading standards functions could be provided on a joint basis.

In addition to their statutory duties, trading standards services provide **1–31** advice to traders on how to comply with legislation. Most also provide advice to consumers. Some have shop front premises where consumers can obtain shopping advice as well as advice about their legal rights. With the creation in the sheriff court of the small claims procedure which permits lay representation, several services have been accompanying consumers to court and acting as their advocates.

Local Authorities Coordinators of Regulatory Services (LACORS)

LACORS (the Local Authorities Co-ordinators of Regulatory Services) **1–32** is the new name for the organisation formerly known as LACOTS. It was set up in 1978 to co-ordinate the enforcement activities of trading standards services and later took on the additional responsibility of co-ordinating food enforcement. Its new name reflects the emerging widened regulatory remit that since April 2002 includes the Registration Service for Births, Deaths and Marriages, public entertainment licensing, liquor licensing and Health and Safety at Work. It provides machinery for trading standards departments to liaise with the Government and industry on technical matters; co-ordinate local practice to ensure uniform enforcement of legislation; and to advise local authorities on the interpretation and enforcement of legislation. A central feature of the work of LACORS is the "home authority principle".

The home authority principle is designed to avoid businesses which **1–33** may have offices and factories in several different parts of the country receiving conflicting advice or being subject to differing interpretations of the law from various local authorities. The main feature of the principle is to prevent infringements by offering advice at source and by encouraging enforcement authorities and enterprises to work in liaison with a particular authority called "the home authority". This is the authority where the decision making base of the enterprise is located and can be the head office, the factory, a service centre or the place of importation. The role of the home authority is to provide advice on policy issues, compliance with the law and adherence to standards and codes of practice. It is the link between enforcement authorities and originating authorities with whom they must liaise. Originating authorities are only relevant where an enterprise operates a decentralised structure and decisions may be made at a number of different places. It will monitor premises within its area at which goods or services are produced. It keeps the home authority informed about significant findings and, if there are problems, it will liaise with it to solve them.

1–34   Each local authority enforces the law in its area. Under the home authority principle when enforcement authorities detect breaches of the law they should consider consultation with the home or originating authority before embarking on detailed investigations or legal action. They should also routinely inform the home authority of enforcement action which they have taken.

INDEPENDENT AND VOLUNTARY ORGANISATIONS

The National Consumer Council

1–35   The National Consumer Council (NCC) was set up in 1975 as a non-departmental public body (or quango) following the White Paper, *A National Consumers' Agency*.[27] It replaced the Consumer Council which, on the recommendation of the Molony Committee,[28] had been set up by the Government in 1963 but abolished in 1971. Technically, it is a company limited by guarantee and its Memorandum of Association states that its purpose is:

> "to promote action for furthering and safeguarding the interests of consumers, to ensure that those who take decisions which will affect the consumer can have a balanced and authoritative view of the interests of consumers before them and to insist that the interests of all consumers including the inarticulate and disadvantaged are taken into account."

1–36   The memorandum then goes into more detail about how these purposes are to be achieved. The Council shall make representations of the views of consumers to central and local government and industry (including the nationalised industries). It may also represent consumers on appropriate government and other organisations including international organisations. While it does not give advice or information to individual consumers, one of the Council's functions is to provide information and advice to consumers in general and to comment on the adequacy of consumer advice services and support facilities.

1–37   This work is directed by a Council of 13 members chaired by a part-time chairman. Members of the Council, who are appointed by the Secretary of State for Trade and Industry, come from a geographically wide range of places and diverse backgrounds. The chairmen of the associate councils, the Scottish and Welsh Consumer Councils, and the General Consumer Council of Northern Ireland are members. There are

[27] Cmnd. 5726 (1975).
[28] Final Report of the Committee on Consumer Protection, Cmnd. 1781 (1962), Ch.20.

usually members with backgrounds in trading standards, the legal profession, industry and commerce and other consumer organisations. The full-time staff of 43, including professional and secretarial staff, are located in central London.

Given the distinctive socio-economic, geographic and cultural issues **1–38** as well as the separate legal, administrative and educational system in Scotland, it was appropriate that a Scottish Consumer Council should have been set up. There is also a similar Welsh Council. The Scottish Consumer Council (SCC), which has offices in Glasgow, is technically a sub-committee of the NCC. Its structure is similar to the parent body. There is a chairman and 13 members who are appointed by the Secretary of State for Trade and Industry in consultation with the Secretary of State for Scotland. All are part-time and they have a similar range of backgrounds to the members of the NCC.

Funding comes mainly from a modest grant-in-aid from the Depart- **1–39** ment of Trade and Industry which provided 73 per cent of the NCC's income in 2002–03. The rest came from research projects carried out for various organisations, mostly in the public sector. In the case of the SCC slightly under half of its income comes in the form of a grant-in-aid channelled through the NCC.[29] In 2002–03 it raised the other half from research projects. In the first edition of this book the fear was expressed that pressure from the Government to generate more income from non-government sources might compromise the independence of the SCC and deflect them from their main role. Happily, this does not seem to have happened.

The NCC and its associate councils adopt the same strategy for **1–40** carrying out their task. As they have no statutory powers they can only achieve their objectives by persuasion. They have built up a formidable record of achievement based on thorough research and effective lobbying and campaigning. They have also been instrumental in assisting other consumer organisations. For example, the NCC has played a central role in the creation and growth of the Consumer Congress.

Since its creation the Scottish Consumer Council has come to play a **1–41** prominent part in public affairs in Scotland. Much of its work involves responding to proposals of the Government but it has also, where possible, attempted to set its own agenda. Good examples of this have occurred in legal reform where the SCC was prominent in the campaign for a small claims procedure and the inclusion of Scotland in the Unfair Contract Terms Act 1977. More recently, it has argued strongly for a review of the civil justice system in Scotland and has supported the creation of the Scottish Sheriff Court Users' Group. It has not confined itself to a narrow definition of consumer issues. Over the years it has done a good deal of work on education and was one of the few

---

[29] SCC, Annual Review 2002–03, p.6.

organisations to argue strongly for the introduction of school boards. It has also built up a strong reputation in health issues and food matters. Given the geography of Scotland it has also paid particular attention to the problems of consumers living in rural areas, as its report Consumer Problems in Rural Areas demonstrates.

Nationalised Industry Consumer Councils

1–42 A diminishing range of goods and services is provided for consumers by nationalised industries. These industries are statutory corporations invested with monopoly, or near monopoly, powers, and this makes it especially important that there should be scrutiny of their activities in the consumer interest. As the Molony Report noted, "the evils of monopolistic control are not the exclusive prerogative of private enterprise".[30] The consumer interest in many of these industries has been represented by the creation of consumer or consultative councils. The consumer bodies associated with the railways are the Rail Passengers' Council which co-ordinates the local Rail Passengers' Committees one of which covers Scotland. They were created by the Transport Act 2000. The interests of users of postal services are protected by the Postwatch and its regional councils one of which is the Postwatch Scotland. Postwatch was set up by the Postal Services Act 2000 as the successor to the Post Office Users' Council.

Consumers' Association

1–43 The Consumers' Association, best known as the publisher of *Which?* magazine, was founded in 1957. In 1987 it became a charity and changed its name to the Association for Consumer Research, a private company limited by guarantee which is entitled to omit the word "limited" from its name. With effect from April 1, 1995 the name again became the Consumers' Association. This company carries on research and charitable functions and, since April 1, 1995 also carries on campaigning functions. A subsidiary, Which? Ltd., now carries on the trading functions which consist primarily of publishing both books and magazines. The Consumers' Association is financed by members' subscriptions, donations and fees for advisory services which it undertakes and the trading profits of its subsidiary. In 2003 the Consumers' Association had 651,000 members, and 976,000 subscribers to its magazines.[31]

1–44 While the Consumers' Association is best known for *Which?*, it also publishes other magazines such as *Holiday Which?*, *Gardening Which?*, *Which? Way to Health, Drugs and Therapeutics Bulletin* and *Legal Services*. These contain reports of comparative tests of products and

---

[30] Final Report of the Committee on Consumer Protection, Cmnd. 1781 (1962), p.296.
[31] Annual Report 2002–03, p.16.

services which have been carried out completely independently. Consumers' Associations' publications carry no advertising and tests are carried out on products purchased anonymously. It also publishes a wide range of books such as *What to Do When Someone Dies* and *The Which? Hotel Guide.* In addition to this work, the Consumers' Association has increasingly been involved in campaigning. It was prominent in the campaigns for the Unfair Contract Terms Act 1977 and has vigorously campaigned on safety issues.

The National Consumer Federation

The National Consumer Federation was formed in 2001 by the amalgamation of Consumer Congress and the National Federation of Consumer Groups. It encourages and co-ordinates the work of voluntary, independent local consumer groups, individual consumers and those who have an interest in consumer affairs through other organisations. It represents their views nationally. NCF and the local Groups are non-party political and non-profit making. The National Federation of Consumer Groups was established in 1963 to bring together local Consumer Groups which were first set up from 1961 with the encouragement of Consumers' Association, publishers of Which?. Its individual membership scheme was introduced in 1977 for people who do not live near enough to a group. Consumer Congress was a separate organisation, funded by government which organised an annual Congress on consumer matters. Its members were mainly larger organisations, including Trading Standards departments, Age Concern and bodies representing disabled groups. **1–45**

The British Standards Institution

The British Standards Institution, incorporated by royal charter in 1929, is an independent, non-profitmaking body which exists to co-ordinate the production of goods by devising, where possible, national standards. A "British Standard" sets out testing requirements, specifications or measurements with which a product should comply. Such standards are devised after consultation with representatives of manufacturers, distributors and users. Of particular relevance to consumers is the Consumer Standards Advisory Committee, which includes representatives of consumer organisations. **1–46**

The Advertising Standards Authority

The Advertising Standards Authority Ltd (ASA) administers the system of self-regulatory control in the print, cinema and poster media. It is a company limited by guarantee whose directors are its chairman and council members. The chairman, currently Lord Borrie, a former Director General of Fair Trading and professor of law, is appointed by the Advertising Standards Board of Finance Ltd (ASBOF); an independent body created by the advertising industry. ASBOF is obliged by **1–47** its articles of association, before making any appointment, to consult with the Department of Trade and Industry, and the appointment is also made in consultation with, and subject to the agreement of, the existing members of the ASA Council. The ASA articles provide that the chairman is not to be engaged in the business of advertising. It is the chairman who chooses the members of the council, normally totalling 12, of whom at least half must be independent. It is present policy to ensure that the proportion of independent to industry members remains at the maximum permissible level of two to one.

1–48   The functions of the ASA are to oversee the work of the Code of Advertising Practice (CAP) Committee in drafting and amending the British Code of Advertising Practice; to act as an appeal tribunal from the CAP Committee from within the industry; to maintain a procedure for investigating complaints from members of the public; and to publicise the existence of the self-regulatory system of control. The ASA has been funded since 1974 by a surcharge of 0.1 per cent on the cost to the advertiser of advertisements other than those appearing in the classified columns of the press. The surcharge is collected by ASBOF.

EUROPE

The European Union

1–49   As with so many areas of law, consumer protection is influenced by the UK's membership of the European Union (EU). Our accession to the EU (or the European Communities as it was then known) coincided with the development of its consumer policy and the creation of its consumer institutions. These institutions are described in Ch.2 (see paras 2-11 to 2-13).

Bureau Europeen des Union de Consommateurs

1–50   To try to ensure that the consumer voice is heard in the councils of the EU, Europe's consumer organisations set up the Bureau Europeen des Union de Consommateurs (BEUC). It is a lobbying organisation with a small staff and is based in Brussels. Its methods are similar to those of the NCC.

CHAPTER 2

EUROPEAN DIMENSION

An English judge once said memorably that EC law was like an **2–01**
"incoming tide. It flows into the estuaries and up the rivers. It cannot be
held back. Parliament has decreed that the Treaty [of Rome] is
henceforward to be part of our law."[1] Like other areas of law, consumer
protection is subject to this process and it is important to appreciate its
impact. For the EC has had an impact on the development of consumer
protection law and policy in the UK. It is an impact which has produced
benefits but can also be argued to have had disadvantages. In this
chapter the origins and implementation of this policy are considered as
well as its benefits and disadvantages.

In an economic community it is a remarkable irony that consumer **2–02**
protection has not had a high profile. There were only four references to
consumers in the original treaty and, with one exception, the translation
is probably not accurate. "End user" rather than "consumer" would
probably be more appropriate. This, no doubt, is explained by the fact
that the Communities were the result of negotiations which took place
in the 1950s, well before consumer protection became the conspicuous
issue that it did in the mid-1960s and 1970s.

The term "consumer protection" first appeared in Art.100a of the **2–03**
Treaty of Rome, as a result of the Single European Act. This Act did not
accord consumer protection the status of a separate policy of the EC in
the way that environmental policy was recognised. That, however, was
achieved by the Maastricht Treaty on European Union, signed in 1992,
which added a Title XI on consumer protection to the original Treaty.
This now appears in a slightly modified form in Art.153 of the Treaty as
modified by the Amsterdam Treaty.

LEGAL COMPETENCE OF THE EC

When looking at any legislative action of the EC it must always be **2–04**
borne in mind that the EC is not a sovereign state, and so one must
always be able to point to some power in the EC treaties permitting the

---

[1] *H.P. Bulmer Ltd and Showerings Ltd v 1. Bollinger SA and Champagne Lanson Pére et
Fils* [1974] 2 All E.R. 1226, *per* Lord Denning at 1231.

action taken. In the field of consumer protection there have, in the past, been some doubts on this score. However, it has long been accepted that where the interests of consumers in health and safety have been at stake the EC has competence.[2] This could be justified by arguments based on the original Art.30 (now Art.28) which are implicitly accepted in the series of cases starting with *Cassis de Dijon*.[3] There had been a little more doubt about legislation dealing with the protection of the economic interests of consumers but, legally, it could be justified by pointing to Art.2 of the original Treaty of Rome which sets out the objectives of the treaty to create a common market and improve living standards. It was argued that differing national laws on advertising, contract terms and marketing practices impede the attainment of a truly common market, and that the improvement of the protection of the consumer is an aspect of a better standard of living. As Professor Bourgoignie has pointed out, "[i]mproving the standard of living . . . could no longer be understood only in a quantitative way (increase in income and purchasing power of individuals) but also qualitatively, aiming to improve, in the widest sense of the term, the living conditions of European citizens."[4]

2–05   With the amendments made to the original treaty by the Single European Act and the Maastricht and Amsterdam Treaties the situation is now clearer. The starting point is Art.3 of the Treaty which sets out the activities which the EC may carry out. Paragraph (h) provides that these include "the approximation of the laws of Member States to the extent required for the functioning of the common market" and para.(t) provides that these may include "a contribution to the strengthening of consumer protection". One then turns to Art.153 (using the new numbering following Amsterdam) which contains the title on consumer protection. This amends this title which was originally inserted by the Maastricht Treaty. It provides in para.1 that:

> "In order to promote the interests of consumers and to ensure a high level of consumer protection, the Community shall contribute to protecting the health, safety and economic interests of consumers, as well as to promoting their right to information, education and to organise themselves in order to safeguard their interests."

2–06   These objectives are to be achieved by two means. The first is by Art.95 (formerly Art.100a) measures relating to the internal market. Such measures can be adopted using the qualified majority voting pro-

---

[2] See Close, "The Legal Basis of the Consumer Protection Programme of the EEC and Priorities for Action", in *Consumer Law in the EEC* (Woodroffe ed., 1984).
[3] *Rewe-Zentrale AC v Budesmonopolverwaltung fur Brantwein* (No.120/78); [1979] E.C.R. 649: see paras 2-33 *et seq.*
[4] Bourgoignie, "European Community Consumer Law and Policy: from Rome to Amsterdam", 1998 Cons. L.J. 443 at 444.

cedures of the Treaty and must "take as a base a high level of protection". In addition, they will be attained by measures which support, supplement and monitor the policy pursued by the Member States. A further important paragraph of Art.153 provides that "[c]onsumer protection requirements shall be taken into account in defining and implementing other Community policies and activities". The reference in Art.153 to supporting and supplementing measures taken by Member States is a reminder that all of this is subject to the principle of subsidiarity. This is now found in Art.5 of the EC Treaty.

This clause, which has been the subject of intense debate, is one of those provisions which can be used by opposing sides in an argument to justify their position. Lord Mackenzie-Stuart, a former President of the European Court of Justice, went so far as to call it "gobbledygook" in a letter to *The Times*.[5] **2–07**

As has been pointed out: **2–08**

"The quest for a definition of subsidiarity is doomed to failure. It has become an intrinsic part of the debate on greater social, political and economic integration, and as such, will be subject to constant evolution, adapting to shifts in policy and opinion. It is a flexible but elusive concept, with the potential both to act as a dynamic for change and as a bulwark of the status quo. The priority for consumers is to ensure that it does not serve as a pretext to block proposals to improve consumer protection at Community level which might otherwise be neglected at national level."[6]

The important point to grasp, which Art.153 supports, is that consumer protection is not just an optional extra for the Community. It is an essential feature of a single market. Such a market can be exploited by the unscrupulous who engage in fraudulent practices across national boundaries. This calls for action at EC level both in the interests of honest traders, who should be protected from such unfair competition, and consumers, who are entitled to protection of their interests. A failure to provide effective protection is bound to weaken consumer confidence and thus the success of the single market. **2–09**

A difficult question is how to decide when action should be taken at Community level and when it should be left to Member States. In a communication to the Council and the European Parliament in October 1992, the Commission proposed three tests to assist in the application of the subsidiarity principle. These were "comparative efficiency", "value added", and "proportionality". In deciding whether there should be Community action the first two would involve the use of a number of criteria, such as whether there was a significant cross-border dimension, **2–10**

---

[5] Dec. 11, 1992.
[6] Gibson, "Subsidiarity: The Implications for Consumer Policy" (1993) 16 J.C.P 323 at 336.

the effects on trade and competition, and the costs of taking action. The proportionality test would be used to ensure that action taken would be no more than necessary to achieve the desired aim. This would require consideration to be given to self-regulatory measures as well as legislation.

INSTITUTIONAL ARRANGEMENTS

2–11 The low status of consumer protection has often been reflected in the institutional arrangements in Brussels. As a result of a heads of state meeting in Paris in 1972 a directorate-general for environment and consumer protection was, for the first time, created in the Commission. After various changes of title the consumer protection functions were moved to a separate Consumer Protection Service with the intention that this service would influence the policies of all directorates which have implications for consumers. In 1995 consumer protection once again became the responsibility of a directorate-general (DG XXIV). In 1998 the mad cow crisis and other health concerns resulted in it being renamed the Directorate-General for Health and Consumer Protection; now commonly referred to as DG Sanco.[7] This reflected the fact that its responsibilities and manpower have been considerably increased as a result of the decision of the Commission to separate the services deciding policy on food and health from those responsible for questions of control which have been transferred to DG XXIV.

2–12 As Professor Bourgoignie notes, while there is reason for pleasure at this increase in the resources and responsibilities for consumer protection there is also cause for caution. The frequent reorganisations of DG XXIV have not been conducive to the creation of an effective and coherent service. He also observes "[t]hat one would also hope that a balance is observed between the new tasks of DG XXIV and its more traditional responsibilities".[8] At least, as a result of these changes the financial stringency that has bedevilled EC consumer protection activities seems to have been eased.

2–13 At the same time as what is now the Consumer Protection Directorate was set up, a Consumers Consultative Committee (CCC) was created. The idea was that this body, consisting of representatives of national consumer organisations and trade union representatives, would be consulted by the Commission on its consumer programme. In October 2003 it was renamed the European Consumer Consultative Group. In practice consultation is sporadic and, in any event, does not have the resources to be an effective commentator on policy issues.

---

[7] This acronym derives from the French name of the directorate: Santé et Protection des Consommateurs.

[8] Bourgoignie, "European Community Consumer Law and Policy: from Rome to Amsterdam", 1998 Cons. L.J. 443 at 457.

CONSUMER PROTECTION PROGRAMMES

It was in 1975 that the Community adopted its first programme for **2–14**
consumer protection[9] which set out to guarantee five basic consumer
rights:

(1) protection of the consumer against health and safety risks.
(2) protection of consumers' economic interests.
(3) improvement of the consumers' legal position through advice,
    assistance, and the right to seek a legal remedy.
(4) improvement of consumer education and information.
(5) appropriate consultation and representation of consumers in
    the taking of decisions affecting their interests.

In May 1981 a second programme along the same lines was **2–15**
adopted,[10] and ever since at regular intervals further programmes have
been published. It cannot be said that a great deal was achieved by these
early programmes. However, it must be remembered that there were
considerable obstacles in the way of this. Until the Single European Act
and the Maastricht Treaty there were doubts about the legal basis for
consumer protection measures. Another formidable hurdle in the early
years was the need for unanimity among the Member States before a
measure could be implemented.

The more recent consumer programmes have shown a change of **2–16**
emphasis in part brought about by the treaty changes that have
established the legitimacy of consumer protection as a community
policy. The Commission's Consumer Action Plan 1996–98[11] included
new priorities. These were the protection of consumers' interests with
regard to public services and financial services as well as in relation to
the information society. It also alluded to the importance of sustainable
consumption, assistance to the countries of central and eastern Europe to
develop consumer protection policies and to Third World countries in
order to improve conditions in relation to basic products.

The 1999–2001 plan[12] identified three areas as the main tasks for **2–17**
consumer policy. These were: a more powerful voice for consumers
throughout the EU; a high level of health and safety for the EU
consumers; and full respect for the economic interests of EU consumers.
The current programme covers the five years 2002–06.[13] The document
notes that: "European consumer policy is central to one of the
Commission's strategic objectives, that of contributing to a better
quality of life for all. It is also an essential element of the Commission's

---

[9] [1975] O.J. C92/1.
[10] [1981] O.J. C133/1.
[11] COM (98) 696.
[12] COM (98) 0696–C4-0035/99.
[13] Consumer policy strategy 2002–06, COM (2002) 208 final–2002/C 137/02.

strategic objective of creating new economic dynamism and modernising the European economy." The programme sets out three objectives: the achievement of a high level of consumer protection; effective enforcement of consumer protection rules; and the involvement of consumer organisations in EU policies. In pursuit of the first objective the main initiatives will be work to follow-up the issues on commercial practices addressed by the Green Paper on EU Consumer Protection and on the safety of services. The priorities for action under the second objective of effective enforcement are the development of an administrative cooperation framework between Member States and of redress mechanisms for consumers. The third objective, involvement of consumer organisations in EU policies, will be pursued by reviewing the mechanisms for participation of consumer organisations in EU policy-making and in the setting up of education and capacity-building projects.

ACHIEVEMENTS SO FAR

2–18 As this recital of the various Community programmes shows, there has been no shortage of good intentions towards consumers. To what extent have there been concrete achievements? In pursuance of its aim of promoting consumer protection the Commission has encouraged debate on the subject, an aspect of its work which should not be underestimated. The Commission organises or funds conferences and research projects throughout Europe for this purpose. This is probably of more importance in those parts of Europe where consumer protection is less well developed. It must be remembered that consumer protection has, until fairly recently, been more prominent in northern Europe. However, there have been, and continue to be, benefits from this aspect of the Commission's work in the United Kingdom in general, and in Scotland in particular. The interest of the Commission in consumer redress influenced the creation of the small claims procedure in the sheriff court through both financial and moral support to the Dundee small claims experiment. Similar encouragement has been given to pilot projects in Belgium and Milan. More recently the Commission gave financial support for joint Scottish and Irish projects on in-court advice. The Scottish part of this project (which is still running) provides an adviser based in Edinburgh Sheriff Court.

2–19   Its interest in consumer redress was indicated in a communication from the Commission on "the out-of-court settlement of consumer disputes" and a recommendation on the principles applicable to the bodies responsible for out-of-court settlement of consumer disputes often referred to as alternative dispute resolution (ADR).[14] This follows

---

[14] COM (1998) 198.

an earlier thought-provoking Green Paper on access to justice,[15] which stimulated discussion on a wide range of issues. Apart from the development of small claims procedures it raises the question of the use of group actions, which is a notable lacuna in the Scottish legal system. There are no practical methods by which those who are the victims of a common misfortune or fraud can band together to sue the perpetrator.

Another type of group action is sometimes referred to as the public **2–20** interest action. This permits an organisation to take action in the public interest to stop some activity inimical to consumers. While available in some European jurisdictions, it is not available in the Scottish, or indeed the English, legal system. European influence may be beneficial here. Provision for such means of redress is contained in individual pieces of European legislation. As a result of the provisions of the Misleading Advertising Directive[16] and the Unfair Contract Terms Directive[17] it has been necessary to provide a version of this type of action. Initially, the OFT was given powers to take action in some circumstances under these directives. As we shall see later, in the case of unfair terms these powers have been extended to a range of other organisations. With the implementation of the Injunctions Directive[18] there has been a further extension of this type of action. This directive addresses the problem of obtaining redress across national boundaries. This is a start and may accustom lawyers and administrators to a new idea. In time, it may be possible to develop a fully-fledged group action.

As part of its concern for safety the Commission has promoted the **2–21** Rapid Information Exchange System (RAPEX). Under this system Member States notify the Commission's Consumer Protection Service when they discover a dangerous product on their market, and the Commission in turn notifies other Member States. EHLASS, the European Home and Leisure Accident Surveillance System, has also been promoted by the Commission. Under it Member States provide the Commission with statistics on home and leisure accidents involving products, to help identify areas where common action is needed.

In discussion of the achievements of EC consumer protection policy **2–22** most attention tends to centre on its legislative achievements. Over the years a considerable number of measures have emanated from Brussels. In the early years progress was slow but it should not be forgotten that even in the very early years legislation which benefited consumers was passed. Various directives whose primary aim was harmonisation of the common market also had the effect of improving consumer protection. Examples from this early period include legislation on the harmonisation of laws on classification, denomination, packaging and labelling of

---

[15] COM (93) 378.
[16] Dir. 84/450.
[17] Dir. 93/13.
[18] Dir. 98/27.

consumer goods as well as those on foodstuffs, animal health, pharmaceutical products, cosmetics and electrical home appliances. In the 1970s and 1980s more overtly consumer protection measures were adopted although the uncertainty over the legal competence of the EC in the area of consumer protection undoubtedly retarded progress. However, it is possible to point to a number of directives from this period directly concerning consumers. Examples are those on the labelling of foodstuffs in 1978, the Misleading Advertising Directive of 1984, the Product Liability Directive and the Door to Door Sales Directives of 1985, and the Consumer Credit Directive of 1986.[19]

2–23   As Professor Bourgoignie has observed,[20] most of these measures related to improving consumer information. It was only with the recognition in the EC Treaty itself of consumer protection as a community policy that more fundamental initiatives have been taken in the last 10 years. To quote Professor Bourgoignie: "[b]eyond solutions of an informational nature which aim to improved the quality of the consent which a consumer gives to his actions, the provisions of the Directives most recently adopted or proposed, seek to alter the very nature of consumer relationships by imposing new obligations, by confirming new rights and by prohibiting certain practices or behaviour". Examples of such new directives are those on package travel, general product safety, unfair contract terms, timeshare, distance contracts, comparative advertising, consumer sales and guarantees, and the Injunctions Directive.[21]

2–24   As has been suggested above, EC proposals can have a beneficial effect on domestic policy. Small claims is an example that has been cited. Added to that might be the control of unfair contract terms. Regulation of such terms has, since the passing of the Unfair Contract Terms Act 1977, been quite effective. In many respects the Unfair Contract Terms Directive[22] duplicates that legislation. The importance of the Directive lies in the extensions which it makes to our law. This is discussed in more detail in the chapter on Unfair Contract Terms and at this stage it is sufficient to point out two salient features. As mentioned above, the Directive requires organisations to be permitted to take action on behalf of consumers. Not only is this important in itself but, as has been argued above, it may lead to the recognition of a wider right to act in this way. The other point is more specific. The Directive applies more widely than the 1977 Act and, with its concept of good faith, introduces a potentially revolutionary tool into our armoury of legal weapons.

2–25   While benefits have undoubtedly been derived from the EC consumer protection policy, it is also possible to argue that it has had its

---

[19] Dir. 87/102.
[20] Bourgoignie, "European Community Consumer Law and Policy: from Rome to Amsterdam", 1998 Cons. L.J. 443 at 449.
[21] For details see relevant chapters.
[22] See n.17.

disadvantages. There are those who consider that EC initiatives can be an impediment to the achievement of desirable reforms in the UK. The example usually given in this context is product liability. The debate on the need for reform was well advanced in the UK when a draft EC directive was published. It may be argued that the desire to produce a detailed proposal put at risk the possibility of achieving any change at all.[23]

In addition to concerns about the content of some of the directives **2–26** there has also been concern about the methods of implementing them and whether enforcement in this country is over-zealous as compared with that in some other Member States. The UK can be said to have a good record in implementing EC proposals.[24]

It is sometimes said that the UK over-implements EC law, including **2–27** single market directives, in that on transposition it includes additional requirements or complexities which are not required by the directive. Combined with this assertion it is not uncommon to find allegations that other Member States do not implement properly and adopt a less rigorous approach to enforcement.

The *Review of the Implementation and Enforcement of E.C. law in the* **2–28** *United Kingdom* considered these issues. On the first point it "found little evidence to support the allegation that the United Kingdom deliberately adds requirements when transposing EC law". Where this did happen it was for two main reasons:

"First, where EC Law has been integrated into existing United Kingdom law there is a tendency to carry over existing national provisions, [with] wider scope and tougher penalties than in other Member States ... Second, the United Kingdom legal system is based on a tradition of precise drafting which aims to eradicate doubt in contrast with the purposive approach of continental jurisprudence on which EC law and that of other Member States is based."[25]

On the question of failure to implement properly in other Members **2–29** States the same report found no evidence to suggest that other Member States have omitted requirements of a directive though they noted that not all the directives which they studied for the purposes of their review had been implemented in some other Member States.

---

[23] See Borrie, *The Development of Consumer Law and Policy—Bold Spirits and Timorous Souls* (Stevens, 1984), pp.116–118. Doorstep selling might be another example.
[24] This is borne out by statistics, see *Review of the Implementation and Enforcement of E.C. law in the United Kingdom* (DTI, July 1993), an efficiency scrutiny report commissioned by the President of the Board of Trade and available, in particular, Ch. 3.
[25] (DTI, July 1993), p.19, n.1.

2–30   It is not uncommon to hear complaints that enforcement is less stringent and more pragmatic in other Member States. The Review considered this issue mainly in relation to a small number of case studies that it undertook. It concluded that it found "no evidence to support the assertion that United Kingdom enforcers were more highly qualified than those in other Member States". It went on to say that "simple comparisons of enforcement practice are not helpful in understanding deep seated differences in culture".[26] The Review then goes on to consider the approach of the Sutherland Report.[27] While critical of some of the report's recommendations as overly bureaucratic it states:

> "Nevertheless, the basic thrust of the recommendations is sensible, and the call for a 'cooperative approach' to be taken to enforcement issues as the 'single most important way of reinforcing mutual confidence between Member States and the Commission' should build on the collaboration that enforcement authorities in all Member States are already developing."[28]

ROLE OF THE EUROPEAN COURT

2–31   It must not be forgotten that the European Court has had a role in the development of the law relating to consumers. Much of this has been based on the exposition of Art.30 (now Art.28) of the Treaty of Rome which establishes the right of free movement of goods. There is also an equivalent in relation to services in Art.59 (now Art.49). The theory behind this is that the removal of barriers to trade between Member States benefits the consumer in permitting greater competition with the benefits that economic theory says will follow from that.[29]

2–32   According to the court, Art.30 covers "all trading rules enacted by Member States which are capable of hindering, directly or indirectly, actually or potentially, intra-Community trade".[30] One of the best known examples of the application of the court's approach to Art.30 is the *Cassis de Dijon* decision[31] where regulations governing the composition of alcoholic drinks which could be marketed in Germany were held to offend against European law. That case also demonstrated that there were circumstances where trade barriers could be justified. The court pointed out that:

---

[26] (DTI, July 1993), p.20.
[27] *The Internal Market After 1992* (Sutherland Report).
[28] (DTI, July 1993), p.20.
[29] For a detailed study of this area of EU law see Weatherhill and Beaumont, *EU Law* (3rd ed., Penguin, London, 1999).
[30] *Procureur du Roi v Dassonville* (No.8/74); [1974] E.C.R. 837.
[31] *Rewe-Zentrale A.G. v Bundesmonopolverwaltung für Brantwein* (No.120/78); [1979] E.C.R. 649.

"obstacles to movement in the Community resulting from disparities between national laws in question must be accepted in so far as those provisions may be recognised as being necessary in order to satisfy mandatory requirements relating in particular to the effectiveness of fiscal supervision, the protection of public health, the fairness of commercial transactions and the defence of the consumer."[32]

The scope for taking advantage of these exceptions on the ground of **2–33** consumer protection is not great, as the case law shows. The court has frequently pointed out that where there are other ways of achieving the same end they should be used. The *German Beer* case[33] illustrates this point. Germany sought to argue that its beer purity laws, dating from medieval times, were justified on consumer protection grounds. The court pointed out that the objectives of the laws could be secured by labeling requirements which would also allow a freer market in beer with greater consumer choice.[34]

In the past few years the Court of Justice has been altering its **2–34** approach in this area. In a series of cases beginning with *Keck* and *Mithouard*,[35] and including *Hunermund*[36] and *Clinique*[37] the court appears to be using a new definition of "measures having an equivalent effect". A distinction is being drawn between rules on the composition and presentation of products, and those restricting and prohibiting certain sales methods. The former are subject to the *Cassis de Dijon* controls but the latter are not regarded as measures having an equivalent effect. One particular problem that this new distinction throws up is that it leaves it unclear into which category advertising falls.

FUTURE OF EUROPEAN CONSUMER PROTECTION

Consumer protection policy in the EU is at an uncertain stage. On the **2–35** one hand the Maastricht and Amsterdam Treaty changes appear to have enhanced its significance. That must be balanced against the meaning given to subsidiarity by some Member States who see it as a means to limit the ability of Brussels to intervene in areas such as this. There does appear to be increasing realisation of the importance of consumers to the

---

[32] *Rewe-Zentrale A.G. v Bundesmonopolverwaltung für Brantwein* (No.120/78); [1979] E.C.R. 649, para.8.

[33] (No.178/84); [1987] E.C.R. 1227.

[34] For a detailed discussion of this area, see Weatherhill, "The Role of the Informed Consumer in European Community Law and Policy" (1994) 2 Consum. L.J. 49.

[35] Cases C-267–268/91; [1993] E.C.R. 1-6097.

[36] Case C292/92 *Hunermund v Landesapothekerkammer Baden-Wurttemberg*, Dec. 15, 1993.

[37] Case 315/92 *Verband Sozialer Wettbewerb eV v Clinique Laboratories SNC* [1994] E.C.R. 1-317.

success of the operation of the Single Market. The Sutherland Report[38] made this point forcibly in pointing out that consumer uncertainty was one of the major obstacles to the realisation of the internal market. If consumers have doubts about the quality of goods from other Member States or their legal rights are obscure, they cannot be expected to participate fully.

2–36   This is one of the most important factors behind the Commission's Green Paper on European consumer protection published in 2001.[39] It argues that the principal problem in guaranteeing consumer protection in the internal market lies in the different national laws concerning commercial practices between businesses and consumers. As a result neither businesses nor consumers are taking full advantage of the potential of the internal market despite the introduction of the Euro and developments in e-commerce. The Green Paper argues that Community rules on consumer protection have not succeeded in adapting to the natural development of the market or to new commercial practices. The solution envisaged involves simplification of national rules and a more effective guarantee of consumer protection.

2–37   The Green Paper put forward two methods of achieving simplification: the adoption of new directives or a framework directive supplemented by a number of targeted directives in specific areas. It should be emphasised that that these proposals deal only with the protection of consumers' economic interests; health and safety matters are not affected. The Commission's clear preference is for a framework directive which would harmonise the general rules on trading fairly found in most EU States though not the UK. This would not override sector specific directives such as the unfair terms directive but would provide a long stop in those areas where there was no legislation or where the legislation did not extend to some new practice. It was envisaged that some existing directives would have to be revised and the framework directive would also be supplemented by increased self-regulation.

2–38   This is an ambitious idea and one which has met with some scepticism. Howells and Wihelmsson argue that "EC consumer law is not yet sufficiently developed to protect the consumer, partly because the constitutional limits on Community activity in this area prevent the adoption of a comprehensive consumer policy".[40] They go on to point out that references to moving from the minimal harmonisation approach of many existing directives to a policy of maximum harmonization as the Green Paper seems to envisage has profound dangers for consumers. Minimum directives which leave Member States free to make their own

---

[38] *The Internal Market after 1992: Meeting the Challenge*, (Sutherland Report).
[39] COM (2001) 531 final.
[40] "European Consumer Law: Has it Come of Age?" (2003) 28 *European Law Review* 370.

more protective rules might not have been agreed to in their present form if it had been thought that they might later become maximum directives. They also question whether the reliance of the Green Paper on information remedies and self regulation is in the interests of consumers. Following a period of consultation the Commission has brought forward a draft directive on unfair commercial practices.[41] Significantly, the draft directive does not propose a duty to trade fairly, rather it outlaws unfair practices. The directive is currently being negotiated by the Member States.

---

[41] Dir. COM (2003) 356.

CHAPTER 3

ADVERTISING AND MARKETING

INTRODUCTION

3–01 Much skill and expense is devoted to persuading consumers to purchase goods and services, and the role of advertising in our economic system is recognised as being important, if controversial. It is essential that advertising be accurate, and thus there is a good deal of legal regulation of this area. The major problems do not concern blatant falsehood but the more subtle issues of claims that are ambiguous or misleading or offend against decency or good taste.

3–02 Much of the statutory control of advertising is of a negative character. However, there are a number of Acts which require that advertisers provide consumers, or potential consumers, with information which will assist them to make a rational purchasing decision. Examples of such provisions which are discussed below are to be found in the legislation on food and drugs, weights and measures and consumer credit legislation.

ROLE OF THE COMMON LAW

3–03 The common law has traditionally tended to ignore advertising. The blatantly false advertisement would, almost certainly, involve criminal liability for fraud, and might give rise to a civil action for fraudulent misrepresentation. This is not, however, the usual kind of case. The common law has taken a tolerant attitude towards sellers' statements promoting their products. Its watchwords have been *simplex commendatio non obligat* (a mere recommendation does not bind). This does seem to have been taken too far on occasions.[1] However, the fact is that in some circumstances a statement will not be regarded as giving rise to legal consequences.

3–04 Despite this laxity in the law, it is possible that statements made about the goods or services by the seller can have legal consequences. As we shall see later, if the statement is considered to have contractual effect

---

[1] Mullins, "An Analysis of Simplex Commendation in Modern Society" (1984) 101 S.A.L.J. 515.

the contractual remedies for breach will apply. If the offending statement does not form part of the contract but is what lawyers call a "mere representation" there are still remedies available to the consumer under the heading of misrepresentation.

To attract legal liability for misrepresentation a statement must be **3–05** material and made in the course of negotiations. It must also be a statement of fact and not one of opinion.[2] Generally, silence will not amount to a misrepresentation but in some circumstances the parties do owe each other a duty to disclose. One of the best known examples of these contracts, *uberrimae fidei* (of the utmost good faith), arises in insurance where it is the duty of the insured to make full disclosure when requesting insurance.[3]

The law recognises three types of misrepresentation: fraudulent; **3–06** negligent; and innocent. Fraudulent misrepresentation occurs where the maker of the statement was aware that his statements were untrue, or made them recklessly, heedless of whether they were true or false, or did not believe them to be true.[4] If fraud can be proved, not only is the contract void, that is, it has no effect, but also the victim may sue for damages.

Negligent misrepresentations occur where one party has failed to take **3–07** reasonable care in making a statement in circumstances where the law says that there is a duty of care to do so. This is an area of law which has developed since the House of Lords decision in *Hedley Byrne & Co. Ltd v Heller & Partners Ltd.*[5] In Scotland, until the enactment of s.10 of the Law Reform (Miscellaneous Provisions) (Scotland) Act 1985, it was not clear whether damages were available for such misrepresentations. That provision now makes it clear that this is the case.

An innocent misrepresentation is one that is made in the belief that it **3–08** is true. The only remedy is to reduce the contract, which can only be done if action is taken without delay and it is possible to restore the parties to their original positions. In addition, the rights of third parties must not have been affected.[6]

Given the limitations on the remedies relating to misrepresentations, **3–09** it is better to be able to show that a statement is a term of the contract rather than a representation that induced it. Distinguishing between terms and representations is not easy, but the test is what the parties intended. This in turn appears to depend on the stage at which the statement was made, whether an oral statement was put into writing, and whether the person who made the statement had special knowledge. In

---

[2] *Bisset v Wilkinson* [1927] A.C. 177.
[3] See *H. Demetriodes & Co. v Northern Assurance Co. Ltd; The Spathari*, 1925 S.C. (H.L.) 6. For discussion of the concept of unfairness in Unfair Terms in Consumer Contracts Regulations 1999 (S.I. 1999 No. 2083), see Ch. 10.
[4] *Derry v Peek* (1889) 14 App. Cas. 337.
[5] [1964] A.C. 465.
[6] See *Boyd & Forest v Glasgow & South-Western Ry*, 1912 S.C. (H.L.) 93.

Scott v Steel[7] a statement about the soundness of a horse made by the seller at the time of sale to clinch the sale was held to be a term of the contract. On the other hand, in *Malcolm v Cross*[8] a gap of almost two months between the statement about the condition of a horse and the making of a contract for its sale resulted in the statement not being regarded as part of the contract.[9]

3–10   In England, the cases of *Oscar Chess Ltd v Williams*[10] and *Dick Bentley Productions Ltd v Harold Smith (Motors) Ltd*[11] have been explained on the basis that in one the maker of the statement was an innocent private individual with no specialist knowledge of cars, while in the other the statement was made by a motor dealer. The dealer's statement was a term of the contract: the private individual's was not.

IMPLIED TERMS ABOUT DESCRIPTION

3–11 The implied term about description found in the Sale of Goods Act 1979 and other legislation about the supply of goods[12] is relevant to advertising. Section 13 of 1979 Act provides that where there is a sale by description there is an implied term that the goods will correspond with the description. If the sale is by sample, as well as by description, it is not sufficient that the bulk of the goods correspond with the sample if the goods do not also correspond with the description.

3–12   Sales are by description in a wide range of situations. An obvious example, in a consumer context, is provided by mail order purchasing where the buyer relies on the description in a catalogue or an advertisement in a newspaper or magazine. As s.13(3) makes clear, the fact that the goods are seen and selected by the buyer does not prevent the sale being one by description. Many goods are packaged and the buyer relies on the label or packaging for identification of the product. *Beale v Taylor*[13] extended this to a situation where the purchaser had examined the goods. Mr Taylor had placed an advertisement for a car in a newspaper, describing the car as "Herald, convertible, white, 1961". After examining the car, Mr Beale decided to buy it. In fact, the car was an amalgamation of a 1961 Herald and another of a different year which had been welded together and was in a very dangerous condition. As this was a private sale, Mr Beale could not rely on the quality terms in s.14, so he had to resort to s.13. The English Court of Appeal held that

[7] (1857) 20 D. 253.
[8] (1898) 25 R. 1089.
[9] See also *Matthew Paul & Co Ltd v Corporation of the City of Glasgow* (1900) 3 F. 119.
[10] [1957] 1 W.L.R. 370; [1957] 1 All E.R. 325.
[11] [1965] 1 W.L.R. 623; [1965] 2 All E.R. 65.
[12] See Supply of Goods and Services Act 1982, Pt 1A (inserted by Sale and Supply of Goods Act 1994, s.6) and Supply of Goods (Implied Terms) Act 1973, s.9.
[13] [1967] 1 W.L.R. 1193.

the words "1961 Herald" formed part of the description which had not been complied with.

The modern tendency is to draw a distinction between disputes about **3–13** quality, which should be reserved for s.14, and those about the identity of the goods, which are appropriate to s.13. This has been asserted in two Scottish decisions; *Britain Steamship Co. Ltd v Lithgows Ltd*[14] and *Border Harvesters Ltd v Edwards Engineering (Perth) Ltd.*[15]

As *Beale v Taylor*[16] demonstrates, almost any words describing the **3–14** goods will be regarded as part of the description. Strict compliance with description has been enforced in some cases.[17] However, as the unusual facts of *Harlingdon and Leinster Enterprises Ltd v Christopher Hull Fine Art Ltd*[18] demonstrate, there are limits. This case resulted from the sale of a painting which the defendants had purchased some time earlier when it had been described as being by the German artist, Munter. On the plaintiff, a specialist in German art, expressing interest in it the defendant emphasised that he did not know much about it, his particular expertise being in a different school of painting. The Court of Appeal held that it must be the intention of the parties that the description should be relied on. On the facts of this case that could not be said to have occurred.[19]

CONTRACTUAL CONSEQUENCES OF ADVERTISEMENTS AND SHOP DISPLAYS

The general rule is that advertisements, like shop displays, are regarded **3–15** as invitations to treat and are not to be considered in contractual terms as offers which, when accepted, give rise to contracts. There does not appear to be any Scottish authority on the status of shop displays. The leading cases are two English cases where, in criminal proceedings, this was the central issue. In *Pharmaceutical Society of Great Britain v Boots Cash Chemists (Southern) Ltd*[20] certain drugs which, under the Pharmacy and Poisons Act 1933, had to be sold by or under the supervision of a registered pharmacist had been sold in a Boots' pharmacy which operated a self-service system. Customers selected their purchases from shelves on which the drugs were displayed, put them into a shopping basket supplied by Boots, and took them to a cash desk at one of the two exits. There they paid the price and it was at this stage that a registered pharmacist supervised the transaction. To avoid

---

[14] 1975 S.C. 110.
[15] 1985 S.L.T. 128.
[16] [1967] 1 W.L.R. 1193.
[17] See *Arcos v E. A. Ronaasen & Son* [1933] A.C. 470.
[18] [1990] 1 All E.R. 737.
[19] Applied in *Drake v T. Agnew & Sons Ltd* [2002] EWHC 294.
[20] [1952] 2 Q.B. 795.

liability under the Act, Boots had to prove that supervision took place at the point of sale. It was held by the English Court of Appeal that the contract was made, not when the customer put the goods in the basket, but when the cashier accepted the offer to buy and received the price.

3–16   *Fisher v Bell*[21] involved a shop window display. Mr Bell displayed a "flick knife" in his shop window together with a price ticket. He was charged with the offence of offering the knife for sale contrary to s.1(1) of the Restriction of Offensive Weapons Act 1959. The justices found that no offence had been committed and the prosecutor appealed. It was held that no offence had been committed. The phrase "offer for sale" must be interpreted in the light of the law of contract, and a display in a shop window with a price ticket was an invitation to treat, not an offer to sell which, if accepted, would produce a binding contract.

3–17   There is good reason for this to be the law. Otherwise, if a display were an offer the shop would be bound to supply anyone who offered the price. This could create problems where the displayed item had been reserved for someone else or its sale was restricted in some way, as is the case with alcohol and cigarettes.

3–18   There is a similar rationale behind the rule that advertisements are presumed to be invitations to treat. Were it otherwise, traders who misjudged demand would find themselves in breach of contract. However, it is quite possible for an advertisement to constitute an offer, as Lord Kinnear acknowledged in *Hunter v General Accident Fire and Life Assurance Corporation Ltd* when he said: "[i]t is suggested that this is making a contract by an advertisement, but it is none the worse for being an advertisement if it is a distinct and definite offer unconditionally accepted."[22]

3–19   In that case the defenders had inserted a coupon in a diary, inviting purchasers to avail themselves of accident insurance by completing and returning the coupon together with a small fee. The Inner House and the House of Lords regarded this advertisement as an offer.

3–20   The classic case of an exception from the rule that advertisements are presumed to be invitations to treat is the English case of *Carlill v Carbolic Smoke Ball Co Ltd*,[23] where a manufacturer placed an advertisement in a newspaper inviting the public to purchase its product, a smoke ball, which, it asserted, would prevent influenza. The advertisement included a promise to pay £100 to anyone who contracted influenza after using the ball as instructed. The advertisement went on to emphasise the company's sincerity by stating that £1,000 had been deposited with a bank. Mrs Carlill used the smoke ball as instructed but contracted influenza. She was held to be entitled to recover £100 from

---

[21] [1961] 1 Q.B. 394.
[22] 1909 S.C. 344 at 348. This passage was approved by Lord Shaw in *A. & G. Patersoll Ltd v Highland Ry*, 1927 S.C. (H.L.) 32 at 46.
[23] [1893] 1 Q.B. 256.

the company because their promise in the advertisement was intended to be legally binding and was sufficiently precise to be enforced.

While the facts of *Carlill* may be regarded as highly unusual, the **3–21** principles underlying it do have modern applications. For example, the not uncommon situation where a retailer offers to refund part of the price if the purchaser discovers that an article could have been purchased more cheaply elsewhere would be decided on similar principles.

STATUTORY CONTROL

Statutory regulation of advertising in the UK has, until recently, been **3–22** piecemeal. There was no general prohibition on false or misleading advertising. However, with the implementation of the European Communities' directive on misleading advertising,[24] the UK has moved towards that position. Before looking at that development it will be useful to look at the heterogeneous collection of statutes prohibiting, with varying degrees of generality, false and misleading advertising, and a limited number of provisions regarding the provision of information. Of these the best known and widest ranging is the Trade Descriptions Act 1968, which controls false and misleading statements relating to goods, services in many situations. While it is relevant to the control of advertising it is discussed in detail in Ch.11.

ADVERTISING FOOD

Section 15 of the Food Safety Act 1990 provides that it is an offence **3–23** falsely to describe, advertise or present food. The first of these three offences makes it an offence to sell, offer or expose for sale food which has a label which falsely describes the food or is likely to mislead as to its nature, substance or quality.[25] It is also an offence to publish, or to be a party to the publication of an advertisement which falsely describes any food, or is likely to mislead as to its nature, substance or quality.[26] The Act defines "advertisement" as including any notice, circular, label, wrapper, invoice or other document, and any public announcement made orally or by any means of producing or transmitting light or sound.[27]

In relation to both these offences it is no barrier to a conviction that **3–24** the label or advertisement contains an accurate statement of the composition of the food.[28] This is intended to catch situations where a

---

[24] Dir. 84/450; [1984] O.J. L250/17.
[25] Food Safety Act 1990, s.15(1). See G. G. Howells, R. Bradgate and N. Griffiths, *Blackstones's Guide to the Food Safety Act 1990* (Blackstone, 1990), Ch. 4.
[26] *ibid.*, s.15(2). For defences, see s.15(4).
[27] *ibid.*, s.53(1).
[28] *ibid.*, s.15(4).

label or advertisement is literally true but the overall effect is deceptive. For the same reason s.15(3) creates a new offence of selling, offering or exposing for sale or having in one's possession for the purpose of sale, any food the presentation of which is likely to mislead as to its nature substance or quality. Presentation of the food includes its shape, appearance and packaging as well as the way it is arranged when exposed for sale and the setting in which the food is displayed with a view to sale. Section 53(1) excludes from this definition any form of labelling or advertising.

3–25 In addition to these general prohibitions, there is a considerable body of regulations controlling the labelling, marking or advertising of food for sale for human consumption. As has been traditional in this area, these regulations are made under powers now contained in the Food Safety Act 1990. Section 16(1)(e) gives a power to make regulations "for imposing requirements or prohibitions as to, or otherwise regulating, the labelling, marking, presenting or advertising of food, and the descriptions which may be applied to food". Numerous regulations were made under similar powers in previous legislation and these remain in force by virtue of s.59.

WEIGHTS AND MEASURES

3–26 Part 4 of the Weights and Measures Act 1985 regulates the sale of goods by quantity.[29] The 1985 Act, together with a vast corpus of regulations, imposes requirements designed to ensure that consumers are accurately informed about the quantity of goods they are intending to purchase.

ADVERTISING MEDICINAL PRODUCTS

3–27 Parts 5 and 6 of the Medicines Act 1968 deal with the promotion, labelling and packaging of "medicinal products".[30] These are defined as substances or articles (other than an instrument, apparatus or appliance) which are for use wholly or mainly for administration to human beings or animals for a medicinal purpose or as an ingredient in the preparation of such a product.[31] It is an offence for a commercially interested party or someone who does so at his request to issue a false or misleading advertisement relating to medicinal products.[32] In addition, there are wide powers to regulate advertisements and representations.[33] These have been exercised in order to control the content of advertisements, to ensure that no advertisement is issued unless the product has a product

---

[29] *i.e.* Weights and Measures Act 1985, Pt 4, ss.21–46. This area of law is under review, see *Fair Measure: A consultation document on modernising the law on the sale of goods sold by quantity* (DTI, 1999).
[30] *i.e.* Medicines Act 1968, Pt 5 (ss.85–91) and Pt 6 (ss.92–97).
[31] *ibid.*, s.130(1).
[32] *ibid.*, s.93(1). For the meaning of "commercially interested party", see s.92(4). For defences, see s.93(5)(a).
[33] *ibid.*, s.95.

licence, and to prohibit the issue of advertisements advocating the use of a medicine for the treatment of certain diseases.[34] Part 5 contains provisions concerning the labelling and packaging of medicines.[35] It is an offence to sell or supply, or to have in one's possession for the purpose of sale or supply, a medicinal product in a container or package which is falsely labelled or misleads as to the nature, quality or uses of the product.[36] Similar provisions apply to leaflets relating to medicines.[37] The appropriate ministers[38] are given wide powers to make regulations controlling the labelling and packaging of medicines and the contents of leaflets supplied with them.[39] These regulations are designed to ensure that medicines are correctly described with adequate instructions and warnings, and also to promote safety in relation to medicines.[40]

TOBACCO PRODUCTS

The Tobacco Advertising and Promotions Act 2002 bans the advertising of most tobacco product advertising in the UK. The Act brings in its prohibitions in several stages. Those affecting advertising in newspapers and periodicals have been in force for some time. Point of sale advertising will be strictly limited with effect from December 21, 2004.[41]   **3–28**

CONSUMER CREDIT

Consumer credit is discussed in Ch.9, but it is relevant to note that the Consumer Credit Act 1974 and the regulations made thereunder regulate the advertising of credit.[42] It is an offence to convey information which in a material respect is false or misleading.[43] The Secretary of State has a duty to make regulations governing the form and content of credit advertisements.   **3–29**

REGULATION OF PRICE MARKING

The Prices Act 1974 permits the Secretary of State for Trade and Industry to make orders regulating the way in which prices are   **3–30**

---

[34] Medicines Act 1968, Pt 6, s.95.
[35] *ibid.*, ss.85–91.
[36] *ibid.*, ss.85(3), 91(2).
[37] *ibid.*, ss.86, 91(1), (2).
[38] For the meaning of "the appropriate minister", see s.1(2).
[39] Medicines Act 1968, ss.85(1), 86(1).
[40] *ibid.*, ss.85(2), 86(1).
[41] Tobacco Advertising and Promotion (Point of Sale) (Scotland) Regulations 2004 (SSI 2004 No. 144).
[42] See Consumer Credit Act 1974, ss.39–47.
[43] *ibid.*, s.46.

indicated.[44] The powers given by s.2 of this 1974 Act were used to make regulations implementing the EC directives on the indication of prices of food and of non-foodstuffs. The Price Marking Order 2004[45] is intended to increase price transparency in the market, thus enabling consumers to know what the price of goods is and to make comparisons. The Order applies to a wide range of goods for retail sale but not those supplied in the course of the provision of a service, such as food sold in restaurants, hotels, and public houses; auction sales; and sales of antiques and works of art.[46] Where a trader indicates that a product is or may be for sale to a consumer its selling price must be indicated. This does not apply to goods sold from bulk or to advertisements. In certain circumstances the unit price, *i.e.* the price for one kilogram, litre, metre, square metre or cubic metre or the one item for goods sold by number, must also be indicated. This will be the case where products are sold loose from bulk, as in the case of fruit and vegetables. It also applies to pre-packaged products which are required by Weights and Measures legislation to be marked with quantity or to be made up in a prescribed quantity. These include most packaged food and drink and a wide range of non-food products such as construction and decorating products, fuel both solid and liquid, aerosol dispensers, cleaning and toilet preparations, cosmetics and pet foods. The requirement to indicate unit prices does not apply to cinema and television advertisements or, in the case of pre-packaged products, to sales in small shops, by itinerant traders or from vending machines.[47] A small shop is defined in art.1 as one with a floor area of less than 280sq.m.

3–31   Whatever price must be indicated it must be indicated in a way that is "unambiguous, easily identifiable and clearly legible", as must any charges for postage, package or delivery. It must be placed in close proximity to the products to which it relates and in such a way as to be available to customers without the need for them to seek assistance from the trader to ascertain it.[48] The latter requirement overrules the decision in *Allen v Redbridge London Borough Council*.[49]

3–32   "Selling price" includes VAT and any other taxes,[50] and must be stated in sterling. If a trader is willing to accept payment in foreign currency the price in that currency may also be displayed provided the price in the foreign currency or the conversion rate to be used is indicated together with any commission to be charged.[51]

---

[44] See Prices Act 1974, s.4 (amended by Price Commission Act 1977, s.16).
[45] SI 2004/102, which replaces the Price Marking Order 1999 (SI 1999/3042).
[46] art.3.
[47] art.5(3), Sch.2.
[48] art.7.
[49] [1994] 1 W.L.R. 139; [1994] 1 All E.R. 728
[50] art.1.
[51] art.6. See DTI guidance note on the order on its website: http://www.dti.gov.uk/ccp/topics1/guide/pricemark2004.pdf.

Another order made under the Prices Act 1974, the Price Marking **3–33**
(Food and Drink Services) Order 2003[52] requires prices of food and
drink to be indicated at premises where food and drink is offered for
consumption on the premises. "Premises" includes vehicles and vessels
with exceptions for certain premises such as members' clubs and staff
canteens. The Order also requires prices to be indicated at premises
selling take-away food. Detailed provisions are laid down as to the
prices and charges that must be indicated. Article 5 specifies how
many prices must be indicated with art.7 providing for the manner in
which prices and charges must be indicated.

Although made under a different Act, the Tourism (Sleeping Accom- **3–34**
modation Price Display) Order 1977, made under the Development of
Tourism Act 1969, has a similar function to the price marking orders. It
requires that hotels display in a prominent position, in the reception area
or the entrance, the price (including any service charge and value added
tax) of various kinds of accommodation.[53]

In all the above cases the sanction for non-compliance is a fine.[54] **3–35**

PRICE COMPARISONS

The control of misleading claims about prices has proved to be a **3–36**
difficult and controversial matter. On the one hand, it is important not to
impede the working of the competitive process by unnecessary restrictions but, on the other hand, it is difficult by simple methods to catch
those determined to exploit the loopholes in legislation. The Trade
Descriptions Act 1968[55] sought to regulate price advertising, but it
proved necessary to buttress it with the Price Marking (Bargain Offers)
Order 1979.[56] This proved unpopular both with traders and trading
standards officers, and Pt 3 of the Consumer Protection Act 1987
introduces a different approach to the regulation of price advertising.

Instead of attempting to prohibit specific practices, as the earlier **3–37**
legislation did, the 1987 Act creates a wide general offence of giving to
consumers a misleading indication as to the price of any goods, services,
accommodation or facilities.[57] There are two main offences. Section
20(1) makes it an offence, "in the course of any business of his",[58] for
someone to give an indication which is misleading. Section 20(2) on the

---

[52] SI 2003/2253. It revoked the Price Marking (Food and Drink on Premises) Order 1979
(SI 1979/361), with effect from Mar. 2, 2004.
[53] SI 1977/1877.
[54] See Prices Act 1974, s.7, Sch.1, para.5 (amended by Price Commission Act 1977,
s.13(5)), and Tourism (Sleeping Accommodation Price Display) Order 1977, arts 4,
5.
[55] *i.e.* Trade Descriptions Act 1968, s.11 (now repealed).
[56] Price Marking (Bargain Offers) Order 1979 (SI 1979/364) (amended by SI 1979/633
and SI 1979/1124).
[57] See Consumer Protection Act 1987, s.20(1).
[58] *Warwickshire CC v Johnson* [1993] A.C. 583; [1993] 2 W.L.R. 1; [1993] 1 All E.R.
299.

other hand applies to a price indication "which, after it was given, has become misleading".[59] An indication of the price, or the method of determining a price, is misleading if what is conveyed, or what consumers might reasonably be expected to infer from the indication or any omission from it, includes any of a number of factors.[60] These are indications:

(1) that the price is less than (or the method of determining it is not what) in fact it is;

(2) that the applicability of the price or the method of determining it does not depend on facts or circumstances on which its applicability does in fact depend;

(3) that the price or method of determining it covers matters in respect of which an additional charge is made;

(4) that a trader has no genuine belief that a price increase or reduction (or alteration of a method of price determination) is imminent; and

(5) that facts or circumstances by reference to which a consumer might reasonably be expected to judge the validity of a comparison are not accurate.[61]

3–38   It is made clear that references to services do not include references to services provided to an employer under a contract of employment[62]; and that references to services or facilities do not include references to services or facilities provided by authorised persons or appointed representatives in carrying on an investment business.[63] However, it is emphasised that the provision of credit[64] or banking or insurance services, the purchase or sale of foreign currency,[65] the supply of

[59] *Thomson Tour Operations Ltd v Birch* (1999) 163 J.P. 465; *The Times*, Feb. 24, 1999. See also *Link Stores Ltd v Harrow LBC* [2001] 1 W.L.R. 1479, QBD; and *DSG Retail Ltd v Oxfordshire CC* [2001] 1 W.L.R. 1765, QBD.

[60] Consumer Protection Act 1987, s.21(1), (2).

[61] Consumer Protection Act 1974, s.21(1)(a)–(e), (2)(a)–(e), (3).

[62] *ibid.*, s.22(2). By virtue of s.22(5), "contract of employment" and "employer" have the same meaning as in Employment Protection (Consolidation) Act 1978 (see s.153(1)).

[63] Consumer Protection Act 1987, s.22(3). By virtue of s.22(5), "appointed representative", "authorised person" and "investment business" have the same meaning as in Financial Services Act 1986 (see ss.1(2), 44, 207(1)).

[64] "Credit" has the same meaning as in the Consumer Credit Act 1974: Consumer Protection Act 1987, s.22(5). For case involving a misleading indication about the cost of credit, see *R v Kettering Justices, ex p MRB Insurance Brokers Ltd* [2000] 2 All E.R. (Comm) 353.

[65] In relation to a service consisting in the purchase or sale of foreign currency references in Consumer Protection Act 1987, Pt 3, to the method by which the price of the service is determined include references to the rate of exchange: s.22(4).

electricity and the provision of off-street car parks and caravan sites[66] are included.[67]

This somewhat curious provision is explained by the fact that all **3–39** these services have been the subject of frequent complaints on account of the quality of price advertising. Reference to accommodation or facilities does not include accommodation or facilities being made available by means of the creation or disposal of an interest in land, except where it is the creation or disposal of the *dominium utile* of land comprising a new dwelling (or a leasehold in such a dwelling) where at least 21 years remains unexpired.[68]

For the most part the defences available are similar to those **3–40** applicable to offences under the Trade Descriptions Act 1968. The due diligence defence set out in the 1987 Act applies.[69] This was successful in *Berkshire County Council v Olympic Holidays Ltd*[70] where the company showed that the misleading price was generated by faulty computer software which it had rigorously tested. It is a defence for a person (1) to show that a price indication complied with regulations made under Part 3[71] of the 1987 Act[72]; (2) that he was a bona fide publisher of an advertisement[73]; or (3) that he was the author of a recommended price and did not offer goods, services, accommodation or facilities himself but reasonably assumed that the recommended price was, for the most part, being followed.

A defence which gave rise to a good deal of controversy during the **3–41** parliamentary progress of the Consumer Protection Bill is that in respect of the code of practice. The Secretary of State, after consulting the Director-General of Fair Trading and such other persons as may be appropriate, may by order approve a code of practice giving practical guidance about price indications.[74] Failure to comply with this code does not by itself give rise to any criminal or civil liability. It will have evidential value[75] in that contravention of the code may be relied on for the purpose of establishing that an offence had been committed, or of

---

[66] "Caravan" has the same meaning as in Caravan Sites and Control of Development Act 1960 (see s.29(1)): Consumer Protection Act 1987, s.22(5).
[67] Consumer Protection Act 1987, s.22(1)(a)–(e).
[68] *ibid.*, s.23.
[69] *ibid.*, ss.24(5), 39. In respect of offences under Pt 3 (ss.20–26), s.39 only applies to the offence of giving a misleading price indication under s.20(1): s.39(5).
[70] (1994) 158 J.P. 421; (1994) 13 Tr. L.R. 251.
[71] *i.e.* Consumer Protection Act 1987, s.26.
[72] *ibid.*, s.24(1). This defence is only available in respect of offences under s.20(1), (2).
[73] *ibid.*, s.24(3). This defence is only available in respect of offences under s.20(1), (2). "Advertisement" includes a catalogue, a circular and a price list: s.24(6). In proceedings for an offence under s.20(1), (2), in respect of an indication published in a book, newspaper, magazine, film or radio or television broadcast or in a programme included in a cable programme service, it is a defence to show that the indication was not contained in an advertisement: s.24(2), (6).
[74] See *ibid.*, s.25(1), (3), (4).
[75] *i.e.* in proceedings for an offence under Consumer Protection Act 1987, s.20(1), (2).

negativing a defence; while compliance with the code may be relied on to show that no offence has been committed or that there is a defence.[76]

3-42   Such a code has been promulgated by the Consumer Protection (Code of Practice for Traders on Price Indications) Approval Order 1988.[77] It gives guidance on the situations in which comparisons may be made. For example, it sets out the circumstances in which a comparisons may be made with the trader's own previous price. The comparison should be with the last price at which the product was offered by that trader in the previous six months. During that period the product should have been available for at least 28 consecutive days in the same shop where the reduction is being made. This harks back to a repealed provision in the s.11 of the Trade Descriptions Act 1968 which proved very difficult to enforce.

3-43   Enforcement of this part of the 1987 Act is the duty of district councils as the weights and measures authorities.[78] The penalties for the offence of giving a misleading price indication are, on conviction on indictment, a fine, and, on summary conviction, a fine not exceeding the statutory maximum.[79]

DETAILS TO BE DISPLAYED ON CARS FOR SALE

3-44 Car dealers are required to display on cars for sale a label giving the results of officially approved tests of fuel consumption and stating that the test results for other cars are available.[80] This information must also be included in other promotional literature.

DISCLOSURE IN BUSINESS ADVERTISEMENTS

3-45 In addition to the mandatory disclosure of information intended to assist the consumer in making a rational purchasing decision, there are some other statutory information disclosure provisions which can be explained on the basis that they are intended to assist consumers to assert their legal rights. A good example is the Business Advertisements (Disclosure) Order 1977.[81] This is designed to eradicate the practice of trade sellers placing advertisements in the classified columns of newspapers or periodicals posing as private sellers. The purchaser from a private seller is much less well protected than the purchaser from a trader — hence the inclination of some traders to adopt such a practice.

---

[76] Consumer Protection Act 1987, s.25(2).

[77] SI 1988/2078.

[78] See Consumer Protection Act 1987, s.27(1).

[79] *ibid.*, s.20(4). As to the time-limit for bringing prosecutions, see s.20(5). "The statutory maximum" means the prescribed sum as defined in the Criminal Procedure (Scotland) Act, s.289B. The only reported case on Pt 3 appears to be *Clydesdale Group plc v Normand*, 1994 S.L.T. 1302; 1993 S.C.C.R. 958.

[80] See Passenger Car Fuel Consumption Order 1983 (SI 1983/1486).

[81] SI 1977/1918.

It is a criminal offence to fail to indicate in an advertisement that goods are for sale in the course of a business.[82]

DISTANCE SELLING

The Consumer Protection (Distance Selling) Regulations 2000,[83] which **3–46** implement the EC Distance Selling Directive, include important protections for consumers thinking of buying goods in circumstances where they and the seller are not in face to face communication. The regulations repealed the Mail Order Transactions (Information) Order 1976[84] which applied only to mail order transactions. They apply to most contracts involving a "means of distance communication" which is defined as, "any means which, without the simultaneous physical presence of the supplier and the consumer, may be used for the conclusion of a contract between those parties".[85] It, therefore, covers transactions effected by the internet, digital television, mail order, including catalogue shopping, telephone and fax. In these cases suppliers must give consumers clear information including details of the goods or services offered, delivery arrangements and payment, the supplier's details and the consumer's cancellation right before they buy[86] and this information must be given in writing.[87]

BROADCAST ADVERTISING

Under the terms of its licence the British Broadcasting Corporation is **3–47** not permitted to transmit advertisements on its radio and television services. The broadcasting services regulated by the Office of Communications (OFCOM) which was set up by the Communications Act 2003 are expressly permitted to do so. Television, and to a lesser extent commercial radio stations, are an attractive medium for advertisers. Broadcast advertising is subject to a range of controls specific to it which encompass an interesting combination of statutory and self-regulatory methods. Broadcast advertising is, of course, subject to the various Acts of Parliament which regulate advertising in general.

The Communications Act 2003 provides that "the inclusion of **3–48** advertising which may be misleading, harmful or offensive in television and radio services" must be prevented[88]; and goes on to provide that OFCOM must ensure "general provision governing standards and

---

[82] See Fair Trading Act 1973, s.23, and Criminal Procedure (Scotland) Act 1975, s.289B (added by Criminal Law Act 1977, s.63(1), Sch.11, para.5, substituted by Criminal Justice Act 1982, s.55(2), and amended by Increase of Criminal Penalties etc (Scotland) Order 1984 (SI 1984/526), art.3).
[83] SI 2000/2334.
[84] SI 1976/1812.
[85] SI 2000/2334, reg.3.
[86] *ibid.*, reg.7.
[87] *ibid.*, reg.8.
[88] Communications Act 2003, s.319(2)(h).

practice in advertising and in the sponsoring of programmes"[89] and that this must be done by codes.[90] The 2003 Act also specifically outlaws subliminal advertising techniques.[91] The predecessors of OFCOM, the Independent Television Commission and the Radio Authority, had drawn up codes to ensure that the similar rules about advertising and sponsorship laid down in earlier legislation were complied with and these have been adopted by OFCOM. Most of these rules are contained in the ITC Code of Advertising Standards and Practice, the ITC Code of Programme Sponsorship and the ITC Rules on Advertising Breaks.[92] However, s.321(2) of the 2003 Act has general rules about advertising which prohibit advertisements by any body whose objects are wholly or mainly of a political nature or relate to an industrial dispute.

3–49   The rules in the ITC code, *inter alia,* require that the advertisements must be clearly distinguishable as such, recognisably separate from programmes, and inserted at the beginning or the end of programmes or in a natural break. They must not be excessively noisy or strident, nor should certain products be advertised in or adjacent to certain programmes. For example, advertisements for alcoholic drinks, liqueur chocolates and pipe tobacco must not be carried in or adjacent to children's programmes.

3–50   Since the beginning of commercial of television there have been controls on the amount of advertising that may be shown. These are now mainly to be found in the ITC Rules on Advertising Breaks.[93] Many of the rules apply to both terrestrial channels and cable and satellite channels, but special provision is made for the latter. This is most marked in relation to home shopping channels where up to eight "tele-shopping windows", that is, advertising features of from 15 minutes to three hours in length may be shown. This compares with the rules for terrestrial channels which permit a daily average of seven minutes advertising in each hour and no more than 12 minutes in any one hour.

3–51   An interesting feature of the regulation of broadcast advertising is the fact that much of the detailed control derives from codes of practice which OFCOM is statutorily obliged to draw up and enforce. The code of advertising standards and practice was drawn up by the ITC in consultation with the Radio Authority, commercial television companies, representatives of viewers and advertisers, those qualified to give advice on advertising, and such others concerned with standards in advertising as the ITC thinks fit. OFCOM is likely to follow a similar procedure.[94]

---

[89] Communications Act 2003, s.321(1)(a).

[90] *ibid.*, s.319(3).

[91] *ibid.*, s.319(.1)(h).

[92] These three documents can be found on the OFCOM website: http://www.ofcom.org.uk.

[93] Rules on Advertising Breaks Consolidated (revised, Dec 1997).

[94] Communications Act 2003, s.16.

The content of the code is very similar to the British Code of **3–52**
Advertising Practice which applies to print media and is discussed
below. It shares with that code the same general principles that
advertising should be legal, decent, honest and truthful and that its
detailed rules are intended to be applied in the spirit as well as the letter.
It suffices at this point to draw attention to some features peculiar to
broadcasting. The code permits the use of special techniques or
substitute materials where technical limitations can make it difficult to
portray a subject accurately. However, the resultant picture must present
a fair and reasonable impression of the product and must not use
unacceptable devices such as glass or plastic sheeting to simulate the
effects of floor or furniture polishes. Cigarettes may not be advertised,
nor may private investigation services or those of betting tipsters,
fortune tellers, unlicensed employment bureaux or private consumer
advisory agencies. Indeed, such are the similarities between the codes
that OFCOM has been consulting on the possibility of delegating its
responsibilities to enforce the broadcasting codes to the Advertising
Standards Authority which enforces the print media codes and has
decided, subject to Parliamentary approval, to do so from November 1,
2004.[95]

Advertising on commercial radio is subject to a similar regulatory **3–53**
regime. This is now overseen by OFCOM which has taken over the
Code of Advertising Standards and Practice and Programme Sponsorship created by the Radio Authority.[96] The code is similar in terms to the
equivalent television codes.

BRITISH CODE OF ADVERTISING PRACTICE

One of the distinctive features of advertising control in the United **3–54**
Kingdom is the role of self-regulation. It has already been noted that
there is an element of this in broadcast advertising through the codes of
advertising standards and practice operated by OFCOM. It might be
argued that this is not pure self-regulation as the codes are mandated by
statute and drawn up not only by representatives of the advertising
industry but also of government and consumers. Self-regulation has an
important role to play in the control of advertising standards in media
other than broadcasting. This is achieved by means of the British Codes
of Advertising and Sales Promotion, the eleventh edition of which came
into force on March 4, 2003.[97]

These codes were drawn up by the Code of Advertising Practice **3–55**
Committee composed of representatives of the advertising industry in
consultation with the Advertising Standards Authority (ASA) and trade

---

[95] See *The Future Regulation of Broadcast Advertising* available on the OFCOM website,
see n. 92.
[96] Available on the OFCOM website: *http://www.ofcom.org.uk.*
[97] Available on the ASA website: *http//www.ASA.org.uk.*

and consumer interests. The Advertising Standards Authority is a company limited by guarantee set up by the Advertising Association to supervise the code and its enforcement. It is composed of a chairman who, under the terms of ASA's article of association, must "not be engaged in the business of advertising" and must be appointed only "after consultation with the Members of the Council of the Authority", a majority of whom must also be independent.[98]

3–56   The Advertising Standards Authority receives complaints about advertisements from members of the public and also carries out a limited amount of monitoring of advertisements on its own initiative. Complaints by one advertiser against another are the responsibility of the Code of Advertising Practice Committee. The main sanction available to ASA is that of adverse publicity, and details of complaints are published by ASA. One of the criticisms of the self-regulatory system has been the inadequacy of its sanctions. Apart from adverse publicity, its only other sanction is to request those companies controlling the media and which adhere to the British Code of Advertising Practice not to publish advertisements found to be in breach of the code and not to accept advertisements from advertising agencies which do not abide by the code. Since 1999 an Independent Reviewer has been added to the process of dealing with complaints. In exceptional circumstances, the Advertising Standards Authority Council can be asked to reconsider its adjudication (including a Council decision not to investigate a complaint). There are two grounds on which such a request can be made: where additional relevant evidence becomes available; or where there is a substantial flaw in the Council's adjudication or in the process by which that adjudication was made.[99]

3–57   In *R v Advertising Standards Authority Ltd, ex p Insurance Service plc*[1] it has been held that the activities of ASA in adjudicating on complaints against advertisements are subject to judicial review. There have been several applications for judicial review most of which have decided in favour of ASA. The relevance of the European Convention on Human Rights was considered in *R v Advertising Standards Authority, ex p Matthias Rath BV*.[2] The claimants sought judicial review of the decision by ASA to publish an adverse adjudication against them regarding a complaint made by a health authority and the refusal of the Independent Reviewer of ASA to reconsider the adjudication. The claimants argued that ASA was a public authority for the purposes of the Human Rights Act 1998. The Advertising Standards Authority did not argue against this, but wished to preserve the right to argue otherwise in a future case. The claimants claimed that Art.10.2 of the Convention permitted interference with freedom of expression only

---

[98] For more detail, see Ch.1.
[99] *British Code of Advertising Practice* (11th ed. 2003), para.60.38.
[1] (1990) 2 Admin. L.R. 77; (1990) 9 Tr. L.R. 169; 133 S.J. 1545, QBD.
[2] [2001] E.M.L.R. 22; [2001] H.R.L.R. 22.

where there were rules prescribed by law and that The British Codes of
Advertising and Sales Promotion were not such rules "prescribed by
law". The judge referred to the Control of Misleading Advertisements
Regulations 1988[3] and concluded that there was

> "no doubt that the advertising code of practice, which had an
> underpinning of subordinate legislation and which was readily
> accessible was prescribed by law. Its provisions were sufficiently
> clear and precise to enable any person who was minded to place
> advertisements to know within what limits they were likely to
> prove acceptable and would also know what were the conse-
> quences if he were to infringe its provisions."[4]

Although the codes did not have direct statutory effect, they met the
purposive intention of Art.10.2.[5]

The Advertising Code has four general principles: that advertise- **3–58**
ments should be legal, decent, honest and truthful. It is also stated that
it will be "applied in the spirit as well as the letter". In addition to these
general principles the code goes into a good deal of detail about various
advertising practices and the manner in which certain products and
services may be advertised. Advertisements must be clearly distinguished as such and comparative advertising is permissible, although
this must be done fairly and without denigrating other products.

A section of the British Code of Advertising Practice sets out rules **3–59**
governing health claims, and there are sections devoted specifically to
advertisements directed at children, advertisements for slimming and
medical products, vitamins, alcohol and cigarettes, as well as mail order
advertisements.

Proponents of the self-regulatory system argue that it provides a **3–60**
positive approach to advertising control which can deal with matters of
taste and decency which it would be impractical to control by statute. It
is also argued that the code can be amended more speedily than
legislation and that it commands a high degree of commitment from the
business community and encourages higher standards in advertising.[6]

Against this, the weakness of the sanctions available to ASA has **3–61**
already been noted. It should be added that such sanctions as there are
operate only after a breach of the code has taken place. There is no
speedy method of taking preventive action against major breaches of the
code. Also, as with all voluntary measures, the code only applies to

---

[3] SI 1988/915.
[4] [2001] E.M.L.R. 22 at para.26; [2001] H.R.L.R. 22 at para.26.
[5] For another decision raising the question of the applicability of Human Rights Act
1998, see *Buxton (t/a The Jewellery Vault) v Advertising Standards Authority* [2002]
EWHC 2433.
[6] See *The Self-Regulatory System of Advertising Control. Report of the Working Party*
(Burgh Report) (DTI, 1980), p.3.

those advertisers and media that subscribe to it. To a limited extent, this criticism of the code has lost some of its force with the implementation of the Misleading Advertising Directive,[7] and it is to consideration of this that we now turn.[8]

EC DIRECTIVE ON MISLEADING AND COMPARATIVE ADVERTISING

3–62 The UK implemented the EC Council Directive on Misleading Advertising, adopted by the Community in 1984,[9] through the Control of Misleading Advertisements Regulations 1988.[10] The purpose of the Directive was to protect consumers and those carrying on trades and professions against the effects of misleading advertising in any form.[11] It has now been amended so as to include comparative advertising.[12] The Directive obliges Member States to ensure that adequate and effective means exist for the control of misleading advertising, and for compliance with its provisions on comparative advertising. This must take the form of legal provisions which permit persons or organisations regarded under national law as having a legitimate interest in prohibiting misleading advertising or regulating comparative advertising to take legal action, or to bring it before an impartial administrative authority competent either to decide on a complaint or to initiate appropriate proceeding, or both.[13]

3–63 In so far as further action was required, the Misleading Advertising Directive has been implemented in the UK by two pieces of legislation, the Financial Services and Markets Act 2000 and the Control of Misleading Advertising Regulations 1988.[14] The Act provides that investment advertisements may only be issued by or with the approval of "authorised persons".[15]

3–64 The regulations deal with other types of advertising which they define in very wide terms.[16] An advertisement is misleading if in any way,

---

[7] Dir. 84/450; [19841 O.J. L250/17.

[8] For two views on the codes, see Middleton and Rodwell, "Regulating Advertising" (1998) 8 *Consumer Policy Review* 88 and Crawford, "If It Ain't Broke, Don't Fix It" (1998) 8 *Consumer Policy Review* 132. And for an independent comment see on the operation of the system, see D. L. Parry, "The Future of Voluntary Regulation of Advertising" (2000) 8(2) Consum. L.J. 137–159.

[9] Dir. 84/450; [19841 O.J. L250/17.

[10] SI 1988/915.

[11] *ibid.*, art.1.

[12] Dir. 97/55.

[13] SI 1988/915, art.4, paras 1, 3.

[14] *ibid.*, as amended by Control of Misleading Advertisements (Amendment) Regulations 2000 (SI 2000/914).

[15] See Financial Services and Markets Act 2000 and *Financial Services Authority Handbook*, "Conduct of Business Manual", Pt 3.

[16] See Control of Misleading Advertisements Regulations 1988 (SI 1988/915), regs 2(1), 3.

including its presentation, it deceives or is likely to deceive the persons to whom it is addressed or whom it reaches; and if, by reason of its deceptive nature, it is likely to affect their economic behaviour or, for those reasons, injures or is likely to injure a competitor of the person whose interests the advertisement seeks to promote.[17] An advertisement is comparative "if in any way, either explicitly or by implication it identifies a competitor or goods or services offered by a competitor".[18] The OFT is required to consider complaints (other than frivolous or vexatious ones) about misleading or comparative advertisements except those relating to commercial broadcasting or cable television.[19] Before it considers a complaint the OFT may require the complainant to satisfy it that appropriate means of dealing with the complaint have been tried and that, despite being given a reasonable opportunity to do so, those means have not dealt with the complaint adequately.[20] Such means might include a complaint to a local authority trading standards department who might take action under the Trade Descriptions Act 1968, or to a self-regulatory body such as ASA.

Where the OFT does decide that it is appropriate for it to take action **3–65** it is given power to bring proceedings in the Court of Session for interdict to prevent the publication or continued publication of an advertisement.[21] Should it decide not to take action it is required to give reasons for its decision.[22]

The new provisions contained in the regulations, to quote the **3–66** Government consultative paper on their implementation, were seen "essentially as a 'long-stop'" which it was hoped would "strengthen rather than diminish the authority of the self-regulatory system". That appears to have been how the system has operated, and the OFT has only had to resort to court action on nine occasions. The first case, *Director-General of Fair Trading v Tobyward Ltd,*[23] was a good example of the "longstop" nature of the regulations.

Tobyward Ltd made a number of sweeping claims for a slimming **3–67** product which led to complaints to ASA that its code, had been breached. The Advertising Standards Authority agreed and advised Tobyward on how it might comply with the code, advice which was ignored. It then referred the matter to the Director-General of Fair Trading (since the enactment of the Enterprise Act 2002 it would be the OFT) who sought an interlocutory injunction to stop the publication of the advertisements. In granting the injunction the judge held that "misleading" in the regulations meant "no more than that it must make

---

[17] SI 1988/915, reg.2(2).
[18] *ibid.*, reg.2(2a), inserted by Control of Misleading Advertisements (Amendment) Regulations 2000 (SI 2000/914).
[19] *ibid.*, regs 4(1), (2), (4).
[20] *ibid.*, reg.4(3).
[21] *ibid.*, regs 2(3), 5(1).
[22] *ibid.*, reg.5(2).
[23] [1989] 2 All E.R. 266.

it likely that [consumers] will buy the product." He went on to say that it was:

> "desirable and in accordance with the public interest to which he must have regard that the courts should support the principle of self-regulation. I think that advertisers would be more inclined to accept the rulings of their self regulatory bodies if it were generally known that in cases in which their procedures had been exhausted and the advertiser was still publishing an advertisement which appeared to the court to be prima facie misleading an injunction would ordinarily be granted."[24]

3–68   In addition to obtaining injunctions, the OFT had accepted undertakings from traders on 30 occasions instead of taking court action. In 1992 an undertaking was given for the first time not only by a trader but also by his advertising agency.[25] Following the creation of a team within the OFT in 2000 to deal with misleading advertisements more undertakings and orders are being sought. The most recent statistics show that in the fifteen month period covered in the most recent annual report 38 undertakings and 11 court orders were obtained.[26]

3–69   OFCOM, the communications regulator whose responsibilities include broadcasting is placed under a similar duty to consider complaints relating to the services for which it has statutory responsibility.[27]

---

[24] The DGFT also obtained an injunction in another case in 1989, see Annual Report of the Director-General of Fair Trading (OFT, 1989), p.53.

[25] See annual reports of the Director-General for the relevant years.

[26] OFT, Annual Report and Resource Accounts, Statistical Annexe (2002–03 HC 906).

[27] See Control of Misleading Advertisements Regulations 1988 (SI 1988/915), regs 8–11, as amended by Control of Misleading Advertisements (Amendment) Regulations 2003 (SI 2003/3183), Sch.1, para.3(5).

CHAPTER 4

ACQUIRING THE GOODS

This chapter deals with a number of issues connected by the fact that **4–01** they relate to problems which may arise at the inception of the transaction. These will include questions such as: what sort of contract is it, legally speaking; when was it concluded?; or what are the consumer's rights if it turns out that the person from whom the goods were bought was not the true owner? Other issues could be included at this stage such as the point at which a contract for the supply of goods is concluded. This topic has been omitted because it is fully covered in textbooks on contract and readers are likely to be familiar with the problems of distinguishing invitations to treat from offers and the rules of offer and acceptance. Contracts for the supply of goods are, in general, no different from other contracts and the general law of contract applies to them.[1]

Many contracts for the supply of goods require no special formalities. **4–02** However, as we shall see in Ch.9, those relating to credit must comply with certain statutory formalities to be valid.

The law relating to the capacity of individuals was amended by the **4–03** Age of Legal Capacity (Scotland) Act 1991. As a result, a person of or over the age of 16 has capacity to enter into any transaction.[2] However, a person under the age of 21 may ask a court to set aside a transaction which was entered into while that person was 16 or over but under 18 years of age. The grounds on which this can be done are that the transaction was prejudicial. "Prejudicial"[3] means "a transaction which (a) an adult, exercising reasonable prudence, would not have entered into in the circumstances of the applicant at the time of entering into the transaction, and (b) has caused or is likely to cause substantial prejudice to the applicant." This protection will be lost if the other party to the transaction was induced to enter into it by a fraudulent misrepresentation as to age or other material fact.

---

[1] For an example of the application of the general law to problems thrown up by the supply of computer software, see *Beta Computers (Europe) Ltd v Adobe Systems (Europe) Ltd*, 1996 S.L.T. 604.
[2] Age of Legal Capacity (Scotland) Act 1991, s.1(1)(b).
[3] *ibid.*, ss.3, 4.

4–04   Children under the age of 16 generally have no legal capacity to enter into any transaction.[4] This rule could be inconvenient as such children do purchase goods, so the Act provides that they shall have legal capacity to enter into transactions "of a kind commonly entered into by persons of their age and circumstances" as long as this is "on terms which are not unreasonable." The purchase of things like sweets and comics by children under the age of 16 should not be open to challenge as a result. The same may be said of other purchases such as some sports equipment, computer software or recreational services. As the value of the goods or services rises and the age of the child diminishes it becomes more difficult to know what a child will be regarded as having capacity to buy.

TYPES OF CONTRACT FOR THE SUPPLY OF GOODS

4–05   It is still necessary in Scotland to distinguish between the various types of legal transaction under which the property in, or the possession of, goods may pass from a supplier to a consumer. The enactment of the Sale and Supply of Goods Act 1994 has clarified and simplified the law in this area to a considerable extent. Nevertheless, it is still necessary to be clear about the legal nature of a transaction because the legal consequences vary in some circumstances.

4–06   One of the most common transactions involving the supply of goods is the contract of sale. This is largely governed by the Sale of Goods Act 1979 which consolidated legislation dating from the original Sale of Goods Act 1893 which had been amended by a number of subsequent Acts. A contract of sale is defined by s.2(1) of the 1979 Act as "a contract by which the seller transfers or agrees to transfer the property in goods to the buyer for a money consideration, called the price." The fact that sale must involve "a money consideration, called the price" distinguishes sale from barter.

4–07   Barter, or exchange as it is sometimes called, "is a contract under which one moveable object is exchanged or bartered for another".[5] In this form barter is rarely encountered[6] but it is very common, especially in the motor trade, for goods to be acquired for a price consisting partly of cash and partly of another piece of moveable property. It is not entirely clear what the legal status of this trading-in transaction is. This is not merely of academic interest for important questions on the rights of the consumer turn on the classification.

---

[4] Age of Legal Capacity (Scotland) Act 1991, s.2(1).
[5] Erskine, *Institutes*, III.iii.13.
[6] It is not unknown as *Ballantyne v Durant*, 1983 S.L.T. (Sh. Ct.) 38 (a case involving the exchange of two cars) and *Widenmeyer v Burn, Stewart & Co Ltd*, 1967 S.C. 85 (a commercial transaction involving the exchange of stocks of whisky) demonstrate.

In the most recent case where the problem arose, *Sneddon v Durant*,[7] **4–08** the pursuer had purchased a van which was on display in the defenders' showroom with a price of £995 attached. He paid for the van by trading in his car which was valued at £845 and entering into a consumer credit agreement with the defender to pay the balance of £150. The sheriff disposed of the question of the type of contract by stating that where money was involved it should be regarded as one of sale. From the point of view of consumer protection there was much to be said for this result as it meant that the transaction was subject to the more satisfactory remedies of sale. An examination of the cases and the views of legal writers, however, demonstrates that this view may be an over-simplification.[8] As far as the terms about title, description, quality and sample to be implied in such contracts are concerned, the problem of classification no longer matters because of the Sale and Supply of Goods Act 1994. This has assimilated barter to sale in these respects. However, it is still possible for the exact nature of the contract to be important for other reasons. The new legislation does not apply to questions about the passing of the property. There would thus be no different result in a case such as *O'Neill v Chief Constable of Strathclyde Police*[9] which concerned title to a car which had been bartered for another which had been stolen.

Goods are also supplied under contracts involving supply on credit. **4–09** These are discussed in Ch.9. The legal significance of transactions under which a contractor agrees to provides goods and services is discussed in Ch.7.

Goods are often supplied in return for vouchers, coupons or stamps. **4–10** One example of this is the trading stamp which is now not as popular as it once was. Sales promotions, especially by petrol companies, encourage brand loyalty by offering vouchers which can be exchanged for various "gifts". Trading stamps have their own legislation, the Trading Stamps Act 1964, but there is some uncertainty about the legal nature of the transactions offering "free gifts". The problem caused a good deal of dissension among the Law Lords in *Esso Petroleum Co. Ltd v Customs and Excise Commissioners.*[10] During the 1970 FIFA World Cup a petrol company offered motorists the opportunity to collect a set of coins each bearing a picture of a member of the England football team. The coins had little intrinsic value. The case turned on whether or not this was a sale. Four of their Lordships agreed that it was not a sale, two considering it to be a gift and two some sort of contract for the

---

[7] 1982 S.L.T. (Sh. Ct.) 39.
[8] For a detailed examination of this question of classification, see Forte, "A Civilian Approach to the Contract of Exchange in Modern Scots Law" (1984) 101 S.A.L.J. 691.
[9] 1994 S.C.L.R. 253.
[10] [1976] 1 W.L.R. 1.

supply of goods. The fifth decided that it was a contract of sale, the motorist's payment buying both petrol and the coins.

4–11   The importance of this case now, with the passage of the Sale and Supply of Goods Act 1994, is that it supports the view that such transactions are contracts for the supply of goods and subject to the new Pt 1A of the Supply of Goods and Services Act 1982 which applies to Scotland.

PRICE AND DELIVERY

4–12 Price does not usually give rise to problems in consumer sales. It is usually perfectly clear what the price is because it is marked on a ticket on the goods or on the shelf. The provisions of s.8 of the Sale of Goods Act 1979 which refer to the methods of ascertaining the price have little relevance. Indeed, if the price has not been explicitly agreed in a consumer sale it is probably strong evidence that there has not been an agreement and that negotiations are still continuing.[11] It is possible that there might be misunderstanding about the price, perhaps in private sales. Where there is genuine misunderstanding about the price to be paid it may be that the contractual doctrine of error may operate to show that there has been no agreement.[12] However, it should be remembered that the courts are slow to allow resort to the doctrine of error.

4–13   It is not uncommon, where a consumer orders goods, for the seller to ask for a deposit. This serves two purposes: if the purchase goes ahead it is looked upon as an advance payment, but its principal purpose, to quote Lord Macnaghten in *Soper v Arnold*,[13] "is a guarantee that the purchaser means business". If the purchaser fails to honour the contract the deposit is forfeited.[14] Should the trader, in breach of contract, fail to provide the goods ordered, the deposit is recovered using the restitutionary remedy *condictio causa data causa non secuta*.

PROBLEMS ABOUT TITLE TO GOODS

4–14 Problems sometimes arise about the right of the seller to sell the goods. Difficult questions may arise involving the buyer, the person from whom the goods were acquired, and the true owner. In contracts of sale the starting point is the implied terms about title in s.12 of the Sale of Goods Act 1979. These implied terms, as a result of the Unfair Contract Terms Act 1977,[15] cannot be excluded. Section 12(1) provides that there is an implied term that the seller has a right to sell the goods. Section 12(2) provides that there is also an implied term that the goods are free

---

[11] Support for this may be seen in the judgement of Sellers L.J. in *Ingram v Little* [1961] 1 Q.B. 31 at 49, where absence of agreement even about the method of payment was considered to indicate the lack of a concluded bargain.

[12] As in *Wilson v Marquis of Breadalbane* (1859) 21 D. 957.

[13] (1889) 14 App. Cases 429.

[14] *Zemhunt (Holdings) Ltd v Control Securities plc*, 1992 S.C.L.R. 151.

[15] s.20(1)(a).

from any charge or encumbrance not disclosed or known to the buyer before the contract is made and that the buyer will enjoy quiet possession of the goods except so far as it may be disturbed by the owner or other person entitled to the benefit of any charge or encumbrance which was disclosed.

McDonald v Provan (of Scotland Street) Ltd[16] provides a bizarre **4–15** example of the operation of s.12. McDonald bought a car from Provan Ltd, who in turn had bought it in good faith. Three months after the sale the car was taken from McDonald by the police because at least part of it was stolen property. It appeared that the car consisted of parts of two separate cars, one of which had been stolen, that had been welded together. McDonald sued for damages for breach of the implied term about title in s.12 and it was held that he was entitled to succeed if he could prove the assertions on which he relied.

The implied terms about title are useful provided that the seller can **4–16** still be found and is worth suing. In many cases raising problems about ownership of goods this is not the case. The facts of *MacLeod v Kerr*[17] provide a typical example. Kerr had advertised his car for sale in a newspaper and sold it to a man who came to see it. He accepted a cheque in payment and permitted the man to take the car away together with the registration document. The man had given a false name and paid with a cheque from a stolen cheque book. On discovering that he had been tricked Kerr immediately informed the police. Meanwhile, the rogue sold the car to a Mr Gibson who knew nothing of these events. The rogue was not worth suing and the question in the case was which of two people who had been duped by him was the legal owner of the car. This unfortunate situation can also arise in other ways as the cases discussed below will demonstrate.

Prior to the passing of the original Sale of Goods Act 1893, problems **4–17** of this sort posed fewer problems at Scots common law. The approach of Scots law, contrasting sharply with that of England, was that, normally, someone could not become the owner of moveable property without *traditio*, which was the physical transfer of the article to the buyer. The 1893 Act changed this in relation to the contract of sale by imposing on Scots law the English idea that the transfer of ownership and possession could be separated. It is this approach which increases the number of situations in which problems akin to that mentioned in the previous paragraph can arise.

NEMO DAT RULE AND ITS EXCEPTIONS

It is a general principle of the law relating to moveable property that **4–18** someone who buys from a person who is not the owner can get no better

---

[16] 1960 S.L.T. 231.
[17] 1965 S.C. 253.

title than that person has. This is sometimes referred to by the Latin tag *nemo dat quod non habet*: no one can give a better title than he himself has. While logical, this can be an extremely inconvenient and unjust rule in some circumstances, and so the Sale of Goods Act 1979 has a number of modifications of this principle.

PERSONAL BAR EXCEPTION

4–19 The first of these exceptions is to be found in s.21 of the 1979 Act which first states the general principle. It reads as follows:

> "Subject to this Act, where goods are sold by a person who is not their owner, and who does not sell them under the authority or with the consent of the owner, the buyer acquires no better title to the goods than the seller had, unless the owner of the goods is by his conduct precluded from denying the seller's authority to sell."

4–20 There are no Scottish cases on this exception, though there are some examples of its operation in English case law. In *Eastern Distributors Ltd v Goldring*[18] it came into play through the owner of a van signing hire-purchase forms in blank, for completion by another person, thus allowing that person to appear to be the owner of the van. Generally, the English courts have construed the exception narrowly, as *Moorgate Mercantile Co Ltd v Twitchings*[19] demonstrates. The parties to this case were both finance companies and both were members of Hire Purchase Information (HPI). Hire Purchase Information is a trade association set up by finance companies to keep a register of hire-purchase agreements relating to cars, and to give information to members, the police and motoring organisations in order to try to reduce hire-purchase frauds. The plaintiffs let out a car on hire-purchase and for some reason, contrary to their normal practice, failed to register the agreement with HPI. The hirer offered to sell the car to the defendant who, after checking with HPI and finding that no agreement had been registered, bought it. By a majority of three to two the House of Lords held that the plaintiff owed no duty of care to the defendant and was not precluded by its conduct from denying the authority of the hirer to sell the car.

4–21 This decision has been subjected to much criticism and it is not binding on the Scottish courts, who are free to come to a different decision in a similar case. It is suggested that it would be appropriate that this should be done. There would be no conflict with the approach of the Court of Session in *Mitchell v Z. Heys & Sons*[20] where a claim that the owner was personally barred failed. There it was held that for such a claim to succeed it would have to be shown that a representation

[18] [1957] 2 Q.B. 600.
[19] [1977] A.C. 890, HL.
[20] (1894) 21 R. 600.

by words or conduct had been made to, and relied upon by, the person claiming now to be the owner.

SALE UNDER A VOIDABLE TITLE

Section 23 of the Sale of Goods Act 1979 provides that when the seller **4–22** of goods has a voidable title to them, but his title has not been avoided at the time of the sale, the buyer acquires a good title to the goods, provided he buys them in good faith and without notice of the seller's defect of title. The facts of *MacLeod v Kerr*[21] are a good example of the sort of situation in which this provision might be relied upon by the buyer. The language of the section is based on English law concepts and it may be misleading to rely on some of the English cases which make subtle distinctions between situations where a contract is void, and therefore of no effect, and those where it is voidable, which means that it has effect until the seller has taken some action to rescind it.[22]

The approach of Scots law, as Professor Gow has cogently argued,[23] **4–23** is that a buyer taking in good faith and for value acquires a title which is unimpeachable unless the seller acquired the goods by theft. The fact that the seller's title was tainted by error or fraud is not relevant. While this reasoning may not have been explicitly adopted in *MacLeod v Kerr*,[24] the decision in the case is consistent with it. It is an approach which has much to commend it on policy grounds. As Professor Gow points out, why should an innocent buyer be "penalised and enmeshed in expensive litigation simply because [the true owner] was so naive, or so credulous, or so gullible as to trust the seller, or so reckless as to take a long chance on his creditworthiness."[25] Indeed, one might argue that the law should be amended to protect the buyer even where the goods have been stolen from the true owner. The true owner will probably be insured against this possibility, to which he may to some degree have contributed, whereas the buyer will not.

SALE BY A BUYER OR SELLER IN POSSESSION

Sections 24 and 25 of the Sale of Goods Act 1994 may protect someone **4–24** who has purchased goods from a person who appears to be their owner. Section 24 deals with the situation where goods have been sold but, for some reason, they are left in the possession of the seller. Depending on the circumstances, the buyer may well have become the owner by this

---

[21] 1965 S.C. 253. See para.4.16.
[22] This view is supported by *Corporeal Moveables: Protection of the Onerous Bona Fide Acquirer of Another's Property* (Scot. Law Com. Memorandum No. 27, (1976)), para.21.
[23] J.J. Gow, *The Mercantile and Industrial Law of Scotland* (W. Green, Edinburgh, 1964), pp.118–122.
[24] 1965 S.C. 253.
[25] Gow, *op cit.*, p.121.

time. What if the seller purports to sell the goods to someone else? The answer given by s.24 is that that person becomes the owner provided that he or she acted in good faith and did not know of the previous sale.

4–25   Similarly, goods which the buyer has bought may come into his possession before he becomes the legal owner. If he sells or otherwise disposes of those goods the sale has the same effect as if the person making the delivery or transfer were a mercantile agent in possession of the goods or documents of title with the consent of the owner. This is conditional on the person to whom he sells having acted in good faith and having no knowledge of the original seller's rights. The significance of the reference to the sale having the same effect as if made by a mercantile agent is that sales by such persons give good title to the buyer. The English Court of Appeal in *Newtons of Wembley Ltd v Williams*[26] has gone so far as to say that this part of the section means that the sale does not simply have the same effect as if it had been made by such an agent but must actually have been made by such agent. This is an impossible situation and it must be open to doubt if a Scottish court would follow this case. There are dicta from Australian and New Zealand cases which take a contrary view and interpret this part of the section in a literal way.[27]

4–26   Before looking at some of the other points in relation to this provision it should be noted that a buyer under a conditional sale agreement[28] and someone who has acquired goods under a hire-purchase agreement are not "buyers" for the purpose of it.[29]

4–27   The protection of s.25 only applies if the buyer is in possession with the consent of the seller. However, the fact that the buyer obtained that consent by deception does not nullify consent for this purpose.[30]

4–28   A point of some uncertainty arises where the seller is not himself the owner of the goods and was not authorised to sell them. This arose in the English case of *National Employers Mutual General Insurance Association Ltd v Jones*,[31] where Mr Jones had acquired a car which had originally been stolen from the plaintiff's insured and then passed through the hands of several parties who had dealt with it in ignorance of this fact. It was held that Mr Jones could not have the protection of s.25 because the person who sold to him did not have title to the car on the *nemo dat* principle. Strictly speaking, he was not a "seller" so Mr Jones could not be a "buyer". In effect, seller was being interpreted to

---

[26] [1965] 1 Q.B. 560.
[27] See *Langmead v Thyer Rubber Co. Ltd* (1947) S.A.S.R. 29 at 39; *Jeffcott v Andrew Motors Ltd* [1960] N.Z.L.R. 721 at 729.
[28] s.25(2).
[29] *Helby v Matthews* [1895] A.C. 471.
[30] *Du Jardin v Beadman Brothers* [1952] 2 Q.B. 712.
[31] [1987] 3 All E.R. 385.

mean "owner". It could, and it is submitted should, be argued that those in the position of Mr Jones are sellers for the purposes of s.25.

DISPOSITIONS OF MOTOR VEHICLES SUBJECT TO HIRE PURCHASE OR CONDITIONAL SALE

Section 27 of the Hire-Purchase Act 1964 was passed to alleviate the **4–29** hardship that was caused where consumers bought cars and later discovered that they were subject to hire-purchase agreements. The seller had no title and so could confer none on the buyer. The finance company financing the transaction was the owner and was entitled to recover the vehicle, leaving the buyer with an action against the seller. The seller would often be untraceable or not be worth suing. Section 27 applies where a motorvehicle has been hired under a hire-purchase agreement or has been agreed to be sold under a conditional sale agreement and, before the property in the vehicle has become vested in the debtor, he has disposed of it to another person. In this situation s.27(2) provides that:

> "Where the disposition . . . is to a private purchaser, and he is a purchaser of the motor vehicle in good faith and without notice of the hire-purchase agreement or conditional sale agreement, . . . that disposition shall have effect as if the creditor's title to the vehicle has been vested in the debtor immediately before that disposition."

Section 27(3) applies this also to the situation where the vehicle has been sold to a trade or finance purchaser who then hire-purchases or sells it to the private purchaser.

It is important to note that this protection only applies to hire- **4–30** purchase and conditional sale agreements. It does not apply to simple hire agreements. Therefore, someone who buys a car from a person who has hired a car or leased it, as it is often termed, does not have the protection of this provisions. With the increasing popularity of leasing as a method of acquiring motorvehicles there is evidence that more innocent purchasers are falling victims to this fraud. "Motor vehicle" is defined as a mechanically propelled vehicle intended or adapted for use on roads to which the public has access."[32] It does not cover caravans or boats, both of which are commonly acquired by hire-purchase.

There must also be a valid hire-purchase agreement, as the recent **4–31** House of Lords decision in *Shogun Finance Ltd v Hudson*[33] demonstrates. Mr Hudson had purchased a car in good faith from a rogue who had acquired it by impersonating a Mr Patel. The rogue had obtained Mr Patel's personal documents and used these and a forged signature to

---

[32] Hire-Purchase Act 1964, s.29(1).
[33] [2003] UKHL 62; [2003] All E.R. (D) 258

convince the finance company that he was Mr Patel and so to accept his offer to enter into a hire-purchase agreement. Mr Hudson sought to rely on s. 27 to assert that he had a good title to the car. The House of Lords held that the hire-purchase agreement was void for mistake and thus the rogue had not acquired title of any sort. There was thus no possibility of Mr Hudson taking advantage of s.27. This decision does turn on the rather obscure English law of contractual mistake but it seems likely that the same result would obtain in Scotland as the rogue would be regarded as having stolen the car and this taints the transaction with a *vitium reale* (fundamental flaw) and so it is void from its inception.

4–32   The term "private purchaser" is somewhat misleading as it includes anyone who is not a trade or finance purchaser; that is, anyone who does not carry on a business involving trading in motor vehicles or providing finance for their hire-purchase or conditional sale. This means that many businesses will also obtain the protection of s.27.

4–33   To obtain the protection the buyer must be able to show that he did not have actual notice of the fact that there was an existing hire-purchase agreement.[34] It is also important to note that the buyer only gets the title of the person who was described as the creditor in the hire-purchase or conditional sale agreement. Suppose that a stolen car is sold to a dealer who then lets it on hire-purchase to someone who sells it before the end of the hire-purchase agreement. Even if the buyer from that person takes in good faith and without notice of the hire-purchase agreement, s.27 does not come to their rescue. This is because the dealer did not have title to the car having bought from a thief who could not pass on a good title.

PROBLEMS CONCERNING PROPERTY AND RISK

4–34 In this section the problems that arise when the goods are damaged or destroyed after the buyer has agreed to buy them are discussed. Here it is assumed that there is nothing wrong with the quality of the goods in the sense that at the time that the contract was made the goods were of satisfactory quality, fit for their purpose and matched any description applied to them. Similarly, it is assumed that none of the problems about title to goods discussed in the previous section has arisen.

4–35   Here we are concerned with the question of who bears the risk of something going wrong. For example, suppose that after the buyer and seller have entered into a contract for the sale of a piece of furniture it is destroyed in a fire at the showroom; or goods ordered by mail are lost or damaged in the post. Until the changes made to the Sale of Goods Act 1979 by the Sale and Supply of Goods to Consumers Regulations 2002[35] came into force on March 31, 2003, the solution to problems like

---

[34] *Barker v Bell* [1971] 1 WL.R. 983.
[35] SI 2002/3045.

these could be quite complex. Since that date the law in relation to consumer transactions has been considerably simplified.

Prior to March 31, 2003, the starting point was to be found in the Sale **4–36** of Goods Act 1979, s.20(1):

> "Unless otherwise agreed, the goods remain at the seller's risk until the property in them is transferred to the buyer, but when the property therein is transferred to the buyer, the goods are at the buyer's risk whether delivery has been made or not."

The Sale and Supply of Goods to Consumers Regulations 2002[36] added a new subs.(4) to that section which provides:

> "In a case . . . in Scotland, where there is a consumer contract in which the buyer is a consumer, subsections (1) to (3) above must be ignored and the goods remain at the seller's risk until they are delivered to the consumer."

This change is complemented by another to s.32 of the Sale of Goods **4–37** Act 1979. That section contains the general rule that where the seller is authorised or required to send the goods to the buyer delivery to a carrier is "prima facie deemed to be delivery of the goods to the buyer". That could have been interpreted to mean that in mail order sales the consumer took the risk of the goods going missing or being damaged in transit though in previous editions of this book it was argued that this would not normally be the case in consumer transactions.[37] The result of these changes is that until the goods are delivered to a consumer the risk is on the seller. For the sake of completeness it should be added that because the definition of "consumer contract", which is that in s.25 of the Unfair Contract Terms Act 1977, excludes sales of second hand goods by auction which individuals can attend in person the old rules could still be relevant. This is a somewhat limited exception which does not justify a discussion of the previous law.[38]

RISK RULES AND FRUSTRATION

In relation to the problems which may arise where the goods are **4–38** damaged or destroyed some other points need to be referred to, though in the context of consumer sales they may not have much relevance. Section 6 of the Sale of Goods Act 1979 provides that where there is a contract for the sale of specific goods, and the goods without the knowledge of the seller have perished at the time when the contract is made, the contract is void. Section 61 defines "specific goods" as

---

[36] SI 2002/3045.
[37] See 2nd ed., para.4–55.
[38] This can be seen in 2nd ed., paras 4–34—4–55.

"goods identified and agreed on at the time a contract of sale is made". In a consumer context an obvious example would be a product selected by the consumer in a shop. This might apply where the seller and buyer have agreed that the seller will sell a specific car identified by make and registration number. If, unknown to him, it was destroyed in a fire on the day before the contract was made the contract would be a nullity.

4–39   Section 7 deals with a slightly different situation. Like s.6 it applies to a sale of specific goods, but here the destruction occurs, without any fault on the part of the seller or buyer, before risk passes to the buyer. In this situation the sale is avoided. In consumer sales, s.7 can have little scope for application when one considers the rules about the passing of risk. A possible example would be where a consumer buys a car which requires some work to be done to it before it is to be collected some days later. The effect of s.18, rule 2 is that the risk does not pass to the buyer so that if, through no fault of the seller, the car were stolen or destroyed in a fire the section would apply.

4–40   In the case of unascertained goods the scope for them to perish in a legal sense is more limited. "Unascertained goods" are not defined in the Act but it is clear that the term is used in contradistinction to specific goods. It covers three situations. Where the goods are to be manu-factured or grown by the seller they will be unascertained. While not common in a consumer context this would include a product made to special order. It also includes generic goods such as a ton of coal or a consumer product referred to by its general description; and an unidentified part of a specific whole such as a case of Beaujolais Nouveau from the shipment in a particular wine merchant's warehouse. An agreement to sell purely generic goods cannot be frustrated by the destruction of the goods and it is of no concern to the buyer that the seller had a particular source in mind as Asquith L.J. explained in *Monkland v Jack Barclay Ltd*[39]:

> "Suppose A has contracted to sell to B unascertained goods by description for example, 'a' Bentley Mark VI (not 'this' Bentley Mark VI), and suppose, further, that the seller expects to acquire the goods from a particular source, which may, indeed, be the only source available, the bare fact, without more, that when the time for delivery comes that source has dried up and that the seller cannot draw on it, does not absolve the seller. He is still, in the absence of some contractual term excusing him, liable for non-delivery."

Late delivery

4–41   What is the position where the goods are delivered late? The starting point is s.10(2) of the Sale of Goods Act 1979 which provides that whether any stipulation, other than one about the time of payment, is of

---

[39] [1951] 2 K.B. 252 at 258.

the essence of the contract depends on the terms of the contract. The buyer can make the delivery date an express term of the contract but the cases show that this must be done in the clearest terms.[40] This is rarely the case in consumer contracts. However, it may occur, as is shown by *Charles Rickard Ltd v Oppenhaim*[41] where the defendant had ordered a car for delivery within six or seven months. Having allowed the supplier more time on several occasions, he lost patience eventually and wrote saying that he would not take delivery after a certain date. It was held that he was entitled to give reasonable notice making time the essence of the contract, and was thus not in breach of contract in not accepting the car when it was delivered after the stipulated date.

TITLE IN OTHER CONTRACTS FOR THE SUPPLY OF GOODS

Implied terms about title following the model of the Sale of Goods Act **4–42** 1979 are to be found in other contracts for the supply of goods. In the case of hire-purchase they are to be found in s.8 of the Supply of Goods (Implied Terms) Act 1973. Where goods are redeemed for trading stamps they are found in s.4(1) of the Trading Stamps Act 1964. As a result of the insertion in the Supply of Goods and Services Act 1982 of Pt 1A which applies only to Scotland, the implied terms in other contracts for the supply of goods are to be found in two sections of that 1982 Act. For contracts of hire this is achieved by s.11H; and for other contracts by s.11B.

As far as other questions concerning ownership of goods subject to **4–43** the non-sale contracts for the supply of goods are concerned the situation is simpler than with sale.[42] Legislation has not been superimposed on the common law in the way that occurred with the Sale of Goods Act 1979. The transfer of title will normally occur through the handing over of possession. As a result, in these contracts one can generally rely on the person in possession being the owner. As Erskine put it:

> "Such is the natural connection between property and possession, that in moveables, even where they have had a former owner, the law presumes the property to be in the possessor; so that till positive evidence be brought that he is not the right owner, he will be accounted such by the bare effect of his possession."[43]

---

[40] See *T. & R. Duncanson v Scottish County Investment Co. Ltd*, 1915 S.C.1106, *per* Lord Guthrie at 1118.
[41] [1950] 1 K.B. 616.
[42] For a detailed and learned discussion of the issues, see D. L. Carey Miller, *Corporeal Moveables in Scots Law* (W. Green, Edinburgh, 1991), esp. Ch.10.
[43] *Institutes*, II.i.24. See also Stair, *Institutions*, II.i.42.

4-44   Lord Cockburn suggested in *Anderson v Buchanan*[44] that "[t]his is a presumption liable to be rebutted, and perhaps liable to be rebutted easily." In *Prangnell-O'Neill v Lady Skiffington*[45] Lord Hunter observed that how easy it might be to rebut the presumption depended on the circumstances. In his view, to overcome the presumption it was necessary to show that the goods had once belonged to the person claiming them and that his or her possession was terminated in such a way that the subsequent possessor could not have acquired a right to them. Theft will fulfil the second requirement but, as was observed in *Prangnell-O'Neill*, so would evidence of removal by force.

4-45   The presumption can be rebutted, but it seems that where the person in possession has acted in good faith and given value for the goods only proof of theft will be sufficient to permit the original owner to recover the property.

---

[44] (1848) 11 D. 270 at 284.
[45] 1984 S.L.T. 282.

Chapter 5

PRODUCT QUALITY

The vast majority of consumer complaints about goods are concerned **5–01**
with their quality. Consumers expect what they buy to be free from
defects. Should their expectations be disappointed what can they do
about it? This chapter explores the standards of quality that consumers
are entitled to expect, concentrating on goods which are defective but
have not caused physical injury. In the next chapter the way in which
consumers are protected against unsafe goods is discussed. It is mainly
the civil law which is relevant in determining what the legal standard of
quality is, but it should not be forgotten that the criminal law has some
role to play as well. The core of the chapter is devoted to the terms
implied in the various contracts under which goods are supplied. The
final section deals with the role of criminal law in setting standards for
products.

The claims made for a product by the seller may be relevant. If these **5–02**
claims have become terms of the contract the buyer is entitled to expect
that they will be fulfilled and if they are not the normal contractual
remedies will be available. If the claims are not regarded as terms it may
be that they will be misrepresentations. These issues are discussed in
Ch.3.

STATUTORY IMPLIED TERMS IN CONTRACTS FOR THE
SUPPLY OF GOODS

The lynch-pin of consumer protection in relation to quality is the **5–03**
implication of terms into the various contracts under which goods are
supplied. The nature of these contracts has been outlined in Ch.4. The
common law implied various terms relating to quality in these contracts.
Starting with the original Sale of Goods Act 1893 the terms relevant to
the contract of sale were put on a statutory footing and are now to be
found in the Sale of Goods Act 1979. Until the Sale and Supply of
Goods Act 1994 added a Pt 1A to the Supply of Goods and Services Act
1982, the only other contracts where there were such statutorily implied
terms were contracts of hire-purchase[1] and contracts under which

---

[1] Supply of Goods (Implied Terms) Act 1973, ss.8–11.

trading stamps were redeemed for goods.[2] With effect from January 3, 1995, the new Pt 1A of the Supply of Goods and Services Act 1982 has implied similar terms into the various other contracts under which goods are supplied. The discussion of the implied terms in this chapter concentrates on those implied in the contract of sale. The other contracts are dealt with more briefly.

5–04   The implied term about description found in s.13 is not discussed at this point but in Ch.3. This is because the modern tendency, as pointed out in that chapter, is to reserve that term for matters relating to the identity of the goods leaving issues of quality to be decided under s.14. However, there is sometimes a fine line to be drawn between these two things as *Beale v Taylor*[3] demonstrates.

5–05   It hardly requires to be stated that as contractual liability is involved it is the supplier who is liable under the various contracts and that only the other party to the contract may invoke the implied terms. Whether this privity principle should be altered is under consideration and this was recommended in a discussion paper issued by the DTI.[4]

IMPLIED TERMS IN CONTRACTS OF SALE

Quality and Fitness for Purpose

5–06   Section 14(1) of the Sale of Goods Act 1979 provides that: "Except as provided by this section and section 15 . . . there is no implied term about the quality or fitness for any particular purpose of goods supplied under a contract of sale." The section then goes on to set out the two terms that are implied: that goods must be of satisfactory quality, and that they must be reasonably fit for any particular purpose for which the goods are being bought. Before discussing these two terms in detail certain points that are common to both will be mentioned.

5–07   The terms implied by s.14 only apply where the "seller sells goods in the course of a business", a term which, according to s.61, includes "a profession and the activities of any government department . . . or local or public authority". In most cases this will cause no difficulty though there will be some doubtful cases. Must the seller be selling something which he habitually sells, or are the implied terms imposed on every trader who happens to sell an item? The latter approach was the one preferred by the Molony Committee in 1962 and by the Scottish Law Commission in a report in 1969.[5] It has also got judicial support in Scotland in the Outer House judgement in *Buchanan-Jardine v Hami-link*.[6] The case arose out of the sale of livestock on the retirement from

---

[2] Trading Stamps Act 1964, s.4. The DTI has announced that this Act is to be repealed probably in late 2004.
[3] [1967] 1 W.L.R. 1193.
[4] See *Consumer Guarantees: A Consultation Document* (DTI, Feb. 1992).
[5] First Report on Exclusion Clauses (Law Com. No.24; Scot. Law Com. No.12, 1969).
[6] 1981 S.L.T. (Notes) 60.

farming of the pursuer. When it was alleged that two of the cattle which he had sold were not of merchantable quality (as the quality term then was) he argued that this had no application in the circumstances. Lord Dunpark stated that:

> "In my opinion anyone who sells any part of his business equipment must sell that part in the course of his business. It can make no difference whether he sells only one item or the whole of the goods used by him for the purpose of a business."[7]

There are several cases in England where the same phrase has been **5–08** interpreted by the courts in the context of other statutes.[8] These have mainly been criminal statutes where there is a tendency to give a narrow construction to a penal provision. It is submitted that in the context of civil liability the interpretation of Lord Dunpark is to be preferred, in that it provides protection for consumers who are in no position, in many cases, to know what the seller's business consists of. It is also in accord with the plain meaning of the statute. The English Court of Appeal recently adopted this interpretation in *Stevenson v Rogers*.[9]

Less reputable traders have been aware of the advantages of appear- **5–09** ing to sell privately, and such was the scale of this practice that it proved necessary to make it a criminal offence.[10]

The provisions of s.14 can, however, apply where the seller is not **5–10** selling in the course of a business in one situation set out in s.14(5). This occurs where someone arranges for a trader to act as his or her agent for the sale of goods. The fact that the principal is not selling in the course of a business is irrelevant unless the buyer knows that this is the case or reasonable steps are taken to bring this fact to his attention before the contract is made. The buyer may sue either the principal or the agent.[11]

It is also clearly established that the liability under s.14 is strict, as **5–11** was pointed out in *Randall v Newsom*[12]:

> "If there was a defect in fact, even though that defect was one which no reasonable skill or care could discover, the persons supplying the article should nevertheless be responsible, the policy of the law being that in a case in which neither were to blame, he,

---

[7] 1981 S.L.T. (Notes) 60.
[8] See *Davies v Sumner* [1984] 1 W.L.R. 405. The same phrase used in Unfair Contract Terms Act 1977 has not been applied to the purchase of a car by a company for the use of one of its directors: see *R. & B. Customs Brokers Co Ltd v United Dominions Trust Ltd* [1988] 1 WL.R. 321.
[9] [1999] Q.B. 1028; [1999] 1 All E.R. 613; [1999] 2 W.L.R. 1064.
[10] See Business Advertisements (Disclosure) Order 1977 (SI 1977/1918).
[11] *Boyter v Thomson* [1995] 3 All E.R. 135, HL.
[12] (1876) 45 L.W.B. 364.

and not the person to whom they were supplied, should be liable for the defect."

5-13   *Frost v Aylesbury Dairy Co Ltd*[13] provides a good example of this principle in operation. The dairy had supplied Mr Frost and his family with milk which contained typhoid germs which caused the death of his wife. The evidence showed that the dairy's processes were extremely careful and that typhoid germs could only be detected by prolonged investigation. Nevertheless, it was held that there was an implied term that the milk would be reasonably fit for consumption. It was irrelevant that the defect could not have been discovered at the time of sale.

5-13   It is important to note that s.14 applies to the "goods supplied under a contract of sale." This means that in determining whether the goods are of the requisite quality the container or other packaging, the instructions, or foreign material inadvertently supplied with the goods contracted for may be relevant. A graphic illustration is provided by *Wilson v Rickett, Cockerell & Co Ltd*[14] where the plaintiff, who had ordered Coalite from the defendants, found that he had also been supplied with a detonator which exploded in his living room when placed on the fire. The defendants had ingeniously argued, no doubt encouraged by the Court of Session's extraordinary decision in *Duke v Jackson*,[15] that there was nothing wrong with the Coalite and that the detonator[16] was not ordered under the contract. The Court of Appeal held that the goods delivered were not of the requisite quality. As Denning L.J. (as he then was) put it in referring to the words "goods supplied under a contract of sale":

> "In my opinion that means the goods delivered in purported pursuance of the contract. The section applies to all goods so delivered, whether they conform to the contract or not: that is, in this case, to the whole consignment, including the offending piece, and not merely to the Coalite alone. . . . Coal is not bought by the lump. It is bought by the sack or by the hundredweight or by the ton. The consignment is delivered as a whole and must be considered as a whole; not in bits. A sack of coal, which contains hidden in it a detonator, is not fit for burning, and no sophistry should lead us to believe that it is fit."[17]

---

[13] [1905] 1 K.B. 608.

[14] [1954] Q.B. 598.

[15] 1921 S.C. 362; 1921 1 S.L.T. 190.

[16] Counsel does not seem to have had the temerity to go quite as far as to add that the detonator was a perfectly good detonator — as the damage to Mr Wilson's livingroom seemed to prove.

[17] [1954] Q.B.598 at 606.

In *Duke v Jackson*[18] the Court of Session had dealt with a very similar **5–14** case and had been seduced by the arguments of counsel into arriving at just this conclusion. Strictly speaking, that case is a binding precedent in Scotland which the English decision of the Court of Appeal is not. It is inconceivable that it would be followed today; and, indeed, two sheriffs principal on whom the decision was binding managed to distinguish it.[19]

The relevance of instructions is illustrated by *Wormell v RHM* **5–15** *Agricultural (East) Ltd*[20] where a farmer argued that the inadequacy of the instructions on tins of weedkiller rendered it unfit for its purpose. In the English High Court it was observed that the goods included not just the weedkiller but also its packaging and instructions:

> "All of these . . . are part of the goods. One must look at all of them as a whole . . . By selling goods with such instructions the seller is warranting that the chemical, when used in accordance with those instruction, will be reasonably fit for its purpose . . . If a retailer . . . sells the goods (that is the chemical together with its container and instructions) and those instructions make the goods not reasonably fit for their purpose, in my view there is a breach of section 14(3) of the Sale of Goods Act 1979."[21]

Implied Term of Satisfactory Quality

The principal quality standard is contained in s.14(2) which states that: **5–16** "Where the seller sells goods in the course of a business, there is an implied term that the goods supplied under the contract are of satisfactory quality."

The term "satisfactory quality" is a fairly recent innovation. It **5–17** replaced "merchantable quality" which had been introduced into the Scots law of sale by the Sale of Goods Act 1893. Although a definition of "merchantable quality" was eventually added, increasing dissatisfaction was felt with it culminating in the recommendation of the Scottish

---

[18] 1921 S.C. 362; 1921 1 S.L.T. 190.
[19] See *Fitzpatrick v Barr*, 1948 S.L.T. (Sh. Ct.) 5 and *Lusk v Barclay*, 1953 S.L.T. (Sh. Ct.) 23, cited by McBryde, "Scots and English Contract Laws" in Birks, *The Frontiers of Liability* (1994), Vol.2, p.146. See also *Gedling v Marsh* [1920] 1 K.B. 668.
[20] [1986] 1 All E.R. 769.
[21] On appeal the Court of Appeal reversed the decision of the High Court because it took a different view of the facts: see [1987] 1 W.L.R. 1091. No doubt was cast on the principle enunciated. It is now underlined by the inclusion in the list of "relevant circumstances" relating to satisfactory quality of a new s.14(2D) of the Sale of Goods Act 1979, which adds: "any public statement on the specific characteristics of the goods made about them by the seller, the producer or his representative, particularly in advertising or on labelling". This was added by Sale and Supply of Goods to Consumers Regulations 2002 (S.I. 2002 No 3045), reg.3.

Law Commission that it be replaced. In its report, *Sale and Supply of Goods*,[22] the Scottish Law Commission observed:

> "If the word 'merchantable' has any real meaning today, it must strictly be a meaning which relates to merchants and trade; the word must be inappropriate in the context of a consumer transaction. The expression 'merchantable quality' is, and always has been a commercial man's notion."

5–18 The change was effected by s.1 of the Sale and Supply of Goods Act 1994 which inserted a new version of s.14(2) and new subss.(2A), (2B) and (2C). It has also been necessary to add a new subs.(2D) to implement the Directive on Certain Aspects of the Sale of Consumer Goods and Associated Guarantees.[23] The opportunity has also been taken to draft the subsection in language which is appropriate to Scots law. Its predecessor spoke of the implied term being a "condition", a term appropriate in this context to English law and its system of remedies. The significance of this will be discussed in detail later when remedies are considered.

5–19 While "satisfactory quality" is a new phrase, the general structure of section 14 is broadly similar to that in the previous version. Before examining the central features of "satisfactory quality" it is necessary to note two qualifications to its operation.

5–20 Section 14(2C) repeats, in slightly different language, the two qualifications found in the previous versions of the Act. First, the term does not extend to any matter "which is specifically drawn to the buyer's attention before the contract is made". It is important to note that the factor must be specifically brought to the buyer's attention. In *Turnock v Fortune*[24] it was held by the sheriff principal that a strong recommendation from a third party not to buy a car did not amount to specifically drawing attention to its unroadworthiness, and thus did not prevent the car from being regarded as unmerchantable.

5–21 Secondly, if a buyer has examined the goods before the contract was made nothing which "that examination ought to reveal" can be relied on to demonstrate that the goods are not of satisfactory quality. There has been some doubt about the interpretation of this proviso as a result of *Thornett & Fehr v Beers & Son*[25] where the slightly different wording of the 1893 Act was interpreted as if it read "a reasonable examination". A commercial buyer who had made a cursory examination of some glue was held to have lost the protection of section 14 despite the fact that his examination was insufficient to have detected the defect. That case may have been wrongly decided, as it seems to be inconsistent with an earlier

---

[22] Law Com. No.160; Scot. Law Com. No.104, Cm. 137 (1987).

[23] Dir. 1999/44; [1999] O.J. L171/12.

[24] 1989 S.L.T. (Sh. Ct.) 32.

[25] [1919] 1 K.B. 486.

Court of Appeal decision, *Bristol Tramways, etc. Carriage Co v Fiat Motors Ltd*,[26] which was not cited. In any event, the present wording is slightly different and would seem to support the view that it is only defects which the type of examination actually carried out should have revealed that are relevant.

Satisfactory Quality

As was the case in the latter days of its predecessor, satisfactory quality **5–22** is defined. Section 14(2A) provides that: "goods are of satisfactory quality if they meet the standard that a reasonable person would regard as satisfactory, taking account of any description of the goods, the price (if relevant) and all the other relevant circumstances."
Section 14(2B) goes on to expand on this by saying that the quality of **5–23** goods:

> "includes their state and condition and the following (among others) are in appropriate cases aspects of the quality of goods—
>
> (a) fitness for all the purposes for which goods of the kind in question are commonly supplied,
> (b) appearance and finish,
> (c) freedom from minor defects,
> (d) safety, and
> (e) durability."

The new definition retains several elements of the previous definition **5–24** of merchantable quality, but what is novel about it is that new factors are to be taken into account.

The new definition is based on the recommendations of the Law **5–25** Commissions. They suggested "acceptable quality", but like the Consumer Guarantees Bill 1990, the Act refers to "satisfactory quality". Moving the second reading of the Bill, its sponsor explained that it was thought that "[a] non-complaining buyer might decide reluctantly that goods he bought were of acceptable quality, even if by objective standards the quality was not satisfactory."[27] In practice this change probably does not matter very much. What is important is that, as the Law Commissions recommended, there is an objective test of quality and one that is given content by the list of factors which are to be taken into account in assessing what is satisfactory in a given case. It remains a standard that can be applied to all kinds of goods whether new or second-hand.

The definition of "satisfactory quality" is in two parts. The basic test **5–26** appears in s.14(2A) and states the general principle. The test is that of the reasonable person, and in deciding if the standard has been met, any

---

[26] [1910] 2 K.B. 831.
[27] *Hansard*, HC, Vol. 237, col. 633 (Feb. 11, 1994).

description applied to the goods must be taken into account as well as the price, if that is relevant, and all other relevant circumstances. As already pointed out, the reference to "a reasonable person" implies an objective standard and this appears to be how the judges confronted by the definition have applied it though they have generally not thought it necessary to spell this out. The reasonable person is "not an expert"[28] and Sedley L.J. observes in *Jewson Ltd v Boyhan*[29] that the "reasonable person" is "a construct by whose standards the judge is required to evaluate the quality of the goods". Who this reasonable person is will depend in part on the description of the product and he gives the homely example of a soft toy where the test will have to be applied by reference to how a toddler might handle it. The reasonable person, he notes, is not one "equipped with the buyer's personal agenda"[30] even if this has been communicated to the seller. In *Jewson* the buyer had sought to argue that it was relevant to take into account under satisfactory quality that he did not simply want central heating boilers but that he wanted boilers which would not have a detrimental effect on his business of property developer in selling the flats. If this could be relevant at all it could only be relevant to the other implied term of fitness for purpose.

5–27   The factors of price, description and other relevant circumstances were set out in the earlier definition of "merchantable quality". A description may affect the standard that can be expected. If goods are described as "second-hand" then it will usually not be reasonable to expect the quality of new goods. On the other hand, statements in advertising material suggesting that the article is at the top end of the range might increase the standard of quality that it would be reasonable to expect. In *Clegg v Andersson* Hale L.J. points out that the buyer of a very expensive, brand new, ocean going yacht is entitled to expect it to be "perfect or nearly so".[31] Similarly, price may be important, though it is an ambiguous signal. The price may be reduced simply to encourage faster sale of the item without implying any diminution in quality. Taken with other factors, such as a statement that the goods are "seconds", or the mileage and general condition of a second-hand car, it might well indicate that a lower standard of quality can be expected. In *Thain v Anniesland Trade Centre*,[32] for example stress was put on the price together with the fact that the car was second-hand, not new, and had a high mileage as factors that lowered the level of quality that could be expected. At the other end of the scale payment of a high price, as the observation of Hale L.J. in the previous paragraph demonstrates, will raise the standard of quality that can be expected.

---

[28] *Clegg v Andersson* [2003] 1 All E.R. (Comm) 721, *per* Hale L.J., para.73.
[29] [2003] EWCA Civ. 1030, para.78.
[30] *ibid.*
[31] [2003] 1 All E.R. (Comm) 721, para.73.
[32] 1997 S.L.T. (Sh. Ct.) 102.

Jewson raises generally the question of what might constitute "other **5–28**
relevant circumstances" which may be taken into account in addition to
price and description. Clarke L.J.'s observation that "a circumstance
would be relevant if a reasonable person would regard it as relevant"[33]
does not take matters very far. As we have just noted, Sedley L.J.
considers that the personal agenda of the buyer will not usually be
relevant. However, he does note that the place of sale could be a relevant
circumstance. He gives the example of a soft toy whose safety and
durability would normally have to be judged in relation to how a toddler
might handle it. If a toddler were to choke on it there might be a breach
of the implied term of satisfactory quality while if the victim were a dog
the only claim would be under s.14(3) as not being fit for a particular
purpose. However, he suggests that the fact that the object had been
bought in a pet shop might be a relevant circumstance allowing the
claim to be brought under s.14(2) in relation to harm to the dog.

In *Britvic Soft Drinks Ltd v Messer UK Ltd*[34] the other "relevant **5–29**
circumstance" appears to have been the commercial context of the
problem and expected consumer reactions. The defendants sold carbon
dioxide to the claimants who, as the defendants knew, intended to use it
in the production of their alcoholic and soft drinks. The carbon dioxide
was contaminated by benzene, a carcinogen, though not in quantities
that posed any threat to health. The level of contamination was
substantially higher than the maximum acceptable statutory limits
subsequently agreed and at a level which led the seller, in consultation
with the manufacturer from whom it had obtained the supplies, to issue
immediate warnings to customers. Both the seller and the claimants
were mindful of the catastrophic commercial repercussions on Perrier
which had resulted from the poor handling of a contamination problem.
As a result the claimants had recalled supplies of drinks thought to have
been contaminated and their claim was for the losses flowing from this
course of action.

The trial judge found: **5–30**

"it impossible to conclude that a reasonable person would regard
the CO2 supplied as meeting a satisfactory standard. Consumers
would not wish to drink products which had inadvertently been
contaminated with a measurable quantity of a known carcinogen,
notwithstanding the quantity was not harmful to their health . . .
The affected products themselves were in a real sense unsaleable in
the sense that no consumer would knowingly buy them and the
manufacturers could not as responsible manufacturers be seen to
attempt to sell them."[35]

---

[33] [2003] 1 All E.R. (Comm) 721, para.67.
[34] [2002] 2 All E.R. (Comm) 321; [2002] EWCA Civ. 548.
[35] [2002] 1 Lloyd's Rep. 20, para.92.

In coming to this conclusion Tomlinson J. was applying the general definition and, in part, specifically referring to one of the factors, description, as the carbon dioxide had been described as suitable for food applications. However, this does also seem to be an example of taking into account "other relevant circumstances" in the form of consumer reactions.[36]

5–31   In addition to the basic principle, s.14(2B) sets out a list of specific factors which, *in appropriate cases*, may be taken into account in assessing satisfactory quality. The words emphasised in the last sentence make it clear that not all the factors would be relevant in every case; and it is also stated that the list of factors is not exhaustive.

5–32   The first factor is that the goods are fit for all the purposes for which goods of the kind in question are commonly supplied. The placing of this aspect of quality is significant. As the Law Commissions noted in its report, this is almost always a very important aspect of quality, but the drafting of the previous definition had over-stressed it. In several decisions usability had been the touchstone and the fact that there were defects affecting the appearance of the product were not considered to be relevant.[37] In addition, the earlier definition had spoken of goods being fit for the purpose or purposes as "it is reasonable to expect". This, it can be argued, had lowered the standard of quality where the seller could establish that goods of the particular type, such as new cars, can reasonably be expected to possess a number of minor defects on delivery. *Millars of Falkirk Ltd v Turpie*[38] can be used in support of this argument.

5–33   The new definition diminishes the importance of fitness for purpose by including it in the list of factors which may be taken into account. As the Law Commissions' report pointed out,[39] a new car should not only be capable of being driven safely and effectively on the roads, but should also do so "with the appropriate degree of comfort, ease of handling and reliability and . . . of pride in the vehicle's outward and interior appearance" to quote Mustill L.J. in *Rogers v Parish (Scarborough) Ltd*.[40]

5–34   It goes further and reverses the previous law under which the test was satisfied if the goods were fit for any of the purposes for which goods of that type could be used.[41] The new version provides that goods must be suitable for "all the purposes for which goods of the kind in question are commonly supplied". If goods have more than one purpose and the

---

[36] The finding that the product was not of satisfactory quality was not challenged on appeal but comments in the judgments of the Court of Appeal suggest that it agreed with these observations: see [2002] Lloyd's Rep. 368, *per* Mance L.J. at para.11.

[37] More recent cases such as *Rogers v Parish (Scarborough) Ltd* [1987] Q.B. 933 have suggested a more realistic approach to fitness at least in relation to consumer goods.

[38] 1976 S.L.T. (Notes) 66.

[39] Law Com. No.160; Scot. Law Com. No.104, Cm. 137 (1987); and see para.3–31.

[40] [1987] Q.B. 933.

[41] *M/S Aswan Engineering Establishment Co v Lupdine Ltd* [1987] 1 W.L.R. 1.

seller intends his product to fulfil only one of those purposes it will be necessary to make this clear. This may be done explicitly or, in some circumstances, other factors such as the price may indicate this fact.

This factor has only been explicitly discussed in *Jewson Ltd v* **5–35** *Boyhan*.[42] This case raised the question, to quote Clarke L.J., "as to how far it is appropriate to have regard to the purposes for which goods are wanted by the purchaser in deciding what circumstances are relevant for the purposes of subss.(2) and (2A)"[43] as opposed to subs.(3). The buyer was a property developer who purchased a number of electric central heating boilers for installation in flats that he was constructing. He discovered that these boilers had poor energy ratings according to government approved tests and feared that the flats would be difficult or impossible to sell. This caused him to abandon the project and when Jewsons sued him for the price of the boilers he counterclaimed for several hundred-thousand pounds based on his loss of profit and increased costs resulting from the installation of the boilers, as opposed to boilers with better energy ratings. He attempted to argue that among the purposes for which the boilers had to be fit was ensuring that they would not render the flats in which they were to be installed difficult or impossible to sell. In effect, the Court of Appeal did not accept that this was one of "the purposes for which goods of the kind in question are commonly supplied". Clarke L.J. recognised that there is scope for debate about which purposes are relevant but went on to suggest the following test:

> "There may be exceptions, but in general a particular purpose which is not one of the ordinary uses for which goods of the relevant type are generally supplied seems to me to be irrelevant. The question in most cases will be whether the goods are intrinsically satisfactory and fit for all purposes for which goods of the kind in question are supplied."[44]

He conceded that "some regard must be had to the use which is likely **5–36** to be made of the goods"[45] but that would only extend in this case to saying that they had to be of satisfactory quality for use in flats, which they were. As Sedley L.J. succinctly put it: "[The buyer] got exactly what he had bargained for: twelve boilers which worked perfectly well".[46]

Appearance and finish, and freedom from minor defects are also to be **5–37** taken into account in determining whether goods are of satisfactory quality. These characteristics are more likely to apply to new rather than

---

[42] [2003] E.W.C.A. Civ. 1030.
[43] *ibid.*, para.69.
[44] *ibid.*, para.69.
[45] *ibid.*, para.70.
[46] *ibid.*, para.79.

second-hand goods. A major uncertainty of the old law is thus removed.[47] The result is, to quote the Law Commissions' report, that:

> "[D]ents, scratches, minor blemishes and discolorations, and small malfunctions will in appropriate cases be breaches of the implied term as to quality, provided they are not so trifling as to fall within the principle that matters which are quite negligible are not breaches of contract at all."[48]

5–38   The regrettable decision in *Millars of Falkirk v Turpie*[49] is thus reversed and, if similar facts were to recur, it seems certain that the car would be regarded as of unsatisfactory quality. The application of this test will, of course, depend on the facts. Second-hand goods may be expected to have some minor marks or defects while, usually, new goods should not. Hale L.J. pointed out *obiter* in *Clegg v Andersson*, a consumer case, that: "In some cases, such as a high priced quality product, the customer may be entitled to expect that it is free from even minor defects, in other words perfect or nearly so".[50] However, certain kinds of product such as earthenware, pottery or natural products may be expected to have minor inconsistencies and blemishes and these may well not render them of unsatisfactory quality. In some cases this test will have no application at all. The Law Commissions gave as examples cars sold as scrap and loads of manure.

5–39   There has never been any doubt that unsafe goods were not of the quality demanded by law[51] and this is explicitly recognised in the definition. The Law Commissions argued that this was necessary, despite the clarity of the existing law, for several reasons. It might make clear that hazardous products which can be used safely only if unusual precautions are taken or warnings given will not meet the standard of satisfactory quality unless those warnings are given; it would rebut the argument that safety was not relevant because it has not been included in the statute; and to omit a reference would be odd since safety is such an important part of the quality of modern consumer goods.[52] Safety was the central factor in *Clegg v Andersson*.[53] A new ocean going yacht costing £250,000 was delivered to the buyer with a keel which was substantially heavier than the manufacturer's specification. Technical evidence showed that this would render the rigging

---

[47] In *Bernstein v Pamson Motors (Golders Green) Ltd* [1987] 2 All E.R. 220 certain obiter remarks suggested that minor defects were not relevant to merchantability, while *Rogers v Parish (Scarborough) Ltd* [1987] Q.B. 933 considered that they were.

[48] Law Com. No.160; Scot. Law Com. No.104, Cm. 137 (1987); and see para.3–40.

[49] 1976 S.L.T. (Notes) 66.

[50] [2003] 1 All E.R. (Comm) 721; [2003] EWCA Civ 320; [2003] 2 Lloyd's Rep. 32, para.72.

[51] *Godley v Perry* [1960] 1 WL.R. 9, CA; *Lambert v Lewis* [1982] A.C. 225.

[52] *op. cit.*, n.48, para.3.45.

[53] [2003] 1 All E.R. (Comm) 721; [2003] EWCA Civ 320; [2003] 2 Lloyd's Rep. 32.

unsafe and, in the circumstances, the Court of Appeal had no difficulty in finding that the yacht did not meet the standard of satisfactory quality.[54]

Somewhat less clear was whether goods had to be durable, though **5–40** this does appear to have been the law.[55] The matter is now put beyond doubt by the new definition. It is important to realise that this term is to be satisfied at the time of delivery and not at some later date. Later events may be relevant in determining whether, at the time of sale, the goods were durable.[56] The criterion is durability not duration. The Law Commissions rejected any suggestion that normal lifespan for classes of goods should in some way be required. They emphasised, and this is reflected in the new definition, that durability is to be a flexible concept requiring that goods should last a reasonable time taking into account whether they have been well or badly treated.

The first case to discuss the new satisfactory quality term was *Thain* **5–41** *v Anniesland Trade Centre*[57] a decision of the sheriff principal of Glasgow and Strathkelvin. Ms Thain had paid £2,995 for a second-hand Renault 19 car which had travelled about 80,000 miles and was about six years old. Two weeks after she purchased it an intermittent droning noise was noticed and this proved to be a failing differential bearing in the automatic gear box. The sellers refused to replace the gear box. Eventually, after about nine to ten weeks, the car was unusable and Ms Thain rejected it. The sheriff principal upheld the sheriff's decision that the car was of satisfactory quality observing:

> "[T]he sheriff's conclusion can only be described as that of the reasonable person. Even a negligible degree of durability may not represent unsatisfactory quality where the secondhand car supplied is as old and as heavily used as the Renault had been. The plain fact is that, given the Renault's age and mileage when supplied, its durability was a matter of luck. Durability, in all the circumstances, was simply not a quality that a reasonable person would demand of it."[58]

One can only marvel at this view of reasonableness and ask how **5–42** many car buyers would think it reasonable that they should take all the risk of a catastrophic breakdown almost immediately after purchase. The decision appears to make a mockery of the express inclusion of durability as one of the factors to be taken into account in assessing satisfactory quality. Perhaps emphasis should be placed on the fact that

---

[54] [2003] 1 All E.R. (Comm) 721, paras 49 and 73.
[55] For a survey, see Ervine, "Durability, Consumers and the Sale of Goods Act", 1984 J.R. 147.
[56] *Crowther v Shannon Motor Co. Ltd* [1975] 1 WL.R. 30.
[57] 1997 S.L.T. (Sh. Ct.) 102; 1997 S.C.L.R. 991.
[58] 1997 S.L.T. (Sh. Ct.) 102 at 106.

this case turns on its own somewhat special facts. There was evidence even from Ms Thain's own expert witness that there was no sign of a problem during the first two weeks that she drove the car and that the part which failed could work well and suddenly deteriorate. Given that nine to ten weeks was regarded as reasonable durability the problem of when the test has to be satisfied never arose. It is sometimes said that that this is the date of the contract, at which point in this case there was no evidence of a defect. That could have been circumvented, as was done by Lord Denning in *Crowther v Shannon Motor Co*,[59] by using the fact of a short lifespan as evidence that the car did not meet the statutory standard at the date of the contract.[60]

5–43   Where it is possible to show that the goods were unsatisfactory because they were not durable the benefits of including durability in the definition of satisfactory quality will not be as great as one might expect. This stems from the fact that while a lack of durability will render goods unsatisfactory, there is no corresponding change in the remedies available. By the time a consumer realises that the goods are not durable it is very likely that the right to reject will be lost. Damages will, therefore, be the only remedy in most of the cases where goods prove not to be durable.[61] It may be that this statement needs to be modified in the light of the new alternative set of remedies to be found in Pt 5A of the Sale of Goods Act 1979 as a result of the Sale and Supply of Goods to Consumers Regulations 2002.[62] Section 48C provides a right to rescind which is not lost in the way that the other right to reject is. However, it is not the consumer's primary right and any reimbursement is subject to a reduction to take account of the use that the consumer has enjoyed.

Fitness for Purpose

5–44   As well as being of satisfactory quality, s.14(3) states that:

> "Where the seller sells goods in the course of a business and the buyer, expressly or by necessary implication, makes known—
>
> (a) to the seller, or
> (b) where the purchase price or part of it is payable by instalments and the goods were previously sold by a credit-broker to the seller, to that credit-broker, any particular purpose for which the goods are being bought, there is an implied term that the goods supplied under the contract are reasonably fit for that purpose, whether or not that is a purpose for which such goods are commonly

---

[59] [1975] 1 W.L.R. 30.
[60] See Ervine, "Satisfactory Quality, Thain v Anniesland Trade Centre", 1998 J.R. 379.
[61] In *Thain* the possibility that the right to reject had been lost was not discussed.
[62] SI 2002/3045.

supplied, except where the circumstances show that the buyer does not rely, or that it is unreasonable for him to rely, on the skill or judgement of the seller or credit-broker."

The reference to a credit-broker is necessary to take account of **5–45** certain kinds of sales financed by a third party. The credit-broker will often be a retailer in whose shop the goods have been displayed and in which negotiations for their purchase have taken place. If the retailer does not provide his own credit facilities what next happens is that the goods are sold to a finance company who then sell to the consumer. Examples of transactions which would be covered would be credit sale and conditional sale.

The features which this term shares with that on satisfactory quality **5–46** have already been commented on above. It will also be noted that there is considerable overlap between the two, as satisfactory quality is partially defined in terms of fitness for purpose. There will be many situations where a product will fail to satisfy either term. The weedkiller in *Wormell v RHM Agricultural (East) Ltd*,[63] which had inadequate instructions, and the defective car in *Rogers v Parish (Scarborough) Ltd*[64] are examples. However, there are circumstances where a product might be of satisfactory quality but not pass the test of fitness for purpose. Suppose that someone has a metal gate which is to be painted. She goes to a DIY store and explains to an assistant that paint suitable for the job is required. The paint which the assistant sells her turns out to be unsuitable, being intended only for application to wood. In this case the customer will succeed in a claim under s.14(3) for breach of the implied term about fitness for purpose. She would not succeed with a claim for unsatisfactory quality because there is nothing wrong with the paint which would be perfectly satisfactory for painting wood.

The relationship between the two implied terms has been explored in **5–47** two recent cases. In *Clegg v Andersson* Hale L.J. observed: "The amendments made to s.14 by the Sale and Supply of Goods Act 1994 also make it clear that fitness for purpose and satisfactory quality are two quite different concepts".[65] It is true that there will be circumstances in which both implied terms are broken but there is a tendency to mark out more clearly the scope of each and this is explored in *Jewson Ltd v Boyham*.[66] There, Sedley L.J. pointed out: "Section 14(2) is directed principally to the sale of substandard goods. This means that the court's principal concern is to look at their intrinsic quality, using the

[63] [1986] 1 All E.R. 769.
[64] [1987] Q.B. 933.
[65] [2003] 1 All E.R. (Comm) 721 at para.72; [2003] EWCA Civ 320; [2003] 2 Lloyd's Rep. 32.
[66] [2003] EWCA Civ 1030.

tests indicated in subsection (2A), (2B) and (2C)."[67] He went on to point out that where it was sought to introduce "factors peculiar to the purposes of the particular buyer" that had to be done under section 14(3).[68] In the same case Clarke L.J. stated: "It seems to me that under the statutory scheme set out in section 14 it is the function of section 14(3), not section 14(2), to impose a particular obligation tailored to the particular circumstances of the case."[69]

5-48   To avail oneself of the protection of this term it is necessary to show that one has, either expressly or by implication, indicated the particular purpose for which the goods are required. As Lord Wilberforce observed of both the s.14 implied terms, they are "readily and untechnically applied to all sorts of informal situations — such as retail sales over the counter of articles whose purpose is well known — and are applied rather more strictly to large scale transactions carried through by written contracts".[70] In many cases it will not be necessary for the customer to have referred expressly to the particular purpose. The burden of proof is on the seller to show that reliance was unreasonable, as was pointed out in *Grant v Australian Knitting Mills Ltd*[71]:

> "The reliance will seldom be express: it will usually arise by implication from the circumstances. Thus to take a case like that in question, of a purchase from a retailer, the reliance will be in general inferred from the fact that a buyer goes to the shop in the confidence that the tradesman has selected his stock with skill and judgement: . . . the main inducement to deal with a good retail shop is the expectation that the tradesman will have bought the right goods of a good make."

5-49   This quotation is redolent of an earlier age before the rise of modern retail methods. Nevertheless, if the customer relies on the staff of a store it will be difficult for it to assert that this was unreasonable, unless it had been made quite plain that they had no specialised knowledge.[72] As this case makes clear, it is not necessary to specify a particular purpose where the goods, such as underpants or hot-water bottles,[73] have only one purpose.

---

[67] [2003] EWCA Civ 1030, para.77.
[68] *ibid.*
[69] *ibid.*, para.47.
[70] *Henry Kendall & Sons v William Lillico & Sons* [1969] 2 A.C. 31 at 123.
[71] [1936] A.C. 85 at 99.
[72] A parallel might be drawn with the cases on services where the tradesman having done a poor job tried to assert that he did not have the specialised skill for the particular job. See cases discussed at paras 7–13 *et seq.*
[73] See *Priest v Last* [1903] 2 K.B. 148.

If the customer does have a particular purpose in mind, which is not **5–50** the common purpose or has some susceptibility, this must be communicated to the seller. *Baldry v Marshall*,[74] where the customer required a car which would be comfortable and suitable for touring, is an example of the first issue; and *Griffiths v Peter Conway Ltd*[75] an example of the second. In the latter case the plaintiff had developed a very severe attack of dermatitis as a result of wearing a tweed coat purchased from the defendants. Mrs Griffiths' skin was unusually sensitive and the evidence showed that there was nothing in the cloth that would have affected a normal person's skin. As Mrs Griffiths had not informed the sellers of her sensitivity they were not liable.

Flynn v Scott[76] makes clear that the particular purpose must be clearly **5–50** specified. There, the subject of the sale was a lorry which could have been used for a number of different functions, though the buyer intended to use it to transport furniture and livestock. A claim for breach of the implied term of fitness for purpose failed because it was not shown that the buyer had communicated his particular purpose.

SALE BY SAMPLE

Section 15 of the Sale of Goods Act 1979 implies various terms in sales **5–52** by sample. There is a term that the bulk will correspond with the sample in quality; and that the goods will be free of any defect rendering them of unsatisfactory quality which would not be apparent on reasonable examination of the sample.

These terms are not limited to sales in the course of a business, no **5–53** doubt because it was not thought likely that they would occur in any other context. They are not especially important in a consumer context, though carpets and wallpaper will often be sold by reference to samples. To some extent, s.15 duplicates other sections in many circumstances. Most sales by sample will attract the protection of the implied term about description and, if the goods are not of satisfactory quality under s.15, they must also fail to satisfy the implied term in s.14(2).

TERMS IMPLIED IN OTHER SUPPLY CONTRACTS

Hire-purchase

Terms in very similar language to that relating to sale, but adapted to the **5–54** specialities of hire-purchase transactions, are to be found in ss.8–11 of the Supply of Goods (Implied Terms) Act 1973. The drafting of these terms has been amended by the Sale and Supply of Goods Act 1994 to reflect the change from merchantable quality to satisfactory quality and

---

[74] [1925] K.B. 260.
[75] [1939] 1 All E.R. 685, approved in *Slater v Finning Ltd*, 1996 S.L.T. 912; [1996] 3 All E.R. 398, HL.
[76] 1949 S.C. 442; 1949 S.L.T. 399.

to be appropriate for Scots law.[77] They have been further amended by the Sale and Supply of Goods to Consumer Regulations 2002[78] in implementation of the EC Directive on Certain Aspects of the Sale of Consumer Goods and Associated Guarantees[79] in a similar manner to s.14 of the Sale of Goods Act 1979.

Trading Stamps

5–55 Section 4 of the Trading Stamps Act 1964 implies terms about quality and description where goods are exchanged for trading stamps. These terms have been amended in the same way as the terms in sale and hire-purchase contracts and now use terminology appropriate to Scots law.

Other Contracts for the Supply of Goods

5–56 In addition to the contracts for the supply of goods already referred to, there are various other transactions which result in goods being supplied to consumers. Although it is not particularly common nowadays in its most basic form, goods are sometimes exchanged or bartered for other goods. Indeed, if trading in is legally barter, then this contract is very common, especially in the car market. There is some doubt, as we have seen in an earlier chapter, about this issue.[80]

5–57 It is common to hire goods of many kinds. Televisions and video recorders are frequently supplied on long-term hire, cars and equipment may be hired for short periods, and it is not uncommon for cars to be acquired for long-term use through a hire arrangement usually referred to as a lease. This is an alternative to purchasing on credit. Goods may also be acquired in exchange for coupons, vouchers or tokens in sales promotions.[81]

5–58 What all these transactions had in common, until the passing of the Sale and Supply of Goods Act 1994, was the absence of a regime of statutory implied terms such as were implied in contracts of sale and hire-purchase. There were, of course, implied terms, but these were implied by common law, and it was not always certain what they were, or easy to discover them. Pt 1 of the Supply of Goods and Services Act 1982 had provided implied terms in such contracts in England but that Act did not then extend to Scotland. Section 6 of the Sale and Supply of Goods Act 1994 provides that a Pt 1A is inserted in the 1982 Act to achieve the same thing in Scotland for contracts entered into after January 3, 1995. This new part is set out in Sch.1 to the 1994 Act. As the terms implied are the same as those for sale, subject to necessary

---

[77] See Sale and Supply of Goods Act 1994, Sch.2, para.4.
[78] SI 2002/3045.
[79] Dir. 1999/44; [1999] O.J. L171/12.
[80] See Ch.4.
[81] The legal nature of this kind of transaction was examined in Ch.4.

verbal changes, it is not necessary to discuss them again.[82] As in the case of the other types of contract discussed above the definition of satisfactory quality has been amended by the Sale and Supply of Goods to Consumers Regulations 2002.[83]

REMEDIES

CONTRACTS OF SALE

The enactment of the Sale of Goods Act 1893 put the law relating to the **5–59** remedies of the disappointed consumer in Scotland into a confused state.[84] The Sale and Supply of Goods Act 1994 effected considerable improvements. The problem stemmed from the fact that the original 1893 Act was drafted with English legal concepts in mind. It was extended to Scotland only at a late stage in its parliamentary progress. The implied terms, for example, were described as "conditions" and "warranties", expressions which do not fit into the scheme of remedies in Scots contract law. An attempt was made to modify the legislation to conform to Scots law, but this was not satisfactory.[85]

The Sale of Goods Act 1979, which had not addressed this basic **5–60** problem, was amended by the Sale and Supply of Goods Act 1994. As we have seen above, the implied terms have been redrafted and are simply described as "terms". The consequences of breach are then separately dealt with for England and Wales and Scotland in ways which are appropriate for each jurisdiction. However, further complication has been added by the necessity to implement the EC Directive on Certain Aspects of the Sale of Consumer Goods and Associated Guarantees[86] which, among other things, requires new remedies to be available to purchasers of goods. Under the scheme of remedies set out in the Directive the primary remedies are repair or replacement whereas under the original Sale of Goods Act the primary remedy is to reject the goods and have the price returned. Strictly speaking, under the original Sale of Goods Act repair or replacement were not legal rights of the consumer, although in practice they were frequently offered. The UK government indicated that implementation of this Directive would be carried out in such a way that there would be no lessening of the protection enjoyed by UK consumers. To achieve this result the original remedy of rejection had to be preserved as well as introducing the new

---

[82] On the 1994 Act, see Ervine, "The Sale and Supply of Goods Act 1994", 1995 S.L.T. 1. Note that the definition of satisfactory quality is split between s.11J (in the case of hire) and s.11D (in other supply contracts) and s.18(1) of Supply of Goods and Services Act 1982, as amended by Sale and Supply of Goods Act 1994, Sch.2, para.6(10).
[83] SI 2002/3045.
[84] See Clarke, "The Buyer's Right of Rejection", 1978 S.L.T. (News) 1.
[85] *ibid.*
[86] Dir. 1999/44; [1999] O.J. L171, pp.0012–0016.

rights of repair or replacement. This has been done by creating two parallel sets of remedies. The original remedies of rejection or damages remain and the new remedies have been created by introducing a new Pt 5A to the Sale of Goods Act 1979. This is clearly headed "Additional Rights of the Buyer in Consumer Cases".

5–61   As a result, it is necessary to consider the two sets of remedies. From an examination of these two sets of remedies it will become clear that there may be situations where the disappointed consumer will have difficult choices to make about which set of remedies to pursue. It will also be apparent that, at least initially, the new situation must cause consumers, their advisers and traders some difficulty in coming to terms with the new dispensation.

Original Sale of Goods Act Remedies

5–62 A new s.15B, inserted in the Sale of Goods Act 1979 by the Sale and Supply of Goods Act 1994, provides that, where the seller is in breach of any term of a contract, whether express or implied, the buyer shall be entitled to claim damages and, if the breach is material, to reject the goods and treat the contract as repudiated. This firmly places the remedies for breach of a contract of sale in the scheme of Scots contract law.[87] The section goes further in the case of consumer contracts. In these contracts, breach of the express or implied terms about the quality or fitness of goods for a purpose, and correspondence with description or sample, is deemed to be a material breach. This makes clear that the primary remedy of a consumer for the common breaches of contract is rejection of the goods. It removes the uncertainty caused by *dicta* in *Millars of Falkirk Ltd v Turpie*.[88] In that case the Lord President had suggested that a finding that goods were not of merchantable quality would not automatically confer a right to reject. The continuing importance of rejection as the main remedy was underlined in *Clegg v Andersson*[89] recently by the English Court of Appeal. In a brief but powerful judgment Hale L.J. (as she then was) pointed out that "the customer has a right to reject goods which are not of satisfactory quality. He does not have to act reasonably in choosing rejection rather than damages or cure" and the fact that this remedy "may be thought to be disproportionate by some is irrelevant".[90] This is an important point of principle emphasising the primacy of the remedy of rejection for consumer (though not non-consumer) buyers. It is especially important given the new alternative set of remedies for consumers brought in by the Sale and Supply of Goods to Consumers Regulations 2002[91] which make repair or replacement of defective goods the primary remedy.

---

[87] See, *e.g. Wade v Waldon*, 1909 S.C. 571.
[88] 1976 S.L.T. (Notes) 66.
[89] [2003] 1 All E.R. (Comm) 721.
[90] *ibid.*, para.74.
[91] SI 2002/3045.

Section 15B does not deem breach of the implied term about title to **5–63** be material. It is difficult to conceive of circumstances where this would not be so. It might be that there could be cases where such a breach was cured almost immediately after the goods were delivered which might justify not treating it as material.

Right to Reject

While it is now clear that rejection is the primary remedy for breach of **5–64** the most important terms in contracts of sale, it is necessary to examine precisely when it may be exercised. It is now assumed that the breach is a material one that justifies rejection.

To exercise the right of rejection, consumers must demonstrate two **5–65** things: that they have effectively intimated rejection to the seller; and that the goods have not been accepted. The first of these requires that the consumer has given the seller an unequivocal indication that the goods have not been accepted. In *Lee v York Coach and Marine*[92] the consumer was held not to have indicated an intention to reject during the period when that was possible. Letters from his solicitors asking the seller to remedy the defects or offer a refund did not amount to rejection. As section 36 of the Sale of Goods Act 1979 makes clear, rejection does not necessarily require the consumer to return the goods to the seller unless it has been otherwise agreed. They would have to be stored carefully and, if the seller fails to collect them, damages may be claimed for any costs involved in storage.[93]

The right to reject ceases to be available when the consumer has **5–66** accepted the goods in the legal sense. When goods are accepted is defined in s.35. It occurs in three circumstances: where the buyer has intimated to the seller that he has accepted the goods; when, on receiving delivery, the buyer does an act inconsistent with the seller's ownership; and when, after the lapse of a reasonable time, the buyer retains the goods without intimating to the seller that he has rejected them.

The first two situations in which acceptance occurs are now clearly **5–67** subject to the right to have a reasonable opportunity to examine the goods for the purpose of ascertaining that they are in conformity with the contract. This is now set out in the new version of s.35(2). In the case of loss of the right to reject through lapse of time, s.35(4) achieves much the same result in a slightly different way. What constitutes a reasonable opportunity to examine goods depends on the circumstances. There do not appear to be any cases in a consumer context which shed much light on this issue. However, it seems that it may involve the use of the goods for a short time.[94] Indeed, in *Clegg v Andersson*[95] it seems

---

[92] [1977] R.T.R. 35, CA.
[93] *Kolfor Plant Ltd v Tilbury Plant Ltd* (1977) 121 S.J. 390, DC.
[94] *Lucy v Mouflet* (1860) 5 H. & N. 229.
[95] [2003] 1 All E.R. (Comm) 721.

to have been accepted without comment that the purchaser of an ocean-going yacht would need to examine it by cruising in it for several days.

Intimation of Acceptance

5–68 The most common situation where rejection by intimation has occurred in a consumer context has been through the signing of "acceptance notes". Consumers often sign such documents when goods are delivered, not realising that they may go further than merely evidencing receipt of the goods. It is not uncommon to find that they contain a statement indicating that the consumer has examined the goods and acknowledges that they are in good condition. Section 35(2) states that buyers who have not previously examined goods which are delivered to them must have a reasonable opportunity of examining them before they are deemed to have accepted them. Section 35(3) makes clear that this opportunity cannot be taken away "by agreement, waiver or otherwise". This means that signing an acceptance note can no longer sign away the consumer's right to reject the goods.

5–69   This aspect of rejection (and others) was discussed in *Clegg v Andersson*,[96] a recent English Court of Appeal decision involving a consumer transaction. Mr Clegg, a wealthy insurance broker, agreed to buy a new ocean going yacht from the defender for £250,000. The yacht was delivered to Mr Clegg with a keel which was almost one tonne heavier than the manufacturer's specification a fact of which he was not informed until the date of delivery. He chose to try out the yacht by cruising in it for several days in August and then between August 2000 and March 1, 2001, he corresponded with the seller on, among other matters, the overweight keel, its consequences, and the available remedies. It was not until February 15, 2001, that he received from the seller the full technical information needed to make an informed decision on the quality of the yacht. This technical evidence showed that the keel as delivered would render the rigging unsafe. On March 6, 2001, the claimant informed the defendants that he was rejecting the yacht. As we have seen, the Court of Appeal had no difficulty in finding that the yacht did not meet the satisfactory quality standard. The defendants argued that Mr Clegg had lost the right to reject because, knowing of the overweight keel, he had said that he liked the yacht, and would decide whether remedial work should be carried out. The court saw these merely as ancillary to his decision whether to reject not statements indicating that he would accept the yacht rather than reject it.

[96] [2003] 1 All E.R. (Comm) 721.

Acceptance by an Act Inconsistent with the Ownership of the Seller

There is little guidance in the case law on what amounts to an act **5–70** inconsistent with the ownership of the seller in the context of a consumer transaction. In commercial transactions the most common situation where this arises is in the resale of goods. There appears to be only one Scottish case, *Hunter v Albancode plc.*[97] Mrs Hunter bought a suite of furniture which proved to be defective and she purported to reject it. When it was not uplifted by Albancode Mrs Hunter continued to use it as she could not afford to replace it until she obtained a refund. The sheriff held that continuing to use the goods amounted to an act inconsistent with the seller's ownership and thus the right to reject had been lost. Further guidance is to be found in the New Zealand case of *Armaghdown Motors Ltd v Gray Motors Ltd.*[98] Gray Motors took a car which they had recently purchased to the premises of the plaintiffs and offered to sell it to them. They applied an incorrect description to the car and were in breach of the equivalent of s.13 of the Sale of Goods Act 1979. The sale took place on June 15, but the plaintiffs did not discover the misdescription until July 7, when they received the vehicle's registration certificate. Four days later they registered the car in their own name and put it on sale in their showroom. It was held that, as the defect was latent, the plaintiffs were entitled to have the period from the date of sale until July 7, to discover the true position. Their actions thereafter, in registering the car in their own name and putting it on sale, were acts inconsistent with the ownership of the seller which brought their right to reject to an end.

Incorporating goods into other goods from which they cannot easily **5–71** be removed may well amount to an act inconsistent with the ownership of the seller.[99] So, for example, if someone buys parts to carry out a repair on a car and after fitting the part it becomes clear that it is defective it may not be possible to reject, though damages would still be available. In *Clegg v Andersson*[1] the defenders argued that Mr Clegg had done acts inconsistent with their ownership by insuring the boat, attempting to register it and indicating to the seller that he might permit remedial work. The latter was dismissed, not surprisingly, given that s.35(6) now provides that actually agreeing to a repair does not amount to acceptance, as were the other two which were requirements of the loan agreement into which he had entered to finance the purchase.

Prior to the amendments to the Sale of Goods Act 1979 made by the **5–72** Sale and Supply of Goods Act 1994 it was unclear whether requesting or agreeing to a repair amounted to an act inconsistent with the ownership of the seller. This matter is now put beyond doubt by the new

---

[97] 1989 G.W.D. 39–1843.
[98] [1963] N.Z.L.R. 5.
[99] *Mechan & Sons Ltd v Bow, McLachlan & Co. Ltd*, 1910 S.C. 758.
[1] [2003] 1 All E.R. (Comm) 721.

version of s.35 of the 1979 Act, which states that the buyer is not deemed to have accepted goods merely because he asks for, or agrees to, their repair by or under an arrangement with the seller.

Lapse of a Reasonable Time

5–73   The third situation in which the right to reject may be lost is where the consumer retains the goods for a reasonable time after delivery without intimating to the seller that he has rejected them. What is a reasonable time is, as s.59 points out, a question of fact, "as if it could be anything else", as Rougier J. sardonically observed in *Bernstein v Pamson Motors (Golders Green) Ltd.*[2] The new version of s.35 gives some important guidance on this point. Section 35(5) states that: "The questions that are material in determining . . . whether a reasonable time has elapsed include whether the buyer has had a reasonable opportunity of examining the goods."

5–74   This is particularly important because under the previous version of the Sale of Goods Act 1979 the right to have an opportunity to examine the goods had no relevance to the loss of the right to reject through lapse of time. In *Clegg v Andersson*[3] this point was emphasised and, in particular, it was pointed out that *Bernstein* could no longer be relied on because of this change in the law. The Court of Appeal in *Clegg* clearly had reservations about the correctness of the much criticised[4] *Bernstein* case even in its own context, but contented itself by pointing out that it does not now represent the law.[5] Sir Andrew Morritt V.C. went on to point out that other factors could be taken into account and that s.35(6)(a) specifically referred to one of these namely, that the buyer "asks for, or agrees to . . . repair by or under an arrangement with the seller".[6] He went further than this because, in addition to stopping the clock while requesting or agreeing to a repair, he added that the time necessary to carry them out is also not to be counted.[7] Further, he specifically finds that the fact that the buyer had been forced to wait for several months for technical information necessary to make a decision was also relevant. In all the circumstances the Court of Appeal found that the three weeks that elapsed between February 15, when Mr Clegg finally received all the information that he needed to make a decision, and March 6 when he finally intimated rejection was not unreasonable.

5–75   This clearly was the intention of Parliament to judge from debate on the bill in the House of Lords where Lord Peston asked for clarification of the phrase "lapse of a reasonable time". The Minister of State,

---

[2] [1987] 2 All E.R. 220.
[3] [2003] 1 All E.R. (Comm) 721.
[4] See (2003) 104 L.Q.R. 8.
[5] [2003] 1 All E.R. (Comm) 721, para.63.
[6] subs. (6)(a) goes on to refer delivery to another under a sub-sale or other disposition but this is unlikely to be relevant in a consumer context.
[7] [2003] 1 All E.R. (Comm) 721, para.64.

Department of Trade and Industry, Earl Ferrers, after reviewing the background to the new section and referring to the fact that *Bernstein* "was unsatisfactory from the point of view of maintaining a fair balance of rights between supplier and consumer" went on to add:

> "If the Act is recast, as it is in the Bill, the provisions which are at present in Sections 34 and 35 will be tied much more closely together. This will make it clear that a material question in determining whether a reasonable time has elapsed — and therefore whether the buyer has accepted the goods — will be whether he has had a reasonable opportunity to examine the goods in order to satisfy himself that they are in fact in conformity with the contract and are what he wanted to buy. This means examination to see whether, among other things, the implied terms of the contract are satisfied.
>
> It is clear, therefore, that the examination must be more than just an examination in general terms. The term 'examine' has to be interpreted in the context of the type of examination which it is necessary to conduct in order to ensure that the goods in question are in conformity with the contract."[8]

The minister then went on to apply this to an example which Lord **5–76** Peston had raised. He had referred to having a new kitchen installed for which he had separately bought a new cooker. The cooker had been delivered in its packaging but not opened immediately because the kitchen fitters had fallen behind schedule. When, some four months after taking delivery of the cooker, it was installed it was found to be defective. The Minister asserted that the "customer would not have examined the goods and would not therefore be deemed to have accepted them."[9]

The new section is thus a valuable clarification of consumer rights. It **5–77** may be said that it builds on *Bernstein* because, even there, the judge was prepared to take into account the personal circumstances of the consumer who had been ill in the period immediately after buying the car. With even greater certainty this can now be done. It might be important in many circumstances. For example, suppose that someone buys a lawnmower in November, in an end of season sale, and is unable to test it until the new season in April. Should the mower prove to be defective the right to reject will not have been lost. Similarly, it would seem that someone who, just before moving house, purchases a product which immediately has to go into storage while the house move is completed, will not lose the right to reject while the product is in store. There are other circumstances which could be taken into account. In

---

[8] *Hansard*, HL, Vol. 557, cols 479, 480 (July 22, 1994).
[9] *ibid.*

Munro & Co v Bennet & Son[10] the time for rejection was extended because the seller had assured the buyer that the goods would be satisfactory after, adjustment.[11]

5–78   Even where there are not special circumstances, such as those just outlined, it would appear that the new Act provides more time to carry out an examination than some of the cases under the old law allowed.[12] It will still be the case that a reasonable time will vary from product to product, a longer time being reasonable in the case of more complex goods; and it will still be advisable to reject at the earliest opportunity. It is also clear that the new Act does little for the victim of the latent defect of which *Bernstein* is such a good example. One might speculate that if the same circumstances were to recur Mr Bernstein would be found not to have lost his right to reject. However, if one assumes the same facts, except that the defect occurs six months after purchase, it is doubtful if, in the absence of some other factors, the right to reject would still be available. However, welcome as the new version of s.35 is, it does not go as far as consumer organisations would wish in introducing a long-term right to reject. This, it can be argued, is needed to make meaningful the inclusion of durability within the definition of satisfactory quality. The fact that there is still a reference to accepting through lapse of time must lead to this conclusion.

Other Aspects of Rejection

5–79 Section 35A of the Sale of Goods Act 1979 deals with partial rejection.[13] Where a buyer has the right to reject goods but is prepared to retain some of them and reject only the remainder, the right to reject is not lost by retaining some of them. Where goods are delivered by instalments the right to reject a nonconforming instalment is not lost by having accepted another instalment.

5–80   Where the seller delivers too few goods, or too many, there is no longer, even in consumer contracts in Scotland, an automatic right to reject all the consignment. Section 30[14] provides that rejection is only possible where the excess or shortfall is material.

---

[10] 1911 S.C. 337.

[11] See also *Peakman v Express Circuits Ltd*, CA, Feb. 3, 1998, unreported, one of the few English cases since the reform of Sale of Goods Act 1979 by Sale and Supply of Goods Act 1994, to relate to novel points, where attempts to repair seem to have extended the time for rejection.

[12] It ought to be remembered that *Bernstein* gained an importance that was not wholly justified. As W. H. Thomas pointed out in an interesting survey of car cases several other judges had been much more liberal in construing a reasonable time: see 1989 N.L.J. 1188.

[13] Inserted by Sale and Supply of Goods Act 1994, s.3(1).

[14] *ibid.*, s.5(2).

Damages

Section 15A of the Sale of Goods Act 1979 provides that damages are **5–81** also a remedy where a contract of sale is breached. This may be the only remedy for the non-material breach of an express term or may be the remedy which must be used where the right to reject has been lost through acceptance. The 1979 Act applies the normal contract rule that the damages should be such as result naturally from the breach in the ordinary course of events.[15] Where the breach is the failure of the seller to deliver the goods, s.51 goes on to say that where there is an available market for the goods the measure of damages is, *prima facie*, to be ascertained by the difference between the contract price and the market or current price of the goods at the time that they ought to have been delivered.

Where the seller delivers the goods but is in breach of one of the **5–82** terms of the contract regarding quality s.53A says how the consumer's loss is to be calculated. It is "the difference between the value of the goods at the time of delivery to the buyer and the value they would have had if they had fulfilled the contract." In addition, other damage may have resulted to the consumer or his or her property. In *Godley v Perry*[16] a defective catapult resulted in the purchaser losing an eye, and the claim for breach of contract was mainly for damages for this injury. Similarly, in *Wilson v Rickett, Cockerell & Co Ltd*[17] the breach of contract consisted in the delivery of defective Coalite and resulted in damage to the buyer's living room for which compensation was awarded. In *Bernstein* the consumer was awarded compensation for the cost of returning home after the car broke down, the loss of a tank of petrol, five days loss of use of the car and £150 for the spoilt day out.

As *Bernstein* demonstrates, it is possible to obtain damages for **5–83** inconvenience or disappointment for breach of a contract of sale. This will only be possible where the seller is aware that breach is likely to have this result as in *Bernstein* or *Jackson v Chrysler Acceptances Ltd*[18] where the sellers of a new car knew that the buyer wanted it for a foreign holiday and thus were liable for damages for the distress caused through a holiday ruined by the car breaking down frequently.

New Remedies—Part 5A of the Sale of Goods Act 1979

As an alternative to using the original remedies set out in the 1979 Act **5–84** a consumer can choose to invoke the new remedies set out in Pt 5A inserted in the Act by Reg.5 of the Sale and Supply of Goods to

---

[15] See ss.51, 53A.
[16] [1960] 1 W.L.R. 9.
[17] [1954] 1 Q.B. 598.
[18] [1978] R.T.R. 474.

Consumers Regulations 2002.[19] This change came into effect on March 31, 2003, 15 months later than required by the Directive[20] which ought to have been implemented by January 1, 2002.

5–85   The additional remedies apply only, to quote s.48A(1), where "there is a consumer contract in which the buyer is a consumer" and, of course, the goods do not conform to the contract at the time of delivery. Before considering what non-conformity means it is first necessary to understand what is meant by a "consumer contract". This phrase has been in the 1979 Act for some time and s.61 of the Act states that it has the same meaning as in s.25 of the Unfair Contract Terms Act 1977. However, to implement the Directive accurately it has been necessary to amend it. It will be recalled that s.25 of the Unfair Contract Terms Act 1977 defines a consumer contract is one where (a) the seller deals in a business capacity, and (b) the goods are of a type ordinarily supplied for private use and consumption. New subss.(1A) and (1B) of s.25 alter this in several ways. First, where the buyer is an individual condition (b) does not apply. This is necessary because the directive does not have this limitation on the type of goods to which it applies. Subsection (1B) goes on to add that where the buyer is an individual a contract will not come within the definition of "consumer contract" if the goods are second-hand goods sold by public auction at which individuals have the opportunity of attending in person. This means that the definition of "consumer contract" does apply, for example, to auctions of new goods (a fairly rare event) and to internet auctions, giving consumers enhanced protection in these situations. To further complicate matters a consumer contract does not include one where the buyer is not an individual and the goods are sold by auction or competitive tender, whether new or second-hand and whether or not there is access in person.

5–86   Non-conformity with the contract is defined in s.48F. It covers breach of an express term of the contract or one of the terms implied by ss.13–15 of the 1979 Act.

5–87   The new regime brought in by the directive provides four remedies where the goods do not conform to the contract. These are set out in s.48A(2) and are repair or replacement, reduction in price and rescission of the contract. The interaction of these remedies lacks the simplicity of the existing remedies. It is, however, clear that they are available in this order and that the consumer cannot, as with the existing remedies, choose between them.

5–88   The first remedy is repair or replacement and it is dealt with in detail in s.48B. Subsection (2) provides that if the buyer requires the seller to repair or replace the goods, the seller must carry out the buyer's preferred option "within a reasonable time but without causing significant inconvenience to the buyer". What amounts to a reasonable time or significant inconvenience is, subs.(5) says, to be determined by

---

[19] SI 2002/3045.
[20] Dir. 1999/44; [1999] O.J. L171/12.

reference to the nature of the goods and the purpose for which they were acquired. If the problem is a defective light bulb in a new car, instant repair might reasonably be expected whereas if the problem was the failure of some more complex mechanical part which might have to be ordered from the manufacturer, a longer time would be reasonable. If the defective product were, say, a wedding dress or video camera intended to film the wedding, the reference to the purpose for which the product was required might indicate that replacement should take priority over repair if repair could not be effected in time for the event. In addition, the seller must "bear any necessary costs incurred in [repair or replacement] (including in particular the cost of any labour, materials or postage)".[21]

However, the buyer cannot require the seller to carry out one of these **5–89** remedies if it is not possible to do so or if the cost of doing so would be "disproportionate" either to carrying out the other remedy, offering a price reduction or rescinding the contract. Subsection (4) offers guidance on when one remedy is disproportionate to another. This will be the case where the cost of a remedy is unreasonable taking into account the value of the goods if they conformed to the contract, the significance of the defect and whether the alternative remedy could be effected without significant inconvenience to the buyer. For example, this will probably mean that if there is a cosmetic defect in a domestic appliance on a part which will not be visible when it is installed, it will be difficult to insist on a repair which might be quite expensive, taking into account labour charges, in comparison to giving a reduction in price. Similarly, where the value of the product is low and the cost of repair would exceed that value it is unlikely that repair could be insisted upon when replacement would be a cheaper option.

The remedies of price reduction and rescission only come into play if **5–90** the first two cannot be, or have not been, carried out. The circumstances where they will be appropriate are set out in s.48C. As we have seen, repair or replacement may be impossible or their cost may be disproportionate compared to a price reduction or rescission. In this case the buyer will have to be content either with rescinding the contract, *i.e.* getting a refund of the purchase price, or a price reduction. Where the buyer has embarked on an attempt to have a repair carried out or requests a replacement, the right to a reduction in price or rescission will revive if the seller is in breach of the requirement of s.48B(2) to achieve this within a reasonable time and without significant inconvenience to the buyer.

Not unreasonably, s.48D provides that where a buyer has embarked **5–91** on a demand for either repair or replacement he or she may not seek an alternative remedy until the seller has been given a reasonable opportunity to carry out the first one. For example, the consumer may not

---

[21] See s.48B(2)(b).

demand a repair and, before the seller has had a chance to carry it out, decide to assert the right under s.15B of the 1979 Act to reject the goods and treat the contract as repudiated.

5–92   The operation of the remedy of rescission as an additional remedy under Pt 5A is subject to an interesting qualification. Any reimbursement to the buyer may be reduced to take into account the use that she or he has had of the goods. This is quite different from rejection under s.15B of the 1979 Act where no reduction for use is required. It is a factor which needs to be taken into account in deciding whether to embark on the additional remedies.

5–93   To enforce the new rights of repair, replacement or reduction in price s.48E gives the court power to make an order of specific implement. Where the consumer seeks one of the remedies the court has power to order one of the other remedies and has wide discretion as to the terms on which it does so. Specific implement is the primary remedy of the victim of a breach of contract, though nineteenth century developments have resulted in it being rarely used in the context of contracts of sale. It may be that the implementation of the directive will give it new relevance.

5–94   The complexity of this system of remedies may be off-putting. There is, however, an advantage in using it. Section 48A(3) provides that "goods which do not conform to the contract at any time within the period of six months starting with the date on which the goods were delivered to the buyer must be taken not to have so conformed at that date". The next subsection disapplies this rule if the seller can show that the goods did in fact conform during that period, or the rule is incompatible with the nature of the goods or the nature of the lack of conformity. This is in contrast to the existing remedies where the burden of proof at all times is on the buyer. To take an extreme example of the application of the new regime, a consumer will get nowhere by arguing that fresh fruit is defective because he or she can show that a month after purchase it has gone mouldy. On the other hand, this provision could be very useful where the product in question is a consumer durable such as a car, a freezer or a computer. It is debatable how great an innovation this is when one recalls the approach of Lord Denning in *Crowther v Shannon Motor Co*,[22] where he found that the emergence of a defect some weeks after purchase indicated that the product had not conformed to the contract at the time of sale.

OTHER CONTRACTS OF SALE

5–95   In the case of the other contracts for the supply of goods the policy has been to extend the same remedies to them as apply to sale and to do so in terminology that is appropriate to Scots law. In the case of contracts of hire-purchase, s.12A of the Supply of Goods (Implied Terms) Act

---

[22] [1975] 1 W.L.R. 30.

1973[23] achieves this. It is an almost exact replica of s.15A of the Sale of Goods Act 1979. In the contracts for the transfer of goods subject to Pt 1A of the Supply of Goods and Services Act 1982 a similar provision appears in s.11E. In applying these provisions it should be noted that there are no rules providing that the right to reject is lost by acceptance. When the right to reject is lost is not at all clear in Scots law. It would appear to depend on the law of personal bar and waiver and it will probably be the case that the right to reject cannot be lost before the consumer knows that the goods are defective.[24]

In addition to the original remedies a new Pt 1B of the 1982 Act **5–96** provides additional remedies for those to whom goods are transferred. These do not apply to hire-purchase contracts or, as is pointed out in the next paragraph, to contracts of hire. In the cases to which they do apply they provide remedies on the same lines as in Pt 5A of the 1979 Act. One special point to note is that these remedies apply only in relation to consumer contracts and the goods do not conform to the contract. A new s.11S states that goods do not conform to the contract in two circumstances. The first is that there is a breach of an express term of the contract or one of the implied terms about description, quality and fitness or transfer by sample. The second is novel in that it applies where installation of the goods is part of the contract and there has been a breach of any rule of law as to the manner in which the installation is carried out. In other words the new remedies can apply where the installer has failed to carry out the work with reasonable skill and care which is the standard that the law requires.

In the case of contracts of hire, although Pt 1A of the 1982 Act also **5–97** sets out implied terms it does not set out the remedies for breach. This is because the Scottish Law Commission considered that the common law remedies were satisfactory. For breach of this contract the consumer has the normal remedies of rejection and damages. As one would expect there are no additional remedies like those in Pt 5A of the 1979 Act.

MANUFACTURERS' LIABILITY

DELICTUAL LIABILITY

So far the discussion has concentrated on the liability of the supplier. In **5–98** addition, it is possible for the manufacturer, or someone else in the chain of production and distribution, to be liable as well. This may be delictual liability or it may be the result of the manufacturer having offered a guarantee.

---

[23] Inserted by Sale and Supply of Goods Act 1994, Sch.2, para.4(8).
[24] See the Law Commissions' report, paras 2.53, 2.54. For an English hire-purchase case where rejection was permitted although the motorcycle had been ridden for 4,000 miles, see *Farnworth Finance Facilities Ltd v Attryde* [1970] 1 W.L.R. 1053.

5–99   Where goods are defective the consumer will normally find it much easier to attempt to make the supplier liable for breach of one of the implied terms under the Sale of Goods Act 1979 or the analogous legislation discussed above.[25] As we have seen, liability is strict. However, there are circumstances where the consumer will not be able to sue the supplier. The seller may have become insolvent or the person who suffered the harm may, like Mrs Donoghue, in *Donoghue v Stevenson*,[26] not be the purchaser. This may result in a delictual action and will often arise from goods being dangerous and not merely shoddy. The possible types of action in these circumstances are discussed in Ch.6.

5–100   One avenue discussed in that chapter is the delictual action for breach of duty which stems from *Donoghue v Stevenson*. That line of authority appears to have been extended in another Scottish appeal to the House of Lords, *Junior Books Ltd v The Veitchi Co Ltd*.[27] It was held that the owner of a factory had a claim in delict against a sub-contractor who had laid a floor negligently, thus causing economic loss. There was no allegation that the floor was dangerous or had caused any physical injury. Liability was said to depend on the degree of proximity of the parties and in this case it was very close. It was expressly said, however, that the decision would not apply to consumer situations where the complaint was that the goods were of poor quality. This, it was said, was because there would not be the requisite degree of proximity between a manufacturer and the ultimate consumer. In view of the influence of mass advertising carried out mainly by manufacturers, and occasional cases where the retailer is little more than a conduit between the consumer and the manufacturer, this seems open to doubt. There may be situations where a consumer wants something made to special order and goes to a retailer who puts him in touch with the manufacturer. The ultimate sale may be routed through the retailer, but discussion about the product will have been directly between the customer and the manufacturer. There would seem to be little difference in principle between such a situation and *Junior Books*.

MANUFACTURERS' GUARANTEES

5–101   A useful supplement to the legal protection regarding quality is often given by manufacturers' guarantees, usually called warranties in the case of cars. These may consist of a written undertaking to the purchaser to replace or repair a faulty product, or to give a refund, should problems develop within a stated period. This is usually one year in the case of domestic appliances and, in the case of cars, it can be longer.

---

[25] paras 5–03 *et seq.*
[26] 1932 S.C. (H.L.) 31.
[27] 1982 S.C. (H.L.) 244; 1982 S.L.T. 492; [1983] A.C. 520.

Such guarantees can be a very useful addition to the consumer's statutory rights. It avoids the problems surrounding the standard of quality which the consumer is entitled to expect under the Sale of Goods Act 1979 and, in particular, can overcome the deficiencies in the legal remedies where goods do not prove to be durable.

Despite their widespread use, the legal status of guarantees was not **5–102** altogether clear,[28] though it was probably the case that they were contracts. This issue is now put beyond doubt so far as consumer guarantees are concerned by reg.15 of the Sale and Supply of Goods to Consumer Regulations 2002[29] which implements Art.6 of the EC Directive on Certain Aspects of the Sale of Consumer Goods and Associated Guarantees.[30] This it does by providing that "the consumer guarantee takes effect at the time the goods are delivered as a contractual obligation owed by the guarantor".

There is no obligation on a manufacturer, or anyone else in the supply **5–103** chain, to offer a guarantee but if one is offered the regulation goes on to impose certain requirements on such a guarantee. It must be set out in plain and intelligible language (which must be English if the goods are offered within the UK) and must include the particulars for making claims. Those who offer guarantees, be they manufacturers, retailers or others, must make them available to potential customers on demand. The definition regulation makes clear that what is controlled is a guarantee given without extra charge whether by the manufacturer or anyone else in the course of a business. It includes the typical manufacturer's guarantee but not extended warranties for which the consumer has to pay separately.

The obligations relating to guarantees are enforceable by the OFT and **5–104** local weights and measures authorities, which in practice means the trading standards departments of local councils. If a guarantor fails to comply with the provisions of the regulation the OFT or a local authority may seek an order for specific performance from the sheriff court or the Court of Session.

In this case the Unfair Contract Terms Act 1977 provides that a **5–105** guarantee relating to goods of a type ordinarily supplied for private use or consumption given by someone other than the supplier of the goods is void in so far as it purports to exclude or restrict liability for loss or damage, including death or personal injury, arising from the goods proving to be defective as a result of a breach of duty by a manufacturer or distributor.[31]

---

[28] For a discussion of this issue, see Cusine, "Manufacturers' Guarantees and the Unfair Contract Terms Act", 1980 J.R. 185.
[29] SI 2002/3045.
[30] Dir. 1999/44; [1999] O.J. L171/12.
[31] s.19(1), (2)(b).

CRIMINAL LAW

5–106 From the consumer's point of view the civil law relating to the quality of goods is the most important aspect of this topic. In addition, there is a good deal of legislation sanctioned by criminal penalties which plays an important part in ensuring that the quality of goods is satisfactory. Under the Food Safety Act 1990 the quality and composition of food is controlled. The detailed control is to be found in a mass of subordinate legislation made principally under powers conferred by the Act. Similar powers in relation to drugs are given by the Medicines Act 1968. The Hallmarking Act 1973 updated one of the oldest forms of consumer protection and governs the quality of gold, silver and platinum.

CHAPTER 6

PRODUCT SAFETY

While it is irritating and can have serious financial consequences to find **6–01** that a product that one has bought is shoddy, this is as nothing to the dangers posed by unsafe goods. This chapter considers the legal response to the problem of unsafe goods. Broadly speaking, this falls into two categories: attempts to provide compensation for the consequences of unsafe goods; and legislation to prevent unsafe goods reaching the market in the first place. The two categories are not exclusive, as the threat of having to compensate a victim of unsafe goods must act as an incentive to a trader to ensure that unsafe goods do not reach the market place.

We have already seen that goods which are dangerous will not be **6–02** regarded as meeting the standard of satisfactory quality, and that damages for personal injury may be an element in the damages for breach of that term of the contract of supply. This is of limited utility as it will only benefit the purchaser. What happens if the injured person is someone other than the purchaser? Until recently the answer to that question was that the injured person could only succeed by bringing an action for breach of duty as Mrs Donoghue did in the famous case. As Lord Atkin put it in that case:

> "[A] manufacturer of products, which he sells in such a form as to show that he intends them to reach the ultimate consumer in the form in which they left him, with no reasonable possibility of intermediate examination, and with the knowledge that the absence of reasonable care in the preparation or putting up of the products will result in an injury to the consumer's life or property, owes a duty to the consumer to take that reasonable care."[1]

That principle has been applied in a wide range of situations, many of **6–03** them outwith the realm of consumer protection. Within the category of consumer examples is *Grant v Australian Knitting Mills Ltd*,[2] where a

---

[1] [1932] A.C. 562 at 599.
[2] [1936] A.C. 85.

consumer contracted dermatitis from negligently manufactured underpants; and *Malfroot v Noxal Ltd*[3] where a motorcycle manufacturer was
held liable to a passenger in a side car which, as a result of the
negligence of the manufacturer, parted company with the motorcycle
and caused injury to her. A more recent example of a manufacturer's
design defect founding this kind of liability is to be found in *Lambert v
Lewis*,[4] where a passenger in a car was killed and others injured when
a trailer being towed behind a Land Rover became unhitched and
collided with the car in which they were travelling.

6–04   It is not only manufacturers who can be liable, as *Fisher v Harrods
Ltd*[5] demonstrates. In that case the well-known London store was held
liable for the injuries suffered by a lady who had been injured when
defective packaging of jewellery cleaning fluid purchased by someone
else damaged her eye. It was shown that the store had obtained the
product from a small company with whom it had never dealt before and
of which it knew nothing. Despite this, it had failed to have the product
tested before putting it on sale. Repairers can also be liable to their
customers, as *Stennett v Hancock & Peters*[6] shows; as can those who
sell reconditioned products[7] or those who hire out products.[8]

6–05   The difficulty with the *Donoghue v Stevenson*[9] principle of liability is
that it depends on showing that the defender has failed to display
reasonable care for the safety of the pursuer. Despite the assistance of
the maxim *res ipsa loquitur* (the facts speak for themselves), this is not
always easy or possible to prove, as the thalidomide tragedy[10] graph-
ically demonstrated. This led to demands to introduce legislation
imposing strict liability on manufacturers of defective products which
have resulted in the enactment of Part 1 of the Consumer Protection Act
1987.

6–06   Before looking at that Act it is important to point out that, despite its
enactment, *Donoghue v Stevenson*[11] liability will, in some circumstances, still be relevant. This is because the Consumer Protection Act
has a limitation period which may rule out claims that could still be
made at common law; and there are some forms of loss which it does
not cover, such as pure financial loss.

---

[3] (1935) 51 T.L.R. 551.
[4] [1982] A.C. 225.
[5] [1966] 1 Lloyd's Rep. 500.
[6] [1939] 2 All E.R. 578.
[7] *Herschtal v Stewart & Ardern Ltd* [1940] 1 K.B. 155.
[8] *Griffith v Arch Engineering (Newport) Ltd* [1968] 3 All E.R. 217.
[9] 1932 S.C. (H.L.) 31.
[10] Thalidomide was a drug widely prescribed to combat morning sickness in pregnant
    women. In a large number of cases it caused their children to be born with serious
    abnormalities.
[11] 1932 S.C. (H.L.) 31.

STRICT LIABILITY OF MANUFACTURERS IN DELICT

Part 1 of the Consumer Protection Act 1987 introduces what is often, **6–07** though somewhat misleadingly, referred to as strict liability for manufacturers. Incidents such as the thalidomide tragedy had led consumer organisations to campaign for the introduction of such legislation paralleling judicial developments in the United States.[12] This was supported in a joint report by the Law Commission and the Scottish Law Commission,[13] and the report of the Pearson Commission.[14] Both the Council of Europe and the EC took up the issue at European level. The immediate spur to legislative action in the UK was the Directive on Product Liability,[15] which Pt 1 of the 1987 Act implements in the UK. The original Directive has been amended.[16] The effect of this is to remove the exemption from the Directive for unprocessed agricultural products, fish and game.

Part 1 of the 1987 Act introduces a regime of strict liability on **6–08** manufacturers of products which prove to cause harm by reason of a defect. For several years almost no use seems to have been made of it but in the past four years there have been several reported cases.[17] It should be noted that s.1(1) refers to the origin of this part of the Act: "This Part shall have effect for the purpose of making such provision as is necessary in order to comply with the product liability Directive and shall be construed accordingly."

In view of the fact that there are several obscure provisions in the Act, **6–09** which in some cases do not appear to conform to the directive, this provision may be of considerable importance. This was recognised by the ECJ when the Commission challenged the implementation of the implementation of the Directive.[18] In *A v National Blood Authority (No.1)*[19] the judge referred almost exclusively to the wording of the relevant parts of the Directive rather than the statute.

The key provision of the 1987 Act is s.2(1): "Subject to the following **6–10** provisions of this Part, where any damage is caused wholly or partly by a defect in a product, every person to whom subsection (2) . . . applies shall be liable for the damage." As pointed out above, the liability under

---

[12] The landmark decision in the US was that of the California Supreme Court in *Greenman v Yuba Power Products Inc.*, 377 P. 2nd 897 (1963).

[13] *Liability for Defective Products*, Cmnd. 6831 (1977).

[14] *Royal Commission on Civil Liability and Compensation for Personal Injury*, Cmnd. 7054 (1978), Ch. 22.

[15] Dir. 85/374.

[16] Dir. 1999/34; [1999] O.J. L141/20.

[17] It appears to be have been one of the grounds on which those harmed by a polluted water supply in the Camelford area of Cornwall were successful: see *A.B. v South West Water Services Ltd* [1993] Q.B. 507, CA. For discussion of possible reasons for the paucity of cases, see National Consumer Council, *Unsafe Products* (London, 1995).

[18] Case C-300/95; *Commission of the European Communities v UK* [1997] All E.R. (EC) 481.

[19] [2001] 3 All E.R. 289.

Part 1 is strict but it is not absolute. The pursuer must prove that he has been injured; that the defendant manufacturer was the producer of the product; and that it was the manufacturer's product that caused the injury.

6–11 As many negligence cases have shown, it is the issue of causation which frequently proves a stumbling block to claimants. An example is *Kay's Tutor v Ayrshire and Arran Health Board*.[20] The causation issue can also defeat a claim where the manufacturer is able to show some other convincing reason for the pursuer's loss, as in *Evans v Triplex Safety Glass Co Ltd*.[21] Such cases may turn on complex scientific evidence and, like negligence actions raising similar issues, can be extremely expensive.[22]

<h2 style="text-align:center">PRODUCTS</h2>

6–12 "Product" is given a very wide meaning for the purpose of Pt 1 of the Consumer Protection Act 1987. The starting point is the definition in s.1(2) which defines a product as: "any good or electricity and . . . includes a product which is comprised in another product, whether by virtue of being a component part or raw material or otherwise." The term "goods" is then amplified in s.45, the definition section of the Act, to include "substances, growing crops and things comprised in land by virtue of being attached to it and any ship, aircraft or vehicle". "Substance", in turn, is defined as: "any natural or artificial substance, whether in solid, liquid or gaseous form or in the form of a vapour, and includes substances that are comprised in or mixed with other goods."

6–13 The effect of s.46(4) is that buildings are not products for the purposes of Pt 1. However, while buildings are not within the Act, s.46(3) makes clear that products incorporated in a building are subject to it. The result seems to be that if a building collapses because of design faults the builder is not liable under the Act. However, if injury is caused by a defective central-heating boiler blowing up there will be liability.

6–14 The original Directive provided in Art.2 for the exclusion of what it called "primary agricultural products" from the new product liability regime. However, Art.15(a) permitted Member States to derogate from this provision and impose liability on producers of primary agricultural products. This the UK did not choose to do. The Directive has now been amended to apply the product liability regime to agricultural products, fish and game, and the Act was amended to take account of this.[23]

---

[20] 1987 S.C. (H.L.) 145.
[21] [1936] 1 All E.R. 283.
[22] See also *Loveday v Renton* [1990] 1 Med. L.R. 117 and Ferguson, *Drug Injuries and the Pursuit of Compensation* (1996), Ch.9.
[23] Consumer Protection Act 1987 (Product Liability) (Modification) (Scotland) Order 2001 (SSI 2001/265).

For convenience it is usual to speak of product liability as the liability **6–15** of the manufacturer, but it should be remembered that the range of people liable is rather wider than this. The following are potentially liable by virtue of ss.2(2)–(4):

(a) producers;
(b) own-branders;
(c) importers;
(d) suppliers.

(a) Producers (s.2(2)(a))

The "producer" of a product is defined in s.1(2) to mean: **6–16**

"(a) the person who manufactured it;
 (b) in the case of a substance which has not been manufactured but has been won or abstracted, the person who won or abstracted it;
 (c) in the case of a product which has not been manufactured, won or abstracted but essential characteristics of which are attributable to an industrial or other process having been carried out (for example, in relation to agricultural produce), the person who carried out that process."

The expression "the person who manufactured it" is not defined in **6–17** the Act. The Directive can be helpful as in Art.3 "producer" is said to mean "the manufacturer of a finished product, the producer of any raw material or the manufacturer of a component part". The manufacturer of the finished product and the producer of a component or raw material are both liable where the finished product is defective by virtue of a defect in the raw material or the component. In this context it is worth noting s.1(3) which states:

"For the purposes of this Part a person who supplies any product in which products are comprised, whether by virtue of being component parts or raw materials, or otherwise, shall not be treated by reason only of his supply of that product as supplying any of the products so comprised."

The provision is not intended to contradict the assertion that the **6–18** manufacturer of the finished product and the raw material or component producer are both liable. The significant word is "only". It appears that the manufacturer cannot be liable for defects in raw material or components if, for some reason, he is not liable for defects in the finished product.

For the most part it is not difficult to appreciate who is a manu- **6–19** facturer. The term "producer" also includes those who have "won or abstracted" a substance. This is the appropriate terminology for substances, such as ores, which are mined. The third category of producers comprises those who do not manufacture, win or abstract, but who produce products, the "essential characteristics of which are attributable to an industrial or other process". This would cover producers of petroleum products who produce their products by refining raw materials. This is uncontroversial. However this phrase is also relevant to the production of foodstuffs.

(b) Own-branders (s.2(2)(b))

6–20 This clumsy heading is used to sum up the group of persons who are liable by s.2(2)(b): "any person who, by putting his name on the product or using a trade mark or other distinguishing mark in relation to the product, has held himself out to be the producer of the product." It is quite common for supermarkets to arrange for the manufacturer of a product to supply them with that product labelled or wrapped with the supermarket's own well-known brand name or logo. It is to both these situations that s.2(2)(b) applies, and the supermarket will be liable under the Act. This will only increase their liability to a limited extent as they have liability without fault to purchasers under the Sale of Goods Act 1979. However, it does mean that in a case such as *Fisher v Harrods Ltd*[24] the pursuer would be able to sue under the 1987 Act rather than having to raise an action for negligence.

(c) Importers (s.2(2)(c))

6–21 To avoid the possibility of injured consumers having to bring actions in far off jurisdictions, s.2(2)(c) provides that the term producer includes: "any person who has imported the product into a Member State from a place outside the Member States in order, in the course of any business of his, to supply it to another." A simple example of the effect of this provision would be the situation where a car is manufactured in Japan and imported into Italy. The Italian importer then sells it to an English dealer who sells it to a customer. The car proves to be defective, the brakes fail, and injury is sustained by the customer. The injured person does not have to sue the Japanese manufacturer; as a result of s.2(2)(c) he or she can sue the Italian importer as the person who imported the product into the EC.

(d) Suppliers (s.2(3))

6–22 The first three categories of persons liable for defective products can be seen as primarily liable to the injured person. The final category comprised in s.2(3) is different: persons in this category become liable only where the person primarily liable cannot be identified. Liability

---

[24] [1966] 1 Lloyd's Rep. 500.

arises if three conditions are fulfilled. The injured person must request the supplier to identify one or more of the persons listed in categories (a) to (c) above; that request must be made within a reasonable time after the damage has occurred and at a time when it is not reasonably practicable for the person making the request to identify those persons; and the supplier must fail to supply the information requested within a reasonable time. An example of a situation where a supplier's liability might be extended occurs where a retailer's goods have injured someone other than the purchaser. If the retailer cannot identify his supplier then under this provision he finds himself strictly liable.[25]

DEFECT

A key concept in the Consumer Protection Act 1987 is that of "defect" **6–23** and this is defined in s.3. The principle part of the definition is contained in s.3(1):

> "Subject to the following provisions of this section, there is a defect in a product for the purposes of this Part if the safety of the product is not such as persons generally are entitled to expect; and for those purposes 'safety', in relation to a product, shall include safety with respect to products comprised in that product and safety in the context of risks of damage to property, as well as in the context of risks of death or personal injury."

It is clear from this definition that the strict liability regime is **6–24** concerned only with safety, not with shoddiness. It provides no remedy where the product is defective in the sense that it does not work or has some other flaw (other than a safety defect) which might render it of unsatisfactory quality. In this situation the purchaser is thrown back on the existing remedies under the Sale of Goods Act 1979, or other legislation setting standards of quality in relation to the supply of goods.

Safety is relative

It is clear that s.3 of the 1987 Act is concerned with relative safety. **6–25** There is probably no such thing as a completely safe product. Even such innocuous substances as cotton wool might, in the hands of an infant, prove dangerous, if the infant put large quantities into its mouth. On the other hand there are other products which are inherently dangerous: sharp knives, cars and matches are examples. The question is, to quote s.3(1), when is the degree of safety "not such as persons generally are entitled to expect"? To answer this question s.3(2) gives some further guidance. After stating that "all the circumstances shall be taken into

---

[25] That traders sometimes cannot identify who their suppliers were is demonstrated in *Lambert v Lewis* [1982] A.C. 225.

account", it goes on to set out a number of specific circumstances which are to be taken into account.

6–26   Before looking at these it is important to point out that the role of the court is to act as what Burton J. in *A v National Blood Authority (No.1)*[26] referred to (quoting one expert) as "the appointed representative of the public at large".[27] The factors set out in s.3(2) are:

> "(a) the manner in which, and purposes for which, the product has been marketed, its get-up, the use of any mark in relation to the product, and any instructions for, or warnings with respect to doing or refraining from doing anything with or in relation to the product;
>
> (b) what might reasonably be expected to be done with or in relation to the product; and
>
> (c) the time when the product was supplied by its producer to another."

6–27   The subsection concludes by stating that the fact that products produced after an injury has occurred have a greater level of safety may not be used to infer that earlier products were defective. These factors will be discussed in turn. It should be noted that while, for the purposes of exposition, it is necessary to discuss them in isolation, in real life they will tend to interact with each other and overlap with such issues as the defences considered below and the question of causation.

(a) Marketing, warnings and instructions

6–28   It is probably the case that these factors only come into play when it is not feasible to make the product safe through better design. It was said in the American case of *Schell v AMF Inc*[28] that "as a matter of policy, it is questionable whether a manufacturer which produces a machine without minimal available safeguards is entitled to escape liability by warning of dangerous condition which could reasonably have been avoided by a better design."

6–29   The importance of warnings is not a novelty: it has been pointed out in negligence cases such as *Clarke v Army and Navy Co-operative Society Ltd.*[29] Mrs Clarke had purchased a bottle of disinfectant, at the defendant's shop. There was no warning on the bottle, despite the fact that the defendant's shop manager had been informed by customers of incidents causing injury. When the plaintiff opened the bottle some of the contents flew out injuring her eyes. She sued, *inter alia,* alleging

---

[26] [2001] 3 All E.R. 289.
[27] *ibid.*, para.31.
[28] 567 F. 2d. 1259 (1977) (3rd Cir).
[29] [1903] 1 K.B. 155.

negligence in failing to issue a warning about this danger. The defendants were held to be in breach of their duty to the plaintiff in failing to attach a warning to the bottle. Collins M.R. said that there was:

> "a duty, if there is some dangerous quality in the goods sold, of which he knows, but of which the purchaser cannot be expected to be aware, of taking reasonable precautions in the way of warning the purchaser that special care will be requisite."[30]

Where the danger is a matter of common knowledge a warning will **6–30** not be necessary,[31] but where warnings should be given they must be adequate, precise and appropriately placed. In this context the distinction between instructions and warnings is sometimes relevant. The function of a warning is to inform the user of the dangers of a product: directions or instructions for use are intended to indicate how the best results may be obtained when using the product. When dangers from failing to follow directions for use are not obvious such directions by themselves may not be sufficient to absolve the manufacturer from liability.

A good example of a warning which was not adequate comes from **6–31** the Californian case of *Boyl v California Chemical Co.*[32] The plaintiff used a liquid weedkiller frequently sold to ordinary consumers for garden use. The warnings given on the label by the defendant included the avoidance of breathing the spray mist, of contact with eyes, skin or clothing, and the necessity of washing after use. It also warned that livestock and poultry would be poisoned if allowed to feed on treated areas, which indicated that the defendant manufacturers knew of the weedkiller's propensity to contaminate the earth. The label also warned that the container should be washed after use and carefully disposed of. After using the weedkiller on her driveway the plaintiff rinsed the container, disposing of the rinsing water on some grass in her garden. Five days later she sunbathed in this area and absorbed some of the weedkiller into her skin causing serious injury. It was held that the defendants were negligent in failing to give an adequate warning of the danger of contact with contaminated earth.

---

[30] The same point was made in *Vacwell Engineering Co. Ltd v BDH Chemicals* Ltd [1971] 1 Q.B. 88 where liability in negligence was found on the breach of a duty adequately to warn of the explosive properties of boron tri-bromide on contact with water. The importance of accurate instructions was demonstrated in relation to the merchantability and fitness for purpose of products in *Wormell v RHM Agriculture (East) Ltd* [1987] 1 W.L.R. 1091 where the problem was the ineffectiveness of herbicide, not personal injury.

[31] See *Yachetti v John Duff & Son Ltd* [1943] 1 D.L.R. 194 where the Ontario High Court found that there was no need to warn of the danger of trichinosis from uncooked pork.

[32] 221 F. Supp. 669 (1963).

6–32   Warnings about the possible of danger of toxic shock syndrome were central to the decision in *Worsley v Tambrands*[33] that the tampons were not defective. Mrs Worsley had used the defendant's tampons for many years and had read and acted on the instructions and warnings supplied with them. On the outside of the packet was a warning of the possibility of toxic shock syndrome (TSS) and a reference to the leaflet inside. The leaflet contained detailed information about the risk of TSS and its symptoms and advised that urgent medical advice be sought if certain symptoms were experienced while using tampons. While using them, in 1994, Mrs Worsley did experience such symptoms but, at first, thought that she was suffering from food poisoning. When she went to her doctor she did not tell him that she was using tampons and he did not diagnose TSS. When her condition did not improve she looked for the leaflet but it had been discarded a few days earlier and she did not have access to the information which would probably have alerted her to the fact that she had the symptoms of TSS. Her condition deteriorated and she was eventually admitted to hospital in a serious condition.

6–33   When she recovered she sued the manufacturers both in negligence and under Part 1 of the Consumer Protection Act 1987. Her claim under the Act was based on the argument that the product was defective because it contained inadequate warnings. The claimant was able to prove that she was using the product at the relevant time although the defendant denied that it had caused the illness. In the event the causation issue did not have to be resolved as the judge found that the product was not defective. She observed:

> "As a matter of common sense, I conclude the duty of the manufacturer, and that to which persons generally are entitled to expect in relation to the product, is that the box contains an unambiguous and clear warning that there is an association between TSS and tampon use and directs menstruating woman to the internal leaflet for full details. TSS is a rare but potentially very serious condition which may be life threatening, but it is necessary to balance the rarity and the gravity. That balance is reasonably, properly and safely struck by the dual system of a risk warning on the box and a full explanation in the leaflet if the former is clearly visible and the latter is both legible and full."

6–34   The product, thus, provided the requisite degree of safety and was not defective.

6–35   Burton J. in *A v National Blood Authority (No.1)*[34] also referred to the fact that no warnings had been given about the danger of infection from blood transfusions in deciding that the product was defective. The importance of warnings was also referred to by Pill L.J. in *Abouzaid v*

---

[33] [2000] P.I.Q.R. 95, QBD.
[34] [2001] 3 All E.R. 289.

Mothercare plc.[35] He observed that the product was defective "because it was supplied with a design which permitted the risk to arise and without giving a warning that the user should not so position himself that the risk arose".

McLauglin v Mine Safety Appliances[36] illustrates that the location of **6–36** the warning can be important. The warning was on the cardboard container in which the defective appliance was boxed, rather than on the appliance itself. It was held that this was not sufficient and the warning should have been on the appliance.

In addition to warnings, the way in which the product is promoted is **6–37** relevant. A good example is to be found in the negligence case of *Watson v Buckley, Osborne, Garrett & Co Ltd*[37] where the fact that a hair dye had been advertised as needing no preliminary tests contributed to a finding that the distributor had been negligent. In *Richardson v LRC Products*[38] this seems to have been important. In that case Mrs Richardson had become pregnant after a condom used by her husband had failed. In essence, following the rejection of evidence that the condom had been damaged during production, her case was that the fact of the fracture in use demonstrated a defect. The judge drew attention to the fact that it was well known that a proportion of condoms fail for no known reason and that the manufacturers do not claim absolute reliability.

(b) Reasonable expectations about use

This criterion raises the difficult question of how far abnormal use, or **6–38** use not intended by the manufacturer, should be taken into consideration in determining whether a product is defective. Cases such as *Yachetti v John Duff & Son Ltd*[39] where the purchaser had not carried out an obvious process will be relevant. There the Ontario High Court found that there was no need to warn of the necessity to cook pork to avoid the danger of trichinosis. The American case of *Reid v Spadone Machine Co*[40] may also be helpful. There it was held to be foreseeable that, if a dangerous machine for cutting up plastic could be used by two persons, it would be so used, because used in that way the job could be done faster. As designed, the machine, though not intended for use by two persons, was dangerous when so used. It was shown that it would have been fairly easy to have designed the machine so that one person could not have set the machine in motion while the other was in a position of danger and so the manufacturer was liable.

---

[35] *The Times*, Dec. 21, 2000, CA.
[36] 181 Ne. 2d. 430 (1960).
[37] [1940] 1 All E.R. 74.
[38] [2000] Lloyd's Rep. Med. 280, QBD.
[39] [1943] 1 D.L.R. 194.
[40] 404 A. 2d. 1094 (1979).

Time of supply

6–39 This factor requires a court to take into account standards applicable
when the product was put into circulation, not those developed since the
product was supplied. Another American case, *Bruce v Martin Marietta
Corp.*,[41] illustrates this point. This action arose out of the crash in 1970
of a plane, which had been manufactured by the defendants in 1952.
When the plane crashed, seats in the passenger cabin broke loose from
their floor attachments and were thrown forward against a bulkhead,
blocking the exit. A fire broke out and it was alleged that the escape of
passengers was impeded by the seats. Evidence was produced by the
plaintiffs to show that seats could now be produced which would
withstand a crash. The defendants showed that when the plane was built
by them it met or exceeded all relevant design requirements, safety
requirements, and other criteria prescribed by the regulatory body. It
was held that the plaintiffs had not shown that the ordinary consumer
would expect a plane made in 1952 to have the safety features of one
made in 1970. "A consumer would not expect a Model T to have the
safety features which are incorporated in automobiles made today. The
same expectation applies to airplanes."

Other Factors

6–40 As s.3 makes clear, the factors listed are not the only ones which may
be taken into account in determining whether a product is defective.
What other factors might a court consider? This issue was extensively
canvassed in *A v National Blood Authority (No.1)*.[42] The claimants had
been infected with hepatitis C through blood transfusions which had
used blood from infected donors. During the period when most of the
claimants had been infected the risk of such infection in this way was
known to exist but was impossible to avoid, either because the virus
itself had not yet been discovered or because there was no way of testing
for its presence in blood. It was for that reason that the claims were
brought under Pt I of the Consumer Protection Act 1987 rather than in
negligence. There was much discussion of the meaning of Art.6 of the
Directive which states that: "A product is defective when it does not
provide the safety which a person is entitled to expect, taking all
circumstances into account".[43]

6–41 In a very detailed judgment following lengthy argument by counsel
Burton J. considered this provision. He emphasised in his judgment the
context of the enactment of the Directive pointing out that it was a
consumer protection measure designed to provide strict liability and
overcome the difficulties for consumers of obtaining reparation through
fault based remedies. "All circumstances", he held, meant all *relevant*

---

[41] 544 F. 2d. 442 (1976) (10th Cir.).
[42] [2001] 3 All E.R. 289.
[43] Dir. 85/374.

circumstances. The defendants argued that among such circumstances in a case like this would be: whether there were tests which could ensure that infection could be avoided; were such tests unreasonably expensive; and the benefit to society or the utility of the product. Burton J. considered that none of these factors could be regarded as relevant circumstances. The first two, in particular, would subvert the purpose of a directive as a measure introducing strict liability by reintroducing ideas more relevant to fault-based liability. They are irrelevant to the issue of consumers' expectations about safety which in this case were that blood was free from infection. It should be remembered that though the risk of infection was known to the medical profession they did not pass on that knowledge to patients, unless they asked, which they rarely did.

In this case Burton J. appears to have adopted a different approach to **6–42** that of Ian Kennedy J. in *Richardson v LRC Products*.[44] The approach to defectiveness was not clearly articulated in that judgment, but there are comments that suggest an approach more appropriate to negligence than to strict liability. The judgment in *Richardson* appears to have considerably influenced the decision in *Foster v Biosil*,[45] a decision of Ms Booth Q.C. sitting as a recorder. The claimant had received silicone gel breast implants in 1994. Five months later the left implant was removed and was found to have ruptured. The claimant brought an action under Part 1 of the 1987 Act alleging that it was defective and had caused her loss. The court found that the implant by reason of the rupture was unsafe and accepted that this had caused her loss. On a literal reading of s.3 it might be thought that this would have been enough for the claim to succeed. The court, however, accepted the defendant's argument that the claimant bore the onus of proving "not merely the fact of the defect but also the cause of the defect". There seems to be no warrant for this in the 1987 Act much less the Directive and the decision in this case must be open to doubt.

In *B (A Child) v McDonald's Restaurants Ltd*[46] the approach in *A v* **6–43** *National Blood Authority (No.1)*[47] was followed in a case where a number of children had been scalded by hot tea and coffee in a McDonalds restaurant. It was argued that tea and coffee provided in containers at such high temperatures were not safe products. It was held that this was not so. The judge pointed out that McDonalds had trained its staff about the dangers and had provided the beverages in cups with lids. Furthermore, he did not consider that customers would have been prepared to accept the beverages at temperatures which would have avoided scalding. In his view the beverages did achieve the "safety which a person is entitled to expect", to quote Art.6 of the Directive.

---

[44] [2000] P.I.Q.R. 164.
[45] (2001) 59 B.M.L.R. 178.
[46] [2002] E.W.H.C. 490
[47] [2001] 3 All E.R. 289.

DEFENCES

6–44 Section 4 Consumer Protection Act 1987 sets out a number of defences open to the producer. The burden of proof is on the producer to establish the defence.

6–45 The manufacturer has a defence if he can show "that the defect is attributable to compliance with any requirement imposed by or under any enactment or with any Community obligation".[48] An example of a situation where this defence might apply is where safety regulations have been made in relation to a specific product under Pt 2 of the 1987 Act. The producer also has a defence if he can show that he did not supply the product to another. This could apply when stocks of a product are stolen from a manufacturer and reach the market through illicit channels.

6–46 Not unreasonably, s.4(1)(d) provides that it is a defence to show that there was no defect in the product at the time that the product was supplied. For this purpose it is important to note that the Act in s.4(2) states what is the "relevant time" for this purpose. The basic idea is that a supplier should only be liable for defects present when he put it into circulation. In the case of manufacturers, own-branders and importers this is the time at which they supplied the product to another. In the case of other persons it is the time when the product was last supplied by one of the producers just referred to. This defence will absolve a manufacturer from liability if he can show that some defect has arisen through damage caused to the product after it left his hands. This may take the form of deterioration through ordinary wear or tear; or the product may have become defective through unskilled servicing or maintenance.[49]

6–47 The final defence in s.4(1)(c) is intended to protect those involved in non-commercial activities such as those who provide homemade goods for a charity sale. They will have a defence where they can show that the only supply of the product to another by the person proceeded against was otherwise than in the course of a business, and that that person is not a producer, own-brander or importer as defined in s.2(2) or, if he is, that he is not acting in that capacity with a view to profit.

State of the Art Defence

6–48 The most controversial defence is that which is popularly known as the state of the art defence, or sometimes the development risk defence. The Directive permits such a defence but also provides that Member States may choose not to include it in their national legislation. The UK has chosen to include the defence although its inclusion was not recommended by the Law Commissions or the Pearson Committee in their

---

[48] Interpretation Act 1978, Sch.1 applies to all legislation the definition contained in of European Communities Act 1972, Sch.1.
[49] For an example from a negligence case, see *Evans v Triplex Safety Glass Co Ltd* [1936] 1 All E.R. 283.

reports.[50] Its inclusion is a weakness of our products liability law though the way that it has been interpreted by the courts suggests that its inclusion may not be as deleterious as had been thought.

The defence is set out in s.4(1)(e) and applies where it can be **6–49** shown:

> "that the state of scientific and technical knowledge at the relevant time was not such that a producer of products of the same description as the product in question might be expected to have discovered the defect if it had existed in his products while they were under his control."

The Commission sued the UK in the ECJ alleging that this formula- **6–50** tion did not properly implement Art.7(e) which provides that a manufacturer shall not be liable if he proves: "that the state of scientific and technical knowledge at the time when he put the product into circulation was not such as to enable the existence of the defect to be discovered." The Commission argued that the Directive sets out an objective test where the Act, with its reference to the possibility of another producer discovering the defect, suggests a subjective test. It is even possible that this formulation of the defence would allow the courts to give the defence the meaning that it has been given in some American states. As was observed in one case " 'state of the art' . . . is sometimes confused with 'standards of the industry' ".[51] The ECJ rejected the challenge by the Commission. It agreed that the test was an objective one and observed:

> "Article 7(e) is not specifically directly at the practices and safety standards in use in the industrial sector in which the producer is operating, but, unreservedly, at the state of scientific and technical knowledge, including the most advanced level of such knowledge, at the time when the product in question was put into circulation."[52]

It went on to add that in order to have a defence: **6–51**

> "the producer of a defective product must prove that the objective state of scientific and technical knowledge, including the most advanced level of such knowledge, at the time when the product in question was put into circulation was not such as to enable the existence of the defect to be discovered. Further, in order for the relevant scientific knowledge to be successfully pleaded against

---

[50] Liability for Defective Products (Law Com. No.82, Scot. Law Com. No.45, Cmnd 6831, 1977) and Royal Commission on Civil Liability and Compensation for Personal Injury Cmnd 7054–I, 1978 Ch.22.

[51] Supreme Court of the state of Washington, *Cantu v John Deere Co.*, 603 P. 2d. 839 at 840.

[52] [1997] All E.R. (EC) 481; [1997] 3 C.M.L.R. 923, para.26.

the producer, that knowledge must have been accessible at the time when the product in question was put into circulation. On this last point . . . the Directive raises difficulties of interpretation which, in the event of litigation, the national courts will have to resolve".[53]

6–52   It concluded that there was no evidence that UK courts would fail to interpret s.4(1)(e) in this way.

6–53   This has been borne out in a passing reference to the state of the art defence by Ian Kennedy J. in *Richardson v LRC Products*[54] who confirmed this view. He observed that "The test provided by the statute is not what the defendants knew, but what they could have known if they had consulted those who might be expected to know the state of research and all available literature sources".[55] In *Abouzaid v Mothercare plc*[56] the Court of Appeal in England also clearly accepted this approach. It rejected the defence based on expert evidence that engineers had not encountered such accidents and that the Department of Trade and Industry's accident database contained no reports of such accidents. Indeed, Pill J. observed that he was:

"very doubtful whether, in the present context, a record of accidents, comes within the category of scientific and technical knowledge. The defence contemplates scientific and technical advances which throw additional light, for example, on the propensities of materials and allow defects to be discovered."

6–54   *A v National Blood Authority (No.1)*[57] also applied the approach of the ECJ and rejected the defendant's state of the art defence. Burton J. held that the defence did not apply where the existence of a generic defect was known or should have been known in the context of accessible information. Once the existence of a defect was known, there was the risk of that defect materialising in any particular product, and it was immaterial that the known risk was unavoidable in the particular specimen of the product.

6–55   Concerns that the formulation of the state of the art defence in the Act might result in UK courts interpreting it less favourably than intended by the Directive have proved groundless. Other fears about the state of the art defence also need to be seen in perspective. As was pointed out in the parliamentary debates, the true undiscoverable development risk is likely to be very rare. It is only to the category of design defects that it is likely to have any relevance. Where the defect is a manufacturing

[53] [1997] 3 C.M.L.R. 923, para.29.
[54] [2000] P.I.Q.R. 164.
[55] *ibid.*, p.172.
[56] *The Times*, Dec. 21, 2000, CA.
[57] [2001] 3 All E.R. 289.

defect it is unlikely to have any relevance; and can have no application where the product is defective through a failure to warn.

Components

Many products contain component parts made by various manu- **6–56** facturers. An excellent example is the motorcar where the manufacturer of the finished product may actually fabricate only the bodywork, the seats and the interior trim, but purchase many other parts such as brakes, gear boxes, tyres and electrical accessories from independent suppliers. As was pointed out above, a component manufacturer is liable as a producer for any defects in products of his which are incorporated in a finished product. In certain circumstances the component manufacturer will have a defence under s.4(1)(f). This is the case where the component supplier can show that the defect in the finished product which resulted from the article supplied by him was wholly attributable to the design of the finished product or to compliance with instructions given by the producer of the finished product.

This defence will be particularly important to manufacturers of **6–57** components which are widely used in industry without the component manufacturer having any control over their use, such as nuts and bolts. Provided the component manufacturer has produced articles without a flaw and has correctly described his product, he will have no further responsibility for problems resulting from the use to which an assembler puts his product.

Contributory negligence

As we have seen already, s.2(1) states that various persons are liable **6–58** "where any damage is caused wholly or partly by a defect in a product". Thus where the damage is caused partly by the defect and partly by some third party the producer is liable to the victim, though he will be able by virtue of s.2(5) to obtain a contribution from the third party. When the damage is caused partly by a defect in the product and partly by the fault of the victim the normal rules of apportionment for contributory negligence apply. These are to be found in the Law Reform (Contributory Negligence) Act 1945.

Causation

The new product liability regime introduced by the Consumer Protec- **6–59** tion Act 1987 does not require proof that the loss suffered by the victim was foreseeable. This does not rule out consideration of causation. It is not enough to show that the product was defective and that the plaintiff was injured by it. It must be shown that there was a casual connection between these two facts. The Act states in s.21(1) that the damage must be "caused wholly or partly by a defect in a product". If the defendant can show some break in the chain of causation he will be able to avoid liability. Questions of causation will undoubtedly overlap with issues of improper use and contributory negligence.

DAMAGE

6–60 For the purposes of liability for defective products damage is defined in s.5 of the Consumer Protection Act 1987 to mean death or personal injury or any loss of or damage to any property including land. There is no mention of economic loss and it is generally assumed by the textbook writers that this is not recoverable under the Act. Although the 1987 Act does not state the basis on which damages are to be calculated, it is reasonable to assume that it will be on the normal delictual principles. Damages for personal injury will include damages for pain and suffering. Art.9 of the Directive[58] states that such damages are to be awarded if, as is the case in Scotland, they are awardable under domestic law. Where the victim has died as the result of his injuries s.6(1)(c) preserves the rights of dependants and relatives to bring actions under the Damages (Scotland) Act 1976. Section 6(3) aligns the Congenital Disabilities (Civil Liability) Act 1976 with the new product liability regime.

6–61 Liability for damage to property is limited in various ways. Damages are not available for any loss of, or damage to, the defective product itself. Compensation for other property is available only where the property is, to quote s.5(3), "of a description of property ordinarily intended for private use, occupation or consumption" and "intended by the person suffering the loss or damage mainly for his own private use, occupation or consumption's Where compensation for property loss is sought s.5(4) provides that there is to be no award unless the amount awarded exceeds £275.

6–62 For the purpose of deciding who has the right to sue for loss to property, and when such loss occurred, s.5(5) provides that it "shall be regarded as having occurred at the earliest time at which a person with an interest in the property had knowledge of the material facts about the loss or damage." Section 5(6) goes on to state that material facts "are such facts about the loss or damage as would lead a reasonable person with an interest in the property to consider the loss or damage sufficiently serious to justify his instituting proceedings for damages against a defendant who did not dispute liability and was able to satisfy a judgement."

6–63 The Directive permits Member States to limit a producer's liability for damage resulting from death or personal injury and caused by identical items with the same defect to be limited to an amount which is not less then 70 million ECUs (approximately £40 million). The UK has chosen not to take advantage of this facility.

---

[58] Dir. 85/374.

TIME-LIMITS

The Prescription and Limitation (Scotland) Act 1973 is amended by **6–64** Sch.1 of the Consumer Protection Act 1987 and provides that product liability actions are extinguished 10 years after the product was supplied by its manufacturer, importer or the person who put his own name on it. In addition, the same action shall be brought three years after the later of the date on which the cause of action accrued and the date of knowledge of the injured person. It is important to note that the 10-year limit can have the effect of abbreviating the three-year limit. Where someone is injured say, nine years after the product was supplied, that person has only one year in which to raise an action. This seems to have been accepted in *Re MMR and MR Vaccine Litigation*[59] although it should be noted that these changes to the normal rules required to be made separately for each jurisdiction.

EXCLUSION OF LIABILITY

It will not be possible to contract out of liability under Pt 1 of the **6–65** Consumer Protection Act 1987. Section 7 makes this clear stating that liability "to a person who has suffered damage caused wholly or partly by a defect in a product, or to a dependent or relative of such a person, shall not be limited or excluded by any contract term, by any notice or by any other provision."

CIVIL LIABILITY UNDER THE CONSUMER PROTECTION ACT 1987, PT 2

The criminal law is used, as is discussed below,[60] to try to ensure that **6–66** only safe goods reach the market place. In addition to incurring criminal liability breach of the safety regulations can lead to civil liability. Section 41 of the 1987 Act is one of those rare provisions in legislation imposing criminal penalties which explicitly states that this is the case. It provides that breach of safety regulations gives a right of action for breach of statutory duty to anyone affected. It is to be noted that while this applies to breach of the safety regulations it does not apply to breach of the general safety requirement. In practice little use seems to be made of this provision and there are no reported cases on it from any part of the UK.

---

[59] [2001] EWCA Civ 2006; [2002] 1 W.L.R. 1662; [2002] C.P. Rep. 20; (2002) 65 B.M.L.R. 79
[60] See para.6–67 *et seq.*

ROLE OF THE CRIMINAL LAW

6–67 The civil law controls on product standards discussed above apply after the harm has occurred. Where the failure of a product to meet the required legal standard may cause personal injury or death it is important to attempt to prevent such a product being put into circulation at all. The Consumer Protection Act 1961[61] was the legislative response to the need identified by the Molony Report[62] for legislation governing dangerous products. Its central feature was the creation of a power to make regulations specifying safety criteria for products. The Consumer Safety Act 1978 followed a review of product safety controls in a government consultative document[63] which revealed inadequacies in the earlier legislation. Among these were: criticisms of slowness in establishing and revising safety standards; the lengthy consultations involved when hazards came to light; and the absence of powers to deal promptly with new products which proved to be hazardous but which were not subject to existing regulations.

6–68 The 1978 Act met these criticisms by introducing three new techniques. Where the Secretary of State considered that a product or a component part of a product was not safe he was empowered to issue a "prohibition order" prohibiting the supply of goods which were considered to be unsafe, or permitting their supply only on such conditions as were specified in the notice.[64] Finally, a "notice to warn" could be served on any person, requiring that person to publish, at his own expense, a warning about unsafe goods which he had supplied. Further improvements to the legislation were made by the Consumer Safety (Amendment) Act 1986 which implemented many of the proposals in the 1984 White Paper.[65] This was concerned mainly with improving the enforcement of the legislation.

6–69 All this legislation was repealed by the Consumer Protection Act 1987,[66] which is primarily a consolidating measure, although it does include some new provisions, most notably the creation of a general safety requirement.[67] While there were other pieces of safety legislation, the law was reasonably clearly set out. That can no longer be said with the enactment of the General Product Safety Regulations 1994.[68] In

---

[61] Consumer Protection Act 1961 was repealed by Consumer Safety Act 1978, s.10(1), Sch.3, on Oct. 1, 1987: Consumer Safety Act 1978 (Commencement No.3) Order 1987 (SI 1987/1681).

[62] Final Report of the Committee on Consumer Protection, Cmnd. 1781 (1962)

[63] Cmnd. 6398 (1976).

[64] See Consumer Safety Act 1978, s.3, Sch.1 (repealed).

[65] Cmnd. 9302 (1984).

[66] Consumer Protection Act 1987, s.48, Sch.5. The repeals came into force on Oct. 1, 1987: Consumer Protection Act 1987 (Commencement No.1) Order 1987 (SI 1987/1680), art.3(k), Sch.1, Pt 1.

[67] As to the general safety requirement, see para.6.84.

[68] SI 1994/2328.

order to try to make sense of the present law it will be necessary to discuss Pt 2 of the 1987 Act and then the new regulations. This is because both are relevant and complement each other. As we shall see, the new regulations refer to the enforcement techniques of Pt 2.

SAFETY REGULATIONS

The Consumer Protection Act 1987, like earlier safety legislation, gives **6–70** the Secretary of State for Trade and Industry extensive powers to make regulations relating to the safety of goods.[69] Regulations may be made to ensure that goods are safe; that unsafe goods are not made available generally, or to persons in whose hands they would be unsafe; and that appropriate information is provided. Section 11(2) goes on to specify a wide range of matters with which the regulations may deal such as their composition, testing and inspection.[70] Before making such regulations the Secretary of State has a duty to consult organisations which appear to him to be representative of interests substantially affected by his proposal and any other persons he considers appropriate.[71]

The power to make safety regulations is exercisable by statutory **6–71** instruments subject to annulment by resolution of either House of Parliament.[72] Under previous legislation regulations were subject to affirmative resolution of both Houses of Parliament. Breach of safety regulations is not itself a criminal offence. It is an offence to supply (as widely defined in s.46[73]) where the regulations prohibit such supply. Offences are punishable on summary conviction by imprisonment for a term not exceeding six months or by a fine not exceeding level 5 on the standard scale or by both.[74]

Prohibition notices and notices to warn

The prohibition notices introduced by the Consumer Safety Act 1978 **6–72** are re-enacted in the Consumer Protection Act 1987, as are notices to warn,[75] and the 1987 Act sets out in detail the procedure to be used when it is proposed to issue such notices.[76] In *R v Liverpool City*

---

[69] See Consumer Protection Act 1987, s.11. For the goods to which s.11 does not apply, see s.11(7).

[70] A large number of regulations have been made covering such goods as toys, see Toys (Safety) (Amendment) Regulations 1993 (SI 1993/1547); cosmetics, see Cosmetic Products (Safety) (Amendment) Regulations 1992 (SI 1992/1525); and see Low Voltage Electrical Equipment (Safety) Regulations 1989 (SI 1989/728).

[71] See s.11(5). This function has been discussed in *R. v Secretary of State for Health, ex p. United States Tobacco International Inc.* [1992] 1 Q.B. 353; [1992] 1 All E.R. 212.

[72] s.11(6).

[73] See *Drummond-Rees v Dorset CC* (1998) 162 J.P. 651, DC

[74] See, generally, s.12. Level 5 is £5,000: Increase of Criminal Penalties etc. (Scotland) Order 1984 (SI 1984/526), art.4.

[75] See s.13.

[76] See s.13(2), Sch.2.

Council, ex p. Baby Products[77] it was held that the council was acting outside its powers in issuing a press release alleging that a product was dangerous. The statutory procedure under the safety legislation was the appropriate way to prevent the sale of goods suspected to be dangerous. The court conceded that this was cumbersome and slow and the Lord Chief Justice commented: "I can imagine circumstances in which an emergency procedure to supplement the s.13 procedure would be desirable. The remedy for a defective statutory procedure is not, however, to ignore or circumvent it but to amend it."[78]

Suspension notices

6–73 The Consumer Safety (Amendment) Act 1986 gave enforcement authorities, in practice trading standards officers, an important new power to deal with dangerous goods when it introduced the suspension notice. This is re-enacted in the Consumer Protection Act 1987. A trading standards officer may serve a suspension notice prohibiting the supply of specified goods if he has reasonable cause to believe that any safety provision has been, or may be, contravened.[79] Such a notice applies beyond the area of the local authority which issued it but may only be enforced in other areas by the local authorities for them.[80] A suspension notice may not extend beyond six months and a further notice may only be served in respect of the same goods if proceedings have first been instituted for breach of a safety provision or for the forfeiture of the goods.[81] The owner of suspended goods may appeal against the suspension notice.[82]

6–74 In *R v Birmingham City Council, ex p. Ferrero Ltd*[83] the English Court of Appeal held that the proper method of challenging a suspension notice was by means of the appeal procedure set out in s.15 of the 1987 Act, not by judicial review. Taylor L.J. (as he then was) said:

> "The real issue was whether the goods contravened a safety provision and the section 15 appeal was geared exactly to deciding that issue. If the goods did contravene the safety provision and were dangerous to children then, surely, procedural impropriety or unfairness in the decision-making process should not persuade a court to quash the order. The determining factors are the paramount

---

[77] (2000) 2 L.G.L.R. 689; [2000] B.L.G.R. 171; [2000] C.O.D. 91, DC.

[78] (2000) 2 L.G.L.R. 689 at 694.

[79] See s.14(1), (5). A suspension notice may also require that the authority be informed of the whereabouts throughout the suspension period of suspended goods: s.14(3). As to the contents of a suspension notice, see s.14(2).

[80] *Brighton and Hove City Council v Woolworths Plc* [2002] EWHC 2565; (2003) 167 J.P. 21; (2003) 167 J.P.N. 52, QBD.

[81] See s.14(1), (4). As to forfeiture of goods, see s.17.

[82] See s.15(1), (2), (4)

[83] [1993] 1 All E.R. 530; (1991) 155 J.P. 721; 89 L.G.R. 977; (1991) 3 Admin. L.R. 613; (1991) 10 Tr. L.R. 129.

need to safeguard consumers and the emergency nature of the section 14 powers."[84]

Where the power to suspend a supply has been exercised, an **6–75** enforcement authority is liable to pay compensation to any person having an interest in the goods, in respect of any loss or damage caused by reason of the exercise of the power, if there has been no contravention in relation to the goods of any safety provision and the exercise of the power is not attributable to any neglect or default by that person.[85]

Defence of due diligence

There is a due diligence defence in the Consumer Protection Act 1987,[86] **6–76** but reliance on information supplied by someone else will not establish this defence unless it can be shown that it was reasonable in all the circumstances to have relied on the information having regard in particular to: (1) the steps which were taken, and which might reasonably have been taken, to verify the information; and (2) whether he had any reason to disbelieve the information.[87]

It has not been easy to take advantage of this defence. In *Riley v* **6–77** *Webb*,[88] a case under the Consumer Protection Act 1961, the defendant, who was a wholesaler, showed that it had a condition on its order forms that orders were placed in the understanding that the goods met any relevant statutory requirements. It also argued that it was a small company and had dealt with the supplier of the unsafe goods for many years. Random sampling, it claimed, would have been unreasonable. The English Divisional Court held that the defendants could have taken a simple step to avoid breaching the Act. It could either have asked for specific assurances about the goods; or it could have imposed contract terms under which its suppliers would have had to ensure that the regulations had been complied with. By using only the general term in its order form it had not exercised due diligence.

In *Rotherham Metropolitan Borough Council v Rayson (UK) Ltd*[89] a **6–78** request to overseas suppliers to report any failures to meet UK standards had been sent to them, and the defendants had tested one packet out of an annual purchase of several thousand. The Divisional Court did not

---

[84] [1993] 1 All E.R. 530 at 539.

[85] s.14(7). Any dispute as to the right to or the amount of any compensation is to be determined by a single arbiter appointed, failing agreement between the parties, by the sheriff: s.14(8).

[86] *i.e.* s.39. The offences in Consumer Protection Act 1987, Pt 2, to which the defence relates are offences under ss.10, 12(1)–(3), offences against safety regulations, and s.14(6) offences in respect of suspension notices: s.39(5).

[87] s.39(4).

[88] (1987) 151 J.P. 372.

[89] [1988] B.T.L.C. 292.

regard this as meeting the due diligence standard. In *P. & M. Supplies (Essex) Ltd v Devon County Council*[90] the appellants had been convicted of an offence against the Toys (Safety) Regulations 1974[91] relating to a soft toy. Evidence showed that 0.49 per cent of stock was tested randomly, and some samples were sent to the public analyst. Dismissing the appeal, the English Divisional Court said that it was for the company to produce evidence, preferably independent statistical evidence, to show the soundness of their sampling methods.

6–79   It is generally believed that a high proportion of dangerous goods are imported. For this reason the provision giving powers to the Commissioners of Customs and Excise to disclose information to those who enforce safety legislation, which was introduced by the Consumer Safety (Amendment) Act 1986, is re-enacted in the Consumer Protection Act 1987.[92] A customs officer may also, for the purpose of facilitating the enforcement of the safety provisions, seize any imported goods and detain them for not more than two working days.[93]

6–80   Where there has been a contravention of the safety provisions the procurator fiscal may apply to a sheriff for an order for the forfeiture of any unsafe goods. The owner, or anyone having an interest in the goods, must be given notice of the application and may appear at the hearing to oppose the making of such an order.[94]

GENERAL SAFETY REQUIREMENT

6–81 The major innovation of Pt 2 of the Consumer Protection Act 1987[95] is the enactment of a general safety requirement. Prior to its introduction, problems could arise where goods which were not the subject of safety regulations were found to be unsafe. If traders did not voluntarily remove them from the market, there were no powers to do so. It is to fill this gap that the general safety requirement was introduced.

6–82   With the enactment of the General Product Safety Regulations 1994[96] the general safety requirement has a much restricted ambit. This is because the new regulations also contain a general safety requirement and provide that where it applies the requirement of the Act does not apply.[97]

6–83   It is a criminal offence to supply, offer or agree to supply, expose or possess for supply any consumer goods which fail to comply with the

---

[90] (1992) 11 Tr. L.R. 52.
[91] SI 1974/1367.
[92] See s.37.
[93] See s.31.
[94] See s.17.
[95] Consumer Protection Act 1987, Pt 2 (ss.10–19), came into force on Oct. 1, 1987: Consumer Protection Act 1987 (Commencement No.1) Order 1987 (SI 1987/1680), art.3.
[96] SI 1994/2328; and see 6–86 *et seq.*
[97] *ibid.*, reg.5.

general safety requirements.[98] "Consumer goods" means any goods which are ordinarily intended for private use or consumption except (1) growing crops or things attached to land; (2) water, food, feeding stuff or fertilisers; (3) gas[99]; (4) aircraft (other than hang-gliders) or motor vehicles; (5) controlled drugs or licensed medicinal products; or (6) tobacco.[1] Goods fail to comply with the general safety requirement if they are not reasonably safe having regard to all the circumstances, including:

"(a) the manner in which, and purposes for which, the goods are being or would be marketed, the get-up of the goods, the use of any mark in relation to the goods and any instructions or warnings which are given or would be given with respect to the keeping, use or consumption of the goods;
(b) any standards of safety published by any person either for goods of a description which applies to the goods in question or for matters relating to goods of that description; and
(c) the existence of any means by which it would have been reasonable (taking into account the cost, likelihood and extent of any improvement) for the goods to have been made safer."[2]

However, goods are not regarded as failing to comply with the **6–84** general safety requirement in respect of anything which is shown to be attributable to compliance with a requirement imposed by any enactment or with any Community obligation.[3] Nor will goods be regarded as failing to comply with this requirement because they go no further than meeting any safety regulations made under the Act or any safety standards provided by that or any other enactment.[4]

Defences in respect of the general safety requirement

It is a defence to a charge that the general safety requirement has been **6–85** breached for the supplier to show: (1) that he reasonably believed that the goods would not be used or consumed in the UK[5]; (2) that, being a retail supplier, he neither knew nor had reasonable grounds for believing

---

[98] s.10(1).
[99] *i.e.* gas which is, is to be, or has been, supplied by a person authorised to supply it by or under Gas Act 1986, ss.6–8 (authorisation of supply of gas through pipes).
[1] s.10(7). For the meaning of "controlled drug", "feeding stuff", "fertiliser", "food", "licensed medicinal product" and "tobacco", see s.19(1).
[2] s.10(2)(a)–(c).
[3] s.10(3)(a).
[4] s.10(3)(b).
[5] s.10(4)(a).

that they did not comply with the general safety requirement[6]; or (3) that the terms on which he supplied or offered to supply the goods indicated that the goods which were to be acquired by someone else were not new.[7]

General Product Safety Regulations 1994

6–86 The General Product Safety Regulations,[8] which implement the General Product Safety Directive,[9] follow the deplorable recent tendency of implementing directives in areas where there is already important domestic primary legislation by means of regulations instead of legislating afresh in the area. New primary legislation would have produced a more coherent and clearer legislative regime than the confusion with which industry, consumers and enforcement agencies have been saddled.

6–87   The central provision of the Regulations is found in reg.7 which states: "No producer shall place a product on the market unless the product is a safe product". The heading in the Regulations calls this "the general safety requirement". This is supported by the following two regulations. Regulation 8 imposes various obligations on producers to give information to consumers and obtain information about the performance of their products. Regulation 9 requires a distributor to "act with due care in order to help ensure compliance with the requirements of regulation 7". In all these situations failure to observe the requirements of the Regulations is a criminal offence.

6–88   Before considering these provisions in more detail it will first be useful to discover what products are covered and who are producers and distributors, remembering that where the safety requirement of these Regulations applies that in the Consumer Safety Act 1987 does not.

6–89   As we have seen,[10] the 1987 Act has a list of products to which it does not apply. The products covered by the Regulations is different and wider. Regulations 2 and 3 define them. Regulation 2 states that a "product" is "any product intended for consumers or likely to be used

---

[6] s.10(4)(b). For this purpose goods are supplied in the course of carrying on a retail business if (1) whether or not they are themselves acquired for a person's private use or consumption they are supplied in the course of carrying on a business of making a supply of consumer goods available to persons who generally acquire them for private use or consumption; and (2) the descriptions of goods the supply of which is made available in the course of that business do not, to a significant extent, include manufactured or imported goods which have not previously been supplied in the UK: s.10(5)(a), (b).

[7] s.10(4)(c).

[8] SI 1994/2328.

[9] Dir. 92/59; [1992] O.J. L228/24.

[10] para.6–83 *et seq.*

by consumers, supplied whether for consideration or not in the course of a commercial activity and whether new, used or reconditioned".

A number of points should be noted about this definition. As the **6–90** definition of "product" goes on to make clear, it does not apply to one used "exclusively in the context of a commercial activity even if it is used for or by a consumer". Unlike the Act, the Regulations apply to second-hand products though, as reg.3 shows, not all second-hand products. Regulation 3 exempts such products if these are antiques. A further important exemption set out in reg.3 is "products supplied for repair or reconditioning before use". This only applies where the supplier clearly informs the person to whom they are supplied that this is the case.

Another important category of products exempt from the Regulations **6–91** is those where there are specific provisions in rules of Community law governing all aspects of the safety of the product. This means that there will be no overlap between these Regulations and other Community product safety rules. For example, various Community directives contain a wide range of specific provisions governing the safety of medicinal products, medicated feeding stuffs and medicinal feed additives. Products which are licensed in the UK in accordance with these Community rules will not be subject to the Regulations. But it is important to note that this exemption applies only where the Community law relates to all aspects of the safety of the product. Regulation 4 makes clear that it does not apply where the product is subject to some other Community law which does not make provision about its safety.

Producers

The Regulations place the primary duty of ensuring that only safe **6–92** products are marketed on "producers" a term which is defined in reg.2. It covers manufacturers established in the Community which, for the purposes of these Regulations, means not just the Member States of the EU but the European Economic Area (EEA), a very much larger group of countries. The term "producer" also includes those who pass themselves off as manufacturers, such as own-branders and those who recondition products. Where the manufacturer is not established in the EEA the producer, his representative or, if there is none, the importer is liable. "Producer" also includes other professionals in the supply chain, in so far as their activities may affect the safety properties of a product. This might bring transport or storage companies within the ambit of the definition.

Distributors

As we shall see, certain duties are placed upon distributors. They are **6–93** defined as "any professional in the supply chain whose activity does not affect the safety properties of a product".

Safety

6–94 The definition of safety in reg.2 bears some resemblance to that in Pt 1 of the Act and is a pragmatic one. A safe product is one:

> "which, under normal or reasonably foreseeable conditions of use, including duration, does not present any risk or only the minimum risks compatible with the product's use, considered as acceptable and consistent with a high level of protection for the safety and health of persons."

6–95 In assessing whether this standard has been met a number factors related to the product are to be taken into account. These are:

(1) its characteristics, including its composition, packaging, and instructions for assembly and maintenance;
(2) its effect on other products where it is reasonably foreseeable that it will be used with them;
(3) its presentation, labelling, instructions for use and disposal and any other indication or information provided by the producer;
(4) the categories of consumers at serious risk when using the product, in particular children.

6–96 However, the fact that higher levels of safety can be obtained, or that there are other products presenting a lesser degree of risk does not of itself mean that a product is unsafe. An example of this in practice might be provided by cars. Some, usually the more expensive, models of cars have anti-lock braking systems. This provision probably means that cars which do not have such systems will not be regarded as unsafe because they do not have such a system.

6–97 In assessing whether a product is safe reg.10 is important. Regulation 10(1) states that there is a presumption that a product which conforms to UK rules laying down health and safety requirements is safe. So, a product which conforms to the safety regulations made under Pt 1 of the 1987 Act would be presumed to be safe. If there are no such rules, reg.10(2) sets out factors to be taken into account in deciding whether a product meets the general safety requirement in reg.7. These are voluntary UK standards which give effect to a European standard, or a Community technical specification. If there are no standards of these types, standards drawn up in the UK, health and safety codes of good practice in the product sector, or the state of the art and technology may be relied upon. In addition, the safety which consumers may reasonably expect is relevant.

Duties of Producers

6–98 In addition to the primary duty not to market unsafe products producers are also under an obligation to provide consumers with relevant information so that they may assess the risks inherent in a product where these risks are not immediately apparent.[11] They must also adopt measures commensurate with the characteristics of their products to enable consumers to be informed of the risks which these products might present and to take appropriate action, including, if necessary, withdrawing the product from the market. Such measures might include marking the products, or product batches, so that these can be identified. This would be important, if a fault were found, in arranging a product recall. Other measures are sample testing, investigating complaints and keeping distributors informed about the results of monitoring.

These requirements are said to apply to a producer "within the limits **6–99** of his activity". This is a peculiarly opaque expression which is copied from the Directive, it would appear to mean something like "in so far as it is within his power".

Duties of Distributors

Distributors as defined in the Regulations are required by reg.9 to act **6–100** with due care in order to help ensure compliance with the general safety duty. In particular, they must not supply products which they know, or should have presumed, on the basis of the information available to them, were dangerous. They must, within the limits of their activities, participate in monitoring the safety of products, pass on information about their safety, and co-operate in action to avoid those risks.

The Regulations are enforced by using the techniques set out in the **6–101** Act. As appropriate, therefore, prohibition notices and notices to warn, suspension notices and forfeiture may be used. Enforcement is in the hands of the weights and measures authorities,[12] *i.e.* the island and district councils. Breach of the general safety requirement, the obligation of a distributor to act with due care to ensure compliance with it, and marketing or supplying unsafe products are criminal offences.[13] A due diligence defence of the type common in consumer protection legislation is provided.[14]

Reform of the General Product Safety Regulations

The 1994 Regulations will have to be revised to ensure that the UK has **6–102** properly implemented the revised General Product Safety Directive.[15] Indeed, as that Directive came into force on January 15, 2004, this should already have happened and the implementation process is some months behind schedule. The first consultation paper was issued by the

---

[11] reg.8(1).
[12] Except for medicine, where it is mainly the responsibility of the Scottish Executive.
[13] regs 12, 13.
[14] reg.14.
[15] Dir. 01/95; [1992] O.J. L11/4.

DTI at the end of 2001 and a second consultation paper was promised in 2002, but at the time of writing had not been published. In the circumstances all that can be done is to indicate what changes are necessary.

6–103   The revised Directive repeals the original General Product Safety Directive[16] and replaces it with provisions which go somewhat further. Like the original Directive, the revised General Product Safety Directive imposes a general safety requirement. This applies to all consumer products not covered by directives relating to specific sectors. For example, there are directives relating to toy safety and the safety of cosmetics. One aim of the revised Directive is to clarify the relationship between the general directive and these sectoral directives. This can be very complex and the Commission has already produced guidance on this issue.[17] The range of products to which the Directive applies has been widened to include two new categories. The first of these is products used by consumers in the "in the context of providing a service". This would include things like gym equipment or supermarket trolleys but not say, a bus or taxi which is used to provide a service but is not operated by the consumer of that service.[18] The second change to the definition brings so-called "migrating products" within the definition.[19] These are products which originally have been used exclusively by professionals but have come to be used also by consumers. Certain types of hire tools might fall into this category and it easy to see that such products can be unsafe if used by consumers who do not have appropriate training. The meaning of "safe product" is expanded in Art.2(b) to take into account the putting into service or installation of a product and its maintenance needs.

6–104   The revised Directive expands the obligations placed on producers and distributors of products. Producers must be in a position to recall products from consumers when other measures are not sufficient to protect them[20] and, as a last resort, enforcement authorities are given power to order the recall of a product.[21] To assist in tracing products in the event of a safety problem distributors are obliged to keep and provide appropriate documentation.[22] Both producers and distributors are required to notify dangerous products to the enforcement authorities

---

[16] Dir. 92/59.

[17] *Guidance Document on the Relationship Between the General Product Safety Directive (GPSD) and Certain Sector Directives with Provision on Product Safety,* Directorate General Health and Consumer Protection, November 2003 available at *http://europa. eu.int/comm/consumers/cons_safe/prod_safe/gpsd/guidance_gpsd_en.pdf.*

[18] See Art.2(a) and Recital 9.

[19] Art.2(a).

[20] Art.5(1).

[21] Art.8(f)(ii).

[22] Art.5(2).

and to co-operate with those authorities on action to prevent risks to consumers.[23] Finally, the export from the EC of dangerous products, which have been banned under the emergency decision procedure established by the Directive, is banned unless the decision provides otherwise.[24]

---

[23] Arts 5(3), (4).
[24] Art.13(3).

CHAPTER 7

SERVICES

7–01 Services encompass a very wide range of activities. These are as diverse as laundry and dry cleaning, furniture removal, home improvements, educational services, car maintenance and servicing and professional services. Even this latter category, which one might have supposed would include a relatively narrow range of services, displays astonishing diversity. The Monopolies Commission, when it was asked to investigate the professions, received evidence from 161 professional bodies, although some of those bodies were concerned with the same, or a closely related, profession. The Commission found it impossible to define the distinguishing characteristics of professions or to establish a definitive list, a feat that has taxed others.[1]

7–02 The service sector of the economy expanded enormously during the twentieth century and the range of services offered to the public is extremely varied. It is sometimes said that in the UK we have become a service economy. This is based on the fact that, like other developed economies, more than half of output is generated by the service sector.

7–03 While the service sector has expanded in economic terms, legally it has been somewhat neglected. The preliminary problem encountered in the range of services is the difficulty in determining into which legal category some kinds of services fall. In the case of most professional services this problem does not arise, the service clearly being *locatio operis faciendi*. As Professor McBryde observes: "This contract is very common in practice but has been somewhat neglected by our textbook writers."[2] Many non-professional services will fall into the same category where the essence of the service is the bringing about of a result as, for example, where a repair is to be effected or a thing is to be cleaned. In other cases classification is much less easy and is not aided by a paucity of authority, both institutional and judicial. The situation in England until recently was not dissimilar.

---

[1] Report on the General Effect on the Public Interest of Certain Restrictive Practices so far as they prevail in relation to the Supply of Professional Services (Monopolies Commission), Cmnd. 4463 (1970), pp.1, 3.

[2] W. W. McBryde, *The Law of Contract in Scotland* (2nd ed., W. Green, Edinburgh, 2001), para.9.22

In England and Wales this was ameliorated by the passing of the **7–04** Supply of Goods and Services Act 1982, Pt 2 of which puts into statutory form some of the main terms to be implied in contracts for services. As Pt 2 does not apply to Scotland it would be a useful service to Scottish consumers if similar legislation were introduced in this jurisdiction.

For the moment it is necessary to try to puzzle out the proper legal **7–05** classification of some service contracts. The best illustration of the conceptual problems that this raises is to be found in what is sometimes referred to as the contract for work and materials. As the Scottish Law Commission pointed out, this is a term of art from English law and it does not seem to be the case that such a contract has been clearly recognised in Scots law.[3] Nevertheless, there are certain contracts into which consumers may enter which involve both the supply of goods and the provision of services. Examples of such situations are contracts for the construction of a building or its repair, the repair of a car, the installation of a central-heating system and the provision of a meal in a restaurant. The problems presented in this area seem never to have been faced squarely in any case, although on occasions they would seem to have been worthy of some discussion. Professor Bell observed[4] that the contract *locatio operis faciendi* implied that the employer should provide the materials, otherwise the contract is one of sale. This is borne out by cases involving ships.[5]

The Scottish Law Commission suggested two other possible classifi- **7–06** cations. The arrangement might be seen as comprising two contracts, one of sale and the other for the hiring of services; or, the correct approach may be to regard it as a contract for services alone. Support for the latter view is available by implication from cases where the problem has been identified as arising not from any defect in the nature of the materials used but from shortcomings in the rendering of the service.[6]

If the arrangement is regarded as a sale combined with the hiring of **7–07** services, the remedy where the materials used turn out to be defective will be those already discussed in relation to sale. Of course, if the employer specifies the materials to be used the contractor cannot be held to stipulate that the goods are fit for their purpose, although he would still be liable if they proved not to be of satisfactory quality as occurred in the English case of *Young and Marten Ltd v McManus Childs Ltd.*[7]

---

[3] *Sale and Supply of Goods* (Scot. Law Com. Memorandum No.58, 1983).
[4] Bell, *Commentaries*, I, 485.
[5] *Nelson v William Chalmers & Co. Ltd*, 1913 S.C. 441; 1913 1 S.L.T. 190; *Reid v Macbeth and Gray* [1904] A.C. 223; 11 S.L.T. 783.
[6] *McIntyre v Gallacher* (1883) 11 R. 64; *Brett v Williamson*, 1980 S.L.T. (Sh. Ct.) 56; *Macintosh v Nelson*, 1984 S.L.T. (Sh. Ct.) 82.
[7] [1969] 1 A.C. 454; [1968] 2 All E.R. 1169.

7–08   If the third possibility is the correct legal categorisation, the consumer in the past may have had the somewhat lower degree of protection afforded by the obligation of the supplier to take reasonable care in selecting the materials to be used. However, Pt 1A of the Supply of Goods and Services Act 1982[8] now applies in so far as goods are transferred. Sections 11B to 11E imply terms in this contract in relation to title, description and quality.[9] This situation may also give rise to problems relating to the transfer of property in the materials. There seems now, as was the case when Professor Bell considered the problem, to be little authority on this point. Bell's view was that "where . . . it is resolvable into a contract for performing a particular piece of labour, of which the articles sent are merely the materials, the act of delivery seems not to be complete till the work be performed".[10]

7–09   In *Simpson v Duncanson Creditors*[11] the situation was somewhat different, Simpson having contracted with Duncanson for the construction of a ship. Duncanson was to supply the materials for the hull, Simpson the mast and some other fitments, and payment was to be made in three stages as work progressed. Duncanson became bankrupt after the first payment had been made, and his trustee sought to include the unfinished ship among the assets available for the creditors. The Court of Session stated that the decision depended on the specific facts of the case and preferred Simpson's argument that the vessel "became his, *specificatione,* the builder being considered merely as a mandatory, who acquired not to himself but to his constituent".[12] As the work proceeded such an appropriation took place as prevented the creditors from attaching the ship without refunding the sums advanced.

7–10   Bearing in mind the problems just discussed about how services are classified legally, it is necessary to consider in more detail how consumers are protected by the civil law when acquiring services. Broadly speaking, the approach is the same as when goods are purchased. The law implies in contracts for services certain terms which, in the absence of any express provision in the contract, will determine the rights and duties of the parties. The discussion of these implied terms will focus on the *locatio operis faciendi,* as this is the most common contract concerning the provision of services.

7–11   Before examining the various terms implied in this contract it is first necessary to note that it will often be important to establish exactly what it was that the consumer and the provider of the service agreed should be done. *Brown v J. Nisbet & Co Ltd*[13] is a good example of this issue.

---

[8] Inserted by Sale and Supply of Goods Act 1994, s.6.
[9] For a discussion of these terms, see Ch.4.
[10] Bell, *Commentaries*, I, 194.
[11] (1786) Mor. 14204.
[12] *ibid.*
[13] (1941) 57 Sh. Ct. Reps. 202.

The defenders had acquired a van which was not in a very good state of repair. They took it to the pursuer who ran a motor repair business and various repairs were carried out. When some problems later developed with the van the pursuers refused to pay for the repairs, alleging that the work had not been carried out properly. They claimed that it had been agreed that a complete overhaul of the van would be carried out. The repairer stated that he had not agreed to this but merely to put the van into good running order. There was evidence that the defenders had first obtained a quotation for the cost of a complete overhaul from another garage and, finding this to be too expensive, had then approached the pursuer who had offered to do work at a much lower cost. Looking at the evidence the sheriff came to the conclusion that "[t]he defenders tried to get along with something much less expensive". He found that the garage's evidence of the nature of the job agreed upon was to be preferred and, having agreed only to carry out limited work on the van, they were not liable for breakdowns which were unrelated to the repair work which they had been asked to do.

Walter Wright & Co Ltd v Cowdray[14] is another example of the **7–12** objective approach which the courts take to this problem of assessing what the parties had agreed should be done. Electric motors on an estate had been damaged by floodwater and the pursuers, who were electrical engineers, were asked to dry out and test them. The engineers carried out this work. The defender refused to pay part of the charge for the work on the ground that it involved expensive repairs to one of the motors which had not been instructed. The sheriff considered the evidence and concluded from it that, looked at objectively, there was no justification for assuming that these repairs had been authorised.[15]

IMPLIED TERMS THAT THE CONTRACTOR WILL EXERCISE REASONABLE SKILL AND CARE

A central issue in the provision of a service is the standard of quality **7–13** which the client is entitled to expect. In contracts for services this is summed up in one of those Latin maxims with which lawyers seek to dazzle the uninitiated, *spondet peritiam artis et imperitia culpae enumeratur.* In English this means that a person is responsible for exercising skill in his trade or profession, and lack of such skill will be regarded as a fault. The standard is that of the reasonable practitioner of the particular trade or profession and there are a number of examples in the law reports.

---

[14] 1973 S.L.T. (Sh. Ct.) 56.
[15] See also *Dalblair Motors Ltd v J. Forrest & Son (Ayr) Ltd* (1954) 70 Sh. Ct. Reps. 107.

7–14   *McIntyre v Callacher*[16] is a good example of the application of the principle. Mr Gallacher was a Glasgow plumber who had been employed to carry out plumbing work in a row of tenements. This included sealing off some pipes. One of the pipes was not properly sealed off and some time later leaked causing damage to property on lower floors for which the landlord, Mr McIntyre, was liable. Evidence proved that the proper and workmanlike method of sealing a pipe was to solder it. In this case Mr Gallacher, or one of his workmen, had only hammered the end of the lead pipe together and it eventually leaked. He was thus liable for failing to carry out the job with the requisite level of skill.

7–15   In *Brett v Williamson*[17] the sheriff principal referred to the fact that in building contracts arranged on either a fixed-price basis or, as in that case, on a "time and lime" basis, the problems resulting from unsatisfactory workmanship are particularly difficult to resolve. In that case the pursuer had undertaken to lay terazzo tiles and having done so in a manner which the defender regarded as unsatisfactory was obliged to bring an action for payment. It was argued for the pursuer that since such tile-laying was a specialist job but had been entrusted by the defender to him (who did not claim to be a specialist) he could not complain that the work was not up to the standard of a specialist. This argument was inspired by *Dickson v Hygienic Institute*[18] where it was said that a contractor need attain only "the skill which he professes or announces". As the sheriff principal pointed out, that did not go far enough for the pursuer's purposes because on examining *Dickson* it will be seen that Lord Dundas held that the standard of care is that of the type of practitioner which the client believed he or she was dealing with. Applying this approach to the case before him the sheriff principal stated:

> "In my view, when a tradesman undertakes to carry out a particular job in his trade, his obligation is to carry it out properly, unless he either makes known to his customer when contracting that the job requires more special skill than he commands, or can show that the customer was aware of that when contracting with him. I consider that a tradesman who accepts instructions professes to be able to carry them out, and it is he not the customer who will normally know whether he has or lacks, the special skill which the job requires."[19]

7–16   This approach has much to commend it especially, as is frequently the case with small building jobs, where the client commissions the work

[16] (1883) 11 R. 64.
[17] 1980 S.L.T. (Sh. Ct.) 56.
[18] 1910 S.C. 352; 1910 1 S.L.T. 111.
[19] *op. cit.*, n.17.

directly from the tradesman and does not engage the services of an architect or surveyor.

Brett v Williamson[20] was applied to slightly different circumstances **7–17** by the same sheriff principal in *Macintosh v Nelson*[21] where the pursuer claimed damages for loss sustained when seriously defective building work was carried out at her house. The defender had been an art teacher for several years before going into business on his own account as an industrial cleaning contractor who also undertook window cleaning, car valeting, external paintwork and landscape gardening. The pursuer had admired a sun lounge which the defender had built at his own home and had inquired whether he could do similar work at her house. While the pursuer understood that the defender was in business as a window-cleaning contractor, it was clear from the evidence that he held himself out as being capable both of drawing up the necessary plans and carrying out the building work in a workmanlike manner. He argued that in the circumstances he should only be held to the standards of an amateur builder. The sheriff principal referred to his decision in *Brett v Williamson* and was:

> "prepared to hold that the same considerations apply where one who is not a tradesman contracts to do work for another. In other words, he must be held to have professed the requisite skill to do the job which he undertakes. Plainly, if he says that the job may be more than he can promise to do well or if the customer is shown to have known that, it would be open to the court to hold that his customer had taken the risk of unsatisfactory work on himself."[22]

A different aspect of the problem of the standard of the work arises **7–18** where the issue is not the competence which the tradesman professes but the advice or warnings which he gave to his customer before carrying out the job. *Terret v Murphy*[23] is a good example. The owner of a furniture shop engaged the pursuer to paint an extension to his shop. He was eager to have the work completed and when the painter reported that supplies of the primer that he wished to use would not be available for several days he persuaded the painter to carry on with the job. This was done despite warnings from the painter that the absence of primer could result in problems later on. Problems did, indeed, arise and the owner of the shop withheld payment. Finding in favour of the painter the sheriff, to whom an appeal had been taken, pointed out that if a householder merely asked for a job to be done then the contractor would be liable if he did not draw attention to a particular risk. He went on:

[20] 1980 S.L.T. (Sh. Ct.) 56.
[21] 1984 S.L.T. (Sh. Ct.) 82.
[22] *ibid.*
[23] 1952 S.L.T. (Sh. Ct.) 51.

"But if, in spite of a clear warning from the painter that the work should be executed in a particular manner, the householder instructs him to proceed in a different way or without some recommended precaution, I cannot see why he should be entitled later on to say that the warning was not loud enough or that it was not repeated often enough or that he did not appreciate the full measure of the risk."[24]

7–19   The result to be expected from the service performed is also related to the agreement between the parties. *Brown v J. Nisbet & Co Ltd*[25] was referred to above in relation to this issue. It is to be noted that it also had implications for the liability of the repairer and the kind of result that the customer was entitled to expect. Had it been proved that he had agreed to a complete overhaul of the van the repairer might well have been liable for a failure to display the requisite level of competence when the van broke down if these were faults which had existed when he had been asked to work on it. As he had only been asked to carry out specific tasks, which it was proved that he had carried out in a workmanlike manner, he was not liable.

7–20   The principle has also been applied to professional services. One of the best known explanations of reasonable skill and care in relation to professional services is that of Lord President Clyde in *Hunter v Hanley*[26] where he said:

"[W]here the conduct of a doctor, or indeed of any professional man, is concerned the circumstances are not so precise and clear cut as in the normal case. In the realm of diagnosis and treatment there is ample scope for genuine difference of opinion and one man clearly is not negligent merely because his conclusions differ from that of other professional men, nor because he has displayed less skill or knowledge than others would have shown. The true test for establishing negligence in diagnosis or treatment on the part of a doctor is whether he has been proved to be guilty of such failure as no doctor of ordinary skill would be guilty of if acting with ordinary care."

7–21   This has been interpreted to mean that if any other professional can be found to agree with the actions of the doctor or other professional sued there is no negligence.[27] A close reading of the case suggests that this is going too far and that McNair J. in *Bolam v Friern Hospital*

[24] *ibid.*, at 55.
[25] (1941) 57 Sh. Ct. Reps. 202.
[26] 1955 S.L.T. 213 at 217.
[27] See Norrie, "Common Practice and the Standard of Care in Medical Negligence", 1985 J.R. 145. For a different view, see Howie, "The Standard of Care in Medical Negligence", 1983 J.R. 193.

Management Committee[28] correctly paraphrased the test when he said of the standard required of a doctor that "it is sufficient if he exercises the ordinary skill of an ordinary competent man exercising that particular art."

This view certainly seems to be consistent with other professional negligence cases. It is the test laid down in *Jameson v Simon*,[29] which involved the supervision of a building contract by an architect. There are numerous cases involving solicitors to similar effect of which *Hart v Frame & Co*[30] is an early example. **7–22**

A professional person does not give an absolute undertaking to achieve a particular result: that would be inappropriate in most cases of professional services. A doctor, in the nature of things, cannot undertake to cure his patients, and a lawyer can give no guarantee to a client that he will win his case. **7–23**

This latter point was emphasised in a medical negligence case, *Eyre v Measday*.[31] Mr and Mrs Eyre decided that they did not wish to have any more children and consulted the defendant, a gynaecologist, to discuss the sterilisation of Mrs Eyre. The defendant explained the nature of the operation and emphasised that it was irreversible and must be regarded as a permanent procedure. He did not explain that there was a small risk of failure. The Eyres believed that the result of the operation would be to render Mrs Eyre incapable of having further children. However, after the operation Mrs Eyre did become pregnant and had another child. She sued the gynaecologist alleging, among other things, that there was an implied term that she would be rendered sterile by the operation. **7–24**

It was held that the defendant had undertaken to carry out a particular type of operation rather than to render Mrs Eyre absolutely sterile and that his statement that the operation was irreversible was not an express guarantee that the operation was bound to achieve its objective. As the judge put it: **7–25**

> "I think there is no doubt that the plaintiff would have been entitled reasonably to assume that the defendant was warranting that the operation would be performed with reasonable care and skill. That, I think, would have been the inevitable inference to be drawn, from an objective standpoint, from the relevant discussion between the parties . . . However, that inference on its own does not enable the plaintiff to succeed in the present case. She has to go further. She has to suggest . . . that the defendant, by necessary implication, committed himself to an unqualified guarantee as to the success of the particular operation proposed, in achieving its purpose of

---

[28] [1957] 2 All E.R. 118.
[29] (1899) 1 F. 1211.
[30] (1839) McL. & Rob. 595.
[31] [1986] 1 All E.R. 488

sterilising her, even though he were to exercise all due care and skill in performing it. The suggestion is that the guarantee went beyond due care and skill and extended an unqualified warranty that the plaintiff would be absolutely sterile.

On the facts of the present case, I do not think that any intelligent lay bystander (let alone another medical man), on hearing the discussion which took place between the defendant and the other two parties, could have reasonably drawn the inference that the defendant was intending to give any warranty of this nature . . . . But, in my opinion, in the absence of any express warranty, the court should be slow to imply against a medical man an unqualified warranty as to the results of an intended operation, for the very simple reason that, objectively speaking, it is most unlikely that he would intend to give a warranty of this nature."[32]

7–26   A case involving professional services which does show that a standard higher than that of due skill and care can be expected in certain circumstances is *Greaves & Co. (Contractors) Ltd v Bayhnam Meikle & Partners.*[33] The plaintiffs, who were building contractors, had agreed to design and build a warehouse for a customer. They employed the defendants, who were structural engineers to design the warehouse and advised them that it was essential that it should be capable of permitting materials to be moved around on forklift trucks. Shortly after the warehouse was handed over to the customer the floor began to crack as a result of vibration caused by the forklift trucks. The plaintiffs accepted that they were liable to their customer and brought this action to recover, by way of indemnity, from the structural engineers the cost of repairs to the building. It was held that on the facts as proved in this case there was a term to be implied into the contract that the engineers would design a building that would be fit for the purpose which the plaintiffs had stipulated.

TIME FOR PERFORMANCE

7–27   A perennial source of complaint from consumers is failure of a contractor to complete a job in good time, or sometimes to complete it at all. The National Consumer Council's report *Service Please*[34] found that this was a very frequent source of annoyance to consumers. Problems in this area tend to fall into two categories. There are those cases where the date for the commencement or completion of the work has been agreed between the parties and subsequently ignored by the

---

[32] *ibid.*, 495. It was held in this case that the plaintiff had been adequately informed of the possibility that the operation might not be successful. For a case where the plaintiff succeeded because an adequate warning of the possibility of failure was not given, see *Thake v Maurice* [1986] Q.B. 644.

[33] [1975] 1 W.L.R. 1095.

[34] Lantin and Woodroffe (NCC, London, 1981).

contractor. The other is where no time has been agreed for the completion of the work but the consumer thinks that the contractor has taken an unreasonably long time to complete the work.

The contract may specify the time by which the service is to be **7–28** completed. This is subject to the proviso that the contractor will not be liable for failure to comply with a time-limit if his failure to do so is the fault of the client. This point was made in *T. & R. Duncanson v Scottish County Investment Co Ltd*[35] where a plasterer was unable to complete his agreed tasks because the client had failed to ensure that other tradesmen, completion of whose work was necessary to allow him to start, had kept to their schedules.

If there is no complication such as that in the case just mentioned, the **7–29** question is whether time is of the essence. There is no problem where the contract explicitly says that this is the case. It should not be necessary to use the particular formula that time is to be of the essence. Any words that clearly indicate that this is the case should suffice.

The problem is more difficult where the contract does not have such **7–30** a provision. Time will be assumed to be of the essence in a commercial contract. It is probably not the case that consumer contracts will fall into this category. Certainly, the reported cases have all been contracts between commercial parties.

If there is no express term about time a consumer is entitled to expect **7–31** that a job will be completed within a reasonable time as was conceded in argument in *Davidson v Guardian Royal Exchange Assurance*,[36] a case involving delay in repairing a car. The point is also illustrated by the English case of *Charnock v Liverpool Corporation*.[37] Mr Charnock's car had been damaged in an accident and he took it to the defendant's for repair. An estimate for the work required was agreed but the job was not completed for eight weeks. Mr Charnock sued the repairers for the cost of hiring a car for three weeks, the period by which, in his opinion, the time taken for the repair exceeded what was reasonable. It was held that there was an implied term that the repairers would carry out the repair with reasonable expedition and on the facts eight weeks was not a reasonable time. Evidence had shown that the job should have taken not longer than five weeks.

Where a time has been stipulated in the contract for completion of the **7–32** service but time is not to be regarded as of the essence of the contract it is open to the customer to make it of the essence. A good example of this comes from the English Court of Appeal case of *Charles Rickards Ltd v Oppenhaim*.[38] Mr Oppenhaim had placed an order in August 1947 with the defendants for the construction of a body on the chassis of his car. The job was to be completed within six months or, at the most,

---

[35] 1915 S.C. 1106.
[36] 1979 S.C. 192.
[37] [1968] 1 WL.R. 1498.
[38] [1950] 1 K.B. 616.

seven months. The job was not completed within seven months and the plaintiff kept pressing for delivery. Eventually, on June 28, 1948 he wrote to the bodybuilders saying: "I regret that I shall be unable . . . to accept delivery . . . after July 25". When the car was not finished by the end of July Mr Oppenhaim cancelled his order and when the car was delivered to him in October 1948 he refused to accept it. It was held that the original stipulation making time of the essence of the contract had been waived but he was entitled to give reasonable notice once again making time of the essence. In determining what is reasonable notice the Court of Appeal drew attention to a dictum of Lord Parker of Waddington in *Stickney v Keeble*[39] where he said:

> "In considering whether the time so limited is a reasonable time the Court will consider all the circumstances of the case. No doubt what remains to be done at the date of the notice is of importance, but is by no means the only relevant fact. The fact that the purchaser has continually been pressing for completion, or has before given similar notices which he has waived, or that it is especially important to him to obtain early completion, are equally relevant facts."

7–33   Applying this approach to the facts of this case it was decided that the notice of June 28, 1948 was a reasonable notice making time of the essence and Mr Oppenhaim was not obliged to take delivery.

COST

7–34   The cost for a service will often be agreed beforehand and in that event it is the price agreed that must be paid even if it is not in accordance with the normal practice in the trade or profession.[40] On occasions a professional man is instructed to carry through some piece of work but no discussion of the fee or payment takes place. The general rule is "that tradesmen and professional men who provide services of the kind by which they earn their livings are presumed not to do so gratuitously and are entitled to reasonable remuneration."[41] *Robert Allan and Partners v McKinstray*[42] is a good example. A firm of architects after a meeting with a client prepared preliminary drawings for a house which he proposed to build. Thereafter the client requested and was supplied with more detailed information to enable a builder to provide an estimate of the cost of construction. When the project was abandoned by the client he refused to pay the architect's fees arguing that the work had been in

---

[39] [1915] A.C. 386. at 419.
[40] *Wilkie v Scottish Aviation Ltd*, 1956 S.C. 198.
[41] *Robert Allan and Partners v McKinstray*, 1975 S.L.T. (Sh. Ct.) 63 at 64, echoing W. M. Gloag, *Contract* (2nd. ed., Edinburgh, 1929), p.291. See also *Bell v Ogilvie* (1863) 2 M. 336, *Landless v Wilson* (1880) 8 R. 289; *Sinclair v Logan*, 1961 S.L.T. (Sh. Ct.) 10.
[42] 1975 S.L.T. (Sh. Ct.) 63.

the nature of an estimate and, the project having been abandoned, no fee was payable. The sheriff principal held that there was no evidence to displace the general rule quoted above and that the architects were entitled *quantum meruit* to a fee for the project.

There is a distinction to be made between cases such as *Robert Allan* **7–35**
and Partners v McKinstray[43] and cases where no more has been done than the submission of an estimate or tender. This was pointed out in *Sinclair v Logan*[44] where a builder had drawn up plans for alterations to licensed premises, negotiated with the police and obtained approval from the licensing court before it became clear that the client was not going to go ahead with the project. In finding that the builder was entitled to a fee for the preliminary work that he had done the sheriff pointed out that:

> "The position of the pursuer is clearly distinguishable from that of a tradesman or contractor who submits a tender or estimate. The tender or estimate is in general submitted without any intention to benefit the person or authority requiring work to be done but purely to benefit the tradesman or contractor. It is generally submitted, in competition with others, so that the employment of the particular person submitting it is not a precondition to its submission."[45]

From this it is clear that the common practice of asking for an **7–36**
estimate for a proposed piece of work does not imply that the tradesman is entitled to charge a fee for this work. This was also held in *Murray v Fairlie Yacht Slip Ltd*[46] where the company, having been asked to prepare an estimate for the cost of repairs, attempted to charge for bringing a yacht ashore and storing it for three months.

To establish a right to a fee more needs to be done than this and, as **7–37**
the quotation from *Sinclair v Logan*[47] makes clear, one element which will be relevant will be whether the client has derived any benefit from the services rendered. This seems to have been decisive in *Landless v Wilson*,[48] where an architect submitted detailed plans for the development of a site in Glasgow which, in the end, the client did not proceed with. There was evidence that the client showed the plans to prospective purchasers of the site, and this and the general presumption referred to above resulted in a finding that the architect was entitled to a fee.

Where there is a contract for services but the amount to be paid has **7–38**
not been stated how is that amount to be calculated? The tradesman or professional is entitled to payment *quantum meruit*. This can be

---

[43] 1975 S.L.T. (Sh. Ct.) 63.
[44] 1961 S.L.T. (Sh. Ct.) 10.
[45] *ibid.*, at 12.
[46] 1975 S.L.T. (Sh. Ct.) 62.
[47] 1961 S.L.T. (Sh. Ct.) 10.
[48] (1880) 8 R. 289.

calculated by referring to a customary rate if there is one. To establish this it must be shown that the custom is reasonable, certain and notorious.[49] Failing this the court will fix reasonable remuneration which will be ascertained from such evidence as has been adduced. Evidence which might be adduced would include the level of charges of other tradesmen or professionals in the area or reference to scale charges of a profession.

DUTY TO TAKE CARE OF GOODS DEPOSITED

7–39   Some services will involve the contractor in taking possession of the customer's goods in order, for example, to effect a repair. In this situation the *locatio operis faciendi is* normally presumed to include as an inherent ingredient an element of *locatio custodiae*. The standard of care which the trader must observe is to take such care as a prudent man would take of his own property in the circumstances.[50] It has sometimes been described as an obligation to take reasonable care.

7–40   The onus of proving that reasonable care has been taken is on the trader. In *Sinclair v Juner*[51] the garage which had undertaken to repair the pursuer's car failed to discharge this onus when it failed to produce any evidence about the cause of the fire which destroyed the customer's car. In *Forbes v Aberdeen Motors Ltd*[52] the defenders were held not to have displayed the requisite degree of care when they left the pursuer's Bentley car in an unsupervised hotel car park in the middle of Aberdeen with the keys in the ignition. It was stolen by an inebriated naval rating whose motoring skills resulted in it suffering serious damage in an accident. Likewise, a garage was held liable for damage caused to a car in its custody when left in the street outside the garage overnight[53]; and, in an example from an earlier age, someone who undertook for reward to break in a horse was liable when it was injured when it bolted on being startled by an explosion under the stables. It was relevant that the explosion was not unexpected as the defender knew that a railway company was constructing a tunnel underneath his premises.[54]

7–41   One might have thought that the liability of a company operating a car park to someone leaving their motorcycle in it might have been the same as in these cases. *Drynan v Scottish Ice Rink Co Ltd*[55] casts doubt on this. In the sheriff court it was held that leaving the scooter in the park and purchasing a ticket created a relationship of licensor and licensee, not that of custody. The correctness of this view must be in

---

[49] *Strathlorne Steamship Co. Ltd v Hugh Baird & Sons Ltd*, 1916 S.C. (H.L.) 134.
[50] *Sinclair v Juner*, 1952 S.C. 35; *Verrico v George Hughes & Son*, 1980 S.C. 179.
[51] 1952 S.C. 35.
[52] 1965 S.C. 193.
[53] See *Vericco v George Hughes & Son*, 1980 S.C. 179.
[54] *Laing v Darling* (1850) 12 D. 1279.
[55] 1971 S.L.T. (Sh. Ct.) 59.

doubt but, as has been observed, "what suffices to create a contract of custody remains to be decided in Scots law".[56]

It is not clear whether the standard of care in cases of custody for reward is the same as in cases of gratuitous deposit. In *Copland v Brogan*[57] a case of gratuitous deposit, the Court of Session spoke of the standard in the same terms as have been used in cases of custody for reward. **7–42**

WHERE THE SERVICE INVOLVES THE PROVISION OF MATERIALS

At the beginning of this chapter the uncertainty about the legal classification of contracts for services which involved the provision of materials was referred to. This is no longer a problem as far as title, description and quality are concerned as the same terms are implied whether the contract is considered to be one of sale as far as the provision of materials is concerned, or something else. This is the result of the insertion of Pt 1A in the Supply of Goods and Services Act 1982. **7–43**

LIABILITY IN DELICT FOR NEGLIGENCE

So far, the standard of care and skill required of those who offer services has been discussed solely in terms of contractual liability. It is important to stress that there is also the possibility of liability for the delict of negligence. Indeed, in some situations there may be no other avenue open to the customer or client. An example of this is the situation of patients who allege that the treatment that they have received under the National Health Service has not been up to the required standard and that they have been harmed as a result. It appears from judicial decisions that such patients have no contractual relationship with the health service and can sue only in delict.[58] Such patients could not avail themselves of the implied terms. Negligence may also be the appropriate type of legal action because, in other circumstances, someone who has not contracted with the provider of the service has suffered loss as a result of his activities. **7–44**

Lawyers will usually have a contractual duty to their clients so delictual liability may not be so important. However, *Ross v Caunters*,[59] an English case, demonstrates where it might be important. Mrs Ross was an intended beneficiary under a will drawn up by Caunters & Co, solicitors. They failed to tell the testator (the person making the will) that if a beneficiary, or the spouse of a beneficiary, witnessed the will the **7–45**

---

[56] W. W. McBryde, *The Law of Contract in Scotland* (2nd ed., W. Green, Edinburgh, 2001), para.9.60.

[57] 1916 S.C. 277.

[58] *Pfizer Corp v Ministry of Health* [1965] 1 All E.R. 450, *per* Lord Reid at 455.

[59] [1980] Ch.297.

gift to that beneficiary would be invalid. Mrs Ross's husband witnessed the signature of the will by the testator and as a result Mrs Ross could not receive the legacy given to her in the will. She sued the solicitors who had drawn up the will for the amount of the legacy that she had lost saying that they had been negligent in not telling the testator that her husband should not act as a witness and in not noticing that he had done so. The solicitors' argument was that they were liable only to their client (now past caring about his will, or at least not in a position to do anything about it), not to people like Mrs Ross. Mrs Ross won. The English Court of Appeal held that the solicitors owed a duty to Mrs Ross who was clearly identified and intended to benefit under the will. There was thus a sufficiently proximate relationship with her to give rise to a duty of care to her.[60]

7–46   It is not clear whether the Scottish courts would reach the same conclusion on similar facts. In *Weir v J. M. Hodge and Son*[61] an Outer House judge declined to follow English authority, feeling bound by *Robertson v Fleming*[62] where the House of Lords had held that in the absence of privity of contract a solicitor was not liable to make reparation to third parties injured by negligent acts or omissions in the course of acting for a client. As the Lord Ordinary observed, this decision is out of sympathy with modern developments in the law of negligence. In *Macdougall v Clydesdale Bank Trustees*[63] Lord Cameron also felt obliged to follow the decision while appearing to hint that it might not survive a challenge in the Inner House. However, in *Tait v Brown & McRae*[64] Sheriff Principal Risk approved of it in relation to disappointed beneficiaries. However, he did emphasise that there were other circumstances in which solicitors, like other professional persons, could be liable in delict to those who were not their clients.[65]

7–47   An advocate does not have a contractual relationship with the lay client and so any action will have to be in delict. Whether an advocate is still immune from action for breach of duty is not clear. There is no direct authority on this point in Scots law, but the House of Lords in an English appeal where, most unusually, 10 Law Lords sat, abolished the advocate's immunity from legal action even for things done in the

---

[60] See *White v Jones* [1995] 2 A.C. 207; [1995] 1 All ER 691, *Walker v G. H. Medlicott & Son* [1999] 1 All E.R. 685; [1999] 1 W.L.R. 727, *Carr-Glynn v Frearsons* [1999] Ch. 326; [1998] 4 All E.R. 225; [1999] 2 W.L.R. 1046, and for a case where a professional non-solicitor will maker was held to have a similar duty of care, see *Esterhuizen v Allied Dunbar Assurance plc* [1998] 2 F.L.R. 668.
[61] 1990 S.L.T. 266.
[62] (1861) 4 Macq. 167.
[63] *Macdougall v Clydesdale Bank Trs*, 1994 S.L.T. 1178; 1993 S.C.L.R. 832.
[64] 1997 S.L.T. (Sh. Ct.) 63.
[65] See *Midland Bank plc v Cameron, Thom, Peterkins & Duncan*, 1988 S.L.T. 611; 1988 S.C.L.R. 209.

course of litigation and it would seem likely that the position is the same in Scotland.[66]

Surveyors may also incur liability to those, such as prospective **7–48** mortgagors, if they are in breach of their duty to take reasonable care. This was established in *Smith v Eric S. Bush & Co*[67] which was followed in *Robbie v Graham & Sibbald*.[68]

REMEDIES

The general principles relating to remedies for breach of contract apply **7–49** to breaches of contracts for services and their application will depend on the particular circumstances of the case. There is a principle that damages are not normally recoverable for injury to feelings occasioned by a breach of contract.[69] It is recognised that there are exceptions to this principle which may be summed up by saying that it does not apply when the purpose of the contract is to provide pleasure. Such contracts are particularly likely to be contracts for the provision of services. In *Diesen v Samson*[70] a photographer failed to turn up to take photographs of the pursuer's wedding and damages were awarded for the disappointment that this caused. In England damages have been awarded on this basis where package holidays have failed to live up to the claims made in the brochure,[71] and the principle was also applied where a firm of solicitors failed to take appropriate legal action to prevent the plaintiff's husband harassing her in breach of an injunction.[72] In *Farley v Skinner*[73] the House of Lords confirmed that damages could be awarded on this basis but that amounts should not normally exceed £10,000.

CRIMINAL LAW

The criminal law has a role to play in protecting consumers of services. **7–50** The main provisions are to be found in the Trade Descriptions Act 1968 and Pt 3 of the Consumer Protection Act 1987 which deals with prices. These are discussed in Ch.11.

---

[66] *Arthur J.S. Hall & Co (A Firm) v Simons* [2002] 1 A.C. 615
[67] [1990] 1 A.C. 831.
[68] 1989 S.C.L.R. 578. The defenders escaped liability because they were protected by an exclusion clause to which, at the time, Unfair Contract Terms Act 1977 had no application in Scotland.
[69] *Addis v Gramophone Co Ltd* [1909] A.C. 488.
[70] 1971 S.L.T. (Sh. Ct.) 49.
[71] *Jarvis v Swans Tours Ltd* [1973] 1 Q.B. 233; *Jackson v Horizon Holidays Ltd* [1975] 1 W.L.R. 1468.
[72] See *Heywood v Wellers* [1976] Q.B. 446; and Jackson, 26 I.C.L.Q. 502 for a review of some of the cases in his area.
[73] [2001] UKHL 49; [200] 2 A.C. 732.

SELF-REGULATION

7–51 In addition to the legal rules which have been discussed above it is important to note that codes of conduct drawn up by members of some trade associations may offer assistance to consumers. The Association of British Travel Agents, the electricity companies, the motor trade and funeral directors are examples of providers of services who subscribe to such codes. Their chief benefit is that codes can attempt to cope with matters which it would be difficult, if not impossible, to deal with statutorily. For example, the code governing electrical repairers provides that where a home visit is needed "the first visit should (wherever possible) be made within three working days from receipt of the request". The Scottish Motor Trade Association code states that members will ensure "sensitive treatment of vulnerable consumers".[74]

CASE STUDY: PACKAGE HOLIDAYS

7–52 The package holiday is an important part of the lifestyle of many consumers and accounts for a significant part of their spending. From a consumer protection perspective it is particularly interesting because it provides an example of various techniques being used to protect the consumer. The criminal and civil law are brought into play as well as self-regulation.

7–53 While it is not the only relevant source of law in this area it will be convenient to structure this discussion around the Package Travel, Package Holidays and Package Tours Regulations 1992.[75] These Regulations were enacted to implement the EC Package Travel Directive.[76] The Regulations came into effect on December 3, 1992. They use both the civil and criminal law to improve the protection afforded to consumers.

7–54 Before looking at the Regulations in detail it is first necessary to look at the definition of a package. Regulation 2 defines it as the pre-arranged combination of at least two of the following elements when offered for sale at an inclusive price, and when the service covers a period of at least 24 hours or includes overnight accommodation. The three elements

---

[74] Available on the website of the Scottish Motor Trade Association: *http://www.smta.co.uk/*.

[75] SI 1992/3288, as amended by Package Travel, Package Holidays and Package Tours (Amendment) Regulations 1995 (SI 1995/1648); Package Travel, Package Holidays and Package Tours (Amendment) Regulations 1998 (SI 1998/1208); Enterprise Act 2002 (Pt 8 Notice to OFT of Intended Prosecution Specified Enactments, Revocation and Transitional Provision) Order 2003 (SI 2003/1376), art.3; and Enterprise Act 2002 (Part 9 Restrictions on Disclosure of Information) (Amendment and Specification) Order 2003 (SI 2003/1400), art.7 and Sch.5.

[76] Dir. 90/314.

are: transport; accommodation; and, other tourist services not ancillary to transport or accommodation and accounting for a significant proportion of the package. The European Court has ruled that 'package' could include a holiday organised by a travel agent at the request of, and in accordance with the specifications of, a consumer or a limited group of consumers.[77]

The Regulations set out various civil obligations of the package **7–55** organiser or retailers. Regulation 4 provides that tour organisers or retailers must not provide consumers with information that is misleading. If they do they are liable to compensate consumers for any loss which is suffered.[78] Particulars in brochures constitute implied terms of the contract unless the brochure states that the information in it may change and the changes are clearly communicated before the contract is concluded.[79] It is an implied term of the contract that the other party to the contract will ensure that the contract contains at least the information specified in Sch.2.[80] This is basic information about price, means of transport, destination, type of accommodation, meals and payment schedule. The contract terms must be set out in writing or such other form as is accessible to the consumer who must be given a written copy of them.

In addition, the Regulations imply various terms into contracts. **7–56** Where the consumer is prevented from proceeding with the package there is an implied term that he or she may transfer the booking to any person who satisfies all the package conditions.[81] Surcharges have been a source of considerable friction in package tours and controls are placed on them. Price revision clauses are void unless they provide for the possibility of upward and downward revision. They must also state precisely how the revised price is to be calculated and that revisions are to be made solely to allow for variations in transport costs, service charges and currency fluctuations. In any event, they cannot be made less than 30 days before departure and the tour operator must absorb the first two per cent of any increase.[82] Further terms are implied by regs 13 and 14. These deal with compensation for cancellation of the holiday and failure to provide a significant proportion of the services contracted for.

In many ways the central feature of the civil law provisions of the **7–57** Regulations is to be found in reg.15. This imposes strict liability on the package organiser or retailer for the proper performance of the contract, whether its obligations are to be performed by him or another supplier.

---

[77] Case C-400/00 *Club-Tour, Viagens e Turismo SA v Garrido and Club Med Viagens Ld* [2002] O.J. C144/10.
[78] *Mawdsley v Cosmoair Ltd* [2002] E.W.C.A. Civ. 587.
[79] reg.6.
[80] reg.9.
[81] reg.10.
[82] reg.11.

Failure to do so renders him liable for any damage caused, unless the
failure is attributable to the consumer or due to unusual and unforesee-
able circumstances beyond the control of the other party.[83] This liability
cannot be excluded but it may be limited in accordance with international conventions; and, in the case of damage other than personal
injury, may be limited, provided that the limitation is reasonable.

7–58   One of the greatest problems that can beset a holidaymaker is the
insolvency of the tour operator or the financial failure of the travel
agent. For some years there have been various methods of ensuring that
holidaymakers will not suffer financial loss in these events. The Civil
Aviation Authority licenses travel organisers who must have an Air
Traffic Organiser's Licence (ATOL) which requires them to provide a
bond. This amounts to 15 per cent of licensable turnover, or 10 per cent
if the licence holder is a member of the Association of British Travel
Agents (ABTA) which has arrangements to cope with these problems.
For more serious failures the Air Travel Trust which succeeded to the
assets of the reserve fund set up under the Air Travel Reserve Fund Act
1975 provides protection.

7–59   One of the most important aspects of the Regulations is contained in
regulation 16, which places an obligation on tour operators and travel
agents to provide evidence of security for the refund of money paid by
customers and for their repatriation in the event of insolvency. This
obligation is sanctioned by criminal penalties. Regulations 17 to 20
provide a choice of methods through which this obligation can be met.
These include taking out a bond, having an Air Travel Organiser's
Licence, being a member of a scheme which operates a reserve fund, or
having insurance or placing money in a trust fund.

7–60   The scope of reg.16 which implements Art.7 of the Directive was
demonstrated in a decision of the ECJ.[84] There it was said that:

> "Article 7 of Directive 90/314 was to be interpreted as covering, as
> security for the refund of money paid over, a situation in which the
> purchaser of a package holiday who had paid the travel organiser
> for the costs of his accommodation before travelling on his holiday
> was compelled, following the travel organiser's insolvency, to pay
> the hotelier for his accommodation again in order to be able to
> leave the hotel and return home."

7–61   The criminal law is also used to ensure compliance with other
requirements of the Regulations. Regulation 5 makes it an offence for a
holiday organiser to make brochures available to potential customers
which do not indicate the price and adequate information about

---

[83] The meaning of "improper performance" was discussed in *Hone v Going Places
Leisure Travel Ltd* [2001] E.W.C.A. Civ. 947.
[84] *Verein fürKonsumenteninformation v Österreichische Kreditversicherrungs AG*, Case
C-364/96 at para.23.

specified matters in a "legible comprehensible and adequate manner". A retailer who makes such a brochure available knowing that it does not comply also commits an offence. Regulation 7 requires tour operators or travel agents to make available before the contract is concluded general information about visa requirements applying to British citizens, information about health formalities, and arrangements for security of money paid over and repatriation arrangements. Failure to comply is also a criminal offence as is failure to provide "in good time before the start of the journey" certain information about what to do in the event of some problem arising during the holiday.

The use of the criminal law is, of course, not new in the package **7–62** holiday world. As we shall see in Ch.11, the Trade Descriptions Act 1968 has had considerable effect in ensuring high standards of accuracy in brochures. The law on price indications contained in Pt 3 of the Consumer Protection Act 1987 also applies to package holidays.

Not only has the law been used to protect holidaymakers, but also the **7–63** industry itself has taken steps to improve matters. One of the more successful codes of practice has been that of ABTA. This covers many of the matters now required by law under the Regulations. Two particularly important features are the compensation arrangements in the event of a travel agent or tour operator facing financial difficulties, and the low cost arbitration provisions. These are discussed in Ch.12.

CHAPTER 8

THE PUBLIC SECTOR

8–01 A number of important goods and services are supplied by nationalised or recently privatised companies. In addition, the state through local and central government provides services and facilities for its citizens. Health, education and the courts are examples. In the latter case there has been an increasing tendency to apply consumer principles to the provision of these services. In this chapter we look at the implications for consumers of the provision of services by these providers.

8–02 In the case of the nationalised and the privatised industries where the consumer complains of defective goods or services the remedy will usually be no different from that pursued against any other supplier. The legislation and common law rules discussed in earlier chapters will be relevant. To this there are some exceptions. The liability of the Post Office (and any other universal service provider) is restricted in relation to the provision of a "universal postal service" by Pt 6 of the Postal Services Act 2000. Section 23 of the British Telecommunications Act 1981 excludes British Telecom's delictual liability for failure to provide a service or apparatus and for errors in telephone directories.

REGULATED INDUSTRIES

8–03 A major feature of the last 25 years has been the privatisation policy pursued by the previous Conservative administration under which many nationalised industries have been returned to private ownership. The major examples have been British Gas, British Telecom, British Airways, the English and Welsh water companies, the electricity and bus industries, the railways and the coal industry. As a result, few major industries are in state ownership, the Post Office being the most notable example.

8–04 While, in theory, these state monopolies have been broken, in practice, in many cases, the privatised companies have near monopoly power. British Telecom does face increasing competition but is by far the dominant enterprise in telecommunications in the United Kingdom. While there is increasing competition in the gas and electricity industries this has been slow to develop and the regional power companies tend to be the dominant suppliers in their areas. The privatisation legislation recognised that, in most cases, there might not be a high level of competition in the markets supplied by the new corporations.

To provide a proxy for the protection afforded to the consumer by **8–05** competition in the market place the solution adopted in the privatisation legislation was the creation of independent statutory regulators who in the original privatisation statutes was usually given the title of Director-General. These regulators had extensive powers to control the industries concerned. More recently as these arrangements have been revised the model of an office with a corporate identity has been adopted, as we shall see in the cases of communications and energy.

COMMUNICATIONS

The Communications Act 2003 completely reorganised the regulation **8–06** of the communications industries in the UK. It covers not only telecommunications but also the internet and broadcasting. The Office of Communications Act 2002 set up Ofcom which has taken over the functions of five regulators in this field. These were the Broadcasting Standards Commission, the Director-General of Telecommunications (Oftel), the Independent Television Commission, the Radio Authority, and the Secretary of State, who had a regulatory role through the Radiocommunications Agency. It is believed that this will give a more coherent form of regulation through a body that has both competition and consumer protection functions. Ofcom is a corporate body with a chairman, chief executive and a number of board members. In addition to its general role as a regulator of communications s.3(1) of the Communications Act 2003 provides that:

> "It shall be the principal duty of Ofcom, in carrying out their functions;(a) to further the interests of citizens in relation to communications matters; and(b) to further the interests of consumers in relevant markets, where appropriate by promoting competition."

Section 16(2) of the 2003 Act requires Ofcom to establish an **8–07** independent consumer panel to advise on the consumer interest in the markets it regulates. The panel is independent of Ofcom and operates at arm's length from it, setting its own agenda and making its views known publicly. It has a responsibility to understand consumer issues and concerns related to the communications sector (other than those related to content of advertising and programming) and will help inform Ofcom's decision-making by raising specific issues of consumer interest. These will include issues affecting rural consumers, older people, people with disabilities and those who are on low incomes or otherwise disadvantaged. To ensure that its recommendations to Ofcom are based on sound evidence, the panel has an appropriate budget to commission its own research, and will be developing new means of communicating with consumers.

8–08   Ofcom has also established Ofcom "Advisory Committees for the Nations" on the whole breadth of its communications responsibilities in Scotland, Wales, Northern Ireland and for the English regions. These will be set up under s.20(1) of the 2003 Act. The advisory committee for each nation will, according to its website, be chosen by open public process, and is currently discussing the committees' structure with those who have special knowledge and interests in each nation.

ENERGY

8–09 The Utilities Act 2000 reorganised the regulation of the UK energy sector. The Offices of the Directors-General of Electricity and Gas (Offer and Ofgas) were abolished and their functions transferred to the Gas and Electricity Markets Authority. This body has the same structure as Ofcom with a chairman and board which make all major decisions and set policy priorities for Ofgem which is the public face of the new regulator. Ofgem's powers are provided for under the Gas Act 1986 and the Electricity Act 1989, as amended by the Utilities Act 2000. It also has enforcement powers under the Competition Act 1998. One of its principal objectives is to protect the interests of consumers, wherever appropriate, by promoting effective competition. In performing its functions it must also have regard to the interests of low income consumers, the chronically sick, the disabled, pensioners and consumers in rural areas.[1] The legislation also gives it powers to impose financial penalties on utility companies for breaches of licence conditions and other specified statutory requirements.[2]

8–10   Part 3 of the Utilities Act 2000 replaced the separate Gas and Electricity Consumers' Councils with one Gas and Electricity Consumers' Council which has adopted the name Energywatch for its activities. The main functions of Energywatch are to keep itself informed of consumer matters and the views of consumers and to provide advice and information to regulatory authorities, government, utility companies and anyone else whose activities may affect the interests of consumers. It also provides information and advice to consumers and publishes information in the interests of consumers. Like Ofgem it has a specific duty to have regard to the interests of the disabled or chronically sick, individuals of pensionable age, those with low incomes and people living in rural areas. Energywatch has a main office in London as well as eight regional offices, one of which is in Glasgow. To assist it a Lay Committee for Scotland was set up in 2001.

---

[1] For the gas industry, see Gas Act 1986, s.4AA; for electricity, see Electricity Act 1989, s.3A.

[2] For the gas industry, see Gas Act 1986, s.30A; for electricity, see Electricity Act 1989, s.27A. For an example of the exercise of these powers affecting two energy companies, see Ofgem press release, Feb. 20, 2004, reporting that npower and Scottish Power had each been fined £200,000 for unfairly stopping customers from switching to a new gas or electricity supplier in breach of licence conditions.

An important aspect of its work is resolving the complaints of **8–11**
consumers who have not been able to settle a complaint directly with
their energy provider. The Annual Report for the first 18 months of
Energywatch covering November 2000 to March 2002 shows that
87,000 complaints were received. Of these 49 per cent related to
accounts, 41 per cent to transfers from one supplier to another and 10
per cent to marketing practices. Energywatch assisted consumers to
recover compensation of £1.5 million from energy companies.[3]

WATER

The restructuring of local government effected by the Local Govern- **8–12**
ment (Scotland) Act 1994 has had implications for water and sewerage
services which were previously services provided by the regional
authorities. In response to public opinion in Scotland these services have
not been privatised. Instead, these were provided originally by three
new regional water authorities. With effect from April 2002 these
authorities were merged to form Scottish Water as a result of Pt 3 of the
Water Industry (Scotland) Act 2002. Scottish Water has a duty to
promote conservation and effective use of water resources, ensure that
there are adequate supplies, and have regard to the interests of
customers especially those with special needs occasioned by a persistent
medical condition or family circumstances.

When the regional water authorities were set up it was the Govern- **8–13**
ment's view that it would not be appropriate for a service which was
still in the public sector to have a regulator based on the model of the
privatised public utility regulators. That view has changed and the office
of the Water Industry Commissioner for Scotland was created by Pt 2 of
the Water Industry Act 1999, and came into operation on November 1,
1999.[4] The primary role of the commissioner is to promote the interests
of customers of Scottish Water who include both business and domestic
users. He is also the economic regulator of the industry. Section 3(1) of
the Water Industry (Scotland) Act 2002 provides that the commissioner
must investigate any complaint made to him or a customer panel by a
current, potential or former customer of Scottish Water as respects any
of its core functions.

These customer panels or Water Customer Consultation Panels, to **8–14**
give them their full titles are created by s.2 of the 2002 Act. Each
customer panel is to have the general function of representing the views
and interests of the customers of Scottish Water in the panel's area in
relation to the provision of services by Scottish Water in the exercise of
its core functions. Five panels have been created and these are required
to publish reports on any matter they consider relevant to the interests
of customers and make such recommendations as they consider appro-

---

[3] Energywatch Annual Report, Nov. 2000–Mar. 2002, p.10.
[4] The office was continued by Water Industry (Scotland) Act 2002, s.1.

priate to the commissioner (and others) as to the promotion of the interests of customers. In addition, they have a statutory right to be consulted by Scottish Water and the commissioner.

CITIZEN'S CHARTER

8–15 Another approach to improving service in the public sector was launched in 1991 through the citizen's charter initiative. In a glossy White Paper, *The Citizen's Charter,*[5] the Government announced a programme to improve the quality of public services. This applied to a wide range of central and local government services as well as the privatised utilities. It recognised that in many of these areas competition has a limited role to play in ensuring high quality services. It stated that there were four main themes in the programme: quality, choice, setting of standards, and value for money. In promoting these themes a number of mechanisms were to be used. In some cases further privatisation was to be the preferred method, in others the possibility of contracting out services was to be explored along with other ways of using competition. An important mechanism was the setting of targets such as the targets for train punctuality. Other important mechanisms were the creation of inspectorates to ensure that standards were being met, more effective complaints systems, and better redress for citizens when things go wrong.

8–16   The original Citizen's Charter set out the basic principles of the initiative but it also envisaged that there would be further charters dealing with specific areas. By the time that the new Labour Government came to review the operation of the charter programme in 1997 there were about 200 national charters. This figure includes 40 that were termed "national charters" by the previous administration and the "Charter Standard Statements" drawn up by executive agencies and non-departmental public bodies.[6] In addition, there are thought to be about 10,000 local charters. Charters cover a diverse range of services including health, education, public utilities and the courts. Of particular interest in Scotland are the *Parents' Charter in Scotland* and the *Justice Charter.* The former deals mainly with what parents can expect of the schools which their children attend; the latter with the court and procurator fiscal system, prisons and related aspects of social work services.

8–17   In June 1998 the new Labour administration, under the title of *Service First,* relaunched the charter initiative. A year later the main elements of *Service First* were incorporated into the Government's White Paper.[7] This foreshadowed the use of "People's Panels" to carry out regular

---

[5] Cm. 1599 (1991).
[6] *Service First: The New Charter Programme* (1998).
[7] *Modernising Government,* Cm. 4310 (1999).

consumer surveys across a range of public services and this initiative ran from 1998 to 2002. The Office of Public Service Reform was set up in 2001 to carry forward the drive to improve public services by improving current structures, systems, incentives and skills to deliver better, more customer-focused public services. The strategy to achieve this was set out in more detail in March 2002.[8] The most recent development in this area took place in February 2004 with the relaunch by the Government of the Chartermark scheme.

How effective the charter initiative has been is difficult to say. **8–18** However, the 1997 Labour Government observed that "[t]here is little doubt among those people who commented on the original Charter programme that it made a major contribution to the improvement in public services during the 1990s".[9] One commentator has observed:

> "[T]he spirit of the original Citizens' Charter lives on—albeit with new nomenclature and as part of a wider agenda of 'modernisation' and consumer focus . . . . The Charter principles have become absorbed into the bloodstream of the public service and are taken largely for granted by both the producers and the users of those services."[10]

LOCAL GOVERNMENT

Related to the *Service First* programme is the *Best Value* initiative. This **8–19** was a manifesto commitment of the Government and it seeks to improve local government performance in the delivery of services to local communities throughout Scotland. It has also been extended to police forces and fire brigades. It aims to ensure that the cost and quality of these services are at a level acceptable to local people. This is to be achieved by increasing the role of local people in deciding the priorities for local government services; improving the way authorities manage and review their business; and building on the experience and expertise of staff. In Scotland, unlike England and Wales, "Best Value has developed on a partnership basis . . . although backed by the threat of the re-imposition of [compulsory competitive tendering] in case of failure".[11]

In July 1997, the Secretary of State and the Convention of Scottish **8–20** Local Authorities (COSLA) set up a joint Task Force on Best Value, comprising the Scottish Office, COSLA and Accounts Commission, to develop and implement best value across local government. In its final report the task force concluded:

---

[8] *Reforming our Public Services: Principles into practice* (pamphlet, Mar. 2002).
[9] *ibid.*, para.2.1.
[10] Drewry, "Whatever Happened to the Citizens' Charter?" [2002] P.L. 9 at 12.
[11] Best Value Task Force, *Final Report: Best Value in Local Government*, para.2.5.

"[A]ll Scottish local authorities have shown a commitment to Best
Value and have attempted to incorporate the essential principles of
Best Value in the way they serve their communities. They have
achieved varying levels of understanding and success in doing so,
and we doubt that any would claim the process to be complete."[12]

8–21   The task force concluded that it would be desirable to provide a
legislative basis for best value but that this should not be highly
prescriptive to allow for flexibility in developing the programme.
Section 1 of the Local Government in Scotland 2003 places a duty on
all Scottish local authorities to secure best value and describes best
value in terms of the continuous improvement of performance of
functions.

---

[12] Best Value Task Force, *Final Report: Best Value in Local Government*, para.1.10.

CHAPTER 9

BUYING ON CREDIT

INTRODUCTION

There can be no doubt about the importance of credit in our society. **9–01**
Even a casual walk down any high street or a glance at newspaper
advertising indicates the prevalence of credit; and the statistics on
consumer credit confirm its immense importance in the economy.
Figures from the Bank of England show that the total level of
outstanding debt to individuals in September 2003 in the UK was £906
billion—of which £737 billion was secured lending and £168 billion
unsecured lending.[1]

The provision of credit has a long and checkered history, becoming **9–02**
especially important in this country following the industrial revolution.
This made credit granting both possible and necessary. If it was to
become feasible for a much-increased volume of goods to be acquired
it would be necessary for much of this increased consumption to be
financed by the extension of credit. To depend on consumption being
paid for out of short-term savings would not have worked. In the latter
half of the nineteenth century with increasing production of mass-
produced consumer goods such as sewing machines and pianos, the
credit market developed. Reliance on personal security alone would
have been commercially imprudent and would have restricted the
development of credit selling. The result was the development of hire-
purchase. The advantage of this was that it provided the lender with
security in the event that the purchaser defaulted. From the consumers'
point of view it enabled them, in the words of the credit card slogan, "to
take the waiting out of wanting". The Crowther Report noted that hire-
purchase "has been one of the chief contributory causes of the great rise
in the material standard of living of the British people in the last generation".[2]

---

[1] *Fair, Clear and Competitive: The Consumer Credit Market in the 21st Century*, Cm.
6040 (2003), para.1.8. Ch. 1 has a very useful overview of the way in which consumers
use credit. The White Paper is accompanied by a consultation document, *Establishing
a Transparent Market: A consultation on proposals for regulations*.
[2] Consumer Credit: Report of the Committee (Cmnd 4596) (1971), Vol. 1, para.2.3.17
(hereinafter "the Crowther Report").

9–03   Hire-purchase could be provided by the seller or manufacturer, though retailers would often not have the resources to finance hire-purchase transactions. There soon grew up finance companies, often companies expanding their activities from commercial financing into the developing area of consumer finance. The consumer credit market developed markedly during the twentieth century, not only in terms of the volume of credit extended, but also in the sophistication and range of methods used. The so-called credit boom of the late 1980s gave considerable impetus to these trends. As the White Paper on consumer credit issued in December 2003 observed: "The consumer credit market has changed fundamentally since the introduction of the Consumer Credit Act 1974".[3] This is because "Specialist lenders are targeting specific sections of the market, and the widespread introduction of new and innovative products means consumers now have an ever-increasing number of credit options available to them".[4] Before considering the legal background to consumer credit it is necessary to summarise the main methods of obtaining credit and then to consider why special attention is paid to the protection of the consumer obtaining credit.

METHODS OF OBTAINING CREDIT

9–04   There is a wide variety of methods of obtaining credit. One way of categorising these methods is, using a classification adopted by the Crowther Report, to divide them into lender credit and vendor credit. Lender credit involves transactions whose legal form is that of a loan of money, whether or not the loan is associated with a particular purchase. Vendor credit relates to transactions that, legally, are not loans but contracts for the sale or hire of goods. As there are some methods of obtaining credit that do not easily fit into either category, a third category of hybrid transactions is added.

LENDER CREDIT

9–05   There are many ways of obtaining loans. Banks offer loans by way of overdraft where the customer is permitted to overdraw on a current account and the rate of interest is liable to fluctuate during the lifetime of the overdraft. There may be no fixed rate at which the customer is to pay off the loan. More common are bank loans, often marketed as "personal loans". In this case the customer borrows a fixed sum at a specified rate of interest and agrees to pay it off by regular instalments.

---

[3] *Fair, Clear and Competitive*, Cm. 6040 (2003), para.1.8.
[4] *ibid.*, para.1.11.

Since the expansion of the facilities which building societies may offer, they, too, provide personal loans. The building societies are best known for offering loans for the purchase of property which are secured by way of mortgage.

Other institutions, such as finance houses, also provide loans and they **9–06** are also available from a number of other sources. Insurance companies may make loans against the cash-in value of a life assurance policy; pawnbrokers will do so in return for the pledge of some item of property; and credit unions will do so for their members.

VENDOR CREDIT

The most common form of vendor credit is hire-purchase. This is an **9–07** arrangement which combines the hire of goods with an option to purchase. Typically, the retailer sells the goods to a finance company which enters into the hire-purchase agreement with the consumer. The consumer agrees to make a series of weekly or monthly payments which are, technically, rental payments, so the consumer is not at this point the owner of the goods and may not dispose of them without the consent of the finance company. The agreement gives the consumer an option to purchase the goods on making a small final payment, an option which, in practice, is normally exercised. The arrangement need not involve a finance company as the retailer may enter into the hire-purchase agreement directly with the consumer.

A very similar transaction is conditional sale. This is an agreement for **9–08** the sale of goods under which the property remains in the seller until payment of the price. The main difference between this and hire-purchase is that in conditional sale the consumer automatically becomes the owner on making the final payment, whereas in hire-purchase the consumer is not obliged to do so.

Hire-purchase and conditional sale both give the person providing **9–09** credit a security over the goods. A third type of transaction, credit sale, is very similar to conditional sale. The difference is that the property in the goods passes immediately to the consumer, so the seller has no security.

Another form of vendor credit is the leasing or rental agreement. **9–10** These have been common for many years in the commercial sphere but have become more common in consumer transactions, especially those relating to cars. The legal form is that of a simple hire agreement similar to that entered into when a car is hired for a short time from a car rental firm. The same legal form can be used to finance a transaction where the lease is for a fixed period at a rent equivalent to the sale price of the goods and the cost of credit. The consumer does not have title to the goods and so cannot pass a good title to anyone else. The provisions of Part 3 of the Hire-Purchase Act 1964, which protect those who acquire cars subject to a hire-purchase agreement, do not apply. As a result, there have been instances recently of innocent purchasers of cars sold by persons who had been leasing them being without a practical remedy when the true owners reclaimed their property.[5]

Check Trading

9–11 The following description is taken from the Crowther Report.[6]

> "Check trading is an outgrowth from the spontaneous development of mutual clubs in the industrial centres of the North of England. A check is a document, issued by the check trader and purchased by the customer, which entitles him to buy goods, of a wide variety, at any of a long list of shops. The customer buys a check for, say £10 or £20 or £30, paying [5p] in the pound at the start, and undertaking to pay a further [5p] in the pound weekly for 20 weeks—that is, a total of [£1.05] of face value. When he uses the check to buy goods, he is charged the cash price, and the amount of his purchase is noted on the back of the check. The check trader then reimburses the retailer, but after deduction of a discount which may range from 12 per cent to 15 per cent. Moreover, settlements are usually made monthly, which means that the average period during which the retailer is out of his money is probably from six to seven weeks."

9–12 In recent years there has been a growth in the issue of high-unit vouchers payable over longer periods by monthly instalments, payment being made by the customer to the check trader direct or through the customer's bank by standing order or direct debit.[7] Check trading is largely confined to the north of England and Scotland and the dominant company is Provident Clothing and Supply. The exact legal nature of cheek trading has never been authoritatively decided.[8]

Credit Cards

9–13 Over the last 30 years credit cards have become increasingly popular in this country. The card is issued by a company specialising in the issue

---

[5] The defrauded purchaser would have a claim against the seller for breach of the implied term about title in Sale of Goods Act 1979, s.12. Often, in these cases, the person sued does not have the means to meet a decree.
[6] Crowther Report, para.2.4.1.
[7] See Goode, *Consumer Credit Law and Practice* (Butterworths Looseleaf) Div. 1A, para.2.35.
[8] There is an English county court decision, *Premier Clothing Co Ltd v Hillcoat*, Feb. 13, 1969, unreported, in which it was held that it was moneylending. It is referred to in the Crowther Report, para.4.1.64.

of cards which arranges that the card can be used to purchase goods and services from various traders.[9] The cardholder receives a monthly statement from the credit card company. In one type of card, sometimes referred to as a "t and e" card (travel and entertainment), of which the best known is American Express, the customer is expected to pay off the full amount each month. Apart from the period between paying for the goods or service with the card and the date by which payment must be made to the credit card company, there is no credit element. The other type of card, such as Access or Visa, gives the customer a choice. The full amount may be paid up and no interest charge incurred; or, subject to the payment of a minimum amount, the customer may choose to pay off the account in succeeding months. For this facility there is a charge which varies between 1.5 to 2 per cent per month. In addition, it is becoming more common for card companies to charge an annual fee. Traders submit their accounts to the credit card company which pays them the amount of the account minus a commission charge.

There has been very little litigation concerning credit cards in any **9–14** part of the UK. In *Re Charge Card Services Ltd*[10] the English Court of Appeal held that payment by credit card discharged the consumer's liability for the price to the trader. The cardholder was liable to pay the credit card company, whether or not the company paid the trader. If, as occurred in this case, the credit card company had failed to pay traders they could not recover from the cardholder.

Budget Accounts

Budget accounts have become common, especially in retail stores. They **9–15** are a form of revolving credit where the consumer agrees to make a regular monthly payment, say £20, and may then purchase goods of up to a certain multiple of this figure, perhaps 10 times or £200. As each payment is made new purchases are permitted provided that the balance outstanding on the account does not exceed £200. A charge which covers interest is made at a specified rate on the amount outstanding at the end of the month.

The precise legal nature of these accounts has never been clear. They **9–16** are not hire-purchase agreements but were thought by some to be money lending transactions. The Crowther Report noted that in the trade they "are usually treated as giving rise to a series of credit sale agreements" and this view derives support from certain Scottish decisions.[11]

---

[9] For a recent illuminating examination of the credit card and related store card industry, see HC Treasury Committee, *First Report: Transparency of Credit Card Charges* (2003–04 HC 125–I), Vol. 1.

[10] [1988] 3 W.L.R. 764; [1988] 3 All E.R. 702; (1988) 4 B.C.C. 524.

[11] Crowther Report, para.4.1.64.

LEGAL REGULATION OF CREDIT GRANTING

9–17 The law on consumer credit was reshaped by the Consumer Credit Act 1974 which adopted many of the recommendations of the Crowther Report on consumer credit. The committee carried out the most comprehensive review of the topic ever undertaken in this country. The report found the state of the law to be gravely defective, one of their most serious criticisms being that legislation regulated transactions on the basis of their form rather than their substance. Hire-purchase, some forms of moneylending and pawnbrokers were subject to strict regulation, whereas loans made by high street banks and the large finance houses were virtually unregulated.

9–18 The Crowther committee considered that tinkering with the law would not be appropriate and recommended a complete revision. They suggested that two new Acts should be drafted: a Lending and Security Act which would rationalise the treatment of security interests and set up a security register, and a Consumer Sale and Loan Act which would govern the treatment of all forms of consumer credit, the linchpin of which would be a Consumer Credit Commissioner. The Consumer Credit Act is essentially the proposed Consumer Sale and Loan Act, the Government having decided that the Lending and Security Act was unnecessary.

9–19 As the Secretary of State observes in her foreword to the recent White Paper on consumer credit, the Consumer Credit Act 1974 "has generally stood the test of time extremely well".[12] However, she notes that "the credit market has developed to an extent never envisaged in the early 1970's" so that "[t]he time is right for a thorough-going modernization of the consumer credit framework"[13]. The White Paper therefore advocates a number of reforms which will be referred to at the appropriate points in this chapter. They will deal with: advertising and other improvements in the information made available to consumers; facilities to enable credit agreements to be concluded online; reform of the law relating to early settlement; strengthening of the licensing regime; removal of the £25,000 limit on the protections afforded by the 1974 Act; and the replacement of the limited test for reopening extortionate credit bargains with a wider unfairness test. How quickly these changes will be made remains to be seen as the White Paper adds that "[the government] will bring legislation forward to effect these reforms as soon as parliamentary time allows."[14]

9–20 As we shall see there is detailed regulation of the credit industry to a degree which is greater than that which normally obtains for protecting the consumer. Why should this be? The Crowther Report[15] summarised

---

[12] *Fair, Clear and Competitive*, Cm. 6040 (2003), p.3.
[13] *ibid.*
[14] *ibid.*, p.8.
[15] For a discussion, see Crowther Report, Ch.6.1.

the factors which prevent the ideal of a fair balance between consumers and credit granters being attained in all cases. An important constraint is consumers' lack of knowledge both of the forms of credit available and their legal rights. In some cases inertia prevents appropriate action being taken. Some consumers are either reckless or improvident in their use of credit; and in other cases, through no fault of their own, families find themselves requiring to borrow because their income is inadequate. As the Crowther committee added, "[t]here is little point in talking of thrift to one who needs money to keep warm or to buy the minimum of food and clothing necessary for subsistence." Such people are particularly vulnerable to harsh and oppressive terms. Inequality of bargaining power and the existence of a small minority of sellers who indulge in trading malpractice causing great hardship were also noted. It should be added that the committee did not delude themselves that all these problems could be solved by legislation.

CONSUMER CREDIT ACT 1974

The Consumer Credit Act 1974 with its 193 sections and five schedules **9–21** has been described by a judge as "an Act of extraordinary length and complexity".[16] And even at this the Act is only a framework on which much flesh has been put by numerous statutory instruments. Such was its complexity that it was not until 1985 that it came fully into force. In addition, it must be remembered that it is not comprehensive. Aspects of the ordinary law of contract, such as the law on formation and misrepresentation still apply, and the Act does not apply to all credit contracts, as we shall see below.[17]

DEFINITIONS

Before looking at the various techniques which the Act uses to protect **9–22** credit consumers it is vital to consider the scope of the Act. The central concept is the "regulated agreement" as, with some exceptions, it is only such agreements that are controlled by the Act. Before the term "regulated agreement" can be understood it is essential to look at various definitions which the Act uses. It will also be convenient at this point to consider some other definitions which will crop up later. The draftsman of the Act invented some new terminology to distinguish various types of credit. In a novel departure from the methods normally adopted by parliamentary draftsmen examples of the terminology were also provided in Sch.2 to the Act.

---

[16] Goff L.J. (as he then was) in *Jenkins v Lombard North Central plc* [1984] 1 W.L.R. 307 at 308.
[17] paras 9–42—9–45.

Fixed and Running Account Credit

9–23 Section 10(1)(a) provides:

> "[R]unning-account credit is a facility under a personal credit agreement whereby the debtor is enabled to receive from time to time (whether in his own person, or by another person) from the creditor or a third party cash, goods and services (or any of them) to an amount or value such that, taking into account payments made by or to the credit of the debtor, the credit limit (if any) is not at any time exceeded."

9–24 Section 10(3) includes provisions designed to prevent circumvention of this definition. Even if the credit limit is above £25,000 (the upper limit for a personal credit agreement) an agreement is still within the definition if at any one time the maximum amount which can be drawn down is under £25,000; or, having regard to all the relevant circumstances it is probable that the limit will not be exceeded. This latter situation is the subject of one of the examples in a schedule to the Act.

9–25 Suppose that an individual runs a small shop which usually carries a stock worth about £5,000. A wholesaler makes a stocking agreement with him under which he undertakes to provide on short-term credit the stock needed from time-to-time without any specified limit. This appears to provide unlimited credit, but because the circumstances show that the shop owner is never likely to be indebted for more than £25,000 the agreement is a consumer credit agreement.

9–26 The most common examples of running account credit are an overdraft or a shop revolving credit account. Fixed-sum credit is any other facility under which credit can be obtained. An obvious example would be a personal loan from a bank or a building society for a specific amount.

Debtor-Creditor-Supplier Agreements

9–27 A debtor-creditor-supplier agreement can arise in three ways.[18] It occurs where a restricted use credit agreement is made to finance a transaction between a debtor and a creditor. An example would be a hire-purchase or credit sale agreement where the supplier provides the finance. Where, as is probably more common, a third party provides restricted use finance this, too, is a debtor-creditor-supplier agreement if made under pre-existing arrangements, or in contemplation of future arrangements between the creditor and the supplier. The typical hire-purchase arrangement, where the finance is provided by a finance company, is a good example, but credit card and check trading transactions provide

---

[18] s.12.

further examples. The third situation deals with the case where a third party provides unrestricted use credit under pre-existing arrangements with the supplier in the knowledge that the credit is to be used to finance a transaction between the debtor and the supplier. This brings within the ambit of debtor-creditor-supplier agreements situations where a supplier, such as a retailer, has agreed to refer customers to a finance company which will provide them with loans which, though technically not limited to the purchase of a specific product, all parties know will be so used.

Debtor-Creditor Agreements

Restricted use credit agreements which would be debtor-creditor- **9–28** supplier agreements but for the fact that there are no pre-existing arrangements between the creditor and the supplier are known as debtor-creditor agreements. Restricted use credit arrangements to refinance any existing indebtedness of the debtor are in the same category. So are unrestricted use credit agreements which are not made by the creditor under pre-existing arrangements with a supplier.[19] Examples are bank overdrafts, moneylenders' advances and loans from pawnbrokers.

Linked Transactions

Certain transactions are said to be linked to a regulated agreement. This **9–29** is important, particularly in relation to withdrawal from, and cancellation of, agreements, as well as the provisions about extortionate credit bargains. A linked transaction is dealt with in s.19 of the Act and does not include a transaction for the provision of a security. Subject to this, it covers transactions entered into in compliance with a term in the principal agreement such as the taking out of a policy of life insurance by the debtor under a loan agreement. In a debtor-creditor-supplier agreement the sale and loan contract are linked; and there is a link where the debtor entered into a transaction in order to induce the creditor to enter into the principal credit agreement.

Total Charge for Credit and Annual Percentage Rate

A central feature of the recommendations of the Crowther Report was **9–30** the necessity for consumers to have better information about credit deals. This, it was hoped, would allow consumers to make rational decisions about credit transactions. It was also expected to benefit them by stimulating competition between lenders who would be exposed to a market where there was greater transparency.

In achieving this aim s.20 of the Act is one of its most important **9–31** provisions. It requires the Secretary of State to make regulations for

---

[19] s.12.

working out the true cost of credit to the borrower. This is known as the "total charge for credit" and is to be contrasted with the credit advanced. This is a most important concept for a number of reasons. For example, in relation to computing some of the monetary limits the total charge for credit is not included, only the amount of credit advanced. As we shall see, it is also relevant to the formalities which must be complied with in drafting a credit agreement, the liability of a debtor after a debtor-creditor agreement has been cancelled and the control of extortionate credit bargains. However, its most important function is probably as the first step in arriving at the annual percentage rate (APR), an important piece of information which must be given to consumers and prospective consumers of credit.

9–32 The detailed working out of the total charge for credit and the related APR are set out in the Consumer Credit (Total Charge for Credit) Regulations 1980.[20] These are necessarily somewhat complex.[21] This is because a credit transaction may not merely include interest. There may well be other charges such as arrangement fees, maintenance charges, or insurance premiums. In giving a true picture of the cost of credit some or all of these charges may have to be taken into account. The main provisions of the 1980 Regulations are regs 4 and 5. Regulation 4 provides that, in calculating the total charge for credit, the total interest charge and any other charges at any time payable under the transaction by or on behalf of the debtor must be taken into account. Regulation 5 then provides that certain charges are to be excluded. Examples are premiums for insurance not taken out as a condition of the loan, or life insurance premiums where the proceeds of the policy will be used to repay the loan.

9–33 Having worked out the total charge for credit it is then possible to calculate the APR. The 1984 Regulations provide three methods which may be used for doing this and there are 15 volumes of consumer credit tables to assist traders.

9–34 The function of the APR is to provide a means of comparison between the cost of various kinds of credit and different credit offers of the same type. It has been argued that consumers have little understanding of APRs and tend to place more reliance on the size and frequency of repayments.[22] However, research by the OFT suggests that understanding of APRs is increasing. It was found that 64 per cent of those surveyed would generally draw the right conclusion from using APRs, even though they might not fully appreciate precisely what they

---

[20] SI 1980/51, as amended by SI 1985/1192; SI 1989/596; and Consumer Credit (Total Charge for Credit, Agreements and Advertisements) (Amendment) Regulations 1999 (SI 1999/3177).

[21] For detailed explanations of the calculation of the total charge for credit and APRs, see R. M. Goode, *Consumer Credit Law and Practice* (Looseleaf ed., Butterworths, London 1999), Div. 1C, paras 29.121–29.300.

[22] *Consumers and Credit* (NCC, 1980), Ch.4.

represented.[23] The report of the House of Commons Treasury Committee revealed: "The APR figure used by consumers to compare [credit] cards is calculated in more than one way. The true cost of cards to the consumer is concealed behind complex interest calculation methods not taken account of in the APR."[24] This is because the industry and the OFT interprets the statutory requirements differently. The White Paper on consumer credit announced that the regulations would be amended by October 2004 to remove this defect.

Regulated Credit Agreements

The meaning of this phrase requires a lengthy trawl through various **9–35** sections of the Act starting with s.189(1), the definition section, which provides: " 'regulated agreement' means a consumer credit agreement, or consumer hire agreement, other than an exempt agreement, and 'regulated' and 'unregulated' shall be construed accordingly."

This raises a number of questions such as "what is meant by **9–36** 'credit'?"; "what are consumer credit and hire agreements?"; and "which agreements are exempt?" "Credit" is very widely defined to include "a cash loan, and any other form of financial accommodation",[25] and section 189 goes on specifically to say that a purchaser on hire-purchase obtains credit.

Consumer Credit Agreement

The definition of a consumer credit agreement is to be found in s.8. **9–37** Section 8(2) defines a consumer credit agreement as "a personal credit agreement by which the creditor provides the debtor with credit not exceeding £25,000."[26] "[A personal credit agreement is] an agreement between an individual ('the debtor') and any other person ('the creditor') by which the creditor provides the debtor with credit of any amount."[27]

It is important to note that the £25,000 limit is calculated by reference **9–38** to the amount of credit advanced; interest charged is not included. For example, in the case of goods purchased on hire-purchase it is not the hire-purchase price of the goods which is relevant but the amount of the balance financed. Take the example of an individual who buys a car, the cash price of which is £26,000. Suppose that a deposit of £3,000 is paid and the finance charges are £7,000. Although the total purchase price at £33,000 is above the upper limit of the Act, the agreement is

[23] *Consumer Credit Deregulation* (OFT, June 1994), para.7.14.
[24] *First Report: Transparency of Credit Card Charges* (2003–04 HC 125–I), Vol. 1, para.19.
[25] s.9(1).
[26] s.8, amended by Consumer Credit (Increase of Monetary Limits) Order 1998 (SI 1998/996), art. 2 (with effect from May 1, 1998).
[27] s.8(1).

within the protection of the Act because the balance financed is only £23,000, *i.e.* the cash price minus the deposit.

9–39   The net result of the definition is that the Act applies to the common forms of instalment credit such as hire-purchase, conditional and credit sale as well as budget accounts, credit cards, loans and overdrafts. In the White Paper on consumer credit the Government announced that it intended to remove the financial limit.[28]

Consumer Hire Agreements

9–40   A consumer hire agreement is defined in section 15 of the Act as one which is made by an individual (the "hirer") for the hiring of goods to the hirer and which is not a hire-purchase agreement, is capable of lasting for more than three months, and does not require the hirer to make payments exceeding £25,000.

WHO IS PROTECTED?

9–41   The definition of "individual" in the Act means that both consumer credit and consumer hire agreements may involve debtors who are not what might usually be thought of as private consumers. This is because "individual" in the Act includes a partnership or other unincorporated body of persons (not consisting entirely of bodies corporate).[29] Defining who should be protected by consumer protection legislation is always difficult at the margin, and the solution adopted in the Act is to make a distinction between corporations (*i.e.* mostly limited companies) and others. The merit of this approach is that it is easy to operate. The disadvantage is that it does not identify all those requiring protection. It can be argued that there are many small businesses which have adopted the corporate form where those in control are just as much in need of protection as private individuals or those who choose to do business through partnerships or as sole traders.[30]

EXEMPT AGREEMENTS

9–42   Having discovered what a consumer credit agreement is, we next must note that some of these agreements will be exempt from the Act where an order has been made by the Secretary of State. This can only apply to agreements where the creditor is a local authority, building society, or one of a number of other organisations listed in the section such as insurance companies, friendly societies, and organisations of workers or

---

[28] *Fair, Clear and Competitive*, Cm. 6040 (2003), para.3.61.

[29] s.189(1).

[30] Following a review of this issue the minister announced, on July 22, 2003, that regulation of credit to businesses will be restricted to sole traders, partnerships of up to and including three partners and other unincorporated bodies. The appropriate changes have not yet been implemented.

employers. An order has been made, the effect of which is to exempt many loans secured on land.[31]

Other parts of the same Order based on other powers in s.16 create the **9–43** following further exemptions:

(1) Debtor-creditor-supplier agreements financing purchases of land which do not gain exemption under the previous exemptions will be exempt if the number of payments to be made does not exceed four.[32]

(2) A debtor-creditor-supplier agreement for fixed sum credit which is not hire-purchase or conditional sale where the number of payments to be made by the debtor in respect of the credit does not exceed four and must be made within 12 months of the date of the agreement. A straightforward example of this would be trade credit on terms such as payment within 30 days of invoice.[33]

(3) A debtor-creditor-supplier agreement which is not for hire-purchase or conditional sale and provides running account credit where the whole of the credit is repayable in one instalment. Examples are American Express or Diners Club cards.[34]

(4) A low interest exemption for debtor-creditor agreements, low being defined as an annual percentage rate which does not exceed one per cent above the highest base rate of an English or Scottish clearing bank in the 28 days prior to the making of the agreement.[35]

PARTIALLY REGULATED AGREEMENTS

Small Agreements

Small agreements as defined by s.17 of the Act are only partially subject **9–44** to the controls in the Act. A small agreement is a regulated consumer credit agreement for credit not exceeding £50 which is not a hire-purchase or conditional sale agreement; or a regulated consumer hire agreement which does not require the hirer to make payments exceeding £50.

Non-commercial Agreements

Non-commercial agreements are also freed from many of the controls of **9–45** the Act such as those on the formalities about agreements and connected lender liability. Such an agreement is a consumer credit or consumer

---

[31] Consumer Credit (Exempt Agreements) Order 1989 (SI 1989/869).
[32] *ibid.*, art.3(1)(b).
[33] *ibid.*, art.3(1)(a)(i). See *Zoan v Rouamba* [2000] All E.R. 620, CA.
[34] *ibid.*, art.3(1)(a)(ii).
[35] *ibid.*, art.4.

hire agreement not made by the creditor or owner in the course of a business carried on by him.[36]

CONTROLLING BUSINESS ACTIVITIES

9–46 Various parts of the Act regulate the way in which those in the credit industry can carry on their businesses. There are controls on advertising, canvassing for business, the marketing of credit cards, and the operation of credit reference agencies. The most important of the controls on the credit industry takes the form of the licensing system.

LICENSING SYSTEM

9–47 The creation of an effective and comprehensive licensing system was one of the central recommendations of the Crowther Report. It pointed out that protective measures focusing on individual transactions, important as they are, have limited efficacy.[37] One of the members of the Crowther committee has explained in more detail the necessity for having a licensing system:

> "No consumer legislation, however sophisticated, is likely to have more than a marginal impact if it is not underpinned by effective enforcement machinery. The Hire-Purchase Acts provided no mechanism whatever for systematic enforcement. The onus was placed on the individual consumer to take the initiative in invoking the Acts. In many cases he was not equipped to do so, through ignorance of his rights, timidity or inability to incur the legal costs that might be involved. The reputable trader or finance house would endeavour to comply with the law. The less scrupulous creditor, against whose activities the legislation was primarily aimed, could afford to cock a Snook—provided he stood clear of the small number of criminal offences provided by the statutes—since at worst he would lose the occasional case, and this loss was far outweighed by the benefits to be derived from diligent and persistent flouting of the statutory requirements and the recovery from uninformed debtors of sums which they could not legally have been compelled to pay."[38]

9–48   The Act set up a licensing system covering, not just moneylending and pawnbroking, as had been the case prior to the Act, but all activities relating to credit. The operation of the licensing system is the task of the OFT.[39]

---

[36] s.189(1).

[37] Crowther Report, para.6.3.3.

[38] R.M. Goode, *Introduction to the Consumer Credit Act 1974* (Butterworths, London, 1974), p.103.

[39] s.1.

Section 21 of the Act provides that licences are required to carry on **9–49** a consumer credit or consumer hire business; and section 147 extends the licensing provisions to "ancillary credit businesses". An "ancillary credit business" means the following:

(1) credit brokerage;
(2) debt-adjusting;
(3) debt-counselling;
(4) debt-collection;
(5) the operation of a credit reference agency.

Most of these are self-explanatory, but the term "credit brokerage" **9–50** requires more comment. In addition to businesses acting as brokers in the ordinary sense of the term it covers many dealers and services providers. It is for this reason that retailers, for example, even though they themselves do not provide credit, must have a licence, because they introduce customers to sources of finance such as hire-purchase companies.

Local authorities and bodies corporate with statutory powers to carry **9–51** on business are not required to have licences.

Applications for licences are made to the OFT and, since 1991, **9–52** licences last for five years. There are two types of licence: a "standard licence" which can be issued to sole traders, partnerships and companies, and "group licences" which are issued where the OFT considers that it is in the public interest to do so, rather than require those affected to apply individually. Group licences, of which there are currently 15, have been issued to the Law Society of Scotland and Citizens' Advice Scotland. The OFT estimate that there are now about 215,000 live licences, and in 2001–02 it dealt with 16,293 applications for new licences, of which 27 were refused, and 11,974 renewals, of which 20 were refused. In addition 18 licences were revoked.

To obtain a licence an applicant must show that the name which the **9–53** business will use is not misleading or otherwise improper; and that "he is a fit person to engage in activities covered by the licence".[40] In deciding on fitness the OFT must have regard to any circumstances appearing to it to be relevant. In particular it will consider evidence tending to show that the applicant has committed offences involving fraud, dishonesty, or violence; broken the law relating to credit; discriminated on the grounds of sex, colour, race or ethnic origin; or engaged in business practices which are oppressive, deceitful, unfair or improper.[41] The record of an associate of the applicant such as an employee or agent or director of a company seeking the licence will also be relevant.

---

[40] s.25(1).
[41] s.25(2).

9–54   In obtaining information about the suitability of applicants the OFT depends on information from various sources, but that from trading standards departments is particularly important. If the OFT is "minded to refuse" an application it must inform the applicant who may make written representations and request an opportunity to make oral submissions.[42] Appeal against a refusal of a licence lies to the Secretary of State.[43]

9–55   In addition to the power to refuse a licence, the OFT may revoke or suspend one that has been issued.[44] The grounds on which this may be done are that the holder has engaged in conduct which would have prevented a licence being granted in the first place. The procedures for dealing with such cases are similar to those where it is intended to refuse a licence.[45]

9–56   As the figures quoted in para.9.52 demonstrate, in practice few licences are refused or revoked. The Comptroller and Auditor General was critical of the effectiveness of the methods used to check on the suitability of applicants and, in particular, noted that arrangements to obtain evidence from trading standards departments are not working well. This seems to be related to a sharp drop in the number of licences revoked since 1995–96 despite a rise in consumer complaints.[46] As the DTI observed: "There is a widespread and general perception that consumer credit licences are not difficult to obtain or to retain. The figures ... on the small number of applications that are denied and licences that are revoked would seem to support this view."[47] To improve the licensing system the White Paper on consumer credit announced a number of proposals.[48] To reduce the administrative burden on the OFT licences will be issued for indefinite periods. The fitness test will be strengthened and the OFT will be given more powers to investigate and more sophisticated compliance tools. At present the only options are approval of a licence or refusal or revocation, which in effect put a trader out of business, and which must therefore be exercised only in serious case.

SEEKING BUSINESS

9–57 In any context accurate information is of importance to a consumer in coming to a rational decision about the purchase of goods and services.

---

[42] s.27.

[43] s.41.

[44] s.32.

[45] The operation of the system is described in the Annual Report of the Director-General of Fair Trading (OFT, 1993), pp.14, 15.

[46] The Office of Fair Trading: *Progress in Protecting Consumers' Interests*, Report by the Comptroller and Auditor General HC 430 Session 2002–2003, March 2003, para.3.21.

[47] *A Consultation Document on the Licensing Regime under the Consumer Credit Act 1974* (DTI, Jan. 2003), para.2.4.2.

[48] *Fair, Clear and Competitive*, Cm. 6040 (2003), para.3.3.

Where a purchase is to be made on credit this is particularly important as consumers contemplating taking on credit commitments are especially vulnerable. There is much pressure through the media to acquire goods and services, and the availability of credit can beguile people into taking on commitments that they cannot afford. In addition, it is not easy to make comparisons between various offers of credit in the absence of common methods of setting major terms such as the rate of interest.

For these reasons the Act has placed considerable importance on pre- **9–58** contractual information. There are controls on advertising, requirements to provide quotations to those considering credit arrangements, and restrictions on canvassing credit agreements and distributing credit cards.

Advertising Controls

Part 4 of the Act regulates advertising in two principal ways. Under s.46 **9–59** it is an offence to publish an advertisement which is false or misleading in a material respect. Section 44 requires the Secretary of State to make regulations as to the form and content of advertisements. These controls are in addition to other more general controls on advertising such, for example, as the Control of Misleading Advertising Regulations 1988.[49]

The controls in the Act cover any advertisements indicating that the **9–60** advertiser is willing to provide credit or hire facilities. There are certain exceptions in s.43 which relate to advertisers who do not carry on a consumer hire or credit business, or a business in the course of which credit secured on land is provided to individuals, and certain agreements subject to foreign law. Also exempt from the advertising controls are those advertisements which indicate that the credit must exceed £25,000 and that no security is required, or that the security is to consist of property other than land; and those directed only to bodies corporate.

The regulations made under the powers in s.44 of the Act are now to **9–61** be found in the Consumer Credit (Advertisement) Regulations 1989.[50] The principles underlying them are that advertisements should contain nothing misleading and should give a reasonable picture of the terms on which credit is to be granted, especially its cost. They also require information about any personal factors which will be taken into account in considering whether to offer credit, and the inclusion of so-called "wealth warnings" in advertisements relating to mortgages. All methods of advertising are covered though amendments[51] have had the effect of exempting certain credit advertisements from the requirement to contain one or both of the warning statements, "Your home is at risk if

---

[49] SI 1988/915.
[50] SI 1989/1125, which came into force on Feb. 1, 1990. They will be replaced on October 31, 2004 by SI 2004/1484.
[51] See Consumer Credit (Content of Quotations) and Consumer Credit (Advertisements) (Amendment) Regulations 1999 (SI 1999 No. 2725), which came into effect in Feb. 2000.

you do not keep up repayments on a mortgage or other loan secured on it" and "The sterling equivalent of your liability under a foreign currency mortgage may be increased by exchange rate movements". This exemption applies to television and radio advertisements broadcast in the course of programming whose primary purpose is not advertising, and to advertisements on film. The same amendments have been made in relation to hire advertisements.

9–62　　The approach of the 1989 Regulations, which do not apply to credit or hire for business purposes, is to divide advertisements into three types: simple, intermediate and full. Simple advertisements can give no more than the name of the credit provider and an indication of the type of business carried on. Intermediate advertisements may consist only of the advertiser's name, address or telephone number and an invitation to obtain written quotations for credit terms. Full advertisements include much more information about the credit or hire facilities and, in particular, involve disclosure of details about the cost of credit, the frequency and amount of repayments and any deposit. Failure to comply with the Regulations is a criminal offence.[52] Any agreement entered into, following an advertisement which did not comply with the Regulations, is not invalid.

9–63　　There have been frequent criticisms of the complexity of the 1989 Regulations and the Director-General of Fair Trading accepted that they require revision. In his review of the Act he recommended that they should be replaced by much less complex regulations focusing on the central information of importance to consumers, such as the cost of credit.[53] The Government said in the White Paper on consumer credit that it accepts that "due to the rapid evolution of the credit industry, the current rules have resulted in a highly technical and complex regime, creating confusion for lenders, enforcers and consumers."[54] It "intends to introduce measures designed to ensure greater consistency and transparency in credit advertising, so that consumers can compare financial products with confidence and make informed purchasing decisions."[55] Such regulations, the Consumer Credit (Advertisements) Regulations 2004 (SI 2004/1484), will come into force on October 31, 2004.

Quotations

9–64　In November 1996, the then Minister for Competition and Consumer Affairs announced that the Government had decided to proceed with some of the recommendations made in the Director-General's report.[56]

---

[52] s.164 and Sch.1.
[53] See *Consumer Credit Deregulation: A review by the Director-General of Fair Trading of the scope and operation of the Consumer Credit Act 1974* (OFT, June 1994), Ch.5.
[54] *Fair, Clear and Competitive*, Cm. 6040 (2003), para.2.6.
[55] *ibid.*, para.2.7.
[56] *op. cit.*, n.53.

As part of the deregulation initiative, the Consumer Credit (Quotations) Regulations 1989,[57] were repealed, without replacement, by the Consumer Credit (Quotations) (Revocation) Regulations 1997.[58] There are, therefore, no current regulations in force. This means that traders who provide credit facilities are no longer under a legal obligation to set out the terms in a specified form when their customers ask for a written quotation. While in most circumstances advertisements for credit or hire facilities must state that written quotations are available on request —and businesses are obliged to supply such quotations when they are asked to do so—the way the necessary information is presented is now solely a matter for individual traders, so long as it does not mislead their prospective clients.

Canvassing

The Moneylenders Acts banned the peddling of loans from door to door. **9–65** Similar but more wide-ranging controls are included in the Consumer Credit Act 1974. Canvassing debtor-creditor agreements (of which the most common type will be personal loans) off trade premises is a criminal offence. So is soliciting the entry of an individual into such an agreement during a visit carried out in response to a request made on a previous occasion, if the request was not in writing and signed by the person making it. "Canvassing" means making oral representations off trade premises. Premises are still trade premises if a business is carried on there by the creditor, a supplier, the canvasser or, even the consumer. It does not matter that the place is only a temporary place of business such as a stand at a trade show.[59]

The Director-General has exercised a power to exempt from these **9–66** rules the solicitation of agreements permitting the debtor to overdraw on certain types of current account, provided that the debtor already keeps an account with the creditor.[60]

Circulars to Minors

In line with the policy of protecting vulnerable consumers, the Act **9–67** makes it a criminal offence to send to a person under 18 years old, with a view to financial gain, any document inviting him or her to borrow money, obtain goods or services on credit, hire goods, or even apply for information about doing any of these things. It is a defence for the accused to show that he did not know and had no reasonable cause to suspect that the person to whom the document was sent was a minor. However, where the address to which the document is sent is a school,

---

[57] SI 1989/1126.
[58] SI 1997/211, as of Mar. 10, 1997.
[59] ss.48, 49.
[60] See determination of the Director-General of June 1, 1977, in *op. cit.*, n.7, Div. IVB, para.2.1.

or other educational establishment for minors, reasonable cause to suspect that the recipient is under 18 years of age will be assumed.[61]

Distribution of Credit Tokens

9–68 Mass mailings of Access cards gave rise to widespread criticism some years ago with the result that this practice is now banned by s.51 of the Act.[62] The section applies to "credit tokens" which are defined as:

> "a card, check, voucher, coupon, stamp, form, booklet or other document or thing given to an individual by a person carrying on a consumer credit business, who undertakes—
>
> (a) that on production of it (whether or not some other action is also required) he will supply cash, goods and services . . . on credit, or
>
> (b) that where, on the production of it to a third party (whether or not any other action is also required), the third party supplies cash, goods and services he will pay the third party for them (whether or not deducting any discount or commission), in return for payment to him by the individual."[63]

9–69 This definition covers two-party cards operated by department stores as well as three-party cards such as American Express, Access and Visa. It also includes checks and vouchers issued by check and voucher trading companies, and cash cards issued by banks and building societies for use at automatic teller machines.

9–70 Credit tokens, such as credit cards, may only be distributed in response to a written and signed request. There are exceptions in the case of renewals and where the agreement is a small debtor-creditor-supplier agreement.[64]

CREDIT REFERENCE AGENCIES

9–71 Those who lend will wish to have as much assurance as possible that borrowers will pay back what they have been lent. In the past lenders may have tended to do this through personal knowledge of clients. With the scale of credit today that is not possible and attempts to interview all borrowers would be prohibitively expensive. Many lenders have stream-lined the process by using credit scoring techniques to determine whether credit should be granted. Credit scoring is a method of assessing applications for credit using statistical techniques and is

---

[61] s.50.

[62] For the only case arising out of a breach of s.51, see *Elliott v Director-General of Fair Trading* [1980] 1 W.L.R. 977.

[63] s.14(1).

[64] For definition, see para.9–77.

widespread among stores and financial institutions throughout the UK. Specialist consultants design individual scorecards for lenders using information about previous credit accounts which have been analysed to show which personal details are associated with good payment records and which with bad. When an individual applies for credit from that company, information on the application form will be combined with information from other sources to obtain a credit score.[65] Usually the other information is obtained from credit reference agencies which are organisations specialising in storing information about people's credit history.

Given the importance of credit scoring and access to credit, the **9–72** accuracy of the information held by credit reference agencies is vital. Their existence also raises other issues related to privacy. For this reason the Act contains protections for consumers. Section 157 imposes a duty on a creditor, owner or negotiator to respond within seven working[66] days to a written request for the name and address of any credit reference agency from which information has been sought about the customer's financial standing. The application must be made within 28 days after the end of antecedent negotiations as defined in s.56.[67]

This obligation is complemented by s.7 of the Data Protection Act **9–73** 1998 which casts a duty on a credit reference agency to give consumers a copy of any file relating to them which they have, putting it into plain English if necessary. This duty only arises where the consumer has made a written request (accompanied by a fee of £3) and given sufficient details to enable the agency to identify the file. As well as providing the information an agency must also send consumers a statement of their right to have mistakes corrected.

This statement refers to the right set out in s.159 of the 1974 Act to **9–74** have wrong and prejudicial information removed from a file or amended. Where the agency complies it must give the consumer a notice stating that it has done so and send a copy of the amended entry. Where the agency and the consumer cannot reach agreement on the issue either side may apply to the Information Commissioner or, in the case of a partnership or other incorporated body, to the OFT which will resolve the matter.

Part 3 of the Data Protection Act 1984 is also relevant and gives **9–75** individuals whose personal data is held by a data user or data bureau an action for damages if loss is occasioned to them through unauthorised destruction, disclosure or access. There is also a right to compensation where loss is caused as a result of the information being inaccurate.

---

[65] For further detail on how credit scoring works, see *Which?*, July 1989, p.316.
[66] See Consumer Credit (Credit Reference Agency) Regulations 1977 (SI 1977/329), reg.3.
[67] See para.9–77 *et seq.*

FORMATION AND CANCELLATION OF THE AGREEMENT

MAKING AN AGREEMENT

Antecedent Negotiations

9–76 In practice there will frequently be situations where an important role in a credit transaction will be played by a person who does not provide the credit or with whom the consumer has no legal relationship because the goods are transferred to the financier before being transferred to the consumer. A typical example would be a hire-purchase transaction where the consumer selects the goods in a shop which does not provide hire-purchase finance itself, but has arrangements with a financier. As we have seen, the consumer's contract is with the hire-purchase company and the shop drops out of the picture. However, what if, in the course of discussions in the shop, false or misleading statements were made to the consumer? Under common law the hire-purchase company would not have any responsibility for the activities of the shop as the courts have not been prepared to find that an independent retailer is the agent of the credit granter.[68] The consumer would have no contractual link with the shop and thus might not be able to obtain redress.

9–77   Section 56 of the 1974 Act seeks to deal with this situation. The central provision is s.56(2) which provides: "Negotiations with the debtor . . . shall be deemed to be conducted by the negotiator in the capacity of agent of the creditor as well as in his actual capacity." The "antecedent negotiations" which are covered by s.56, in addition to those carried out by the owner or hirer, are set out in s.56(1). The first are those "conducted by a credit-broker in relation to goods sold or proposed to be sold by the credit-broker to the creditor before forming the subject-matter of a debtor-creditor-supplier agreement within section 12(a)".

9–78   Section 12(a) refers to restricted-use credit. The typical situation would be a hire-purchase transaction where the credit-broker is the shop which sells the goods to the hire-purchase company which then hire-purchases them to the consumer.

9–79   The second situation is where negotiations have been "conducted by the supplier in relation to a transaction financed or proposed to be financed by a debtor-creditor-supplier agreement within section 12(b) or (c)".

9–80   This covers negotiations such as those conducted by a supplier before putting consumers into contact with a finance house which, under pre-existing arrangements, provides them with loans enabling them to purchase goods or services from the supplier.

9–81   The creditor will be liable under s.56(4) for contractual statements and misrepresentations made by the negotiator during the antecedent

---

[68] *Branwhite v Worcester Works Finance Ltd* [1969] 1 A.C. 552; [1968] 3 All E.R. 104, [1999] G.C.C.R. 397.

negotiations. These begin when the negotiator and the consumer first enter into communication, and for this purpose an advertisement can constitute communication. It is important to note that s.56(3) prevents attempts to exclude liability under the section.

Section 56 does not apply to implied terms or to hire contracts, as **9–82** opposed to hire-purchase contracts.[69] It will sometimes over lap with s.75.[70] Indeed, the two Scottish decisions on s.75 should really have been decided under s.56.[71]

Creditors or owners can be liable for a very wide range of representa- **9–83** tions. It must be noted that the liability is for antecedent negotiations "in relation to goods sold or proposed to be sold" in the case of s.56(1)(b) and "in relation to a transaction financed or proposed to be financed" in the case of subs.(1)(c). However, in *Powell v Lloyds Bowmaker Ltd*[72] a narrow and unrealistic view of s.56(1)(b) was taken. Mr Powell had traded his Vauxhall in part exchange against a Toyota which he wished to purchase. The vendors negotiated finance on the deal and agreed that it would settle an existing hire-purchase commitment (with a finance company called AM) on the vehicle being traded in. The vendors did not settle the commitment and Mr Powell raised an action for damages basing his claim on the proposition that by virtue of s.56(1)(b) the vendors were the deemed agents of Lloyds Bowmaker, who were thus liable for the failure to pay off the earlier hire-purchase commitment. The sheriff disagreed with a decision of an English county court judge in *UDT v Whitfield*[73] where, on very similar facts, the finance company was held liable. He accepted that "the legislation is intended to benefit consumers and that the Crowther Report laid some stress on the need to base the law on commercial reality as opposed to legal abstractions". While agreeing that it could have applied to a representation about the price of the car he did not consider that it applied to the promise to pay off the existing hire-purchase debt.

The English Court of Appeal decided *Forthright Finance Ltd v* **9–84** *Ingate*,[74] shortly after *Powell*. Staughton L.J. examined the decisions of *UDT v Whitfield* and *Powell v Lloyds Bowmaker Ltd* and the legislative origins of s.56. He stated:

---

[69] See *Lloyds Bowmaker Leasing Ltd v MacDonald* [1993] C.C.L.R. 65; [1999] G.C.C.R. 3443, Sh Ct; and the English Court of Appeal decision, *Woodchester (Equipment Leasing) Ltd v British Association of Canned and Preserved Food Importers and Distributors Ltd* [1995] C.C.L.R. 51; [1999] G.C.C.R. 1923.

[70] See para.9–117.

[71] See *United Dominions Trust v Taylor*, 1980 S.L.T. (Sh. Ct.) 28 and *Forward Trust Ltd v Hornsby and Windermere Aquatic Ltd* [1996] C.C.L.R. 18, discussed at paras 9–122—9–125. The same error occurred in the English case of *Porter v General Guarantee Corp. Ltd* [1982] R.T.R. 384.

[72] 1996 S.L.T. (Sh. Ct.) 117; [1999] G.C.C.R. 3523.

[73] [1987] C.C.L.R. 60.

[74] [1997] 4 All E.R. 99.

"In my judgement what s. 56(1)(b) means is that there must be goods sold or proposed to be sold by the credit-broker to the creditor, which will form the subject matter of a debtor-creditor-supplier agreement. If that condition is fulfilled, one next inquires whether there were negotiations in relation to those goods. If there were, then all that was said by the credit-broker in those negotiations is deemed to have been said on behalf of the creditor. On the other hand, what is said in any other negotiations which do not relate to those goods, is not deemed to be said on behalf of the creditor. The question is then a simple one of fact, were the negotiations in this case all relating to the goods to be sold?"[75]

9–85   On the facts he found that only one transaction was involved and that *UDT* was rightly decided. Henry L.J., in agreeing, indicated that s.56 should be construed widely, stating:

"[A] narrow construction of the words would not only be artificial but would fly in the face of the clear purpose of this Act to protect consumers. While I would favour a wide construction of the words on that ground alone, subs. (4) of s. 56 seems to be to put the matter beyond doubt in favouring a wide construction."[76]

Form and Content of Agreements

9–86 In a further attempt to ensure that consumers know exactly what they are doing, the Act requires the Secretary of State to make regulations as to the form and content of regulated agreements.[77] These must have provisions to ensure that a debtor or hirer is made aware of:

(a) the rights and duties conferred or imposed on him by the agreement;
(b) the cost of credit;
(c) the protection and remedies available under the Act;
(d) any other matters which it is desirable that creditors should know.

9–87   The regulations may require that specified information be included in a particular way, be excluded, or be brought clearly to the attention of a debtor or hirer.

9–88   The Consumer Credit (Agreement) Regulations 1983[78] set out in great detail the form, content, legibility and signature of documents containing regulated consumer credit and hire agreements. Different

---

[75] [1997] 4 All E.R. 99, at 105.
[76] *ibid.*
[77] s.60.
[78] SI 1983/1553.

types of agreement require different types of information to be given and the Regulations set out the requirements for each type in schedules. These have in common the fact that the kind of information which must be given falls into five main categories:

(1) heading on the first page of the document prominently stating the legal nature of the agreement;
(2) name and address of each party;
(3) financial information, such as the subject-matter of the agreement, the timing and amount of payments, and the cost of credit, including the APR;
(4) other information about the agreement, such as details of any security provided and charges payable on default;
(5) protection and remedies available under the Act.

The 1983 Regulations also require that there should be a signature **9–89** box in an agreement and go into detail on exactly how this is to be set out. In the case of credit-token agreements the name, address and telephone number of the person to whom notice is to be given of loss or misuse must be included.

Failure to comply with the 1983 Regulations can have serious **9–90** consequences for the creditor or hirer. Before dealing with that issue it is better to consider first the related rules in the Act dealing with the signing of agreements, the provision of copies to the debtor, and rights to cancel or withdraw.

Proper Execution of an Agreement

Execution of an agreement is the technical term for the signing of it by **9–91** both parties. The Act has stringent requirements about proper execution of an agreement which go well beyond simply ensuring that both parties put their names to it. To be properly executed, as the Act calls it, the following requirements must be complied with:

(1) the document must be in the prescribed form containing all the prescribed terms and conform to the agreement regulations;
(2) it must contain all the terms of the agreement apart from the implied terms;
(3) it must be legible;
(4) the requirements of ss.62 and 63 about supplying copies[79];
(5) the cancellation provisions of section 64 or the special provisions of s.58 for a consideration period where there is a heritable security[80];

---

[79] See para.9–93.
[80] See para.9–94.

(6) it must be signed in the prescribed manner by the debtor and the creditor or owner.[81]

9–92 The 1983 Regulations require the debtor or hirer to sign within the signature box in the agreement. Where the debtor or creditor is a partnership or unincorporated association the signature may be that of someone signing on its behalf.

Copies of the Agreement

9–93 The debtor or hirer must get at least one copy of an agreement and ss.62 and 63 of the Act have detailed rules about this. If the debtor signs an agreement at the same time as the creditor, a copy of the executed agreement must be given to the debtor then and there. Where an unexecuted agreement is presented to the debtor and he or she signs it but the creditor does not sign at that time, the debtor must then and there be given a copy of the unexecuted agreement. In addition, within seven days of the agreement being signed by the creditor a further copy must be sent. Where an agreement is sent to the debtor a copy must also accompany it. If the agreement has already been signed by the creditor and so becomes an executed agreement on the debtor signing it, no further copy need be sent. If, however, the creditor has not signed it at that stage a copy of the executed agreement must be sent within seven days of being signed by the creditor. Copies of credit token agreements need not be given within seven days of being made as long as they are given before, or at the same time as, the credit token is given to the debtor.[82]

Special rules for cancellable agreements

9–94 In the case of cancellable agreements[83] these rules are modified. A copy of a cancellable agreement must contain a notice in the form prescribed by the 1983 Regulations,[84] drawing attention to the right to cancel and saying how and when it may be exercised as well as the name and address of a person to whom notice may be given. As we have seen, in some cases a second copy of an agreement must be sent. In the case of a cancellable agreement it must be sent by post.[85] Where a second copy

---

[81] Requirements 1–3 and 6 are found in s.61.

[82] See s.63(4). Because of the practical difficulties in some cases of complying with the requirements about copies Consumer Credit (Cancellation Notices and Copies of Documents) Regulations 1983 (SI 1983/1557) derogate from the full rigour of the copies rules. They also prescribe the form and content of documents to be issued as executed copies.

[83] For discussion of cancellable agreements, see paras 9–103—9–116.

[84] See s.64(1)(a) and Consumer Credit (Cancellation Notices and Copies of Documents) Regulations 1983 (SI 1983/1557).

[85] s.63(3).

of an agreement is not required a notice containing the information about cancellation must be sent by post.

Consequences of Improper Execution

Where an agreement has not been properly executed it can, at best, only **9–95** be enforced against a creditor or hirer by an order of the sheriff court.[86] In some circumstances it cannot be enforced at all. There is a dramatic example of such a situation in *Wilson v First County Trust Ltd*.[87] The defendant pawnbroker lent the claimant borrower a sum of money for six months on the security of her car. The agreement was a regulated agreement and was not properly executed unless the document signed contained all the prescribed terms one of which was the amount of the credit. The English Court of Appeal[88] held that the agreement did not contain the amount of the credit and was accordingly unenforceable with the result that the borrower was entitled to keep the amount of her loan, pay no interest and recover her car.

The Court of Appeal subsequently made a declaration under s.4 of the **9–96** Human Rights Act 1998 that s.127(3) of the 1974 Act was incompatible with two of the rights guaranteed to the pawnbroker by the European Convention for the Protection of Human Rights and Fundamental Freedoms 1950.[89] This decision was overturned by the House of Lords[90] who found that s.127(3) was a proportionate response to a perceived social problem. Lord Nicholls noted:

> "[M]oney lending transactions as a class give rise to significant social problems. Bargaining power lies with the lender, and the social evils flowing from this are notorious. The activities of some lenders have long given the business of money lending a bad reputation. Nor, becoming more specific, do I have any difficulty in accepting, in principle, that Parliament may properly make compliance with the formalities required by the Consumer Credit Act regarding 'prescribed terms' an essential prerequisite to enforcement. In principle that course must be open to Parliament. It must be open to Parliament to decide that, severe though this sanction may be, it is an appropriate way of protecting consumers as a matter of social policy. In making its decision in the present case Parliament had the benefit of experience gained over many years in the working of the Moneylenders Act 1927 and the hire purchase legislation, and also the views of the Crowther committee."[91]

---

[86] s.65(1).
[87] [2003] UKHL 40; [2003] 4 All E.R. 97.
[88] [2001] Q.B. 407 at 417; [2001] 2 W.L.R. 302.
[89] *Wilson v First County Trust Ltd (No.2)* [2002] Q.B. 74; [2001] EWCA Civ 633; [2001] 3 W.L.R. 42; [2001] 3 All E.R. 229.
[90] [2003] UKHL 40; [2003] 3 W.L.R. 568; [2003] 4 All E.R. 97.
[91] *ibid.*, para.75.

9–97   Where an agreement is improperly executed because requirement 1 (document to be in the prescribed form) is not complied with the agreement cannot be enforced even with a court order according to s.127(3). However, the severity of this provision is qualified and the sheriff has power to order enforcement of the agreement even though there has been a failure to comply with the 1983 Regulations. This is the case if the signed document contains all the prescribed terms that should have been in the agreement and has been signed, albeit not necessarily in the manner set out in the Regulations.

9–98   In the case of a cancellable agreement, if the requirements of ss.62 and 63 of the Act about the provision of copies have not been complied with no enforcement order is possible unless the creditor supplies a copy of the executed agreement before legal proceedings are commenced. Providing the debtor or hirer with a copy at this time, of course, gives them the right to cancel.[92] If the creditor or hirer has omitted to give notice of the right to cancel a cancellable agreement, as required by s.64, the omission is regarded as so serious that there can be no enforcement of the agreement in any circumstances.[93]

WITHDRAWAL AND CANCELLATION

Withdrawal

9–99 It is a general principle of contract law that an offer may be revoked prior to acceptance. There is such an opportunity in the context of a consumer credit agreement where the debtor signs the agreement before the creditor or owner signs it. At this point there is an offer by the prospective debtor which has yet to be accepted by the creditor. The consumer, therefore, has an opportunity to withdraw from the agreement.

9–100   The Act clarifies how this may be done. Section 57 provides that no special form of wording is required; all that is required is that it "indicates the intention of the [consumer] to withdraw from a prospective regulated agreement"[94] The notice of withdrawal can be written or oral. The same section also sets out the list of persons to whom such a notice can be given. Notice can, of course, be given to the creditor or hirer, but, in addition, it can be given to others who are deemed to be agents of the creditor or hirer. A credit-broker or supplier who is the negotiator in antecedent negotiations is deemed to be such an agent. Surprisingly, perhaps, so is any person who, in the course of a business carried on by him, acts on behalf of the debtor or hirer in any negotiations for the agreement. This means that if, for example, a solicitor was carrying on negotiations on behalf of a client it would be

---

[92] s.127(4)(a).
[93] s.127(4)(b).
[94] s.57(2).

sufficient for the client to give notice of withdrawal to his own solicitor.[95]

Withdrawal has the same effect as cancellation and is discussed **9–101** below.[96]

Cancellation

In some circumstances someone who has entered into a consumer credit **9–102** or hire agreement may cancel it. The period during which an agreement may be cancelled is popularly known as the "cooling off" period. The reasons for such protection in the context of the Hire-Purchase Acts, which is where it was first introduced, are succinctly set out by Professor Goode:

> "It was aimed primarily at the doorstep salesman who, taking advantage of the unsuspecting housewife, would there and then sign her up . . . to an onerous agreement for goods she might not be able to afford, frequently inducing her entry into the agreement by oral misrepresentations of various kinds, secure in the knowledge that no-one else was present to overhear him and that the organisation he represented would rely on the agreement to disclaim any responsibility for his statements."[97]

The present cancellation provisions apply to a much wider range of **9–103** agreements than the Hire-Purchase Acts rules did. They are set out in ss.67 to 73 of the 1974 Act.

A regulated consumer credit or hire agreement may be cancelled if **9–104** two conditions are met. First, oral representations by an individual acting as, or on behalf of, the negotiator must have been made in the presence of the debtor or hirer during the course of antecedent negotiations. In addition, the subsequent agreement must not have been signed by the debtor or hirer at trade premises of either the creditor or owner, or the negotiator, or any party to a linked transaction (other than the debtor or hirer or a relative of his). While it is often said that the cancellation provisions apply to doorstep sales it should be noted that they can apply in other circumstances. If, for example, the consumer discusses the proposed transaction at a shop or in the offices of a finance company but takes the agreement away and signs it at home it will be cancellable.

The "cooling-off" period begins when the debtor or hirer signs the **9–105** unexecuted agreement. It ends five days after the second statutory notice or copy is received by the debtor or hirer. To exercise the right to cancel

---

[95] s.175 provides that the deemed agent is under a contractual duty to the creditor or owner to transmit the notice to him forthwith.

[96] See paras 9–110—9–112.

[97] R.M. Goode, *Introduction to the Consumer Credit Act 1974* (Butterworths, London, 1974), p.196.

a notice must be served within the cancellation period on one of a number of people. This notice, unlike a notice that one is withdrawing from a prospective agreement, must be in writing. However, it need not be in any particular form. It is sufficient if it "indicates the intention of the debtor or hirer to withdraw from the agreement".[98] If it is posted it is deemed to be served on the recipient at the time of posting, whether or not it ever arrives.[99]

9–106 The notice can be given to any one of several people. These are the same people to whom an intention to withdraw from a prospective agreement may be sent,[1] as well as anyone specified in the statutory cancellation notice.[2]

9–107 The effect of a notice of cancellation is to cancel the agreement and any linked transaction; and to withdraw any offer by the debtor or hirer, or a relative, to enter into a linked transaction.[3] To this there are some exceptions. Where the agreement is a debtor-creditor-supplier agreement for restricted-use credit to finance the doing of work or the supply of goods to meet an emergency it cannot be cancelled. If the same sort of agreement is used to finance the supply of goods which have been incorporated in land or something else before service of the notice of cancellation it cannot be cancelled.[4]

9–108 Section 71 makes clear that where an agreement other than a debtor-creditor-supplier agreement for restricted-use credit is cancelled it still remains alive for the purposes of repayment of credit and the payment of interest. This provision would be important where the credit under a personal loan had been advanced before the end of the cooling-off period. It would be inequitable if the consumer could simply keep the loan. While s.71 prevents this, its other provisions are likely to discourage lenders from advancing loans early as there are considerable disadvantages from their point of view.

9–109 Some linked transactions also survive the cancellation of an agreement. These are insurance contracts, guarantees, and deposit and current accounts.[5]

Consequences of cancellation

9–110 The debtor or hirer can recover any sum paid under the agreement or linked transaction except for the first £5 of any fee or commission charged by a credit-broker. Any sum payable by the debtor or hirer or

---

[98] s.69(1).
[99] s.69(7).
[1] See para.9–100.
[2] s.69(1).
[3] See para.9–29.
[4] s.70(2).
[5] Consumer Credit (Linked Transactions) (Exemptions) Regulations 1983 (SI 1983/1560). Insurance contracts might be cancellable under Insurance Companies Act 1982.

his relative under the agreement ceases to be payable. For any sum repayable the consumer has a lien on any goods in his possession under the cancelled agreement.[6]

Should the consumer have acquired goods under a restricted use **9–111** debtor-creditor-supplier agreement which is subsequently cancelled, they must be restored to the person from whom they were obtained. All that is required of consumers is that they should, if they receive a written request, hand them over at their own premises. While the goods are in their possession they must take reasonable care of them. This obligation does not apply to perishable or consumable goods which are consumed prior to cancellation. In this case the consumer will receive a windfall.[7]

Should goods have been given in part exchange, the debtor or hirer is **9–112** entitled to their return in substantially the same condition as when they were given. This must be done within 10 days of cancellation by the consumer, otherwise the debtor or hirer is entitled to a sum equal to the part-exchange allowance.[8]

Certain conveyancing transactions

Because of the conveyancing difficulties that would arise, the cancella- **9–113** tion provisions do not apply to agreements secured on heritable property. Instead there is a "consideration period" during which the consumer can reflect on the wisdom of the proposed transaction and, if he or she has second thoughts, withdraw from it. The way that this works is that the creditor or hirer must, at least seven days before sending an agreement for signature, send a copy. With this copy must be sent a notice in the prescribed form indicating the consumer's right to withdraw and saying how and when the right may be exercised. During the period for consideration the creditor must not approach the consumer in any way except in response to a specific request from the consumer.[9]

This consideration period does not apply in two situations.[10] The first **9–114** is where the agreement is a restricted-use credit agreement to finance the purchase of the heritable property which is the subject of the security. The other is where the agreement is for a bridging loan in connection with the purchase of the land subject to the security, or other land. The reason for this is that in both these situations speed may be of the essence if the deal is not to fall through.

---

[6] s.70.
[7] s.72.
[8] s.73.
[9] ss.58, 61(2).
[10] s.58(2).

Implied Terms

9–115 In a credit transaction there will be terms relating to the credit and others relating to the goods or services supplied. We will first look at the latter. This leads to discussion of terms relating to the quality of the goods or services, the title of the supplier and the date of delivery. In all credit transactions there will be implied terms relating to such matters. The source of these terms will depend on the type of contract concerned. In many credit transactions the goods will be supplied under a contract of sale and the implied terms will be those to be found in ss.12–14 of the Sale of Goods Act 1979. This is so in the case of conditional sale, credit sale and the supply of goods paid for by means of a credit card. In the case of hire-purchase the implied terms are almost exactly the same but they are to be found in ss.8–11 of the Supply of Goods (Implied Terms) Act 1973 as redrafted by the Consumer Credit Act 1974. The exact wording is to be found in Sch.4, para.35. As these terms are so similar to those in the Sale of Goods Act 1979 reference should be made to the discussion in Ch.5. The ability of a trader to exclude these terms is restricted and this is discussed in Ch.10.

9–116 As a result of the insertion in the Supply of Goods and Services Act 1982 of a Part 1A applying to Scotland[11] there are now statutory implied terms for hire. These are set out in ss.11H–11K. They are very similar to those in contracts of sale and other contracts for the supply of goods.[12]

Connected Lender Liability

9–117 While the use of implied terms in credit transactions is nothing new, there is a novel provision relating to the liability of those involved in such transactions. In certain circumstances, the consumer has a claim not only against the supplier of the goods or service but also the provider of the credit. Section 75(1) of the 1974 Act provides:

> "If the debtor under a debtor-creditor-supplier agreement falling within section 12(b) or (c) has, in relation to a transaction financed by the agreement, any claim against the supplier in respect of a misrepresentation or breach of contract, he shall have a like claim against the creditor, who, with the supplier, shall accordingly be jointly and severally liable to the debtor."

9–118 This is what is commonly known as "connected lender liability" and it has considerable advantages for consumers where it applies. For s.75 to apply four conditions must be met:

---

[11] By Sale and Supply of Goods Act 1994, s.6 and Sch.1.
[12] For discussion, see Ch.4.

(1) the cash price of the goods or service being supplied must exceed £100 but not be more than £30,000 (including VAT);
(2) there must be a debtor-creditor-supplier agreement regulated by the Act, *i.e.* an agreement where credit of not more than £25,000 is advanced to an individual and which is not exempt under the Act;
(3) the provider of the credit is in the business of giving credit and the credit agreement is made in the course of that business; and
(4) the credit is advanced under pre-existing arrangements, or in contemplation of future arrangements, between the provider of credit and the supplier.

One of the most common situations where connected lender liability **9–119** applies is a credit card transaction such as Access or Visa. It would also apply where a consumer wished to buy a car from a motor dealer and the dealer arranged finance with a finance company with whom he had pre-existing arrangements. It would not apply where the consumer wished to buy the car and went to his bank and arranged a personal loan, even where the bank was aware that the loan was specifically for the purchase of the car. In this case the credit is not advanced under pre-existing arrangements between the supplier and the bank and there is not a debtor-creditor-supplier agreement. It should also be noted that debit cards provided with current accounts are not within this protection, nor are payment cards like Diners Club or American Express where credit must be paid off at the end of each month.

Section 75 has no relevance to hire-purchase, conditional sale or **9–120** credit sale agreements, despite the comments of the judge in *Porter v General Guarantee Corp.*[13] in relation to a hire-purchase agreement. This is because of the way in which such agreements are structured. The dealer sells the goods to the finance company which then supplies them to the consumer. Any claim for breach of the supply contract must be against the finance company which is both creditor and supplier as far as the consumer is concerned.

There has been practically no litigation on this section. An OFT **9–121** report says that there have been no reported or unreported cases in the English High Court.[14] The only reported case seems to be the sheriff court decision in *United Dominions Trust Ltd v Taylor.*[15] In that case Mr Taylor had purchased a second-hand car from a dealer in Glasgow. The purchase was financed through a loan from the defenders which had been arranged by the dealer who had arrangements for this purpose. This was, therefore, the kind of transaction to which s.75 could apply.

---

[13] [1982] R.T.R. 384.
[14] See *Connected Lender Liability: A review by the Director-General of Fair Trading of section 75 of the Consumer Credit Act 1974* (OFT, Mar. 1994), p.11.
[15] 1980 S.L.T. (Sh. Ct.) 28. Followed in *Forward Trust v Hornby*, 1995 S.C.L.R. 574.

The car proved to be so unsatisfactory that after several months Mr Taylor sought to rescind the contract of sale. He also stopped making payments to the finance company and, when sued, invoked s.75. He argued that because the dealer had made misrepresentations to him about the condition of the car he had an action for rescission against the dealer. By virtue of s.75 he said that he had a like claim against the finance company, *i.e.* a claim to rescind the loan contract. This the sheriff principal accepted.

9–122 The case has been the subject of considerable academic criticism and is generally thought to have been wrongly decided.[16] The sheriff principal relied on the policy of the Act and the wording of s.75 to justify his decision. Both, it is submitted, are weak arguments. The policy argument that credit and supply contracts that are linked stand or fall together is simply not consistently applied throughout the Act. The policy of the section is to make the creditor vicariously liable for the actions of the supplier. Where the debtor has a claim against the supplier, say for breach of the implied term about satisfactory quality, he or she may assert it against either the supplier or the creditor. The argument on the language of the section would seem to point that way too. The use of the word "claim" suggests a monetary claim rather than a right of rescission.

9–123 Ironically, in this case, had Mr Taylor been better advised and a better case presented to the sheriff principal, the same result could have been achieved by a legally correct route. It is not clear why Mr Taylor did not invoke s.56.

9–124 While, in Mr Taylor's situation, s.56 would have allowed him to escape from the credit transaction, it will not work in some other cases. However, someone in the predicament in which Mr Taylor found himself may well not wish to continue with the loan. If it is accepted that *United Dominions Trust Ltd v Taylor*[17] is wrongly decided is there another solution? It is suggested that there is. A court might accept that the credit contract was void for frustration, though there must be some doubt about this.[18] Alternatively, the debtor might invoke the early repayment provisions of the Act. They provide only a partial solution because the rebate takes into account the setting-up charges involved in credit transactions and the debtor will still be out of pocket. The part of the loan which the debtor cannot recover through the early repayment provisions could be regarded as loss flowing directly from the supplier's breach of contract. This could be included in a claim against the supplier or against the creditor as part of a s.75 claim.

---

[16] For a comment by a Scottish commentator, see Davidson, "The Missing Linked Transaction" (1980) 96 L.Q.R. 343. Other criticisms are to be found in 1981 J.B.L. 179, and E. Lomincka and P. Dobson, *Encyclopaedia of Consumer Credit Law* (Sweet and Maxwell, London), p.2074/3.

[17] 1980 S.L.T. (Sh. Ct.) 28.

[18] See 1981 J.B.L. 179.

While creditors are liable under s.75 it should be noted that they are **9–125** entitled to be indemnified by suppliers for any liability incurred. They can, and this is the policy of s.75, protect themselves by ensuring that dealers with whom they enter into arrangements are reputable.

In relation to s.75 liability there are some grey areas, mostly in **9–126** relation to credit card transactions. Credit card companies take the view that it does not apply where the card was first taken out prior to July 1977, the date when the section came into force. However, they voluntarily accept s.75 liability in such cases but limit it to the amount of the transaction charged to the cardholder's account. They also argue, but with much less plausibility, that transactions by authorised users are not covered by s.75 and that in some situations payments for travel and package holidays are not covered.[19]

Some credit granters take the view that s.75 liability is unfair to them, **9–127** and during the review of it conducted by the Director-General of Fair Trading lobbied hard to persuade him to restrict it.[20] In a 1994 report he observed that "connected lender liability is, and remains, an important consumer protection measure that has proved its worth over the years. It is an integral part of the safeguards for consumers built into the Act".[21] However, in a second report issued in 1995, he recommended that in credit card transactions liability should be limited to the amount charged to the card in respect of the purchase in question.[22]

INFORMATION REMEDIES

As part of the policy of ensuring that consumers have appropriate **9–128** information, the Act provides in ss.77 and 78 that they have the right to obtain information from the creditor about such matters as the amount already paid and the amount owing. To supplement the early repayment provisions in ss.94 and 95, s.97 obliges the creditor to inform consumers of the amount required to settle their accounts. Those hiring goods have similar rights under s.79. Those who have agreed to act as sureties are entitled, on payment of a fee, to similar information.[23]

NOTICE ABOUT CERTAIN ACTIONS

Agreements will often allow creditors to demand early repayment, **9–129** recover possession of goods or land, or treat any right under the agreement as terminated. Such action cannot be taken without giving the

---

[19] For arguments against the views of the credit card companies, see *Connected Lender Liability: A review by the Director-General of Fair Trading of section 75 of the Consumer Credit Act 1974* (OFT, Mar. 1994), pp.28–31. Litigation to clarify this issue is pending in the English High Court.

[20] *ibid.*

[21] *ibid.*, p.33.

[22] *Connected Lender Liability: A second report by the Director-General of Fair Trading on section 75 of the Fair Trading Act 1975* (OFT, May 1995).

[23] See ss.107–109.

consumer at least seven days' notice in an approved form.[24] Debtors must be given at least seven days' notice of variations of agreements before they can become effective.[25]

Appropriations of Payments

9–130 A debtor who has more than one agreement with a creditor may not be able to make a payment which discharges the total sum due under the agreements. Section 81 provides that each agreement should be credited with that proportion of the payment which each sum due bears to the whole sum due under the various agreements. For example, suppose that there are two agreements under which £100 and £50 are due and the debtor can only afford to pay a total of £90. £60 will be appropriated to the agreement under which £100 was due and £30 to that under which £50 was due.

Liability of Credit Card Holders

9–131 Unless the card has been used with the consent of the cardholder, the maximum liability of the cardholder is £50. However, if someone has acquired the card with the consent of the cardholder there is no limit on liability. Once the cardholder has given notice of loss or misuse there is no further liability. Notice is effective when received. If given orally the credit token agreement can stipulate that it is not effective unless confirmed in writing within seven days.[26]

TERMINATION AND DEFAULT

9–132 In this section we are, with the possible exception of the early settlement rules, dealing with cases where consumers have run into financial difficulties. In such a situation they are particularly vulnerable and the policy of the law is to provide a measure of protection against the worst excesses of some elements of the credit industry. As a practical point, it may be said in passing that consumers encountering difficulties are well advised to seek help sooner rather than later. Generally speaking, creditors are willing to be accommodating where, as is usually the case, the difficulties stem from some unexpected cause such as domestic problems, unemployment or illness.

Termination

9–133 At this point termination is being considered in the sense of the statutory right of the debtor or hirer voluntarily to bring the agreement to an end.

---

[24] s.76 and Consumer Credit (Enforcement, Default and Termination Notices) Regulations 1983 (SI 1983/1561), amended by SI 1984/1109.
[25] s.82 and Consumer Credit (Notice of Variation of Agreements) Regulations 1977 (SI 1977/328), amended by SI 1979/661 and 667.
[26] s.84(5).

Later, we shall be discussing the circumstances surrounding termination by the creditor or hirer.[27]

As a response to financial difficulties, termination, using the rights **9–134** given in ss.99 to 101 of the Act will rarely be in the consumer's interests. However, the facility is available.

Regulated hire-purchase and conditional sale agreements may be **9–135** terminated by the debtor at any time before the final payment falls due by giving notice to anyone who is entitled to receive payments under the agreement. To this right there are two exceptions, both relating to conditional sale agreements. Such an agreement relating to land, title to which has passed to the buyer, or one relating to goods where the property has vested in the debtor who has transferred the goods to someone else, cannot be terminated.

Termination only operates for the future. Section 99(2) makes clear **9–136** that liability which has accrued prior to termination is not affected. On termination the debtor must pay the difference between what has been paid and half the total price of the goods. In making this calculation any installation charge is deducted first and the whole of that charge added as it is clearly reasonable that such a charge should be payable. It is possible that the amount due could be less if it can be shown that the creditor's loss is less.

In the case of a consumer hire agreement there is also a right to **9–137** terminate, but the earliest time at which this can occur is 18 months after the making of the agreement. Notice of not less than the shorter of the shortest payment interval or three months must be given. Because early termination can cause hardship to the owner there are three circumstances in which the right is not available. These are: where the total payments, ignoring sums payable on breach, exceed £1,000 in any year; where the goods are let out for the hirer's business and were selected by him and acquired by the owner at his request from a third party; and, finally, where the hirer requires the goods to re-let them in the course of business.

EARLY SETTLEMENT

At any time during a regulated consumer credit agreement the debtor **9–138** may give notice to the creditor of an intention to complete payments early.[28] This is only economic if there is a rebate on the total charge for credit and regulations prescribe how this is to be calculated.[29] These provisions, including the calculation formula known as "the rule of 78" are not always operated in a way that is fair to the borrower. In addition, as research[30] has shown, many consumers are unaware of the charges

---

[27] See para.9–139 *et seq.*
[28] s.94.
[29] See Consumer Credit (Rebate on Early Settlement) Regulations 1983 (SI 1983/1562), amended by SI 1989/596.
[30] *Consumer Credit Awareness Survey* (DTI, 2003).

made when they pay off early. As a result the White Paper[31] announced that legislation would be introduced abolishing the rule of 78 and introducing a new actuarial method to calculate the early resettlement figure as well as measures to ensure that consumers are aware of the costs associated with early repayment.[32]

<h3 style="text-align:center">DEFAULT</h3>

9–139 Where the debtor is in default of the obligations under a regulated consumer credit or hire agreement the Act provides various protections. We have already seen that before a creditor can take action against a debtor a default notice must be served specifying the breach and what action needs to be taken to remedy it. If it is not capable of remedy the amount of compensation required and the date by which this must be paid has to be stated. *Eshun v Moorgate Mercantile Co Ltd*[33] is an example of the result of failure to comply with the similar provisions of the Hire-Purchase Act 1965. The defendant finance company was ordered to pay compensation to the debtor for the loss caused by terminating his agreement.

9–140 A remedy which is open at common law to creditors in the case of hire-purchase and conditional sale is repossession of the goods. Under these agreements the consumer does not acquire title to the goods initially and it is usual for agreements to provide that there shall be this right in case of default. This can operate very harshly where the consumer has paid a substantial proportion of the price, and in the past some creditors abused their rights. As a result, "snatch back" provisions were enacted in the Hire-Purchase Act 1938. Similar provisions are now found in ss.90 and 91 of the 1974 Act.

9–141 Under these provisions, if the debtor has paid one third or more of the total price of the goods, and the property in the goods remains in the creditor, the goods are known as "protected goods". This means that the creditor is not entitled to recover possession from the debtor except on an order of the sheriff court. Where an installation charge is part of the total price the amount relevant for deciding whether the goods are protected is calculated by adding the installation charge to one third of the remainder of the total price. It is not possible for a creditor to circumvent this protection by making a fresh agreement which includes goods additional to those which were protected under an earlier agreement, or by modifying an agreement.[34]

---

[31] *Fair, Clear and Competitive*, Cm 6040 (2003), para.2.46.
[32] *ibid.*, paras 2.46–2.52. The new regulations, SI 2004/1483, come into force on May 31, 2005.
[33] [1971] 1 W.L.R. 722; [1971] 2 All E.R. 402.
[34] ss.90(3), (4).

This protection also applies where the debtor has died. In this case the **9–142** person in possession of the goods benefits initially from the protection and, after confirmation has been granted, the executor.[35]

The protected goods provision only applies where the goods have **9–143** been recovered "from the debtor". This includes anyone to whom the debtor has entrusted the goods, such as a garage in which a car has been left for repair, or someone to whom the goods have been lent. However, if the goods have been abandoned the restrictions on repossession do not apply. This is illustrated by *Bentinck Ltd v Cromwell Engineering*[36] where the debtor had obtained a car on hire-purchase. After the car had become protected goods he defaulted on the repayments and the car was seriously damaged in an accident. Following the accident the debtor took the car to a garage and then disappeared and could not be traced. The hire-purchase company did manage to trace the car, which by then had been at the garage for some months, and repossessed it. In this action against the defendants, who had agreed to act as sureties, it was held that there was such clear evidence of an intention to renounce all rights to the goods that the equivalent of s.90 did not apply.

Protected goods may be repossessed without a court order if the **9–144** debtor consents. The cases show that the courts will wish to be satisfied that the consent is a genuine and informed consent. In *Chartered Trust v Pitcher*[37] the debtor, having lost his job, telephoned the hire-purchase company to say that he could not keep up the payments on his car and was advised to write to them asking them to repossess the car. The letter that he wrote clearly showed that he did not want to do this and that he was hoping that some other solution might be possible. Without telling him that the car was protected goods, and that on an application to repossess the court might reschedule the payments, the car was repossessed. It was held that this was in breach of what is now s.90.[38]

Where the debtor does not choose to hand over the goods it is **9–145** arguable that in Scotland it is always necessary to obtain a court order to recover them. This is certainly the case where the goods are on someone's premises whether or not they are protected goods. Section 92(1) of the Act provides: "Except under an order of the court, the creditor or owner shall not be entitled to enter any premises to take possession of goods subject to a regulated hire-purchase agreement, regulated conditional sale agreement or regulated consumer hire agreement."

---

[35] s.90(6).
[36] [1971] 1 Q.B. 324.
[37] [1988] R.T.R. 72.
[38] The facts of this case are less likely to recur now as the statutory default notice must give more detailed information about a debtor's rights than was the case at the time of this case or the harsh and unrealistic decision in *Mercantile Credit Co Ltd v Cross* [1965] 2 Q.B. 205.

9–146   Section 173 provides that this provision cannot be overridden by anything in the agreement between the debtor and the creditor.[39]

9–147   This leaves the question of the creditor's right to repossess goods which are not on "premises". In practice this means repossessing goods found in the street or a public road and will apply mainly to cars, motorcycles, caravans and the like. Before there can be any question of repossession the debtor must be in breach of an agreement which has a term allowing the creditor in those circumstances to repossess the goods (which invariably agreements do have). The creditor must also have served a default notice (as required by s.87) which has expired.

9–148   The reason that it is suggested that it is never possible to repossess goods under Scots law is that the policy of the law is against such a self help remedy as the nineteenth century institutional writer, Professor Bell, explained:

> "Possession attempted to be acquired by force may be resisted by force; but possession, being once obtained in this way, must be reclaimed by the true creditor judicially; the party who has ceased to possess being bound to trust to the protection of the law for restitution, and not to the strength of his own arm."[40]

9–149   If this is the case where possession has been obtained by force how much more powerful where possession has initially been obtained perfectly legally under a hire-purchase or conditional sale agreement. Professor Walker expresses similar views,[41] though he would allow more latitude to those recovering property.[42] Nevertheless he points out that the repossession must be carried out without committing trespass, assault or any other wrong. This will often be quite difficult to achieve if, for example, the hirer is in the vicinity. In short, Professor Gow's observation[43] that "it seems that the owner who resorts to self help acts at his peril" has still much to commend it. The parliamentary draftsman also thinks so to judge by the statement in the notice required by para.7 of Sch.2 to the Consumer Credit (Enforcement, Default and Termination Notices) Regulations 1983.[44] After pointing out that protected goods can only be recovered by the creditor against the wishes of the debtor by means of a court order it adds "[i]n Scotland he may need to get a court order at any time".

JUDICIAL CONTROL

9–150 As part of the policy of trying to provide adequate protection for those involved in credit transactions, the Consumer Credit Act 1974 gives

---

[39] If the goods are on someone else's premises, *e.g.* a garage, it would appear that the consent needed is that of the owner of those premises.

[40] *Dictionary and Digest of the Law of Scotland* (7th ed., Edinburgh, 1890), p.826.

[41] D.M. Walker, *Civil Remedies* (W. Green, Edinburgh, 1974), p.39.

[42] *ibid.*, pp.263, 264.

[43] J. J. Gow, *The Law of Hire Purchase* (2nd ed., W. Green, Edinburgh, 1968).

[44] SI 1983/1561.

wide powers to the sheriff court in relation to credit agreements. Such powers do, of course, suffer from the inherent disadvantage of private law remedies that consumers must take some action. It is well known that consumers rarely invoke these protections and as a result the White Paper announced the Government's intention to consult on the possibility of creating an alternative dispute resolution (ADR) procedure for dealing with consumer credit disputes.[45]

Before considering the various ways in which the courts can regulate **9–151** agreements it is worth noting the rules about jurisdiction. We have already seen that actions relating to consumer credit agreements must be brought in the sheriff court. This is an advantage for consumers in that expenses in that court are lower than in the Court of Session. In addition, the jurisdiction rules assist the consumer in that actions relating to the enforcement of such agreements, and most other actions relating to them, must be brought in the sheriff court of the place where the debtor is domiciled or carries on business.[46] However, if the purpose of the action is to determine proprietary or possessory rights or security rights over moveable property, the action may be brought in the sheriff court of the place where the property is located.[47]

ENFORCEMENT ORDERS

We have already seen that in certain circumstances an agreement can **9–152** only be enforced by means of a court order. Indeed, in the case of a cancellable agreement, if the rules about supplying copies have not been complied with there is no possibility of enforcing, even by means of a court order. This is also the case where the agreement has not been properly executed. However, enforcement is still possible if all the prescribed terms have been set out in a document even if the statutory formalities have not been complied with.

Where an application has to be made to the sheriff s.127(1) of the Act **9–153** provides that it must be dismissed only if the sheriff considers that it is just to do so taking into account two sets of circumstances. First, account must be taken of the prejudice caused to any person by the contravention, and the degree of culpability for it. In addition, the powers which the court has under ss.135 and 136 must also be taken into account. These give wide powers to vary agreements; and the implication of referring to them in this context is that, by using them, it may be possible to remove any disadvantageous aspects of an agreement by their use.

---

[45] *Fair, Clear and Competitive*, Cm. 6040 (2003), at para.3.46. See also consultation paper, *The Provision of Alternative Dispute Resolution for Disputes arising under the Consumer Credit Act 1974* (DTI, Dec. 2003).
[46] ss.141(3A)(a), (b), which were added by Civil Jurisdiction and Judgments Act 1982, Sch.12, Pt 2, para.4.
[47] s.141(3A)(c).

TIME ORDERS

9–154 Section 129 of the Act gives wide powers to the sheriff to make time orders. These are orders which permit the sheriff to adjust the rate and time of payments of installments by debtors, hirers or sureties. In addition, they can be used to specify the time within which a breach of an agreement, other than non-payment of money, should be rectified.

9–155 A time order may be made in a variety of circumstances. It is possible where there has been an application for an enforcement order or in any other action to enforce a regulated agreement or a security, or to recover possession of goods or heritable property to which an agreement relates. Debtors or hirers can apply for a time order where default notices have been served on them.

9–156 In deciding on the making of a time order the sheriff must consider whether it is just to do so taking into account whether the sum suggested is reasonable, having regard to the means of the debtor, hirer or surety. Section 130 deals with the situation where the debtor has made an offer to pay installments which has been accepted by the creditor. In such a case a time order may be made without hearing evidence of means. In the case of hire purchase and conditional sale agreements only, time orders dealing with installments may deal with sums not yet due.[48] Sheriff Fitzsimmons has held that wide as these powers are they do not extend to varying the rate of interest.[49] In England, the Court of Appeal has held in *Southern and District Finance plc v Barnes*[50] that this is possible under s.136 and approved of the decision of a county court judge who used this power.

FINANCIAL RELIEF FOR HIRERS

9–157 Those who hire goods do not have the benefit of the protected goods rule which applies only to hire-purchase and conditional sale agreements. Prior to the 1974 Act they could find themselves in a particularly difficult and unfair position when they ran into financial difficulties.[51] They might have had use of the goods for only a short time yet, on failure to keep up payments, might become liable to pay substantial sums. Section 132 now provides a solution in this situation. It applies where an owner has recovered possession of goods otherwise than by court action. The hirer may ask the sheriff to order that the whole or part of any sum paid should be repaid, and that the obligation to pay any sums owed should cease.

9–158 The only reported case on s.132 appears to be *Automotive Financial Services Ltd v Henderson.*[52] The defenders had leased a car, the

---

[48] s.130(2).
[49] See *Murie McDougall Ltd v Sinclair*, 1994 SLT (Sh. Ct.) 74; 1994 S.C.L.R. 805.
[50] [1996] 1 F.C.R. 679.
[51] See, *e.g. Galbraith v Mitchenhall Estates Ltd* [1965] 2 Q.B. 473.
[52] 1992 S.L.T. (Sh. Ct.) 63.

purchase price of which was £8,144, from the pursuers. After the agreement had run for six months they got into financial difficulties, stopped making the rental payments, and the pursuers repossessed the car. By this time the defenders had made payments of £2,150 under the lease. The car was sold by the pursuers for £6,000 and they then sued for £3,840 as an amount due under the terms of the agreement. The defenders asked the sheriff principal to exercise his discretion under s.132 but he refused to do so saying:

> "To suggest that somehow the payments made should entitle the defenders to relief seems to me an unlikely proposition unless the defenders can set out a good reason why the pursuers should be satisfied in the commercial sense with what they have received. The defenders have not attempted to do so. Looking at the matter another way they have not even started to suggest that the payment sought is by way of a penalty."[53]

The sheriff principal upheld the decision on appeal saying that this **9–159** was an exercise of discretion based on a proper assessment of relevant materials. He did not think that it was appropriate to use either of the formulae which the defenders had put forward to justify invoking the section's protection. These were to base the operation of s.132 on the interest and administration costs incurred by the lessors during the period during which the defenders had the car; or the monetary value of the depreciation of the car during the same period.

On the facts this seems a suitable case for the exercise of s.132. For **9–160** a car, the purchase price of which was £8,144, the pursuers were found to be entitled to recover just short of £12,000 from the defenders within six months of entering into the agreement. Even allowing for the fact that the pursuers will have incurred various costs this seems excessive. The problem may have been that the sheriff did not feel able to exercise his discretion on the basis of the financial information put before him by the defenders. The moral of this case may be that more sophisticated accounting information should be produced to support an application.

SPECIAL POWERS RELATING TO HIRE PURCHASE AND CONDITIONAL SALE AGREEMENTS

In cases of hire purchase or conditional sale agreements s.133 of the Act **9–161** contains special provisions involving "return orders" and "transfer orders". Such orders may be made where an application for an enforcement order or time order has been made, or where the creditor has brought an action to recover possession of goods. These powers can be exercised together with the power to make a time order or vary an

---

[53] 1992 S.L.T. (Sh. Ct.) 63 at 64.

agreement. The return order is self explanatory, being an order for the return of goods to the creditor.

9–162 A transfer order can only apply where the agreement relates to more than one item of goods. In such a situation an order can be made transferring to the debtor the creditor's title to some of the goods and the return to the creditor of the remainder. Such an order can only be made where the debtor has already paid an amount at least equal to the part of the total price which relates to the goods transferred and one third of the unpaid balance of the total price. The goods transferred shall be "such of the goods to which the agreement relates as the court thinks just".[54]

EXTORTIONATE CREDIT BARGAINS

9–163 One of the most far-reaching powers given to the courts is the power in ss.137–140 of the Act to reopen a credit bargain which it finds to be extortionate so as to do justice between the parties. This power has its origins in the provisions of the Moneylenders Acts but goes much further. Unlike most of the other provisions of the Consumer Credit Act 1974, it applies not only to regulated credit agreements but also to all credit agreements with individuals. This means that a loan of £25,000 to an individual could be challenged on this ground. It does not apply to hire agreements where s.132 may be seen as the nearest parallel.

9–164 It is one of the weaknesses of this part of the Act that s.139(1) provides that a sheriff can reopen a credit bargain on the grounds of extortion only on the application of the debtor or a surety. It was held in *United Dominions Trust v McDowell*[55] that the sheriff cannot do so of his own volition.[56]

9–165 Section 138(1) provides that a credit bargain will be extortionate if either it: "(a) requires the debtor . . . to make payments . . . which are grossly exorbitant, or "(b) otherwise grossly contravenes ordinary principles of fair dealing."

9–166 In making a judgment on these matters sheriffs are to have regard to evidence adduced on prevailing interest rates, the age, experience, business capacity and health of the debtor. They must also take account of the financial pressure that he or she was under at the time the bargain was entered into, as well as any other relevant considerations. From the creditor's point of view the sheriff must consider the degree of risk taken, having regard to any security provided, the relationship to the debtor, and whether or not a colourable cash price was quoted for any goods or services. This latter point is included to prevent a transaction

---

[54] s.133(3).

[55] 1984 S.L.T. (Sh. Ct.) 10.

[56] *Tackling Loan Sharks and More* (DTI, Mar. 2003), a consultation document stated that judicial fears about compromising their impartiality had resulted in ideas about giving judges power of their own motion to reopen agreements being dropped.

being dressed up to seem as if the rate of interest is lower than, in truth, it is by inflating the alleged purchase price.

An important point to note is that dealing with the burden of proof. **9–167** Section 171(7) provides that where a debtor or surety alleges that a bargain is extortionate it is for the creditor to prove the contrary. This can be important, particularly if the matter is finely balanced. It is, of course, necessary for the debtor to produce some sort of evidence to give substance to the allegation, rather in the way that, in a criminal trial where a defence such as provocation is alleged, the accused must produce some evidence to show that there is an issue to discuss.

It is important to note that the test applies to the credit bargain, not **9–168** just a credit agreement. If one or more other transactions are to be taken into account in computing the total charge for credit the test applies to the credit agreement and those other related transactions. These might include various fees such as arrangement fees.

If a sheriff finds that a credit bargain is extortionate there are wide **9–169** powers "for the purpose of relieving the debtor or a surety from payment of any sum in excess of that fairly due and reasonable".[57] The whole, or any part, of any obligation imposed by the credit bargain may be set aside and the creditor may be made to repay the whole, or any part, of a sum paid under the credit bargain or any related agreement by the debtor or a surety. In addition, the sheriff has power to alter the terms of the credit agreement or any security instrument and direct the return to a surety of any property provided as security.

These are potentially draconian powers and it is, perhaps, not **9–170** surprising to find that little use has been made of them. The White Paper on consumer credit[58] notes that they have been raised in only about 30 cases, in only ten of which was the debtor successful. There seems to have been no Scottish case in which a debtor has raised the issue, although there is passing reference to it in two reported cases.[59]

One reason for the small number of cases may be the absence of **9–171** guidance in those that have been reported; and the evidence that they contain that the courts will not easily be persuaded that a bargain is extortionate. There has been some division of opinion on whether the courts should look for guidance to the Moneylenders Acts. In one of the few English High Court decisions, *Ketley v Scott*,[60] it was said that "sections 137–140 are a completely new set of provisions and it is idle to seek guidance from the old Moneylenders Acts of 1900 and 1927 to

---

[57] s.139(2).

[58] *Fair, Clear and Competitive*, Cm. 6040 (2003), para.3.29.

[59] In *Bank of Scotland v Davis*, 1982 S.L.T. 20 there is a reference to the potential relevance of the power; and in *United Dominions Trust v McDowell*, 1984 S.L.T. (Sh. Ct.) 10 the sheriff seems to have decided that the bargain was extortionate. His decision was overruled on appeal on other grounds and the sheriff principal expressed doubt about the correctness of the view that the bargain was extortionate.

[60] [1981] I.C.R. 243.

try to interpret them". However, in a later Court of Appeal decision[61] Russell L.J. notes with apparent approval the view in *Halsbury's Statutes*[62] that "it seems that the word extortionate is to be equated with the words 'harsh and unconscionable'", which appear in the Moneylenders Acts. Neither of these cases is binding on a Scottish court, but it is submitted that *Ketley v Scott* demonstrates the correct approach. If Parliament had intended to use the previous test it would have used the earlier language. In providing new language it must be assumed to have intended to alter the test.

9–172   What factors seem to have been important in the successful cases? In *Barcabe v Edwards*[63] an English county court substituted a flat rate of 40 per cent which would have given an APR of 92 per cent under the original terms of a loan. The debtors had borrowed £400 for the purchase of a car at a flat rate of almost 100 per cent, an APR of 319 per cent. The fact that they had little business capacity, that there was no unusual risk for the lender, and that one of the debtors could not read were taken into account, as was evidence that similar lenders were charging flat rates of 20 per cent.

9–173   In *Devogate v Jarvis*[64] the debtors had borrowed £10,000, on security, to pay off existing debts at an APR of 39 per cent. An APR of 30 per cent was substituted, despite the fact that the original rate was not unusual for the type of loan, the court taking into account the fact that there was security justifying a lower rate. Also relevant was the inequality of bargaining power flowing from the desperate financial circumstances of the debtors. The relatively low risk and the fact that the loan was secured were also important in the judge reducing the flat rate of interest from 42 per cent to 21 per cent in *Prestonwell Ltd v Capon*.[65] The fact that the debtors were under financial pressure, had little business acumen and did not have access to proper legal advice were also relevant. An interesting aspect of this decision is that the judge did not limit comparisons of interest rates to the consolidation loans sector of the market in which it had been obtained.

9–174   Another successful case is *Shahabinia v Giyachi*[66] where loans with flat rates of interest of 78 per cent, 104 per cent and 156 per cent were considered extortionate and reduced to a flat rate of 30 per cent.

9–175   *Falco Finance Ltd v Michael Gough*[67] is one of the few cases where the agreement was found to be extortionate under s.138(1)(b), on the ground that it grossly contravened ordinary principles of fair dealing rather than involving grossly exorbitant payments. This involved a dual

---

[61] *Shahabinia v Giyachi* [1989] G.C.C.R. 1352.
[62] *ibid.*, at 1357.
[63] [1983] C.C.L.R. 11.
[64] 1987, county court, unreported.
[65] 1988, county court, unreported.
[66] See n.61.
[67] (1999) 17 Tr. L.R. 526.

rate mortgage under which the "normal" interest payments of 13.99 per cent (flat rate) were initially discounted to 8.99 per cent, providing every monthly payment was made on time. This concession was lost permanently for the life of the mortgage if any payment was missed or was in any way deficient. The court viewed this as unacceptable as there was no attempt to calculate, in any genuine way, the loss to the company by late payment, or conversely any gain received by prompt payment; the conditions to retain the concession were so harsh that it was almost impossible to comply with them for the whole period; and there was no possibility of reclaiming the concession.

Some guidance can be obtained from unsuccessful cases. The OFT report[68] notes that the highest rate of interest not held to be extortionate has been 48 per cent. One of these was *Ketley v Scott*,[69] where the debtor had business experience and the risk was relatively high. The judge also observed that even if he had found the extortion test had been satisfied he would not have given relief on the ground that this would not have been just between the parties. The reason for this was that the debtor had been deceitful in not disclosing the full extent of his financial commitments and had falsified the value of the house on the security of which the loan was given. **9–176**

While it is not easy from case reports to assess the fairness of decisions it is difficult to dispel the impression that in some cases the courts have been less than realistic and unwilling to make full use of the width of the definition of extortionate. A good example is *Wills v Wood*.[70] An elderly lady with little business experience and no capital, except her cottage, borrowed £3,000 secured on the cottage at 12 per cent. The county court judge found the bargain extortionate on the second limb of the definition, observing that the debtor was in severe financial difficulties with no source of income or capital from which to meet her liabilities. He added that had "she received independent advice I am satisfied she would have been strongly advised against borrowing". The Court of Appeal upheld the creditor's appeal stating that the debtor was of full age and capacity and no "unworldly recluse". It was suggested that she could have sold her cottage to meet her debts. The Master of the Rolls noted that the word was *extortionate*, not *unwise*, and that the situation came nowhere near one in which the court could reopen the bargain. **9–177**

Coldunell Ltd v Gallon[71] is another case the result of which might occasion some surprise. The borrowers were a man of 86 and his wife of 91 who borrowed money on the security of their home which was their only capital asset. The creditor knew that the money was needed to help their son, who promptly ran off with it, and that they had not had **9–178**

[68] Unjust Credit Transactions, 1991.
[69] [1981] I.C.R. 243.
[70] (1984) 128 S.J. 222.
[71] [1986] 1 All E.R. 429, CA.

independent legal advice. In the English Court of Appeal Oliver L.J. said that a creditor could discharge the burden of proof "by showing that the bargain was on its face a proper and not extortionate commercial bargain and that [the creditor] acted in the way that an ordinary commercial lender would be expected to act".[72] In finding that this bargain was not extortionate he added that there was no obligation on the creditor to ensure that the couple had obtained independent legal advice or that the security was executed in the presence of a solicitor.

9–179 In the circumstances it is not surprising that the OFT believes that the extortionate credit provisions have not dealt adequately with the problem of socially harmful lending which the Crowther Report identified.[73] This it believes is because the drafting of the Act is unnecessarily restrictive, or has been interpreted in that way, with undue emphasis on the cost of credit. New forms of lending have emerged into which no sensible person with independent advice would enter but which creditors have induced them to do by exploitation or deception. Another reason is consumer ignorance of the law and a reluctance to resort to the courts because it might jeopardise future access to credit. This is in addition to the various practical, cultural and financial factors which tend to inhibit going to court.

9–180 The OFT recommended sweeping reforms[74] as did the DTI.[75] The White Paper on consumer credit announced the Government's intention to carry out reform though this will occur only "as soon as Parliamentary time is available".[76] The central change will be to widen the definition of extortionate to take account not only of the cost of credit but also the practices of lenders. To quote the White Paper:

> "Legislative factors and guidance from the OFT will give a clear message to businesses, the courts, and, if appropriate, ADR adjudicators in determining the fairness of credit transactions. They will enable account to be taken of relevant practices in the current market and ensure that a balance is struck between the duty of the lender to behave fairly and responsibly and the need for borrowers to provide accurate information, borrow sensibly and take responsibility for their own financial decisions."[77]

9–181 The factors which legislation may include in an assessment of the fairness of an agreement are whether the lender has engaged in practices such as misleading, harassing, coercing or otherwise unduly influencing the borrower. Lenders will also be expected to lend responsibly by

---

[72] [1986] 1 All E.R. 429 at 434, CA.
[73] *Unjust Credit Transactions*, para.4.18.
[74] *ibid.*
[75] Consultation Paper: *Tackling Loan Sharks and More* (DTI, Mar. 2003).
[76] *Fair, Clear and Competitive*, Cm. 6040 (2003), Ch.6, "Implementation Plan".
[77] *ibid.*, para.3.34.

taking steps to ensure a consumer's creditworthiness. Other factors that might be taken into account could be the borrower's circumstances including his or her age, experience, health and the degree to which he or she was under pressure. Whether the borrower has dealt honestly and openly with the lender will be relevant as will the degree of risk accepted by the lender, whether the transaction involves an inflated cash price and whether ancillary transactions such as insurance have reasonably been included.

The White Paper acknowledges that this alone will not be enough and **9–182** that it must be buttressed by better information for consumers to allow them to shop around and to understand what they are committing themselves to. A particularly interesting idea is to protect consumers by extending the provisions of Pt 8 of the Enterprise Act 2002[78] to enable designated organisations to take action on behalf of the collective interests of consumers in relation to credit practices. Codes of conduct have also been identified as having a role to play in effecting changes to practices within the credit industry.

These proposals, as the White Paper acknowledges, are not a **9–183** complete answer to the problem of socially harmful lending. They need to be complemented by enforcement action against illegal money-lending and those who regularly act oppressively against consumers. Better advice and information would also alleviate the problem for consumers. The development of other forms of lending would also be beneficial. Credit unions have not had the success in Scotland (or the United Kingdom as a whole) that they have had, for example, in Ireland or North America. Even the advent of all these measures would still not solve the problems of those most at risk and there is no escape from the conclusion that wider questions of social policy are involved in this issue.

---

[78] For discussion, see Ch.11.

CHAPTER 10

UNFAIR CONTRACT TERMS

INTRODUCTION

10–01 This chapter is concerned with the problem of the fairness of terms found in contracts. It will deal mainly, but not exclusively, with exclusion clauses. Such clauses are often unfair to consumers but other terms of a contract can also be unfair and, as we shall see, to some extent these too can be controlled.

10–02 The problem of exclusion clauses or exemption clauses, as they are also called, is one that has a long history. It is common to find one party to a contract limiting or excluding entirely the legal liability that would otherwise attach. Everyday examples are to be found in any package holiday brochure, car hire contract or a furniture remover's contract. The following are some examples:

(1) All cars parked at the owner's risk.
(2) All photographic materials are accepted on the basis that their value does not exceed the cost of the material itself. Responsibility is limited to the replacement of films. No liability will be accepted, consequential or otherwise, however caused.[1]
(3) In the case of loss or damage the liability of the company is limited to the value of the garment.
(4) All claims must be notified to the company within seven days
(5) Our liability to you in contract law or in tort or delict or otherwise howsoever arising in relation to this contract is limited to £1,000,000 for any one incident or related series of incidents and £2,000,000 for any series of incidents related or unrelated in any period of 12 months.

10–03 Such clauses are frequently found in standard form contracts. These are contracts drawn up by one party setting out the terms on which it will do business. Such contracts are not necessarily objectionable. Indeed, they can be seen as the legal or administrative counterpart of

---

[1] See *Woodman v Photo Trade Processing Ltd*, Exeter County Court, June 20, 1981, unreported.

mass production and marketing. Using such forms cuts out the necessity for detailed negotiation in every transaction and saves time and money. Standard forms and their exclusion clauses work best where both parties know and understand their significance and can take appropriate action to protect themselves against any potential hardship resulting from the other side limiting its liability.

These are conditions which generally do not exist in the typical consumer transaction. How many of us even realise that when we travel by rail, for example, that we are travelling on the rail companies' conditions of carriage which contain exclusion clauses? Even where we do know that there are exclusion clauses in the small print of, say, a car hire contract, how often do we stop to read them. If we did read them would we understand them and would it make any difference? Lord Denning answered that question in his usual forthright way. "The big concern said, 'Take it or leave it.' The little man had no option but to take it." [2]   **10–04**

The underlying approach of the law has been informed by the doctrine of freedom of contract. This fails to take account of the power imbalances in consumer situations, a fact which has been recognised both by the common law and by legislation. How the law has intervened to control the use of exclusion clauses is discussed below under three main headings. First, we consider the role of the common law; then the intervention of the legislature, mainly through the Unfair Contract Terms Act 1977; and finally, the regulations implementing the Unfair Contract Terms Directive [3] are discussed.   **10–05**

COMMON LAW CONTROLS

In controlling exclusion clauses the common law applies two techniques. The first is to consider whether the clause is part of the contract, *i.e.* has it been incorporated into the contract? If so, the second question is: does it cover the situation that has arisen? These techniques are in addition to the various doctrines referred to below under which contracts may be struck down because of some other element of unfairness. The protection of those under the age of 18 whose contracts may be reopened if "prejudicial" is also relevant as is the law on extortionate credit bargains. [4]   **10–06**

INCORPORATION

The parties may have agreed that the exclusion clause is to be part of the contract. The easiest way to demonstrate this is to show that a document   **10–07**

---

[2] *George Mitchell (Chesterhall) Ltd v Finney Lock Seeds Ltd* [1982] 3 W.L.R. 1036 at 1043.
[3] Dir. 93/13; [1993] O.J. L95/29.
[4] See Ch.9.

including that clause has been signed. There can then be no argument, in the absence of fraud or misrepresentation, that the consumer is bound by the agreement. Support for this proposition can be found in *Henderson v Stevenson* where, in a Scottish appeal to the House of Lords, the Lord Chancellor observed that where a document had been signed "there might, indeed, be a question what was the construction of the contract, or how far the contract was valid. But there could be no question whatever that the contract, such as it was, was assented to and entered into by the person who received the ticket".[5]

10–08 A case where this principle did not apply because the effect of the clause had been misrepresented to the consumer is *Curtis v Chemical Cleaning and Dyeing Co.*[6] Staff at a dry cleaners incorrectly assured a customer that a clause exempted the cleaners only for limited kinds of damage when it covered any kind of damage. Fraudulent conduct by the party seeking to rely on the clause would have the same effect. It should be remembered that the concept of fraud in Scots law in relation to the annulment of obligations is wide and, as Professor Smith pointed out, can cover not only what Bell in his *Principles* called "a machination or contrivance to deceive", but also conduct inconsistent with bona fides.[7]

10–09 Quite commonly there is no signed document and the trader relies on an unsigned document such as a railway ticket, a receipt for dry-cleaning or a notice on the premises. The notice or ticket may itself contain the exclusion clause or it may refer, as for example, railway tickets do, to another document. What is the effect of such documents or notices? It must first be shown that the exclusion clause is contained in a contractual document, as *Taylor v Corporation of the City of Glasgow*[8] demonstrates. Mrs Taylor had gone to public baths run by the corporation. On entering she paid for the facility that she wished to use and was given a ticket. On the front were the words "For conditions see other side" and on the reverse were words excluding the corporation's liability for injury caused to users of the baths. As a result of the negligence of the corporation Mrs Taylor sustained serious injuries in a fall. The corporation sought to rely on the exclusion clause on the ticket. The Inner House held that the clause did not protect the corporation because it was not a contractual document. It was merely "a domestic check in the defenders' running of their establishment, the register and the ticket having taken the place of the old-fashioned turnstile. It also performed the function of a receipt . . . this voucher aspect of this

---

5 (1875) 2 R. (H.L.) 71 at 74. The English case of *L'Estrange v Graucob* [1934] 2 K.B. 394 provides an example of the harsh consequences of this rule in operation. It has been argued that the case could have been decided differently.
6 [1951] 1 All E.R. 631.
7 See B. Smith, *A Short Commentary on the Law of Scotland* (W. Green, Edinburgh, 1962), p.833.
8 1952 S.C. 440.

'ticket' was the significant aspect". The court refused to attach the same significance to this kind of ticket as courts have traditionally done to tickets relating to contracts of carriage or deposit.

To be effective the exclusion clause must be brought to the attention **10–10** of the other party before the contract is made. This is the rationale of *Olley v Marlborough Court*[9] where a couple booked and paid for a room on arriving at the reception desk of an hotel. In their room was a notice exempting the hotel from liability for loss of personal belongings. Some of their belongings were stolen from the room and the hotel sought to rely on the exemption clause. It was held by the English Court of Appeal that the guests' contract had been concluded when they booked the room and the notice which they saw subsequently was not part of that contract. This approach was also one reason for the decision in *McCutcheon v MacBrayne*,[10] a Scottish appeal to the House of Lords.

Where the document containing the exclusion clause can be said to be **10–11** contractual in nature it is still necessary to show that the party relying on the clause has done, to quote Lord Dunedin in *Hood v Anchor Line (Henderson Brothers) Ltd*, "what was reasonably sufficient to bring to [the other party's] notice the existence of the condition."[11] It was stated in the same case that what is reasonable notice depends on the facts.

As indicated above, it appears that the courts will be more easily **10–12** satisfied that reasonable notice has been given where contracts of carriage or deposit are concerned. The high point was probably reached in the English case of *Thompson v London Midland & Scottish Ry*,[12] where it was held that an illiterate lady whose niece had bought a ticket for her had been given reasonable notice of a clause by a reference on the ticket to the fact that it was issued subject to the conditions set out in the company's timetable. The conditions could be found on page 552 of that timetable which could be purchased for 6d. The Inner House came to a similar decision in *Gray v London and North Eastern Ry*.[13] Mr Gray had bought his own ticket and admitted that he knew that there was writing on it, though he had not read it.

The courts have not found notice to be sufficient where a ticket for a **10–13** ferry crossing contained an exclusion clause on the back but there was no reference to this on the face of the ticket.[14] The same result occurred where the face of the ticket did refer to conditions on the back but the reference was in the smallest known type and presented in such a way as easily to be overlooked.[15]

---

[9] [1949] 1 K.B. 532.
[10] 1964 S.C. (H.L.) 28.
[11] 1918 S.C. (H.L.) 143 at 149.
[12] [1930] 1 K.B. 141.
[13] 1930 S.C. 989.
[14] *Henderson v Stevenson* (1875) 2 R. (H.L.) 17.
[15] *Williamson v North of Scotland and Orkney and Shetland Navigation Co*, 1916 S.C. 554.

10–14   In other situations the courts have been less inclined to incorporate exclusion clauses. In *Grayston Plant Ltd v Plean Precast Ltd* it was said in the Inner House that it is wrong to apply "the principles of the 'ticket' cases, which are based on matters of practicability and reasonableness peculiar to 'ticket' contracts . . . to a very different kind of case".[16] The court went on to refer with approval to the dictum of Denning L.J. in *Spurling v Bradshaw*[17] that "the more unreasonable the clause is, the greater the notice which must be given of it". In *Thornton v Shoe Lane Parking Ltd*[18] Lord Denning had suggested that there were some clauses that were so oppressive that they would only be effective if placed in a box in red print with a hand pointing to them.

10–15   In theory it seems that an exclusion clause might be incorporated even though no notice was given on the occasion when a problem arose if it was merely one of a number of occasions when the parties had contracted. This is referred to as incorporation by means of a course of dealing and might arise where a consumer has frequently contracted with the same trader and their contracts have normally contained an exclusion clause. This argument was put forward in *McCutcheon v MacBrayne*,[19] where the pursuer's car had been lost when MacBrayne's ferry sank. The pursuer was a frequent customer of MacBraynes both for transporting vehicles and livestock. It was their usual, though not invariable practice, to require the customer to sign a risk note which contained an exclusion clause. They did not do so on the relevant occasion but argued that the pursuer, through a course of dealing with them, knew that goods were shipped on standard terms containing such a clause. This argument failed in the House of Lords. It was accepted that there could be incorporation in this way, but the course of dealing must be both consistent and lengthy. In this case the evidence showed that the pattern of dealings was not consistent, a risk note having to be signed on some occasions but not on others. While there are examples of incorporation by means of a course of dealing in the law reports none concerns a consumer contract.

CONSTRUCTION

10–16   If it is established that the clause is part of the contract the next step is to consider whether it protects the party relying on it in the circumstances. With the passage of the Unfair Contract Terms Act 1977 the courts will probably not resort to some of the mental gymnastics that were necessary in the past to do justice. However, it is still true that the

---

[16] 1976 S.C. 206.
[17] [1965] 1 W.L.R. 461.
[18] [1971] 2 Q.B. 163. See also *Interfoto Picture Library Ltd v Stiletto Visual Programmes Ltd* [1988] 1 All E.R. 348, CA.
[19] 1964 S.C. (H.L.) 28.

courts will construe exclusion clauses strictly and against a party seeking to rely on them. The principle, often known by the Latin tag, the *contra proferentem* rule, can be traced back to Stair[20] and has frequently been employed by the courts. In *McKay v Scottish Airways Ltd* it was said in the Outer House in a judgment approved by the Inner House that:

> "It is well settled that clauses exempting a carrier from liability fall to be construed strictly and *contra proferentem* . . . Only clear and unambiguous language will suffice to exclude a common law liability, and as the language used in conditions expressed on a ticket is language framed and devised by the carriers themselves, it will . . . fall to be construed in the sense most unfavourable to the carrier who sells the ticket and most favourable to the passenger who buys it."[21]

An example of the principle in operation in a consumer context *is* **10–17** *Graham v Shore Porters Society.*[22] Mr Graham arranged to have his belongings moved from Glasgow to Aberdeen by the defenders. While in their custody they were destroyed by fire. The carriers argued that they were protected by the following clause in the contract: "The contractors shall not be responsible for loss and damage to furniture and effects caused by or incidental to fire or aircraft, but will endeavour to effect insurance on behalf of the customer on receipt of instructions."[23]

Applying the *contra proferentem* rule, the Court of Session held that **10–18** this clause did not protect the carriers. They were liable to their customer under the contract to take reasonable care of his goods and also had a statutory duty to him. The court considered that the clause only excluded liability for statutory duty and that the carriers still owed their contractual duty of care to the customer.

The courts look with particular disfavour on clauses seeking to **10–19** exempt one party from the consequences of negligence on the ground that it is inherently unlikely that this is what the parties intended. It has, however, always been accepted in Scotland, which did not flirt with the doctrine of fundamental breach as the English courts did, that a properly worded clause could exclude any kind of liability. With the passing of the Unfair Contract Terms Act 1977 the House of Lords has made clear that it will approach construction of clauses in a less hostile manner. In

---

[20] "*Verba sunt interpretanda contra proferentem* (words must be construed unfavourably to those who drafted them) where the parties are skilful, or are known to have trusted skilful persons in forming of the writs; and therefore the same should be as much extended in favour of the other party, as their sense can bear.": *Institutes* (More's ed.), IV. 42. 21.

[21] 1948 S.C. 254 at 256.

[22] 1979 S.L.T. 119.

[23] *ibid.*

particular, it has been stated that clauses limiting liability will be treated less unfavourably than those entirely excluding it.[24] The cases in which this point has been made are commercial cases and may not be relevant to consumer situations.[25]

A Wider Principle?

10–20 It is arguable that Scots common law had the capacity to control terms in contracts, including exclusion clauses, on more general grounds.[26] In *McKay v Scottish Airways Ltd*[27] Lord Cooper observed that the:

> "remarkable feature of these conditions is their amazing width, and the effort which has evidently been made to create a leonine bargain under which the aeroplane passenger takes all the risks and the company accepts no obligation, not even to carry the passenger or his baggage nor even to admit him to the aeroplane."

10–21 He went on to note that it had not been "argued that the conditions were contrary to public policy nor that they were so extreme as to deprive the contract of all meaning and effect as a contract of carriage". He reserved his opinion on these matters but was clearly inviting lawyers to develop a wider principle for attacking exclusion clauses. This has not been done and there is now less need or scope for such an approach with the enactment of the Unfair Contract Terms Act 1977 and the Unfair Terms in Consumer Contracts Regulations 1999.[28]

STATUTORY INTERVENTION

10–22 In the absence of some wider principle, such as Lord Cooper appeared to be advocating, the common law controls on exclusion clauses were bound to have limited power to protect consumers even in the hands of the most sympathetic judges. With care, it was possible to ensure that exclusion clauses were incorporated in contracts, and careful drafting could ensure that they were appropriate to exclude or limit the liability of the trader. As Lord Reid recognized: "This is a complex problem which intimately affects millions of people and it appears to me that its

---

[24] *Ailsa Craig Fishing Ltd v Malvern Fishing Co Ltd*, 1982 S.L.T. 377.

[25] See *Mars Pension Trs v County Properties and Developments Ltd*, 1999 S.C.L.R. 117, IH, where Lord Prosser considered the proper approach to construing contracts where there was an attempt to exclude liability which would otherwise attach. This was in the context of a case to which the legislative controls did not apply.

[26] See McBryde, "Extortionate Contracts", 1976 J.L.S.S. 322 where a number of cases are referred to.

[27] 1948 S.C. 254 at 263.

[28] SI 1999/203, which replaced the original regulations of the same name. See SI 1994/3159.

solution should be left to Parliament."[29] Legislative action has been taken in a number of forms; the most important of which are the Unfair Contract Terms Act 1977 and the Unfair Terms in Consumer Contracts Regulations 1999.[30]

UNFAIR CONTRACT TERMS ACT 1977

The Unfair Contract Terms Act 1977 followed the second report on **10–23** exemption clauses by the Law Commissions[31] and was introduced as a private member's bill. The title of the Act is confusing in that it both understates and overstates its scope. The title of the original bill, the Avoidance of Liability Bill, more accurately describes its purpose. The Act does not deal with all terms in contracts which might be considered unfair. It may be the case that the price is thought to be too high or the contract gives wide latitude to the supplier in relation to delivery. Neither of these terms would be within the scope of the Act. On the other hand, the title is too narrow in that it applies not only to contract terms but also with notices attempting to restrict or exclude liability for negligence.

It is important to note that before one need consider the relevance of **10–24** the Act it must be established that the clause is validly incorporated into the contract. This point is expressly made in s.24(2), so the common law on incorporation is still relevant. Similarly, even if the clause is validly incorporated it must be demonstrated that it covers the breach that has occurred.

Part 2 of the Act applies exclusively to Scotland, and Pt 3, which **10–25** applies to the whole of the UK, is also relevant. The Act applies to more than just consumer transactions, but it is only with these that this chapter is concerned.

Scope

The approach of the Act is to set out those types of contract to which it **10–26** applies. This covers a wide range of contracts and certainly includes many contracts which would be regarded as consumer contracts, such as contracts for the supply of goods and services.[32] Contracts relating to the liability of an occupier of land to persons entering or using it are covered. This is important as it will cover situations such as attendance at cinemas, theatres, zoos and sporting events. Since April 1, 1991 the controls of the Act apply to non-contractual notices.[33] A notable exception to the scope of the Act is insurance contracts. The insurance

---

[29] *Suisse Alantique Societe d'Armement Maritime SA v NV Rotterdamsche Kolen Centrale* [1967] A.C. 361 at 406.
[30] SI 1999/203.
[31] See Exemption Clauses: Second Report (Scot. Law Com., No.39, 1975).
[32] See s.15.
[33] As a result of Law Reform (Miscellaneous Provisions) (Scotland) Act 1990, s.68.

industry argued that it would be very difficult to distinguish between a genuine attempt to define the insured risk and an exclusion of liability.

10–27   The Act does not define an exclusion clause. There are various references to terms which "exclude or restrict" liability and s.25(3) amplifies what this means. It makes clear that it includes making the liability or its enforcement subject to any restrictive or onerous conditions. Clauses requiring claims to be notified within a short time-limit would be covered by this. Clauses which exclude or restrict any right or remedy or hamper someone in pursuing a remedy are also caught. An example would be a clause limiting a consumer to a remedy in damages where he or she would otherwise be entitled to rescind the contract. A third way in which the phrase is amplified is by stating that it covers clauses excluding or restricting any rule of evidence or procedure.

10–28   Section 23(5) is important in that it states that references to excluding or restricting liability for breach of an obligation or duty "shall include a reference to excluding or restricting the obligation or duty itself". This is an anti-avoidance provision designed to stop attempts to get round the controls on exclusion clauses by saying that one party has no legal obligation in the first place. For example, it is clear that s.20 of the Act covers attempts to exclude or restrict the obligation to provide goods of satisfactory quality. What s.25(3) makes clear is that this cannot be subverted by clauses stating that the subject-matter of the sale is an article not guaranteed to meet those standards.[34] In *Ferguson v Littlewoods Pools Ltd*[35] the "honour clause" seeking to make the arrangement between a pools company and its clients one that gave rise to no legal obligations was considered. In *obiter dicta* it was considered that such a clause might be subject to the Act. This, presumably, would be by applying s.23(5). In *Halloway v Cuozzo*[36] the English Court of Appeal in a very similar situation appear to have assumed that the provisions of the Act did not affect the existence of a contract and, even if they did, the honour clause would be found to be reasonable.

10–29   The Act is aimed at exclusion of liability by businesses. "Business" is defined in s.25(1) as including "a profession and the activities of any government department or local or public authority".

Consumer Contracts

10–30   The term "consumer contract" is used in several sections of Pt 2 of the Act and, by and large, the controls on consumer contracts are more

---

[34] See Peel, "Making More Use of the Unfair Contract Terms Act 1977: *Stewart Gill Ltd v Horatio Myer & Co Ltd*" (1993) 56 M.L.R. 98.
[35] 1997 S.L.T. 309, OH.
[36] Feb. 9, 1999, unreported.

stringent than on contracts between businesses. It is therefore advantageous for the person faced with an exclusion clause to be able to show that they come within the definition. It is helpful to consumers that the party claiming that the contract is not a consumer contract bears the burden of proving that proposition. The term "consumer contract" was originally defined in s.25(1) as follows:

> "a contract (not being a contract of sale by auction or competitive tender) in which
>
> (a) one party to the contract deals, and the other party to the contract ('the consumer') does not deal or hold himself out as dealing, in the course of a business, and
> (b) [where the contract involves the transfer of the ownership or possession of goods] the goods are of a type ordinarily supplied for private use or consumption".

This definition has been amended with effect from March 31, 2003, **10–31** by reg.14 of the Sale and Supply of Goods to Consumers Regulations 2002[37] which implement the EC Directive on certain aspects of the sale of consumer goods and associated guarantees.[38] Where the consumer is an individual a new subs.(1A) provides that para.(b) shall be ignored. This removes a potentially difficult problem in deciding what sort of goods should be considered to be supplied for private use and consumption. Regulation 14 removed the introductory words "not being a contract of sale by auction or competitive tender" to allow the exclusion of auction sales from the definition to be altered. A new subs.(1B) provides that where the buyer is an individual consumer contracts do not include auction sales of second-hand goods where the buyer has the opportunity of attending in person. The fairly rare auction of new goods would come within the definition where individual consumers are concerned. For the sake of completeness it should be added that buyers who are not individuals cannot come within the definition of the consumer contract where they purchase goods sold by auction or competitive tender.[39]

This definition shows that consumers can have exclusion clauses **10–32** imposed on them when buying at auctions. The status of consumer is lost, not only if the dealing is in the course of a business, but also if it occurs while holding oneself out as so dealing. This points out the pitfalls for those private individuals who, for example, gain access to wholesale stores that make it clear that they deal only with trade customers.

---

[37] SI 2002/ 3045.
[38] Dir. 1999/44; [1999] O.J. L171/12.
[39] See subs.(1B)(b).

10–33   It appears that businesses can in some circumstances come within the definition of consumer. Suppose that a firm of solicitors buys a carpet for its office. This is an article which is "ordinarily supplied for private use or consumption", but is it to be regarded as purchased "in the course of a business"? The view of the English courts has been that it is not.[40]

Clauses controlled by the Act

10–34   The Act controls attempts to exclude or restrict liability by means of contracts or notices in four main situations. These are in relation to breach of duty; consumer and standard form contracts; indemnities and guarantees; and terms implied in contracts for the supply of goods.

Breach of duty

10–35   The Law Commissions in their second report on exemption clauses concluded that "clauses or notices exempting from liability for negligence are in many cases a serious social evil". It is hardly surprising that s.16 of the Act should control their use. Section 16 covers more than just liability for negligence. It speaks of breach of duty which covers a number of different situations, as the definition of breach of duty in s.25 of the Act makes clear. The first of these is breach of any obligation to take reasonable care or exercise reasonable skill which arises from the express or implied terms of a contract. Thus, exclusion clauses in a wide range of trades and professions are covered. These would include contracts by professional people such as accountants, solicitors or architects, as well as non-professional services provided by garages or dry cleaners. All these service providers have an obligation to perform their services with reasonable skill and care.

10–36   The definition also applies to any common law duty to take reasonable care or exercise reasonable skill. This covers situations where the delictual duty of care arises as developed in the line of cases originating with *Donoghue v Stevenson*.[41] Finally, it also includes the common law duty to take reasonable care under s.2(1) of the Occupiers Liability (Scotland) Act 1960. In a consumer context this might be relevant where attempts to exclude liability are made at playgrounds, funfairs and other places of amusement or recreation.

10–37   Where a clause or notice attempts to exclude liability for death or personal injury arising from breach of any of these duties it is void and of no effect. This is a most important and wide-ranging provision. Cases

---

[40] See *Peter Symmons & Co v Cook* (1981) 131 N.L.J. 758. The approach of the English Court of Appeal in *Stevenson v Rogers* [1999] Q.B. 1028, a decision on the meaning of in the course of a business in Sale of Goods Act 1979, s.14, suggests that a narrower view should be taken of the meaning of consumer in the 1977 Act.

[41] 1932 S.C. (H.L.) 31.

such as that of *Taylor v Corporation of the City of Glasgow*[42] would now never reach the courts as, no matter what the ticket said or whether it could be regarded as a contractual document, anything which purported to exempt from liability for personal injury or death could have no effect.

Where an exclusion clause seeks to exclude liability for other loss or **10–38** damage arising from breach of duty it can be relied on, but only to the extent that it is "fair and reasonable" to do so.[43] What is fair and reasonable is discussed later. This provision redresses the balance between consumers and those who provide them with such services as dry-cleaning, car-parking or furniture removing.

The controls in s.16 are not intended to affect the defence of *volenti* **10–39** *non fit injuria*. This is a defence to a delict action which applies where it can be shown that a person willingly accepted the risk of injury. It could be argued that although an exclusion clause could not protect a defender from liability it could prevent liability arising in the first place if it were interpreted as a warning of a risk. Section 16(3) prevents this result by providing that where a contract term is void by virtue of s.16 the fact that a person agreed to, or was aware of, that term *"shall not of itself* be sufficient evidence that he knowingly and voluntarily assumed any risk".[44]

Consumer and standard form contracts

Section 17 of the Act controls attempts in consumer and standard form **10–40** contracts to exclude contractual liability. It overlaps with other sections of the Act and it must be remembered that it may be more advantageous to use one of those other provisions. For example, as we shall see below, in some circumstances it is not possible to exclude liability imposed by the implied terms found in the Sale of Goods Act 1979. This is clearly more useful than relying on this provision which applies only a reasonableness test.

Section 17 deals with both consumer and standard form contracts. As **10–41** we are concerned only with consumers all references will be to consumer contracts, the meaning of which has been discussed at para.10–30. The reasonableness test is applied to three situations. It applies where a trader tries to limit liability when in breach of contract; claims to be entitled to perform the contract in a way substantially different from that which was reasonably expected of him; or claims that he is entitled to render no performance at all.

In practice, s.17 is likely to apply most frequently to contracts for **10–42** services. *McKay v Scottish Airways Ltd*[45] contains the sort of clause

---

[42] 1952 S.C. 440.
[43] s.16(1)(b).
[44] (emphasis added).
[45] 1948 S.C. 259.

which would be subject to the first and third of the situations which the section deals with. The second part could apply to the sort of clause often found in package holiday contracts which permits the tour operator to alter the itinerary or the dates of the holiday.[46]

Indemnities

10–43 Indemnity clauses are clauses that require one party to a contract to take responsibility for the legal liability of someone else. Such clauses are not unusual in the contracts of cross channel ferry firms. While, strictly speaking, not exclusion clauses they have a similar effect and are made subject to a reasonableness test by s.18 of the Act.

Guarantees

10–44 Guarantees are often given by manufacturers of products and can be a very useful addition to the rights which a consumer has under the Sale of Goods Act 1979 against the retailer. There have been examples of such guarantees conferring additional advantages on consumers but excluding the manufacturer's common law liability under *Donoghue v Stevenson*.[47] Section 19 of the Act renders void attempts to do this. The section applies only to goods "of a type ordinarily supplied for private use or consumption", the meaning of which has been discussed above.[48]

Terms implied in contracts for the supply of goods

10–45 In Ch.5 we saw that certain terms relating to title, description and the quality of goods are implied in contracts of sale by ss.12–15 of the Sale of Goods Act 1979. Similar terms are implied in contracts of hire-purchase by the Supply of Goods (Implied Terms) Act 1973. Section 20 of the 1977 Act renders void clauses purporting to exclude or restrict these terms in consumer contracts.[49]

10–46   There are several other contracts under which goods may be transferred. Until the amendment of the Supply of Goods and Services Act 1982 by the Sale and Supply of Goods Act 1994, the implied terms in such contracts were found, not in statute, but the common law. The 1994 Act, which came into force on January 3, 1995, added a Pt 1A to the 1982 Act setting out implied terms which are very similar to those implied in contracts of sale.[50] In consumer contracts transferring the property in goods clauses purporting to exclude or restrict such terms are void. Contracts affected will include those for work and materials

---

[46] For an example in a case which arose before the Act, see *Anglo-Continental Holidays Ltd v Typaldos Lines (London) Ltd* [1967] 2 Lloyd's Rep. 61.
[47] 1932 S.C. (H.L.) 31.
[48] See para.10–31.
[49] These provisions first appeared in Supply of Goods (Implied Terms) Act 1973.
[50] The terms are discussed in Ch.5.

and barter. This is achieved by an amended version of s.21 of the 1977 Act.

Contracts of hire, which are not contracts for the "transfer of property **10–47** in goods", are treated slightly differently. Exclusion clauses in these contracts are controlled by s.21 of the 1977 Act. Attempts in consumer contracts to exclude the implied terms about correspondence with description or sample, quality, or fitness for purpose are void. However, exclusion of the terms about the right to transfer possession and the enjoyment of quiet possession are subject to the test of fairness and reasonableness.

Reasonableness Test

In some circumstances an exclusion clause is only effective if "fair and **10–48** reasonable". To assist in determining what this means there is guidance in the Act. Before looking at those guidelines there are two points that need to be kept in mind. The first concerns the onus of proof. Section 25(4) states that this falls on the party asserting that the clause is reasonable. The other point concerns the time at which any test of reasonableness should be applied. The Act draws a distinction between contractual terms and non-contractual notices. In the case of contractual terms s.24(1) states that the test must be satisfied having regard "to the circumstances which were, or ought reasonably to have been, known to or in the contemplation of the parties when the contract was made." In the case of non-contractual notices s.24(2A) states that one must have "regard to all the circumstances obtaining when the liability arose or (but for the provision) would have arisen."

The English case of *Bellamy v Newbold*[51] turned on the question of **10–49** when the test should be applied. Following the discovery of defects in a house the sellers paid compensation to the purchaser who had signed a form acknowledging that this payment was in full and final settlement of all present and future claims. Some time later there was a dispute about the boundaries of the property and the sellers sought to apply this statement to that claim. It was held that the statement did not apply to the boundary dispute as this had not been in the contemplation of the parties at the time that it had been drawn up.

The Act provides not one but three sets of guidelines. The most **10–50** elaborate guidance is given in relation to clauses relating to the supply of goods controlled by ss.20 and 21. As far as consumers are concerned the only situation where these sections apply a reasonableness test is where, in a contract of hire, a clause excludes the implied term about the right to transfer possession or the enjoyment of quiet possession of the goods. In this case s.24(2) directs that regard shall be had to the guidelines in Sch.2 of the Act. These guidelines are as follows:

---

[51] CA, 1986, unreported.

> "(a) the strength of the bargaining positions of the parties relative to each other, taking into account (among other things) alternative means by which the customer's requirements could have been met;
>
> (b) whether the customer received an inducement to agree to the term, or in accepting it had an opportunity of entering into a similar contract with other persons, but without having to accept a similar term;
>
> (c) whether the customer knew or ought reasonably to have known of the existence and extent of the term (having regard, among other things, to any custom of the trade and any previous course of dealing between the parties);
>
> (d) where the term excludes or restricts any relevant liability if some condition is not complied with, whether it was reasonable at the time of the contract to expect that compliance with that condition would be practicable;
>
> (e) whether the goods were manufactured, processed or adapted to the special order of the customer."

10–51   If the clause or notice seeks to restrict liability to a sum of money two further guidelines are included in s.24(3). These are:

> "(a) the resources which the party seeking to rely on that term could expect to be available to him for the purpose of meeting the liability should it arise;
>
> (b) how far it was open to that party to cover himself by insurance."

10–52   In the other cases where the Act applies a reasonableness test to consumer contracts, such as s.16 dealing with breach of duty leading to loss other than death or physical injury and the consumer contracts covered by s.17, the only guidelines are the two just referred to. These can only operate where liability is limited to a specified sum. However, one reason for setting out the Sch.2 guidelines in full, despite their limited application, was that they encapsulate the factors which judges would take into account even if they had not been set out. Indeed, in the English Court of Appeal it has been observed that "the considerations there set out are normally regarded as being of general application to the question of reasonableness".[52]

10–53   Relatively few cases have come before the courts on the issue of reasonableness and most of the specifically consumer cases are decisions of the English county courts. Some guidance on the approach of the appellate courts is set out by Lord Bridge in *George Mitchell (Chesterhall) Ltd v Finney Lock Seeds Ltd.*[53] The case was decided

---

[52] *Stewart Gill v Horatio Myer & Co* [1992] 1 Q.B. 600 at 608.
[53] [1983] 2 A.C. 803 at 815.

under the earlier Supply of Goods (Implied Terms) Act 1973, but Lord Bridge expressly said that his comments were relevant to the 1977 Act:

> "It would not be accurate to describe such a decision as an exercise of discretion. But a decision under [the Supply of Goods (Implied Terms) Act or the Unfair Contract Terms Act] will have this in common with the exercise of a discretion, that . . . the court must entertain a whole range of considerations, put them in the scales on one side or the other and decide at the end of the day on which side the balance comes down. There will sometimes be room for a legitimate difference of judicial opinion as to what the answer should be, where it will be impossible to say that one view is demonstrably wrong and the other demonstrably right. It must follow, in my view, that, when asked to review such a decision on appeal, the appellate court should treat the original decision with the utmost respect and refrain from interference with it unless satisfied that it proceeded on some erroneous principle or was plainly and obviously wrong."

One can see an example of this approach in the speech of Lord **10–54** Griffiths in the only consumer cases on this point to reach the House of Lords, *Smith v Eric S. Bush & Co*; *Harris v Wyre District Council*.[54] While emphasising that it is impossible to draw up an exhaustive list of factors to be taken into account and that he was dealing with dwelling-houses of relatively modest value, he was able to isolate certain matters which should always be considered. These were the relative bargaining strengths of the parties; the practicality of obtaining advice from another source taking into account time and cost; the difficulty of the task undertaken by the service provider; and the financial consequences of the decision on reasonableness. In these cases where the valuation of a house was concerned the factors all pointed in the direction of finding it unreasonable for a surveyor to exclude liability. The disclaimer was imposed on the client who had no effective power to object; given the value of the house it was unreasonable for the buyers to seek an alternative valuation; the task was straightforward; and the consequences of being made liable could be covered by insurance.[55] In *Melrose v Davidson & Robertson*[56] it was stated that for the reasons given by Lord Griffiths in those cases it could not be disputed that the disclaimer was not fair and reasonable.[57]

---

[54] [1990] A.C. 831; [1989] 2 All E.R. 514.

[55] [1989] 2 All E.R. 514 at 531, 532.

[56] 1993 S.C.L.R. 365.

[57] The Scottish cases are reviewed in Stewart, "15 Years of Fair Contracts in Scotland", 1993 S.L.T. (News) 15. See also *Bank of Scotland v Fuller Peiser*, 2002 S.L.T. 574; 2002 S.C.L.R. 255.

10–55   In *Woodman v Photo Trade Processing Ltd*[58] the relevance of choice was an important issue. The plaintiff had taken photographs of a friend's wedding to the defendants for processing. They failed to return the photographs and when sued relied on a clause in their contract limiting liability to the replacement cost of the film. It was held that this clause was unreasonable because it excluded liability for negligence as well as accident. The evidence showed that there was no alternative to the defendant's terms as all other processors used the same terms. It was also relevant that the defendant's could have insured against the liability. In *Moores v Yakeley Associates Ltd*,[59] on the other hand, in a case where an architect's limitation of liability clause was found to be reasonable, the facts that the consumer had been advised by a solicitor, the clause was clearly brought to the client's attention and the market for architects' services was highly competitive were considered to be relevant.

10–56   In *Waldron-Kelly v British Railways Board*[60] a clause in British Rail's conditions of carriage relating compensation to the weight of the goods, not to their value, was held to be unreasonable. The plaintiff's suitcase had been lost by British Rail. On its basis of calculating compensation £27 would have been payable, whereas the value of the contents was £320.

10–57   Although far removed from the consumer sphere, *Stag Line v Tyne Ship Repair Group; The Zinnia*,[61] a shipping case, has some pointers to the attitudes of the courts in relation to reasonableness. Staughton J. observed:

> "I would have been tempted to hold that all the conditions are unfair and unreasonable for two reasons: first they are in such small print that one can barely read them; secondly the drafting is so convoluted and prolix that one almost needs an LL.B. to understand them."[62]

10–58   These remarks were obiter but it is interesting that they should have been made in the context of a commercial contract where the parties were of equal bargaining strength and had suitably qualified persons to scrutinise their contracts. It seems almost certain that a consumer contract of which the same criticisms could be made would be considered to be unreasonable.

---

[58] Exeter County Court, 1981, unreported.
[59] High Court, 1998, unreported.
[60] [1981] 3 C.L. 33.
[61] [1982] 2 Lloyd's Reps. 211.
[62] *ibid.*, at p.222.

Unfair Terms in Consumer Contracts Regulations 1999[63]

These Regulations implement the EC Directive on Unfair Contract **10–59** Terms[64] of April 5, 1993, and replace the 1994 Regulations of the same name which came into effect on January 1, 1995.[65]

The Directive is based on Art.100a of the Treaty of Rome which is **10–60** primarily concerned with the establishment of the single market. The recitals in the Directive point out that the many disparities in contract terms in the Member States create a distortion of the market and may deter consumers in entering into cross-border transactions. In *Oceano Grupo Editorial SA v Rocio Murciano Quintero)*[66] the ECJ has held that a national court dealing with a dispute involving a contract term which might be unfair can consider the issue of its own motion. The ECJ justified this approach by pointing out:

> "[T]he court's power to determine of its own motion whether a term is unfair must be regarded as constituting a proper means both of achieving the result sought by Art.6 of the Directive, namely, preventing an individual consumer from being bound by an unfair term, and of contributing to achieving the aim of Art.7, since if the court undertakes such an examination, that may act as a deterrent and contribute to preventing unfair terms in contracts concluded between consumers and sellers or suppliers."[67]

The criticisms of the method of implementation of the General Safety **10–61** Directive[68] apply with even greater force to this Directive. As it adds to the law relating to unfair terms the obvious course would have been to implement it by means of primary legislation recasting this whole area of law.[69] Instead, the Regulations are superimposed on the existing Unfair Contract Terms Act 1977. In the case of the General Safety Directive such a course could be justified on the ground that the primary legislation and the regulations implementing the directive were complementary. No such answer is available in the case of the Unfair Contract Terms Directive. The 1977 Act and the Regulations overlap. Anyone seeking to ascertain whether a term is valid must check it against both the Act and the Regulations. It is quite possible that a term

---

[63] SI 1999/2083.
[64] Dir. 93/13; [1993] O.J. L95/29.
[65] Those Regulations, SI 1994/3159, came into force on July 1, 1995, six months after the date set out in the directive for implementing it.
[66] [2002] 1 C.M.L.R. 43, ECJ.
[67] *ibid.*, para.28.
[68] Dir. 92/59.
[69] The English and Scottish Law Commissions are currently considering this issue and published a consultation paper in August 2002. See *Unfair Terms In Contracts: A Joint Consultation Paper* (Law Com. Consultation Paper No. 166; Scot. Law Com. Discussion Paper No.119, 2002). They hope to publish a final report with draft legislation in 2004.

would survive scrutiny under the Act but be found to be unfair under the Regulations.

10–62   The central provision of the Regulations is reg.8(1) which provides that "[a]n unfair term in a contract concluded with a consumer by a seller or supplier shall not binding on the consumer". This short sentence introduces a potentially revolutionary rule into our contract law. While this provision looks very similar to the controls introduced by the Act, and does indeed overlap with them to some extent, there are also important differences.

10–63   An obvious difference is that the Regulations apply to unfair terms in contracts. The Act, as we noted,[70] is misleadingly named, for it applies, in the main, only to clauses excluding and limiting liability. There are many other situations where a term can be unfair but, because it is not such a clause, it is not subject to the controls of the Act. The Regulations apply much more widely. For example, they can apply to terms about delivery dates, terms which give the supplier the right to increase the contractual charges unilaterally, or to terminate the contract without adequate notice. Bankers' contracts with their customers often permit the bank to close an account or withdraw a bank card with little notice. None of these would be regarded as exemptions or exclusions of liability and would not be subject to the Act. They can be challenged under the Regulations.

10–64   An important similarity between the existing common law and the new Regulations is that both apply the *contra proferentem* rule. Regulation 7 enjoins traders to "ensure that any written term of a contract is expressed in plain, intelligible language" and goes on to say that "if there is doubt about the meaning of a written term, the interpretation most favourable to the consumer shall prevail". This rule does not apply to proceedings brought by the OFT and others for an interdict which are discussed below.[71] The point of this is to prevent traders, in effect, taking advantage of the *contra proferentem* rule in proceedings for an interdict. Were they to do so and succeed in opposing the award of an interdict banning use of a term they would be at liberty to use a term which was to some degree obscure.

10–65   There is an important difference between the scope of the Regulations and the Act. Regulation 4(1) states that they apply "in relation to unfair terms in contracts concluded between a seller or supplier and a consumer". The definition of "consumer" in reg.3 is narrower than that in the Act. For the purposes of the Act businesses can, in certain circumstances, be regarded as consumers as occurred in *R. & B. Customs Brokers Co. Ltd v United Dominions Trust*.[72] This is not the case under the Regulations as "consumer" is defined as "any natural

---

[70] See para.10–23.
[71] See para.10–96.
[72] [1988] 1 All E.R. 847.

person who ... is acting for purposes which are outside his trade, business or profession".

"Seller" and "supplier" are also defined differently in the Regula- **10–66** tions.[73] In both cases they mean "any natural or legal person who ... is acting for purposes related to his trade, business or profession, whether publicly or privately owned". In *R (On the application of Khatun) v Newham LBC*[74] it was decided that a local authority when acting as a landlord fell within this definition "Related to" is much wider than the equivalent phrase in the Act which is "in the course of a business". In *R. & B. Customs Brokers Co Ltd*[75] it was held that to come within that test "the transaction should be an integral part of the business concerned, or one which he or she carries out with sufficient regularity or a one off adventure in the nature of a trade." "Related to" will bring under the control of the Regulations transactions such as the isolated sale of a capital item by a business which does not deal in that sort of item.[76]

There is a significant difference between the definition of seller or **10–67** supplier in the 1999 Regulations and that in the original set. The 1994 Regulations[77] referred to sellers of goods and services. This assumed that the Directive did not apply to contracts relating to heritage. It is not clear from the Directive whether such contracts are covered by it, but the DTI's guidance notes took the view that they were not and this was reflected in the 1994 Regulations.[78] The 1999 Regulations indicate a change to a neutral stance as the definitions of seller and supplier make no reference to the supply of goods or services. The definition follows that in the Directive precisely. In *R (On the application of Khatun) v Newham LBC*[79] the English Court of Appeal has decided that the 1999 Regulations do apply to contracts relating to land. This vindicates the practice of the OFT which, from the beginning, had taken the view that heritage was covered and have persuaded traders to delete or amend unfair terms in such contracts.

Terms not covered by the Regulations

Schedule 1 of the 1994 Regulations[80] excluded certain types of contract. **10–68** It is no surprise to find that this schedule is not reproduced in the 1999 Regulations as it would not have occurred to anyone that most of the

---

[73] See reg.3.
[74] [2004] E.W.C.A Civ. 55; *The Times*, Feb. 27, 2004.
[75] [1988] 1 All E.R. 847.
[76] *cf. Davies v Sumner* [1984] 1 W.L.R. 1301.
[77] SI 1994/3159.
[78] See *Implementation of the E.C. Directive on Unfair Terms in Consumer Contracts: A Consultation Document* (DTI, Oct. 1993). Footnote 1 to the commentary to draft reg. B(1) cites four recitals which plainly refer to suppliers of goods.
[79] [2004] E.W.C.A. Civ. 55; *The Times*, Feb. 27, 2004.
[80] SI 1994/3159.

excluded types of contract would have been subject to the regulations anyway. They included contracts relating to employment, the incorporation or businesses, contracts relating to succession rights, and contracts relating to rights under family law. The only reason that they appeared in the 1994 Regulations seems to have been because they are referred to in one of the recitals to the Directive. It is understood that their appearance there was an oversight and as they do not appear in the body of the Directive they have been excised from the 1999 Regulations.

10–69   Two other types of terms to which the regulations do not apply appeared in Sch.1 to the 1994 Regulations, and they have been preserved in the 1999 Regulations. These are terms which reflect mandatory statutory or regulatory provisions including Community legislation which has direct effect; and the provisions or principles of international conventions to which the Member States or the Community are party. The latter would exempt from the controls of the regulations clauses in transport contracts which comply with the Warsaw Convention. These exclusions, which are drafted in terms much closer to the wording of the Directive, are now to be found in reg.4(2).

10–70   It is important to emphasise that insurance contracts are subject to the Regulations. They are one of the most important exclusions from the Act but did not escape the controls in the Directive. However, the exclusion of the so-called "core provisions" of a contract[81] from consideration for unfairness means that insurance contracts do get some protection from control under the Regulations.

10–71   It is not all contract terms to which the Regulations apply. Regulation 5(1) makes clear that it is only those "where the term has not been individually negotiated". According to reg.5(2) a term shall "always be regarded as not having been individually negotiated where it has been drafted in advance and the consumer has therefore not been able to influence the substance of the term". The fact that some terms or parts of terms have been individually negotiated will not prevent the Regulations applying "if an overall assessment of [the contract] shows that it is a pre-formulated standard contract". Regulation 5(4) is important here in that it puts the burden of showing that a term was individually negotiated on the supplier or seller. This definition sounds rather like a way of saying in statutory terms what the Law Commissions in their *Exemption Clauses—Second Report*[82] thought it best to leave unsaid in the Act. It is useful in making clear that a contract does not cease to be a standard form contract because some parts of it have been negotiated. For example, in a contract for double glazing the vast majority of the terms will be standard form terms on which there will be no negotiation. The customer will probably not even read them and, would be an unusual customer if he or she fully understood them.

---

[81] See para.10–76.
[82] Law Com. No. 69; Scot. Law Com. No.39, para.157.

However, there will be some terms which will be discussed. The price will be one and the delivery dates another.

Article 9 prevents the controls in the Regulations being circumvented **10–72** by attempts to say that the contract is governed by the law of a state outside the Community.[83] They apply in such a case if the contract has a close connection with the territory of a Member State."

The key aspect of the Regulations is the meaning of unfairness which **10–73** is the criterion by which terms are to judged. Superficially, there are similarities with the Act. The degree to which this is helpful is limited for the concept of unfairness in the regulations is somewhat different. The core of the definition of unfairness is to be found in reg.5(1) which provides: "A contractual term . . . shall be regarded as unfair if, contrary to the requirement of good faith, it causes a significant imbalance in the parties' rights and obligations arising under the contract, to the detriment of the consumer."

Unfairness

How will this be applied? Regulation 6(1) goes on to say that the time **10–74** for applying the test is the time of the conclusion of the contract. It also states that "the nature of the goods or services for which the contract was concluded", the circumstances attending its conclusion, and all other terms of the contract or of another contract on which it is dependent must be taken into account.

From this list of things which may be taken into account in deciding **10–75** on the fairness of the terms of a contract there are two exceptions. Regulation 6(2) provides:

"In so far as it is in plain, intelligible language, the assessment of fairness of a term shall not relate—

(a) to the definition of the main subject matter of the contract, or

(b) to the adequacy of the price or remuneration, as against the goods or services supplied in exchange."

This excludes two kinds of clause from the fairness test. The **10–76** definition of the subject-matter exception is designed to exclude clauses describing what the deal is about. From the recitals to the Directive it can be discovered that insurance contracts are in mind here, though they are not the only possible examples. Insurance contracts were excluded from the Act on the ground that it would be very difficult to distinguish

---

[83] The "Community" means the European Economic Community and the other states of the European Economic Area; and "member state" means a State which is a contracting party to the EEA Agreement signed at Oporto on May 2, 1992 and adjusted by the protocol signed at Brussels on Mar 17, 1993. Liechtenstein, however, is not included until the EEA Agreement comes into force in relation to it: see reg.2(1).

between exclusion clauses and those clauses which defined the insured risk. The Directive and the Regulations do not go as far as this. Their approach is to say that terms defining or circumscribing the risk are not on their own to be subject to the fairness test. However, contracts of insurance are still subject to the Regulations. In addition, the price of the goods or service are not subject to the fairness test. This will be seen as a major gap in the Regulations, as one of the most significant features of a transaction is the price. However, it clear that these exclusions are to be given a narrow interpretation. In *Director-General of Fair Trading v First National Bank plc*[84] the English Court of Appeal held that a term setting out the consequences of default did not define "the main subject matter of the contract" and this was not challenged on appeal to the House of Lords.

10–77 On appeal to the House of Lords in *Director-General of Fair Trading v First National Bank plc*[85] it was argued by the Bank that the default clause was a "core provision" in that it concerned the adequacy of the remuneration. The House of Lords agreed with counsel for the Director-General that that this was not so. Lord Bingham emphasised that this aspect of the Regulations was to be given a narrow ambit:

> "The object of the Regulations and the Directive is to protect consumers against the inclusion of unfair and prejudicial terms in standard-form contracts into which they enter, and that object would plainly be frustrated if regulation 3(2)(b) [6(2)(b) in the 1999 Regulations] were so broadly interpreted as to cover any terms other than those falling squarely within it. In my opinion the term, as part of a provision prescribing the consequences of default, plainly does not fall within it. It does not concern the adequacy of the interest earned by the bank as its remuneration but is designed to ensure that the bank's entitlement to interest does not come to an end on the entry of judgment."[86]

10–78 This aspect of *First National Bank plc* has been applied in the English High Court case of *Bairstow Eves London Central Ltd v Smith*.[87] That case involved an agreement between an estate agent and the seller of a flat. The term challenged was one which provided that the commission would be 1.5 per cent of the purchase price but if that sum were not paid in full within 10 days of completion of the transaction the rate of commission was to be 3 per cent. It was held that on a proper construction of the agreement the reference to the 3 per cent rate was a

---

[84] [2000] 1 All E.R. 240.
[85] [2000] All E.R. 759, CA.
[86] *Director-General of Fair Trading v First National Bank Plc* [2002] 1 A.C. 481, para.12.
[87] [2004] EWHC 263, QB; [2004] All E.R. (D) 354.

default provision and thus did not fall within the exclusion relating to terms about the adequacy of the price or remeuneration.

However, it must be stressed that both these exceptions are subject to **10–79** qualification. Both apply only "in so far as the term is in plain, intelligible language". It is not clear what standard this is imposing. Does it mean language that is intelligible to a lawyer—which is a standard that many standard clauses barely meet at present. Or does it mean language that the average person finds intelligible. From the recitals it would appear that it is the latter. The relevant recital after referring to the need for plain language states that the consumer should be given the opportunity to examine all the terms. This envisages the ordinary person reading the contract and therefore the kind of language used must be such that he or she will find plain and intelligible. This is certainly the approach of the OFT who have stated that[88] it takes the view "that the standard of 'plainness' and 'intelligibility' of contract terms must normally be within the understanding of ordinary consumers without legal advice". A good many standard form contracts do not survive scrutiny on that ground. Insurance contracts are a prime example, but there are many more.

The other qualification to the exclusion of these two factors from the **10–80** fairness test is that while they are not subject to it on their own, they can still be relevant to the fairness of other terms. This is not at all clear from the Regulations but is clearly set out in the recitals to the Directive. So, for example, if it can be shown that a service at the high price charged is usually accompanied by the supplier taking full legal responsibility for its provision then a clause exempting from that liability might be regarded as unfair. On the other hand, if the price were considerably lower the exemption clause might be regarded as fair.

With these considerations disposed of we are left with the central **10–81** features of unfairness of a term. These are that it is one that "contrary to the requirement of good faith . . . causes a significant imbalance in the parties' rights and obligations arising under the contract, to the detriment of the consumer".[89]

The last of these criteria, detriment to the consumer, is probably the **10–82** easiest to explain. It would seem simply to be making the point that only the consumer can take advantage of the Regulations.[90]

The requirement of "significant imbalance" would seem to mean no **10–83** more than the application of a *de minimis* rule eliminating minor imbalances in the rights and obligations of the parties. As Willet has argued,[91] it can hardly mean that the imbalance is particularly extreme. This would run counter to the idea of the having an "Indicative and

---

[88] *Unfair Contract Terms Bulletin* (OFT, Issue 2, Sept. 1996), para. 2.13.
[89] Reg.5(1).
[90] See "Unfair Contract Terms Directive" in *Welfarism in Contract Law* (Brownsword, Howells and Wilhelmsson ed., Dartmouth, Aldershot, 1994).
[91] "Directive on Unfair Terms in Consumer Contracts" (1994) 2 Cons. L.J. 114.

Illustrative List of Terms Which May be Regarded as Unfair" in Schedule 3. In *Director General of Fair Trading v First National Bank plc*[92] Lord Bingham explained:

> "The requirement of significant imbalance is met if a term is so weighted in favour of the supplier as to tilt the parties' rights and obligations under the contract significantly in his favour. This may be by the granting to the supplier of a beneficial option or discretion or power, or by the imposing on the consumer of a disadvantageous burden or risk or duty. The illustrative terms set out in Schedule 3 to the regulations provide very good examples of terms which may be regarded as unfair; whether a given term is or is not to be so regarded depends on whether it causes a significant imbalance in the parties' rights and obligations under the contract. This involves looking at the contract as a whole."

Good faith

10–84 This brings us to the concept of good faith. The central aspect of unfairness is that the term is "contrary to the requirement of good faith". There has been much comment about the novelty of this is in English and Scots law. Whatever may be the case in English law the fact is that it does have antecedents in Scots law. Professor Smith asserted in his that it was an underlying feature of the Scots law of obligations. He pointed to the various doctrines such as facility, force and fear, undue influence and control of minors' contracts on what is now the ground of prejudice, and argued that these were but specific examples of the wider principle of good faith.[93] Professor Gow notes that "Sale is a bargain bonae fidei"[94] and goes on to point out that:

> "Our doctrine of bona fides is of considerable importance *in re mercatoria* [in commercial matters] and its vigorous restatement, especially in an era of instalment credit and buyers, whose pockets appear large enough to impel them into an activity now become essential to the national economy but are not large enough to enable them lightly to embark upon litigations, is urgently required."[95]

10–85 Professor Smith also went on to argue that "the principles of bona fides which are latent in the Scottish law of contract could with

---

[92] [2000] All E.R. 759, CA.

[93] T.B. Smith, *A Short Commentary on the Law of Scotland* (W. Green, Edinburgh, 1962).

[94] J.J. Gow, *The Mercantile and Industrial Law of Scotland* (W. Green, Edinburgh, 1964), p.161.

[95] *ibid.*, pp.178, 179.

advantage be resuscitated to deal with problems of the twentieth century".[96]

Both writers acknowledged that the principle had fallen into disuse. **10–86** The implementation of the Directive is an opportunity to begin its revival. Surprisingly, the 1999 Regulations give less assistance than the 1994 Regulations in interpreting the concept of good faith. The original reg.4(3) had directed that in determining whether a term satisfied the good faith requirement regard should be had to the criteria set out in Sch.2. These criteria contained more than a passing similarity to the criteria in Sch.2 of the Act. They included such matters as the parties' bargaining strength, whether the consumer received an inducement to agree to the term, whether the goods or services were supplied to a special order and the extent to which the supplier had dealt fairly and equitably with the consumer. Their inclusion was clearly intended to placate the fears of English lawyers, in particular, about the use of the unfamiliar concept of good faith so familiar to civil lawyers. In one of the few reported case in which the fairness of a term has been raised in litigation between private parties, *Falco Finance Ltd v Gough*[97] the judge placed considerable emphasis on these criteria.

The absence of these guidelines from the 1999 Regulations does not **10–87** mean that they are no longer relevant. Here we have one of the disadvantages of slavish adherence to the copy-out technique in implementing EC directives. Those less familiar with the regulations and their European background will find the application of the fairness test more difficult. In practice there should be no difference in application between the two sets of regulations. This is because the recitals clearly state that the factors formerly set out in Sch.2 to the 1994 Regulations are to be taken into account in determining fairness. As the regulations implement an EC directive it is legitimate, as *Litster v Forth Dry Dock & Engineering Co*[98] demonstrates, to refer to the recitals to assist in interpreting the regulations.

While the Sch.2 guidelines have disappeared from the Regulations **10–88** the somewhat delphic "indicative and non-exhaustive list of terms which may be regarded as unfair", to quote reg.5(5), remains and is now to found in Sch.2 to the 1999 Regulations. Neither the Regulations, nor the Directive nor its recitals give any further guidance on the status of this "grey list" as it has come to be known. There is no indication that terms appearing in it should be presumed to be unfair. However, given the nature of many of the terms this is the conclusion to which one must come.

This grey list has many similarities to the sort of terms, which are **10–89** controlled by the Act. Included are terms which exclude liability for

---

[96] Smith, *Short Commentary*, p.46.
[97] [1999] Tr.L. 526; see also *Gosling v Burrard-Lucas*, [1999] 1 C.L. 197; and *Kindlance Ltd v Murphy*, NI Chancery Division, 1997.
[98] [1990] 1 A.C. 546.

death or personal injury or the implied terms in contracts for the supply of goods and services; those which give the seller or supplier the right to end or extend the contract at his discretion; or in other ways to alter the terms of the contract. As one might expect, terms imposing harsh obligations to pay compensation in the event of breach as well as barriers to the use of the courts to decide disputes are also in the list. A common characteristic of the list is that the terms included are very much to the advantage of the trader.

10–90   It was argued in earlier editions of this book that the concept of good faith covered both what is sometimes referred to as procedural good faith and substantive good faith. This was the view of the English Court of Appeal in the only case relating to the regulations to be heard in one of the higher courts in the United Kingdom. In *Director-General of Fair Trading v First National Bank plc*[99] they pointed out that "'good faith' has a special meaning in the Regulations, having its conceptual roots in civil law systems". Although the House of Lords in that case took a different view on the fairness of the term in issue they did not disagree with this approach. Lord Bingham observed that the Directive and the Regulations lay "down a composite test, covering both the making and the substance of the contract, and must be applied bearing clearly in mind the objective which the Regulations are designed to promote".[1] He acknowledged that it covered unfairness in the way in which the bargain is arrived at, sometimes referred to as unfair surprise, as well as unfairness because the bargain is very much weighted in favour of the seller or supplier.

10–91   In this case the Director-General was challenging the fairness of a term in a loan agreement subject to the Consumer Credit Act 1974. The term provided that if the borrower defaulted on a repayment the bank could demand repayment of the outstanding balance on the customer's account and interest at the rate set out in the loan agreement. It went on to add that where court action was necessary, interest would be payable at this rate on the judgment. The significance of this is that interest on the judgment would not otherwise have been payable. In practice what happens in cases of default is that after a court action has commenced borrowers agree to pay off the debt by installments and the action is settled without a proper court hearing taking place. Despite making the agreed repayments to pay off the debt the borrower finds that further sums are owed to the bank by way of interest at the contractual rate on the judgment. The Director-General's argument was that this rendered the term in the agreement unfair because when a borrower took out a loan it was not made clear that this could be one of its effects. It also meant that, in practice, borrowers did not have an opportunity to avail themselves of the opportunity to apply for time orders under the

---

[99] [2002] 1 A.C. 481.
[1] *Director-General of Fair Trading v First National Bank plc* [2002] 1 A.C. 481, para.17.

Consumer Credit Act 1974 which could have provided that interest should not be payable. At first instance[2] Evans-Lombe J. had considered this term to be fair. The Court of Appeal disagreed and found that it "does create unfair surprise".[3] The House of Lords disagreed with the Court of Appeal and held the term to be fair. They considered that any unfairness flowed, not from the term, but from weaknesses in the procedures of the English county courts which resulted in debtors in default failing to obtain the benefits of those facilities in the Consumer Credit Act 1974 designed to protect them.

In coming to this decision their Lordships gave useful guidance on the meaning of good faith. Lord Bingham observed: **10–92**

> "The requirement of good faith in this context is one of fair and open dealing. Openness requires that the terms should be expressed fully, clearly and legibly, containing no concealed pitfalls or traps. Appropriate prominence should be given to terms which might operate disadvantageously to the customer. Fair dealing requires that a supplier should not, whether deliberately or unconsciously, take advantage of the consumer's necessity, indigence, lack of experience, unfamiliarity with the subject matter of the contract, weak bargaining position or any other factor listed in or analogous to those listed in Schedule 2 to the [1994] Regulations."[4]

Lord Millet suggested a practical way to test fairness: **10–93**

> "There can be no one single test of this. It is obviously useful to assess the impact of an impugned term on the parties' rights and obligations by comparing the effect of the contract with the term and the effect it would have without it. But the inquiry cannot stop there. It may also be necessary to consider the effect of the inclusion of the term on the substance or core of the transaction; whether if it were drawn to his attention the consumer would be likely to be surprised by it; whether the term is a standard term, not merely in similar non-negotiable consumer contracts, but in commercial contracts freely negotiated between parties acting on level terms and at arms' length; and whether, in such cases, the party adversely affected by the inclusion of the term or his lawyer might reasonably be expected to object to its inclusion and press for its deletion. The list is not necessarily exhaustive; other approaches may sometimes be more appropriate."[5]

---

[2] *Director-General of Fair Trading v First National Bank plc* [2000] 1 All E.R. 240.
[3] [2000] Q.B. 672; [2000] 2 W.L.R. 1353; [2000] 2 All E.R. 759.
[4] [2002] 1 A.C. 481, para.17. The factors listed in Sch. 2 to the 1994 Regs can be found in the recitals to the Directive.
[5] *ibid.*, para.54.

10–94   The fairness test was considered in *Standard Bank London Ltd v Apostolakis (No. 2)*[6] where it was decided that a jurisdiction clause which increased the cost and inconvenience of litigation contravened the regulations. In *Picardi v Cuniberti*,[7] the English High Court held that a clause in a contract between an architect and a client which required the client to submit disputes to the adjudication procedure under the Housing Grants, Construction and Regeneration Act 1996 which does not normally apply to residential properties was unfair. In both these cases reference was made to the fact that the clauses fell under one of the headings in the "indicative and non-exhaustive list of the terms which may be regarded as unfair" contained in an Annexe to the Directive. These are terms which have the object or effect of "[e]xcluding or hindering the consumer's right to take legal action or exercise any other legal remedy." Considerable importance was placed by the judge on the failure of the architect to draw the clients' attention to unusual terms and to explain their significance. In *Oceano Grupo Editorial SA v Rocio Murciano Quintero*[8] the ECJ had founded on this paragraph in holding that a jurisdiction clause which confers exclusive jurisdiction on a court in the territorial jurisdiction of which the seller or supplier has his principal place of business must be regarded as unfair.

10–95   In a number of cases the Directive has added nothing to the protection Scottish consumers already have under the Act. In other ways it has extended considerably that protection. How far it does this will depend on the interpretation of the regulations by the judiciary and the limited evidence so far available suggests that they are applying them in the spirit intended. This assumes that consumers are able to obtain access to the courts. The Regulations take account of the danger that this may not occur in the procedures for enforcing the new rules to which we now turn.

Enforcement

10–96   It is a trite observation that consumer protection laws are of very little value if they cannot be enforced. As we will see in Ch.12 this is a major problem in Scotland, as in many other jurisdictions. Giving individual rights to consumers is of limited value especially where those against whom they must be asserted are much more powerful. Article 7 of the Directive requires Member States to "ensure that in the interests of consumers and of competitors, adequate and effective means exist to prevent the continued use of unfair terms." It goes on to add that the means referred to:

---

[6] [2001] Lloyd's Rep. Bank. 240.
[7] [2002] E.W.H.C. 2923; [2003] B.L.R. 487.
[8] Case C240/98; [2002] 1 C.M.L.R. 43.

"shall include provisions whereby persons or organisations, having a legitimate interest under national law in protecting consumers, may take action according to the national law concerned before the courts or before competent administrative bodies for a decision as to whether contractual terms drawn up for general use are unfair, so that they can apply appropriate and effective means to prevent the continued use of such terms."

Originally, this was implemented by giving the OFT powers, mod- **10–97** elled on those in the Control of Misleading Advertisements Regulations 1988,[9] to seek an interdict in the Court of Session. The Unfair Terms Regulations require the OFT[10] to consider complaints about unfair terms and to apply for an interdict "against any person appearing . . . to be using, or recommending use of, an unfair term drawn up for general use in contracts concluded with consumer.[11] The OFT have also been given new powers[12] to assist investigations of allegedly unfair terms. A major innovation of the 1999 Regulations is the extension of the power to enforce to various other "qualifying bodies" set out in Schedule 1. This followed the launching of litigation in England by the Consumers' Association asserting that the 1994 Regulations had not properly implemented the enforcement provisions of the Directive. Two groups of organisations now have enforcement powers. The first group of "qualifying bodies" to which enforcement powers have been extended are 11 statutory bodies: Information Commissioner, Gas and Electricity Markets Authority (Ofgem), Directors-General of Electricity Supply and for Gas for Northern Ireland, as well as the Office of Communications (Ofcom) and of Water Services, Rail Regulator and, most recently, Financial Services Authority.[13] Also included in this part are the weights and measures authorities in Great Britain as well as the Department of Enterprise Trade and Investment in Northern Ireland which is the weights and measures authority there. This means that trading standards departments of local authorities now have enforcement powers under the 1999 Regulations. In addition, the Consumers' Association also is a qualifying body.[14] These organisations may only seek an interdict after they have given the OFT notice of their intention to do so. This is part of a process of ensuring the co-ordination of action and the avoidance of duplication of effort.[15] A number of these qualifying bodies have

---

[9] SI 1988/915.

[10] SI 99/2083, reg.10.

[11] *ibid.*, reg.12(1).

[12] *ibid.*, reg.13.

[13] The FSA was added to the list when the Financial Services and Markets Act 2000 was enacted.

[14] The reason for the distinction is that the power to require information from those allegedly using unfair terms is not extended to qualifying bodies falling into the second category of which the Consumers' Association is the only example at present.

[15] See *Unfair Contract Terms Bulletin* (OFT, Issue 8, Dec. 1999), pp.4, 5.

used their powers among whom local authorities and Oftel (now subsumed in Ofgem) have been prominent.[16]

10–98   The court to which an application for an injunction or interdict may be made is the Court of Session or the sheriff court, and in the rest of the UK the High Court or the county court. Conferring jurisdiction on the sheriff court and the county court is an innovation which follows the model of Pt 8 of the Enterprise Act 2002, which permits the OFT to take action against traders who do not comply with their obligations to consumers. This facility will be particularly useful for trading standards departments who are likely to take action against local traders; and will also be appropriate where other bodies entitled to seek interdicts sue local businesses.

10–99   The approach of the OFT and the qualifying bodies which have powers under the Regulations, has been to seek to persuade traders to remove or amend terms. The OFT has put considerable resources into the creation of an unfair terms unit, and its operation must be one of its greatest successes. To see the practical effect of the Regulations, it is to the results of the OFT's enforcement that one should look rather than the small number of court decisions on individual cases. By the end of September 2003 it had received 8,300 complaints. Approximately 37 per cent of these were not proceeded with either because they were duplicate or defective complaints or could be dealt with more appropriately under other legislation or were not about contract terms. Eight per cent of complaints were about terms which were not considered to be unfair. It was possible to deal with 25 per cent by advice or warning. In 10 per cent, or 888 cases, an informal undertaking to stop using the term was given by a business, and in 27 cases businesses were required to give formal undertakings. In only one case has it been necessary to obtain a court order.[17] Two spectacular examples of the benefits of the Regulations are contained in a recent report which shows that the agreement of a mortgage company to remove unfair penalties in its loan agreements has saved consumers £65.2 million and amendments to mobile telephone contracts is estimated to save consumers between £60 and £80 million.[18]

OTHER STATUTORY CONTROLS

10–100   The Unfair Contract Terms Act 1977 and the Unfair Terms in Consumer Contracts Regulations 1999[19] are, undoubtedly, the most important controls on exclusion clauses. Brief mention should be made of some other statutory controls. Section 29 of the Public Passenger Vehicles Act 1981 invalidates a provision in a contract for the conveyance of

---

[16] See *Unfair Contract Terms Bulletin*, ss.24 and 25 (OFT, 686, Dec. 2003), p.171.
[17] *ibid.*, p.155.
[18] *The Office of Fair Trading: Protecting the Consumer from Unfair Trading Practices* (Comptroller and Auditor General, 1999–00 HC 57), p.53.
[19] SI 1999/203.

passengers in a public service vehicle which purports to restrict the liability of a person in respect of death or personal injury. The Warsaw Convention on carriage by air which is given effect to by the Carriage by Air Act 1961 controls their use in contracts of air travel. Section 6(3) of the Defective Premises Act 1972 renders void any attempt to contract out of the provisions of the Act. The Trading Stamps Act 1964 prevents the implied terms relating to the title of the promoter of the trading stamp scheme and the quality of the goods being excluded. There are many examples in the Consumer Credit Act 1974 of provisions designed to protect debtors and hirers out of which it is not possible to contract as a result of s.173 of that Act. Similarly, s.7 of the Consumer Protection Act 1987 provides that it is not possible to contract out of the strict delictual duty imposed on producers of defective products.

CHAPTER 11

CONTROL OF TRADING PRACTICES

11–01 This chapter deals with the control of unfair trading practices. There has been a traditional reluctance by government in this country to intervene in this area. Nevertheless, there are several areas where the law does impose specific controls on certain types of trade practices and a number of these are discussed below. In addition, it should be noted that the material on exclusion clauses might well have been included here instead of in a separate chapter. Similarly, while the Trade Descriptions Act 1968[1] is discussed in this chapter there is other material in Ch.3 which deals with controlling trade practices. Attention is also drawn to Ch.9 where the control of trade practices relating to credit are discussed. The credit licensing system provides a good example of one technique which may be used to regulate trade practices.

11–02 A number of methods are used to control unfair or deceptive trade practices. The criminal law is sometimes used to ban or control a practice; statute may intervene to alter the civil law, as it does in relation to exclusion clauses; or a combination of criminal and civil law controls may be used. More recently, administrative methods have been introduced, originally through the Fair Trading Act 1973 and now by Pt 8 of the Enterprise Act 2002. In addition to the use of legal techniques it has become increasingly common to resort to self-regulation of industry through codes of practice. This chapter begins by looking at the most important example of the use of the criminal law to control trading practices—the Trade Descriptions Act 1968 and the related Property Misdescriptions Act 1991. A varied collection of practices which are statutorily controlled by criminal and civil methods is then discussed after which the use of administrative techniques is considered. There follows a look at the role of self-regulation.

11–03 Before looking at how the law intervenes it is worth considering why such intervention is necessary at all. There are some who argue that intervention by the state to control unfair or deceptive trading practices is unnecessary. They assert that competition will usually ensure that those who promote unfair methods of trading will not flourish and that consumers who have been injured by unfair practices can resort to

---

[1] Hereinafter "the Act".

traditional legal remedies.[2] It is true that there are common law crimes that might be seen as having some role to play; and that the common law doctrines of fraud, facility and circumvention, undue influence, and force and fear might have relevance. In practice, such private law remedies are of limited use. The cost of invoking them, if their availability is known, is often prohibitively expensive. In any event, in the more serious cases of malpractice the trader may be difficult to find by the time that the consumer realises that he or she has been the victim of a swindle. This argues for measures which will deter and for institutions with the muscle to police the market.

STATUTORY CONTROL

TRADE DESCRIPTIONS

Introduction

The Trade Descriptions Act 1968 has an important role in the protection **11–04** of purchasers of goods and services through the criminal law. The Act aims to protect consumers against false or misleading claims about goods and services. Legislation of this kind is not new; the earliest example is the Merchandise Marks Act 1862, which was replaced by the more effective Merchandise Marks Act 1887. While the consumer derived some benefit from the Merchandise Marks Acts 1887 to 1953,[3] these Acts were not designed primarily to protect consumer interests.

It was part of the remit of the Molony Committee[4] to review this **11–05** legislation, and it made four main recommendations in this regard. It recommended that the definition of a "trade description" should be widened considerably to include characteristics of goods which were of significant interest to consumers. Powers to define the meaning of terms used in trade and to require that the consumer be provided with essential information about goods were advocated. The committee also laid stress on the need to ensure that new legislation should cover any trade description likely to be taken as relating to goods, whether in advertisements or elsewhere. Its final main recommendation, and one of immense importance, was that there should be specific provisions about enforcement which should be the duty of local weights and measures authorities.

---

[2] See, *e.g.* Posner, "The Federal Trade Commission" (1969–70) 37 University of Chicago L.R. 47.

[3] Merchandise Marks Acts 1887–1953 comprised Merchandise Marks Act 1887, 1891, 1911, 1926 and 1953, Merchandise Marks (Prosecutions) Act 1894, and Patents etc. (International Conventions) Act 1938.

[4] Final Report of the Committee on Consumer Protection, Cmnd. 1781 (1962) (Molony Report).

11–06   The Trade Descriptions Act 1968 incorporated most of the proposals of the Molony committee and, indeed, went further. The most significant excursions beyond the Molony committee's recommendations were in relation to services and prices which are discussed below.[5]

11–07   The Act protects the purchaser of goods by creating criminal offences relating to the making of false trade descriptions and the importation of goods bearing false indications of origin or bearing infringing trade marks. The Act also enables regulations to be made defining terms used in connection with goods[6] and the display of information in advertisements.

Trade Descriptions and Goods

11–08   The two principal criminal offences in relation to goods are set out in s.1 of the Act. Any person who, in the course of a trade or business (1) applies a false trade description[7] to any goods, or (2) supplies or offers to supply any goods to which a false trade description is applied, is guilty of an offence. As was pointed out by the Lord Justice-Clerk (Grant) in an early decision on this part of the Act, "the offences created by section 1 are offences of strict liability subject only to the statutory defences provided".[8]

11–09   It is to be noted that the trade description must be applied "in the course of a trade or business" a phrase which is not defined in the Act. In *Roberts v Leonard*[9] it was held that professional people were included in the Act. The trade or business need not be retail, nor need the offender's business be primarily concerned with transactions of the kind which give rise to the prosecution.[10]

11–10   This was made clear in the *Havering London Borough v Stevenson*,[11] where a car-hire firm which regularly sold off cars from its fleet of cars when it wished to replace them was held to be doing so in the course of its trade or business as a car-hire firm. This decision was distinguished in the House of Lords in *Davies v Sumner*[12] on its facts but, as Lord Keith of Kinkel, who delivered a speech with which his brethren concurred, observed, its correctness was not challenged by counsel for the accused. *Davies v Sumner* decided that goods are not dealt with "in the course of a trade or business" unless there is a degree of regularity in such dealing as part of the normal practice of the business. Thus, the trading-in of a used car by the accused who was a self-employed courier

---

[5] See para.11–35.
[6] See 1968 Act, s.7.
[7] *ibid.*, s.1(1)(a), (b).
[8] *Macnab v Alexanders of Greenock Ltd*, 1971 S.L.T. 121.
[9] (1995) 14 Tr. L.R. 536.
[10] Sales in members clubs are not regarded as being in the course of a business, see *John v Matthews* [1970] 2 Q.B. 443; [1970] 2 All E.R. 643.
[11] [1970] 1 W.L.R. 1375.
[12] [1984] 1 W.L.R. 1301; [1984] 3 All E.R. 831, HL.

who used his car almost exclusively for his business was held not to be done in the course of a business. *Havering London Borough v Stevenson* was different for there the car-hire company regularly sold off its used stock. Sporadic sales of pieces of equipment, which were no longer required by a business, would, likewise, not be considered to fall within the purview of the Act.

In *Elder v Crowe*[13] the High Court of Justiciary dealt with a case **11–11** raising the question whether there was a course of trade. Trading standards officers found 300 bottles of counterfeit perfume, many of them in cellophane wrappers, in a house occupied by the appellant and he was charged with offering to supply goods to which a false trade description had been applied. He argued that the goods were not offered for supply in the course of a trade or business as what was involved was merely a "one-off" transaction. He was convicted and appealed to the High Court. There the dictum of Lord Keith in *Davies v Sumner*,[14] that a one-off adventure in the nature of trade, carried through with a view to profit, can itself constitute a trade, was approved. As there was evidence entitling the sheriff to conclude that this was such a case the appeal was refused.

For the purposes of the Act, statements published in newspapers, **11–12** books, periodicals, in films or sound or television broadcasts are not deemed to be made in the course of a business unless they form part of an advertisement.[15]

Offences, as the vast majority of the reported cases demonstrate, **11–13** normally arise from descriptions applied to goods for sale, but they may also arise from a purchase. This occurred in *Fletcher v Budgen*,[16] where a car dealer informed a private customer that his car was irreparably damaged and fit only for scrap. Nevertheless, the seller, who was paid £2 for the car by the dealer, later saw it advertised at £135. It transpired that repairs costing £56 been carried out to put it in a saleable condition. The dealer was convicted of applying a false trade description. The English Divisional Court held that the Act applied to buyers in the course of a business as well as those selling in the course of a business.

"Any person" includes bodies corporate or unincorporated by virtue **11–14** of the Interpretation Act 1978.[17] Limited companies are thus subject to the 1968 Act, as are partnerships, which, in any event, had been held in *Douglas v Phoenix Motors Ltd*[18] in relation to a Scottish partnership to

---

[13] 1996 S.C.C.R. 38.
[14] [1984] 1 W.L.R. 1301 at 1305.
[15] 1968 Act, s.39(2) (amended by Broadcasting Act 1990, s.203(1), Sch.20, para.11).
[16] [1974] 1 W.L.R. 1056; [1974] 2 All E.R. 1243, DC.
[17] Interpretation Act 1978, s.5, Sch.1.
[18] 1970 S.L.T. (Sh. Ct.) 57.

be bodies corporate, being legal persons distinct from the partners of whom they are composed, under the Partnership Act 1890.[19]

11–15 A person applies a trade description to goods if he (1) affixes or annexes it to or in any manner marks it on or incorporates it with (a) the goods themselves, or (b) anything in, on or with which the goods are supplied; or (2) places the goods in, on or with anything which the trade description has been affixed or annexed to, marked on or incorporated with, or places any such thing with the goods; or (3) uses the trade description in any manner likely to be taken as referring to the goods.[20]

11–16 It is to be noted that, contrary to the recommendation of the Molony committee,[21] trade descriptions may be applied orally as well as in written form.[22] However, where an oral misdescription is alleged, a prosecution must be brought within six months of the commission of the offence[23] and not 12 months which is the normal time-limit for summary proceedings.[24]

11–17 "Goods" includes ships and aircraft, things attached to land and growing crops.[25] It was widely accepted, despite the reference to things attached to land, that houses were not within the scope of the 1968 Act.[26] This omission has now been repaired by the Property Misdescriptions Act 1991 which is discussed below.[27]

11–18 The 1968 Act prohibits "false" descriptions. Ironically, this is itself somewhat misleading when one considers the manner in which it is amplified. The Act, of course, prohibits those trade descriptions which are blatantly deceptive, but it also encompasses that which, though not false, is misleading; that is to say, likely to be taken for such an indication of any of the matters specified as trade descriptions.[28] To secure a conviction it is not sufficient that a trade description be false in the above sense; it must be false to a material degree.[29]

---

[19] s.4(2).
[20] 1968 Act, s.4(1)(a)–(c).
[21] Final Report of the Committee on Consumer Protection, Cmnd. 1781 (1962) (Molony Report).
[22] 1968 Act, s.4(2).
[23] *ibid.*, s.19(4), and Criminal Procedure (Scotland) Act 1975, s.331(1).
[24] *ibid.*, s.19(3).
[25] *ibid.* s.39(1). "Ship" includes any boat and any other description of vessel used in navigation.
[26] Review of the Trade Descriptions Act 1968, Cmnd. 6628 (1976), p.27.
[27] See para.11–67.
[28] 1968 Act, s.3(2). Anything which, though not a trade description, is likely to be taken for an indication of any of those matters and, as such an indication, would be false to material degree is deemed to be a false trade description: s.3(3). A false indication that any goods comply with a standard specified or recognised by any person or implied by the approval of any person is deemed to be a false trade description if there is no such person or no specified standard, recognised or implied: s.2(4).
[29] *ibid.*, s.3(1).

In determining whether a description is false the relevance of **11–19** disclaimers has been a controversial issue.[30] The Act is silent on their effect, but in a number of cases their use has been accepted, albeit within very strict limits. There is no Scottish case in which this issue has arisen, although it seems significant that one of the findings in fact made by the sheriff in *Beattie v Tudhope*[31] was that there was no disclaimer. One may speculate and hope that the Scottish courts would take as vigorous an approach to this problem as have English courts. The leading decision is *Norman v Bennett*[32] where, in one of the many "clocking" cases, that is cases involving car odometers which have been turned back, the Lord Chief Justice laid down the following principle:

> "[W]here a false trade description is attached to goods, its effect can be neutralised by an express disclaimer or contradiction of the message contained in the trade description. To be effective any such disclaimer must be as bold, precise and compelling as the trade description itself and must be as effectively brought to the notice of any person to whom the goods may be supplied. In other words, the disclaimer must equal the trade description in the extent to which it is likely to get home to anyone interested in receiving the goods."[33]

Even where the disclaimer meets this test the courts will look at its **11–20** wording to see if that may create a false impression on the mind of the reader. *Corfield v Starr*[34] is a good example. There the disclaimer read "[w]ith deep regret due to the Customers' Protection Act we can no longer verify that the mileage shown on this vehicle is correct". The English Divisional Court regarded this reference to a fictitious statute, with its implication that the mileage was correct but could not be so stated, as rendering the disclaimer ineffective.

Some confusion has been introduced into this area by misunderstand- **11–21** ing of *Kent County Council v Price*.[35] A market trader had copies of various items of clothing bearing well-known brand names such as *Adidas, Levi's* and *Reebok* which he was selling at very low prices. Beside these items was a notice with the words "brand copy". On appeal the English Divisional Court refused to overturn the decision of the magistrates to acquit the defendant on the ground that the notice was an effective disclaimer. This has sometimes been seen as a counter-feiters' charter but looked at more carefully the decision is explicable as

---

[30] Bragg, "More Mileage in Disclaimers" (1982) 2 L.S. 172.
[31] 1984 S.L.T. 423; 1984 S.C.C.R. 198.
[32] [1974] 1 W.L.R. 1229; [1974] 3 All E.R. 351, D.C.
[33] [1974] 1 W.L.R. 1229 at 1232; [1974] 3 All E.R. 351 at 354.
[34] [1981] R.T.R. 380, DC.
[35] (1993) 12 Tr. L.R. 137 (1994) 158 L.G. Rev. 78, DC.

an example of the reluctance of an appeal court to alter the findings of fact of a trial court. The comments about disclaimers were obiter and a number of issues were not explored in detail.[36]

11–22 In the light of the strict attitude of the courts it is suggested that the review of the Act was right in recommending that the matter be left to be regulated by case law rather than amending the Act. Among those bodies favouring incorporation of the principles presently found in the case law into the Act was the Law Society of Scotland.[37]

11–23 The term "trade description" is defined comprehensively in the Act. It is an indication, direct or indirect, and by whatever means given, of any of the following matters with respect to any goods or parts of goods; that is to say:

(1) quantity,[38] size or gauge;
(2) method of manufacture, production, processing or reconditioning;
(3) composition;
(4) fitness for purpose, strength, performance, behaviour or accuracy;
(5) any physical characteristics not included in heads (1) to (4);
(6) testing by any person and results thereof[39];
(7) approval by any person or conformity with a type approved by any person;
(8) place or date of manufacture, production, processing or reconditioning;
(9) person by whom manufactured, produced, processed or reconditioned;
(10) other history, including previous ownership or use.[40]

11–24 The cases under the Merchandise Marks Acts 1887 to 1953 provide examples of what might be regarded as a misdescription in relation to composition. For example, it has been held to be a false description to

---

[36] Simmonds, "A Counterfeiter's Charter", Trading Standards Review, August 1993, p.22 and Smith "A Licence to Sell Counterfeit Goods?", Sol Jo 20 August 1993, p.822; and see the comments on the case in Trading and Consumer Law (Butterworths) 3-267.

[37] Review of the Trade Descriptions Act 1968, Cmnd. 6628 (1976), p.51.

[38] "Quantity" includes length, width, height, area, volume, capacity, weight and number: 1968 Act, s.2(3).

[39] It should be noted that the provisions under heads (6) and (7) may be seen as being buttressed by the provision which includes in the definition of "false trade description" statements that goods comply with specified standards or are approved by specified standards or are approved by specified persons even if such standards or persons are fictitious: see 1968 Act, s.34.

[40] 1968 Act, s.2(1). Approval marks applied to motor vehicles in respect of any international agreement to which the UK is a party are deemed to be a trade description: see Road Traffic Act 1972, s.63. See also Motor Vehicle (Designation of Approval Marks) Regulations 1979 (SI 1979/1088).

describe artificial silk stockings as "silk".[41] In addition, it has been held that "composition" is wide enough to cover the different articles which are comprised in a package of goods, as where a gas cooker was described as being supplied with a hand-held battery torch for ignition.[42]

Fitness for purpose

Fitness for purpose, strength, performance, behaviour or accuracy have **11–25** frequently been relevant to the description of second-hand cars. For example, auctioneers have been convicted for having applied the description "good condition" to a car which was not roadworthy.[43] In England the courts have been prepared to hold that expressions such as "beautiful car" and "immaculate condition" could be false descriptions within this provision in appropriate circumstances when applied to a car which to external examination seemed in good condition but internally was not.[44]

Somewhat controversially, in *Formula One Autocentres Ltd v Bir-* **11–26** *mingham City Council*[45] it was held that the term "Formula One Master Service" was a trade description within this paragraph. This arose from a check on the quality of the servicing offered by a garage. Trading standards officers arranged to have a car serviced by the appellants having first noted that there were various faults that the service ought to have rectified. When the car was returned without several of these faults having been attended to as the servicing schedule promised, a prosecution was brought under s.1 of the 1968 Act rather than s.14 which relates to services. It was held that there were false trade descriptions, first of "performance" and second, of "accuracy". It was also held that a false trade description had been applied to goods, namely the Rover car.[46]

Whilst the vast majority of the cases on fitness for purpose, etc. have **11–27** involved cars, *Sherratt v Gerald's the American Jewellers Ltd*[47] demonstrates that it can be applied to other products. In that case the misdescription was to describe as a "diver's watch" a timepiece which, on immersion in a bowl of water, filled with water.

---

[41] *Allard v Selfridge & Co Ltd* [1925] 1 K.B. 129.
[42] *British Gas Corp v Lubbock* [1974] 1 WL.R. 37; [1974] 1 All E.R. 188.
[43] *Aitchison v Reith and Anderson (Dingwall and Tain) Ltd*, 1974 J.C. 12; 1974 S.L.T.
[44] *Kensington and Chelsea Royal LBC v Riley* [1972] R.T.R. 122, DC; *Robertson v Dicicco* [1972] R.T.R. 431, DC; *R v Ford Motor Co Ltd* [1974] 1 W.L.R. 1220, CA; [1973] 3 All E.R. 489.
[45] *The Times*, Dec. 29, 1998, DC (transcript ref. CO/3641/98).
[46] The necessity to resort to s.1 in this way to overcome the need to prove mens rea under s.14 will disappear when the promise in the White Paper to amend s.14 is implemented.
[47] (1970) 114 S.J. 147, DC.

Details of manufacture, etc.

11–28 Statements which mislead about origin are caught by the provision in respect of place or date of manufacture, etc. and there are a number of examples from the Merchandise Marks Acts case law.[48] The provision in respect of the person by whom goods are manufactured, etc. has recently become important in the campaign to combat commercial counterfeiting. It can be the appropriate provision to invoke in cases of video piracy or the counterfeiting of computer equipment.[49]

Other history

11–29 Undoubtedly the most frequently invoked category of misdescription is the provision in respect of other history, including previous ownership or use. The vast majority of cases under the rubric have been those involving the altering of car odometers. Since *Macnab v Alexanders of Greenock Ltd*[50] there has been no doubt that this is appropriate. In that case Lord Justice-Clerk (Grant) stated: "The distance which a car has travelled seems to me to be just as much a part of its history as the places where it has been and the persons who have owned it. The mileometer figure is, if accurate, a silent historical record of previous use."[51]

11–30 Trade Descriptions, where they relate to animals, include sex, breed or cross, fertility and soundness, and in relation to semen, include the identity and characteristics of the animal from which it was taken and measure of dilution.[52] The 1968 Act excludes from the ambit of the term "trade description" various marks and descriptions applied in pursuance of the Consumer Protection Act 1987 and a number of statutes relating to agriculture and horticulture.[53] Where food and drug legislation has already prohibited the application of a description, such a description is deemed not to be a trade description within the meaning of the 1968 Act.[54] A similar provision applies to descriptions prohibited by the Medicines Act 1968.[55]

---

[48] *Holmes v Pipers Ltd* [1914] 1 K.B. 57, DC; *Sandeman v Cold* [1924] 1 K.B. 107, DC.

[49] Rowell, "Commercial counterfeiting—Analysis of Trading Standards Statistics" (1984) 92 *Monthly Review* 202. A trade mark could contribute to a misleading trade description, see *Re Swiss Miss Trademark* [1998] R.P.C. 889, CA.

[50] 1971 S.L.T. 121.

[51] *ibid.*, at 124. See also *Tarleton Engineering Co Ltd v Nattrass* [1973] 1 W.L.R. 1261; [1973] 3 All E.R. 699, DC.

[52] 1968 Act, s.2(2).

[53] 1968 Act, s.2(4) (amended by Agriculture Act 1970, ss.6(4), 87(3), 113(3), Sch.5, Pt. 5; European Communities Act 1972, s.4, Sch.3, Pt.3, Sch.4, para.4(2); Consumer Safety Act 1978, s.7(8); and Consumer Protection Act 1987, s.48(1), Sch.4, para.2(1)(a)).

[54] *ibid.*, s.2(5)(a) (amended by Consumer Safety Act 1978, s.7(8); Food Act 1984, s.134(a), Sch.10, para.11; and Consumer Protection Act 1987, Sch. 4, para. 2(1)(b)). See also *H.P. Bulmer Ltd and Showerings Ltd v Bollinger SA and Champagne Lanson Pere et Fils* [1978] R.P.C. 79; [1977] 2 C.M.L.R. 625, CA.

[55] *ibid.*, s.2(5)(b) (added by Medicines Act 1968, Sch.5, para.16).

Conclusion

As the above analysis demonstrates, the scope of the term "trade **11–31** description" is very wide. It has been argued by consumer organisations that to make it even more extensive the 1968 Act should adopt the practice adopted in some other countries and enact a general prohibition on the use of misleading descriptions.[56] The review committee rejected this view on the basis that the precision of the present method was desirable in a criminal statute and helpful to enforcement authorities and traders alike. It also pointed out that few suggestions for additions to the list of trade descriptions[57] have been made. Nevertheless it did recommend some extensions to the present list. Indications of the identity of a supplier or distributor and the standing, commercial importance or capabilities of a manufacturer, producer or supplier of goods were recommended as "[w]e very much doubt whether the provisions of s.2(1)(i) go anything like far enough to provide the protection which we think desirable."[58] Another proposal was that false and misleading indications of the contents of books, films and recordings, including their authorship should be brought within the scope of the Act.[59] To resolve a possible doubt about the scope of the Act relating to testing[60] it was recommended that, unless the contrary is expressed, an indication that goods have been tested should mean that they have either passed the test or would do so if tested.[61] Like the other recommendations in the review of the Act these useful proposals have not been acted upon.

Trade Descriptions in Advertisements

Advertisements present special problems, some of which are dealt with **11–32** in the Act.[62] Advertisements are, by nature, general statements about categories of goods and, therefore, trade descriptions contained in advertisements are to be taken as referring to all goods of the class, whether in existence at the time the advertisement was published or not.[63] In determining whether goods fall into a class, regard must be had, in addition to the form and content of the advertisement, to all matters which would affect a customer's judgement on this matter including the time, place, manner and frequency of the advertisement.[64]

---

[56] Review of the Trade Descriptions Act 1968, Cmnd. 6628 (1976), p.39.
[57] *i.e.* under 1968 Act, s.2(1).
[58] Review of Trade Descriptions Act 1968, Cmnd. 6628 (1976), p.127.
[59] *ibid.*, p.128.
[60] *i.e.* the scope of 1968 Act, ss.2(1)(f), 3(3).
[61] Review of the Trade Descriptions Act 1968, Cmnd. 6628 (1976), p.129.
[62] *i.e.* where in an advertisement a trade description is used in relation to any class of goods: 1968 Act, s.5(1). S.5 applies to Hallmarking Act 1973.
[63] See 1968 Act, s.5(2).
[64] *ibid.*, s.5(3).

11–33   A false statement is made when it is communicated to someone, so that in the case of a written advertisement it is made when the advertisement is read by each reader.[65] Thus, there are as many offences as there are readers of an advertisement. In Scotland the problem of multiple prosecutions which this may give rise to appears to be dealt with appropriately by means of administrative procedures adopted by the prosecuting authorities.[66]

11–34   The Act enables orders to be made requiring advertisements about goods to contain or refer to information, whether or not a trade description.[67]

Trade Descriptions and Services

11–35   Despite the fact that the Molony Report[68] did not so recommend, the Act applies to the provision of services, accommodation and facilities. It is an offence for any person in the course of any trade or business to make a statement which he knows to be false, or recklessly to make a statement which is false, about any of five matters relating to the provision of services, accommodation or facilities.[69] These are (a) their provision or nature; (b) the time, manner in which or persons by whom they are provided; (c) their location; or (d) that they have been examined, approved or evaluated by any person.[70]

11–36   The terms "services", "accommodation" or "facilities" are not defined, or fully defined, in the Act.[71] There has been some doubt whether professional services are regulated by the Act but in *R v Breeze* the argument that they were not was rejected.[72] In the only reported Scottish case[73] to deal with the meaning of the term "facilities" it was held, adopting the same approach as the English decisions, that to provide a facility was to provide someone with the wherewithal to do something for himself. Thus the provision of a guarantee with a television set was a facility. A closing down sale has been held not to be a facility within the meaning of the Act.[74]

---

[65] *Wings Ltd v Ellis* [1985] A.C. 272.

[66] Review of the Trade Descriptions Act 1968, Cmnd. 6628 (1976), p.84.

[67] See 1968 Act, s.9 and Trade Descriptions (Sealskin Goods) (Information) Order 1980 (SI 1980/1150).

[68] Cmnd. 1781 (1962).

[69] 1968 Act, s.14(1)(a),(b). "Services" does not include anything done under a contract of service: s.14(4). In relation to any services consisting of or including the application of any treatment or process or the carrying out of any repair, the matters specified in s.14(1) are to be taken to include the effect of the treatment, process or repair; s.14(3). The Secretary of State of Trade and Industry may make orders defining terms for the purpose of s.14.

[70] *ibid.*, s.14(1)(i)–(v).

[71] As to "services", see 1968 Act, ss.14(3), (4).

[72] [1973] 1 W.L.R. 994; [1973] 2 All E.R. 1141, CA.

[73] *Smith v Dixons Ltd*, 1986 S.C.C.R. 1.

[74] *Westminster City Council v Ray Alan (Manshops) Ltd* [1982] 1 WL.R. 383, DC.

Meaning of "false"

"False" means false to a material degree.[75] Anything (whether or not a **11–37** statement as to any specified matters[76]) likely to be taken for such a statement as to any of those matters as would be false is deemed to be a false statement as to that matter.[77] A statement made regardless of whether it is true or false is deemed to be made recklessly, whether or not the person making it had reasons for believing that it might be false.[78]

It has been commonplace to draw attention to the differing bases of **11–38** liability under ss.1 and 14 of the Act.[79] Section 14 is often said to be markedly different in requiring proof of *mens rea*. In the light of the House of Lords discussion of s.14 in *Wings Ltd v Ellis*[80] it is necessary to revise this assessment. As Lord Scarman put it, "the basic issue between the parties is whether . . . section 14(1)(a) creates an offence of strict, or more accurately, semi-strict, liability or is one requiring the existence of full *"mens rea"*.[81] Lord Scarman found that it fell into the category of "semi-strict" liability in so far as it "can be committed unknowingly, *i.e.* without knowledge of the act of statement."[82] This he justified on the ground that it advanced the social purpose of the legislation which was, in a simple and straightforward way, to protect consumers. He also pointed out that the Act is "not a truly criminal statute. Its purpose is not the enforcement of the criminal law but the maintenance of trading standards. Trading standards, not criminal behaviour, are its concern".[83] In these circumstances he deduced that the intention of the legislature was not to include *mens rea* as an ingredient of the offence. The Government announced its intention in a White Paper in 1999 to align the requirements for liability under ss.1 and 14.[84]

An offence is committed if a statement known to be false is made on **11–39** the defender's behalf in the course of a business. It is irrelevant that the defender did not know that the statement had been made. This was the case in *Wings Ltd v Ellis*, where a holiday firm was convicted when one of its brochures, containing a false statement was read, some months after first being issued, by a customer who obtained it from a travel agent.[85] As *Wings Ltd v Ellis* shows, statements are made not only on

---

[75] 1968 Act, s.14(4).
[76] *i.e.* the matters specified in 1968 Act, s.14(1): see para. 11–35.
[77] 1968 Act, s.14(2)(a).
[78] *ibid.*, s.14(2)(b).
[79] White Paper, para.3.19, the Government indicated that, subject to consultation, they intended to remove the distinction.
[80] [1985] A.C. 272.
[81] *ibid.*, at 290.
[82] *ibid.*, at 295.
[83] *ibid.*, at 293.
[84] *Modern Markets: Confident Consumers*, Cm. 4410 (1999), para.3.19.
[85] *op. cit.*, n.83.

first publication of a document, but on all later occasions when members of the public read them.

11–40   In the only other decision on s.14 of the Act by the House of Lords, the difficult problem of distinguishing between statements of fact, which if false are contrary to s.14, and statements as to future conduct, which are not, was discussed.[86] The bald assertion of this dichotomy conceals some of the problems. The existence of an intention can be a fact like anything else and thus within the prohibition. In a number of cases the difficulty has been that it could not be shown that the accused had at the time he made the assertion no intention to do what he promised.[87] However, *British Airways Board v Taylor*[88] demonstrates that assertions about future conduct can be within the Act. In that case a passenger who had a return ticket from London to Bermuda received from BOAC a written confirmation that he had a booking on a specific flight. When he arrived at the airport he was informed that the flight was full and he was not permitted to travel on that flight. It was shown that BOAC, in common with other airlines, adopted a policy which could lead to this situation. In these circumstances its assertion that the passenger was assured of a seat on the flight was, to its knowledge when made, false. This principle was applied in *Herron v Lunn Poly (Scotland) Ltd.*[89]

Miscellaneous Provisions in respect of Trade Descriptions, etc.

Marking orders

11–41 The Secretary of State for Trade and Industry is empowered by the Act to make orders requiring that goods be marked with or accompanied by certain information.[90] Failure to comply is a criminal offence.[91]

Imported goods

11–42 The Act makes it a criminal offence to import into the United Kingdom goods bearing false indication of their place of origin.[92]

False representation as to royal approval, etc.

11–43 In addition to the prohibitions relating to false trade descriptions already discussed in relation to the supply of goods and services the Act bans false representations as to royal approval or award. It is an offence in the course of a trade or business to give a false indication that goods or services are of a kind supplied to or approved by any member of the

---

[86] *British Airways Board v Taylor* [1976] 1 W.L.R. 13; [1976] 1 All E.R. 65, HL.
[87] *Beckett v Cohen* [1972] 1 W.L.R. 1593; [1973] 1 All E.R. 120, DC.
[88] [1985] A.C. 272.
[89] 1972 S.L.T. (Sh. Ct.) 2.
[90] 1968 Act, s.8.
[91] *ibid.*, s.8(2).
[92] *ibid.*, s.16.

royal family.[93] It is also an offence to make unauthorised use of any device or emblem signifying the Queen's Award to Industry.[94]

False representations as to supply of goods or services

The Act creates an offence of falsely claiming that goods or services **11–44** supplied by a person are of a kind supplied to any person.[95] This is a strict liability offence, but is subject to the general defences set out in the Act.

Defences

Like other consumer protection measures sanctioning behaviour by **11–45** means of strict criminal liability, the severity of the Act offences is mitigated by the defence of due diligence.[96] There is also a defence of innocent publication of advertisements.[97] Although strictly speaking the provision regarding offences due to the fault of another person is not a defence, it is convenient to deal with it here.[98] There has been some doubt as to whether the defences apply in respect of the offence of making false or misleading statements as to services,[99] but this has been dispelled by the decision of the House of Lords in *Wings Ltd v Ellis*.[1]

In *R v Southwood*[2] it was held that the defences could not be used **11–46** where the charge was one of applying a false description to goods. In that case a motor trader had "clocked" a car. The invoice given to the purchaser contained a disclaimer on which the defendant relied as demonstrating that he came within the reasonable precautions defence. The English Court of Criminal Appeal found such a course of action illogical and refused to countenance this as a defence.

Defence of due diligence

To establish the defence of due diligence the accused must establish two **11–47** things: (1) that the commission of the offence was due to his[3] mistake, or reliance on information supplied to him or to the act or default of another person, an accident or some other cause beyond his control[4]; and (2) that he took all reasonable precautions and exercised all due diligence to avoid the commission of the offence by himself or by

---

[93] 1968 Act, s.12(1).
[94] *ibid.*, s.12(2).
[95] *ibid.*, s.13.
[96] *ibid.*, s.24.
[97] *ibid.*, s.25.
[98] *ibid.*, s.23.
[99] *ibid.*, s.14.
[1] [1985] A.C. 272.
[2] [1987] 1 W.L.R. 1361.
[3] *Birkenhead and District Co-operative Society Ltd v Roberts* [1970] 1 W.L.R. 1497; [1970] 3 All E.R. 391, DC.
[4] 1968 Act, s.24(1).

anyone under his control. Where the accused is relying on the act or default of, or on information supplied by, another person he must give, at least seven days before the date of the hearing, written notice to the prosecution giving such information as he has identifying the other person.[5]

11–48   These defences apply to all the offences created by the Act. However, in addition there is a separate defence in respect of the offence of supplying or offering to supply goods to which a false trade description has been applied,[6] which provides that it is a defence to prove that the accused did not know, and could not with reasonable diligence have ascertained, that the goods did not conform to the description or that the description had been applied to the goods.[7]

11–49   The defence of due diligence has given rise to frequent litigation. The part of the defence involving ascription of fault to "another person" has revealed a weakness in the Act where large corporate traders[8] are concerned. It has been held that a branch manager of a large retailing chain was "another person", it not being possible to identify him as the *alter ego* of the company.[9] Only very senior members of the company could be so regarded. The extent to which reliance on this defence may undermine the purpose of the Act should not be over-emphasised. In another case it was pointed out that the defence was not available unless all reasonable inquiries had been made to try to establish the actual person responsible for the offence and that it was not sufficient simply to produce a list of all the staff who might have been responsible.[10]

11–50   It should also be noted that shifting the blame to another person is only one ingredient of the defence, the other being that the accused took all reasonable precautions and exercised all due diligence. The courts have not been easily satisfied on this score. The case law would seem to support the proposition that to avail himself of this part of the defence the accused must show that he had set up a system designed to prevent errors and also that that system was adequately operated. The two Scottish cases which discuss the reasonableness of precautions and due diligence certainly set high standards. In one of these cases the defence was not available, but the High Court of Justiciary would not have held it to have been satisfied.[11]

11–51   The circumstances were that a car sold by the accused company had been serviced by it some months before and the company was not considered to have taken all reasonable precautions to avoid a mis-description of the car's mileage because it was proved that it had taken

---

[5] 1968 Act, s.24(2).
[6] *ibid.*
[7] *ibid.*, s.24(3).
[8] As to offences by corporations, see 1968 Act, s.20.
[9] *Tesco Supermarkets Ltd v Nattrass* [1972] A.C. 153; [1971] 2 All E.R. 127, HL.
[10] *McGuire v Sittingbourne Co-operative Society Ltd* [1976] Crim. L.R. 268, DC.
[11] *Macnab v Alexanders of Greenock Ltd*, 1971 S.L.T. 121.

no steps to check its own records. In the other case the failure of the accused's managing director to check that his instructions had been carried out showed want of due diligence.[12] It was also stated by the High Court of Justiciary that where auctioneers applied descriptions concerning the condition of cars which they offered for sale it was not sufficient, to meet the reasonableness requirement of the defence, merely to carry out a cursory external examination. The Lord Justice-Clerk (Wheatley) observed that the accused "were under no obligation to give any description of the condition of the car, but, if they elected to do so they should have taken some reasonable steps to see that their description was warranted."[13]

A similarly strict line was taken by the High Court of Justiciary in **11–52** *Ford v Guild*,[14] in which a motor dealer appealed against a conviction for supplying a car to which a false trade description had been applied. The dealer had bought the car from D, a private individual, who told him that the mileage reading was correct. It was slightly above average for the age of the car but appeared to be consistent with its condition. D gave his name and address and the name and address of B, the previous owner, but could not produce any service documents. The address of B proved to be false and he could not be traced. The appeal was dismissed. Although the dealer had no reason to disbelieve D's information he had made no attempt to confirm that B existed and the sheriff had been entitled to find that he had not established under s.24(3) of the Act that he could not have ascertained the truth.

Offence due to the fault of another person

Sometimes referred to as the "by-pass" provision, s.23 of the Act **11–53** enables a prosecution to be brought against a person whose act or default has caused another person to commit an offence, even if that other person has not been prosecuted. It is a provision that has been borrowed from the food and drugs legislation, where it has a long history. The version used in the Act is not clearly drafted and, read literally, it is difficult to make sense of it. It could be argued that the first person would not have committed an offence if he could bring himself within the due diligence defence of s.24 by proving that the offence was due to the act or default of another and that he had exercised due diligence. In *Coupe v Guyett*[15] Widgery L.C.J. suggested that ss.23 and 24 could be fitted together. Where the first person referred to in s.23 has a defence on the merits and without reliance on s.24, it is not possible to operate s.23 so as to render guilty the person whose act or default gave rise to the matter in complaint. He argued that s.23 comes into play

---

[12] *Aitchison v Reith and Anderson (Dingwall and Tain) Ltd*, 1974 J.C. 12; 1974 S.L.T. 282.

[13] 1974 J.C. 12 at 17, 18; 1974 S.L.T. 282 at 287.

[14] 1990 J.C. 55; 1990 S.L.T. (Sh. Ct.) 502; 1989 S.C.C.R. 572.

[15] [1973] 1 W.L.R. 669; [1973] 2 All E.R. 1058, DC.

only where the first person escaped prosecution by taking advantage of the due diligence defence of s.24.

11–54   Unlike the other sections of the Act creating criminal offences, s.23 is not prefaced by the words "in the course of a business". It has been held in England that a private individual not acting in the course of a business can be prosecuted under it.[16]

Enforcement and Penalties

11–55 Enforcement of the Act is the duty of the district councils as the local weights and measures authorities.[17] Prosecutions are carried out by the procurator fiscal, who decides whether a prosecution should be brought. There has been some disquiet in Scotland that the level of prosecutions is significantly lower than in England and Wales.[18]

11–56   In order to carry out their duties under the Act, trading standards officers are given various powers. They may make test purchases,[19] enter premises at all reasonable hours to ascertain if the Act is being observed and, if they have reasonable cause to suspect that an offence has been committed, may require production of books and documents and seize goods.[20] On obtaining a warrant from a sheriff or justice of the peace admission to premises, by force if necessary, is permissible.[21] Where goods are seized in exercise of these powers, the enforcement authority may in certain circumstances be liable to pay compensation to a trader.[22] Obstruction of an enforcement officer in the exercise of his duty is a criminal offence.[23]

11–57   The penalties for most offences under the Act are, on summary conviction, a maximum fine not exceeding the prescribed sum[24] and, on indictment, a fine or a term of imprisonment not exceeding two years, or both.[25] The offence of obstructing an enforcement officer in the exercise of his duty[26] carries a fine not exceeding level 3 on the standard scale.[27]

---

[16] *Olgeirsson v Kitching* [1986] 1 W.L.R. 304; [1986] 1 All E.R. 746, DC. See also Ervine, "Private Sellers and the Trade Descriptions Act", 1986 S.L.T. (News) 217.

[17] Weights and Measures Act 1985, s.69(3).

[18] Purdom and Walker, *The Enforcement of the Trade Descriptions Act in Scotland, Scottish Consumer Council* (1980).

[19] See 1968 Act, s.27. As to notice of test and intended prosecution, see s.30(1).

[20] *ibid.*, s.28 (amended by Consumer Credit Act 1974, s.192(3)(a), Sch. 4, para. 28, and Consumer Protection Act 1987, s.48(1), Sch.4, para.2(2)).

[21] See 1968 Act, s.28(3).

[22] *ibid.*, s.33.

[23] *ibid.*, s.29.

[24] *ibid.*, s.18(a). The prescribed sum is now £5,000: Criminal Procedure (Scotland) Act 1975, s.289B (added by Criminal Law Act 1977, s.63(1), Sch.2, para.5, substituted by Criminal Justice Act 1982, s.55(2), amended by Criminal Justice Act 1991, s.17(2)).

[25] 1968 Act, s.18(b).

[26] Consumer Protection Act 1987, s.29(1).

[27] *ibid.*, s.29(1), and Criminal Procedure (Scotland) Act 1975, ss.289F(8), 289G(2) (added by Criminal Justice Act 1982, s.54).

MISLEADING PRICES

The control of misleading indication of prices has proved to be a **11–58** difficult and controversial matter. On the one hand it is important not to impede the working of the competitive process by unnecessary restrictions but, on the other hand, it is difficult by simple methods to catch those determined to exploit the loopholes in legislation. Section 11 of the 1968 Act sought to regulate price advertising, but it proved necessary to buttress it with the Price Marking (Bargain Offers) Order 1979.[28] This proved unpopular both with traders and trading standards officers, and Pt 3 of the Consumer Protection Act 1987[29] introduces a different approach to the regulation of price advertising.

Instead of attempting to prohibit specific practices, as the earlier **11–59** legislation did, the 1987 Act creates two general offences of giving to consumers misleading indications as to the price of any goods, services, accommodation or facilities. These are found in s.20. The first is in s.20(1) which provides as follows:

> "Subject to the following provisions of this Part, a person shall be guilty of an offence if, in the course of any business of his, he gives (by any means whatever) to any consumers an indication which is misleading as to the price at which any goods, services, accommodation or facilities are available (whether generally or from particular persons)."

The other offence is in the s.20(2): **11–60**

> "Subject as aforesaid, a person shall be guilty of an offence if—
>
> (a) in the course of any business of his, he has given an indication to any consumers which, after it was given, has become misleading as mentioned in subsection (1) above; and
>
> (b) some or all of those consumers might reasonably be expected to rely on the indication at a time after it has become misleading; and
>
> (c) he fails to take all such steps as are reasonable to prevent those consumers from relying on the indication."

The difference between these offences is that the first is aimed at price **11–61** indications which are misleading when made; the second at those which were originally accurate but subsequently became inaccurate. This is illustrated in two prosecutions arising from price matching claims. In *The Link Stores Ltd v London Borough of Harrow*[30] a customer

---

[28] SI 1979/364 (amended by SI 1979/633 and SI 1979/1124).
[29] Hereinafter "the 1987 Act".
[30] [2001] 1 WLR 1479.

purchased a mobile phone from the appellant's store having seen a notice saying that if he found a lower price locally within seven days the difference would be refunded. The customer did find a lower price locally but the appellant refused to make a refund. A prosecution under s.20(2) failed because there was no evidence that the offer was originally intended to be honoured but later there was a change of mind. On the other hand, in *DSG Retail Ltd v Oxfordshire County Council*[31] in somewhat similar circumstances a prosecution succeeded, but there it had been brought under s.20(1).

11–62   An indication of the price or the method of determining a price is misleading if what is conveyed, or what consumers might reasonably be expected to infer from the indication or any omission from it, includes any of a number of factors.[32] These are indications:

(1) the price is less than, or the method is not what, in fact it is;
(2) the applicability of the price or method does not depend on facts or circumstances on which its applicability does in fact depend;
(3) the price or method covers matters in respect of which an additional charge is made;
(4) a trader has no genuine belief that a price increase or reduction or alteration of a method is imminent; and
(5) facts or circumstances by reference to which a consumer might reasonably be expected to judge the validity of a comparison are not accurate.[33]

11–63   It is made clear that references to services do not include references to services provided to an employer under a contract of employment[34] and that s.20 does not apply to investment business.[35] However, it is emphasised that the provision of credit[36] or banking or insurance services, the purchase or sale of foreign currency,[37] the supply of electricity and the provision of off-street car parks and caravan sites[38]

---

[31] [2001] 1 WLR 1765.
[32] Consumer Protection Act 1987, s.21(1), (2).
[33] *ibid.*, ss.21(1)(a)–(e), (2)(a)–(e), (3).
[34] *ibid.*, s.22(2). By virtue of s.22(5), "contract of employment" and "employer" have the same meaning as in Employment Protection (Consolidation) Act 1978 (see s.153(1)).
[35] See s.20(5A) which was inserted by SI 2001/3649, art.309. Misleading price claims about investments are dealt with by Financial Services and Markets Act 2000 s.397.
[36] "Credit" has the same meaning as in Consumer Credit Act 1974: Consumer Protection Act 1987, s.22(5).
[37] In relation to a service consisting in the purchase or sale of foreign currency references in Consumer Credit Act 1974, Pt 3, to the method by which the price of the service is determined include references to the rate of exchange: Consumer Protection Act 1987, s.22(4).
[38] "Caravan" has the same meaning as in the Caravan Sites and Control of Development Act 1960 (see s.29(1)): Consumer Protection Act 1987, s.22(5).

are included.[39] This somewhat curious provision is explained by the fact that all these services have been the subject of frequent complaints on account of the quality of price advertising. Reference to accommodation or facilities does not include accommodation or facilities being made available by means of the creation or disposal of an interest in land, except where it is the creation or disposal of the *dominium utile* of land comprising a new dwelling or a leasehold in such a dwelling where at least 21 years remains unexpired.[40]

For the most part the defences available are similar to those **11–64** applicable to offences under the 1968 Act. The due diligence defence set out in the 1987 Act applies.[41] It is a defence for a person (1) to show that a price indication complied with regulations made under Pt 3[42] of the 1987 Act[43]; (2) that he was a bona fide publisher of an advertisement[44]; or (3) that he was the author of a recommended price and did not offer goods, services, accommodation or facilities himself but reasonably assumed that the recommended price was, for the most part, being followed.[45]

A defence which gave rise to a good deal of controversy during the **11–65** parliamentary progress of the Consumer Protection Bill is that in respect of the code of practice. The Secretary of State, after consulting the OFT and such other persons as may be appropriate, may by order approve a code of practice giving practical guidance about price indications.[46] Failure to comply with this code does not by itself give rise to any criminal or civil liability, but it will have evidential value[47] in that contravention of the code may be relied on for the purpose of establishing that an offence had been committed or of negativing a defence, while compliance with the code may be relied on to show that no offence has been committed or that there is a defence.[48]

Enforcement

The enforcement of the provisions in respect of misleading price **11–66** indications is the duty of district councils as the weights and measures

---

[39] Consumer Protection Act 1987, s.22(1)(a)–(e).

[40] *ibid.*, s.23.

[41] *ibid.*, ss.24(5), 39. In respect of offences under Pt 3 (ss.20–26), s.39 only applies to the offence of giving a misleading price indication under s.20(1): s.26.

[42] *ibid.*, s.24(1).

[43] This defence is only available in respect of offences under s.20(1), (2).

[44] Consumer Protection Act 1987, s.24(3). This defence is only available in respect of offences under s.20(1), (2). "Advertisement" includes a catalogue, a circular and a price list: s.24(6). In proceedings for an offence under s.20(1), (2), in respect of an indication published in a book, newspaper, magazine, film or radio or television broadcast or in a programme included in a cable programme service, it is a defence to show that the indication was not contained in an advertisement: s.24(2),(6).

[45] *ibid.*, s.24(4). This defence is only available in respect of an offence under s.20(1).

[46] *ibid.*, s.25(1), (3), (4).

[47] *i.e.* in proceedings for an offence under 1987 Act, s.20(1), (2).

[48] 1987 Act, s.25(2).

authorities.[49] The penalties for the offence of giving a misleading price indication are, on conviction on indictment, a fine, and on summary conviction, a fine not exceeding the statutory maximum.[50]

PROPERTY MISDESCRIPTIONS

11–67 Although house purchase is most people's most expensive purchase it was generally agreed that houses for sale did not come within the ambit of the 1968 Act.[51] Despite a recommendation as long ago as 1976[52] that this omission should be rectified, this did not happen until the Property Misdescriptions Act 1991 was passed.[53] It makes it a criminal offence to make false or misleading statements about various matters in the course of an estate agency or property development business. The prescribed matters are set out in the Property Misdescriptions (Specified Matters) Order 1992.[54] They include location or address, aspect, view, outlook and environment, availability and proximity of services and facilities, accommodation and measurements, physical characteristics, surveys, history, and the identity of the builder. In addition, various matters relating to the tenure and incidents of ownership as well as rates and charges are included.

11–68 Like the offences in s.1 of the 1968 Act the offence created by this Act is one of strict liability. The Act also has a due diligence defence in s.2 in the interpretation of which the cases on the similar defence in the Act will be relevant. The false statement must be made in the course of an estate agency or property development business, "otherwise than in providing conveyancing services". A statement is made in the course of an estate agency business if (but only if) the making of the statement is a thing done as mentioned in section 1(1) of the Estate Agents Act 1979. This means anything done for the purposes of introducing a client to a third party who wishes to dispose of or acquire an interest in land.[55] Given the fact that solicitors offer estate agency services in Scotland, it may be difficult to decide when they are offering estate agency services and when they stray over the line into conveyancing service.

11–69 Enforcement is in the hands of the district councils as weights and measures authorities.[56] The penalty for a breach of the Act is, on

---

[49] 1987 Act, s.27.

[50] *ibid.*, s.20(4). As to the time-limit for bringing prosecutions, see s.20(5). "The statutory maximum" means the prescribed sum as defined in Criminal Procedure (Scotland) Act 1975, s.289B.

[51] See Review of the Trade Descriptions Act 1968, Cmnd. 6628 (1976), para.70.

[52] Cmnd. 6628 (1976).

[53] See Styles, "The Property Misdescriptions Act 1991" (1992) 37 J.L.S.S. 486.

[54] SI 1992/2834, which came into force on April 4, 1993.

[55] There is a similar provision in relation to the making of statements in the course of a property development business.

[56] Property Misdescriptions Act 1991, s.3 and Sch.

summary conviction, a fine not exceeding the statutory maximum which is currently £5,000[57]; and, on indictment, to an unlimited fine.

DOORSTEP SELLING

Complaints about high pressure selling methods employed by some **11–70** sales representatives when they visit consumers in their homes are not uncommon and this issue is the subject of a super complaint by the National Association of Citizens' Advice Bureaux to the OFT. They are particularly prevalent in relation to the sale of double glazing and encyclopaedias, but have arisen in other sectors as well.[58] The Doorstep Selling Directive[59] which was implemented in this country by the Consumer Protection (Cancellation of Contracts Concluded away from Business Premises) Regulations 1987[60] provides a civil remedy.

Although often referred to as a control on doorstep selling, the **11–71** Regulations apply more widely. Regulation 3 provides that they apply where a trader makes a contract relating to goods or services[61] during an unsolicited visit to the home of a consumer,[62] or to another person's home; and also to a person's workplace. They can also apply to a visit which was requested if it results in a contract to supply goods or services other than those concerning which the consumer requested the visit. For the Regulations to apply in those circumstances the consumer must not have known, or could not reasonably have known, when the visit was requested, that the supply of those goods or services formed part of the trader's business activities. Finally, the Regulations also apply to contracts concluded during an excursion organised by a trader away from trade premises.

The 1998 amendment to the Regulations seeks to close loopholes in **11–72** the Regulations by amplifying the meaning of "unsolicited visit" in a new reg.3(3). A visit by a trader is considered to be unsolicited if it follows an earlier unsolicited visit during which he, or someone acting in his name or on his behalf, indicated that he, or the trader in whose name or on whose behalf he was acting, was prepared to make a

---

[57] See n.45.

[58] Life assurance is notorious and since Insurance Companies Act 1982 there has been a right to cancel certain policies of insurance. See para.11–94.

[59] Directive to Protect the Consumer in Respect of Contracts Negotiated away from Business Premises, Dir. 85/577; [1985] O.J. L372/31.

[60] SI 1987/2117 (as amended by Consumer Protection (Cancellation of Contracts Concluded away from Business Premises) (Amendment) Regulations 1988 (SI 1988/958); and Consumer Protection (Cancellation of Contracts Concluded away from Business Premises) (Amendment) Regulations 1998 (SI 1998/3050)).

[61] The ECJ has ruled, in Case C-45/96 *Bayerische Hypotheken-und Wechselbank A.G. v Dietzinger* [1998] All E.R. (EC) 332, that the directive does not apply to a contract of guarantee concluded by a natural person who was not acting in the course of his trade or profession where repayment of a debt contracted by another person who was acting in the course of his trade or profession was being guaranteed.

[62] "Consumer" means a person, other than a body corporate, who, in making a contract is acting for purposes which can be regarded as outside his business: see reg.2(1).

subsequent visit to the consumer. The definition is also amended to make it clear that it covers a visit following an unsolicited telephone call where the person who visits the consumer is not the same as the person who made the telephone call, but the person who made the telephone call was acting in his name or on his behalf.

11–73   Not all contracts are subject to the Regulations. As we have seen, the Consumer Credit Act 1974 has provisions for a cooling off period for "cancellable agreements".[63] Where these apply they should be followed, even if the contract would also fall under these Regulations.[64] Contracts for the provision of credit of less than £35, other than hire-purchase and conditional sale contracts, are exempt, as are other contracts under which the consumer will not make payments of more than £35. There is an important exception also for the supply of food, drink or other goods intended for current consumption by use in the household and supplied by regular roundsmen. Obvious examples would be milk or bread deliveries. Catalogue traders who leave their catalogues with their customers and expect to have a continuous relation with them are exempt from the Regulations if their catalogues and contracts contain a prominent notice that the consumer may return the goods within seven days of their receipt.[65]

11–74   Also excluded from the Regulations are contracts for the sale of land, heritable securities and bridging finance in connection with the purchase of land. Contracts for the construction or extension of a building are exempt. However, the Regulations explicitly state that they do apply to a contract to supply goods and incorporate them in a building; and a contract for the repair of a building.[66] Contracts for fitted kitchens or double glazing are, therefore, clearly within the Regulations. Investment agreements under the Financial Services and Markets Act 2000 and contracts of insurance governed by the Insurance Companies Act 1982 are also exempt.

11–75   Where the Regulations apply, consumers have a cooling-off period of seven days from the making of the contract. During this period they may cancel the contract by giving written notice of cancellation. This need be in no particular form as long as it indicates the intention of the consumer to cancel the contract. The fact that there is a cooling-off period must be brought to the attention of consumers by an easily legible notice which must be given at least as much prominence as any other information in the document. It must contain the information set out in the schedule to the Regulations and a cancellation form in the form set out there. The notice must be given to the consumer at the time of making the contract or, where consumers offer to enter into a contract in their homes, when they make that offer. Failure to comply with this requirement means that

---

[63] See para.9–102.
[64] reg.4(2).
[65] reg.3(2)(c).
[66] reg.3(2)(a).

the contract is not enforceable and that the trader commits a criminal offence.[67]

Where consumers exercise their rights to cancel, any money that they **11–76** have paid becomes repayable and there is a lien for its repayment over any goods supplied under the contract which may be in the possession of a consumer. Subject to this lien, consumers who are in possession of goods are under a duty to take reasonable care of them pending their return to the supplier. Although under no obligation to deliver the goods to the supplier other than at their own homes, consumers may choose to return them to the person on whom a cancellation notice could have been served. These duties to take reasonable care of the goods and to return them are statutory duties and are actionable as such.[68] There are detailed provisions in the Regulations dealing with the return of goods given in part exchange[69] and the repayment of credit.[70]

DISTANCE SELLING

Distance selling by which is meant a sales method where the buyer and **11–77** supplier do not come face to face up to and including the moment at which the contact is concluded is becoming increasingly important. Mail order selling is an important and long-standing example and telephone sales and tele-shopping are other examples. E-commerce is an increasingly important growth area with sales over the Internet growing steadily. Few aspects of distance selling were subject to statutory regulation in the UK beyond those controls which apply generally to the supply of goods and services. This has changed with the implementation of the Distance Selling Directive[71] by the Consumer Protection (Distance Selling) Regulations 2000.[72]

The Regulations apply to contracts for goods or services to be **11–78** supplied to a consumer where the contract is made exclusively by means of distance communication and reg.25 provides that it is not possible to contract out of them. Regulation 3 defines "means of distance communication" as any means used without the simultaneous physical presence of the consumer and the supplier and Sch.1 contains an indicative list of examples such as contracts made by telephone, email, letter of fax. Regulation 5 contains a number of exceptions such as contracts relating to the supply of financial services, certain contracts relating to land, those concluded through automated vending machines, auctions and those concluded through a telecommunications operator using a public pay-phone. As a result of reg.6 the Regulations have limited application to contracts for the supply of groceries by regular delivery

[67] regs 4, 4A.
[68] reg.7(8).
[69] reg.8.
[70] reg.6.
[71] Dir. 97/7; [1997] O.J. L144/4, p.19.
[72] SI 2000/2334, which came into effect on Oct. 31, 2000

and contracts for the provision of accommodation, transport, catering or leisure services.

11–79   The Regulations require the supplier to provide the consumer with the information referred to in reg.7 prior to the conclusion of the contract. This includes information on the right to cancel the distance contract, the main characteristics of the goods or services, and delivery costs where appropriate. Regulation 8 requires the supplier to confirm in writing, or another durable medium which is available and accessible to the consumer, information already given and to give some additional information, including information on the conditions and procedures relating to the exercise of the right to cancel the contract. Regulation 8(3) requires the supplier to inform the consumer prior to conclusion of a contract for services that he will not be able to cancel once performance of the service has begun with his agreement.

11–80   An important aspect of the Regulations is the provision of a cooling-off period to enable the consumer to cancel the contract by giving notice of cancellation to the supplier. The effect of giving notice of cancellation under the Regulations is that the contract is treated as if it had not been made. Where the supplier supplies the information to the consumer on time, the cooling-off period is seven working days from the day after the date of the contract, in the case of services, or from the day after the date of delivery of the goods. Where the supplier fails to comply with the information requirement at all, the cooling-off period is extended by three months. Where the supplier complies with the information requirement later than he should have done but within three months the cooling-off begins from the date he provided the information.[73]

11–81   Certain contracts are excluded from the right to cancel unless the parties agree otherwise, such as a contract for the supply of goods made to the consumer's specifications.[74] If consumers cancel, they must be reimbursed within a maximum period of 30 days[75] and any related credit agreement is automatically cancelled.[76] Regulation 17 provides that on cancellation of the contract the consumer is under a duty to restore goods to the supplier if he collects them and in the meantime to take reasonable care of them. The Regulations do not require the consumer to return goods but if he is required to under the contract and does not do so, he must pay the cost to the supplier of recovering them.

11–82   Unless otherwise agreed the supplier must perform the contract within 30 days beginning with the day after the day on which the consumer sent the order to the supplier. However, where the supplier is not able to provide the goods or service ordered, substitutes may be offered provided this possibility was included in the contract and

---

[73] SI 2000/2334, regs 8–10.
[74] reg.13.
[75] reg.14.
[76] reg.15.

formed part of the information supplied to the consumer and this was done in accordance with reg.7.[77]

Regulation 21 amends the Consumer Credit Act 1974 by removing **11–83** the potential liability of the debtor under a regulated consumer credit agreement for the first £50 of loss to the creditor from misuse of a credit-token in connection with a distance contract where the consumer's payment card is used fraudulently. Where the consumer's payment card is used fraudulently in connection with a distance contract the consumer will be entitled to cancel the payment. If the payment has already been made the consumer will be entitled to a re-credit or to have all sums returned by the card issuer.

TRADING STAMPS

Trading stamps are a much less popular method of promoting the sale of **11–84** goods and services than was the case a few years ago. Their use is regulated by the Trading Stamps Act 1964, which makes it a criminal offence for trading stamp schemes to be promoted by entities other than companies registered under the Companies Act 1985 or an industrial and provident society.[78] The Government has announced its intention to repeal the 1964 Act and it is expected that this will be done by means of an order under the Regulatory Reform Act 2001 by the end of 1994.[79] Further detail on the 1964 Act is contained in the previous edition of this book.

PYRAMID SCHEMES

Various get-rich-quick schemes appear from time-to-time which depend **11–85** on participants obtaining benefits by recruiting others. These money circulation or "snowball" schemes (which are not to be confused with genuine multi-level marketing operations) are often little more than consumer frauds. As a judge explained in a recent case:

> "The number of persons who are sufficiently gullible to be persuaded to join may be very large but it is obviously finite. So is the amount of money which can be raised by a scheme of this kind. The scheme is bound to come to an end sooner or later. When it does, most of its members will have lost their money. This is not merely likely, it is a mathematical certainty."[80]

---

[77] reg.19.
[78] See 1964 Act, s.1(1), (3), (4) (amended by Companies Consolidation (Consequential Provisions) Act 1985, s.30, Sch.2). For the meaning of "trading stamp", see 1964 Act, s.10(1) (substituted by Consumer Credit Act 1974, s.192, Sch.4, para.26(3)), and for the meaning of "trading stamp scheme", see 1964 Act, s.10(1).
[79] *Repeal of the Trading Stamps Act 1964: Summary of Responses* (DTI, Nov. 2003).
[80] Millet L.J. in *Re Senator Hanseatische Verwaltungsgesellschaft GmbH* [1996] 4 All E.R. 933 at 942.

11–86   In the past some of these schemes have been closed down because they were illegal lotteries.[81] In a further attempt to control them the pyramid selling provisions in Pt 11 of the Fair Trading Act 1973 have been amended by the Trading Schemes Act 1996.[82]

UNSOLICITED GOODS AND SERVICES

11–87   In the late 1960s the practice of inertia selling developed. It consists of sending out goods which have not been ordered, either by themselves or with other goods that have been ordered, in the hope that the recipient will in fact pay for them. Demands for payment of increasing hostility then follow, often alarming the recipient, who will frequently be unaware of his legal rights. On general contractual principles no obligation could be created in this way, but whether the recipient had any duty to keep the goods safely or any right to appropriate them to his own use was obscure. To combat this problem the Unsolicited Goods and Services Act 1971 was enacted. As far as consumers are concerned reg.24 of the Consumer Protection (Distance Selling) Regulations 2000 have replaced the 1971 Act.[83]

11–88   The Regulations attack the problem in two ways. First they clarify the civil law by providing that the recipient of unsolicited[84] goods "may, as between himself and the sender, use, deal with or dispose of the goods as if they were an unconditional gift to him".[85] This assumes that the recipient has no reasonable cause to believe that they were sent with a view to their being acquired for the purposes of a business and that the recipient has neither agreed to acquire nor agreed to return them.[86] The criminal law is also invoked to control this abuse by making it a criminal offence, without reasonable cause, to demand or assert a right to payment for unsolicited goods.[87] It is also an offence for the sender to threaten legal proceedings, cause the recipient's name to be placed on a list of defaulters or debtors, or threaten to do so, or have any other collection procedure invoked.[88] The Regulations make detailed provision for the form and content of invoices accompanying unsolicited material if they are to avoid being regarded as demands for payment.[89]

---

[81] The case referred to in the previous fn. involving the Titan scheme is an example.

[82] See also Trading Schemes Regulations 1997 (SI 1997/ 30) and Trading Schemes (Exclusions) Regulations 1997 (SI 199731).

[83] SI 2000/2334, with effect from Oct. 31, 2000

[84] "Unsolicited" means, in relation to goods sent or services supplied to any person, that they are sent or supplied without any prior request made by or on behalf of the recipient: SI 2000/2334, reg.24(6).

[85] SI 2000/2334, reg.24(2).

[86] *ibid.*, reg.24(1).

[87] *ibid.*, reg.24(4).

[88] *ibid.*, reg.24(5).

[89] See Unsolicited Goods and Services (Invoices, etc.) Regulations 1975 (SI 1975/732).

The only reported case in respect of demands of payment is *Readers'* **11–89**
Digest Association Ltd v Pirie[90] which suggests a basic weakness in the
legislation. Readers' Digest, as the result of errors by junior employees,
had demanded payment for unsolicited goods. Its conviction was
quashed by the High Court of Justiciary on the ground that there was no
evidence to show that anyone (who could be regarded as acting as the
company) did not have reasonable cause to believe that there was a right
to payment.

It is a criminal offence to send anyone a book, magazine or leaflet (or **11–90**
advertising material for such a publication) which is known to be
unsolicited and which describes or illustrates human sexual techniques.[91] It has been held that even to send an advertisement for such a
publication even though it did not itself illustrate human sexual
techniques is a crime.[92]

RESTRICTIONS ON STATEMENTS

The now discontinued procedure under Pt 2 of the Fair Trading Act **11–91**
1973 produced three sets of regulations governing trading practices.[93]
The Consumer Transactions (Restrictions on Statements) Order 1976[94]
makes it a criminal offence to display, at any place where consumer
transactions[95] are effected, notices which would be void under the
obligations implied by law in consumer transactions[96] or the similar
terms implied under the Trading Stamps Act 1964.[97] It is also forbidden
to make such statements in advertisements, on goods or containers in
which goods are supplied or in documents given to a consumer or
someone likely to enter into a consumer transaction.[98] Where statements
about a consumer's rights are made, whether on the goods or their
packaging or in a document, a clear and conspicuous statement must be
added explaining that the purchaser's statutory rights are not affected.[99]
This applies both to manufacturers' guarantees and notices and statements made by retailers.[1]

---

[90] 1973 J.C. 42; 1973 S.L.T. 170.
[91] See Unsolicited Goods and Services Act 1971, s.4.
[92] *DPP v Beate Uhse (UK) Ltd* [1974] Q.B. 158; [1974] 1 All E.R. 753, DC.
[93] *i.e.* Consumer Transactions (Restrictions on Statements) Order 1976 (SI 1976/1813);
Mail Order Transactions (Information) Order 1976 (SI 1976/1812); Business Advertisements (Disclosure) Order 1977 (SI 1977/1978).
[94] SI 1976/1813 ("the 1976 Order").
[95] For the meaning of "consumer transaction", see 1976 Order, art.2(l) (substituted by SI
1978/127).
[96] *i.e.* under Unfair Contract Terms Act 1977, s.20, which entrenches the terms implied by
Sale of Goods Act 1979. 1976 Order, art.3(a)(i) (substituted by SI 1978/127).
[97] *i.e.* 1976 Order, s.4(1)(c) and art.3(a)(ii).
[98] 1976 Order, art.3(b)–(d). For the meaning of "advertisement", "consumer" and
"container", see art.2(1).
[99] SI 1976/1813, art.4.
[1] *ibid.*, art.5.

Mock Auctions

11–92 The Mock Auctions Act 1961 seeks to control spurious auctions. The objection to such auctions is that "they may be described as a sale conducted by a person . . . whose ultimate aim is to sell goods to the gullible purchasers at highly inflated prices".[2] The auctioneer often begins by giving away or selling at very low prices some inexpensive goods. Somewhat higher priced goods will then be offered and the highest bidder, possibly an unidentified accomplice of the auctioneer, receives an unexpected rebate of the purchase price. Then, with an atmosphere of excitement created, other articles are put up for sale. These will probably not have been available for inspection and may be of inferior quality.

11–93   The 1961 Act seeks to regulate the above practices by making it a criminal offence to promote, conduct or assist at a mock auction.[3] A mock auction is one where goods are sold by way of competitive bidding and the highest bidder pays an amount less than his highest bid or part of the price is repaid or credited to him.[4] Alternatively if, during the course of an auction, articles are given away or offered as gifts or the right to bid for any lot is restricted to those who have bought or agreed to buy other articles, the 1961 Act is breached.[5] Judging by some of the reported cases this piece of legislation is an extreme example of seeking to protect the gullible from their own folly.[6]

Insurance

11–94 Following disquiet about the practices of some insurance salesmen there is a cooling-off period in respect of ordinary long-term insurance business. "Long-term business" includes life assurance, contracts to pay annuities on human life and insurance on death which is to remain in effect for not less than five years.[7] The insurance company may not enter into such contracts unless it sends a statutory notice in the prescribed form either before or at the time the contract is entered into.[8] The principal point of this notice is that it must inform the client that he

---

[2] *Organisation for Economic Co-operation and Development Annual Report on Consumer Policy* (Paris, 1974), p.11.

[3] s.1(1).

[4] s.1(3)(a). A sale of goods is not taken to be a mock auction if it is proved that the reduction in price, or the repayment or credit, as the case may be, was on account of a defect or of damage discovered or sustained after the bid was made: s.1(4). For the meaning of "sale of goods by way of competitive bidding" and "competitive bidding", see s.3(1).

[5] s.1(3)(b), (c).

[6] *Aitchison v Cooper*, 1982 S.L.T. (Sh. Ct.) 41 where the auctioneer invited bids of £50 for "what was on his mind".

[7] See Insurance Companies Act 1982, s.1(1), Sch.1.

[8] *ibid.*, s.75.

or she has a statutory right to cancel the insurance policy.[9] This can be done by serving a cancellation notice on the insurer or his agent within 10 days of receiving the statutory notice or before the end of the earliest day on which he knows both that the contract has been entered into and that the first or only premium has been paid, whichever is the later.[10]

TIMESHARE

Timeshare is a right to use accommodation at a holiday development or **11–95** resort for a specified number of weeks each year over a specified period of time or in perpetuity. To acquire this right an "owner" pays a lump sum to a "developer". In addition, there are usually annual service charges and there may also be optional annual fees for participation in a scheme to exchange timeshares with others. A report[11] by the Director-General of Fair Trading acknowledged that most timeshare owners were satisfied with their purchases. It also noted that there was also a great deal of evidence to suggest that all too often timeshare was not sold in a healthy market where well-informed consumers dealt with responsible traders. The Government responded to proposals in the report for increased protection by bringing forward the Timeshare Act 1992. That Act was extensively amended[12] to implement the Timeshare Directive.[13] These Regulations were made under the European Communities Act 1972 and apply to the United Kingdom. The Regulations amend the Timeshare Act 1992, in particular the provisions under that 1992 Act for ensuring that purchasers of timeshares are given information about their rights to cancel, as well as the application of the 1992 Act to cross-border timeshare purchases.

The approach of the 1992 Act is first to try to ensure that consumers **11–96** make a properly informed decision to buy a timeshare, and then to give a period for reflection during which they can cancel the arrangement. To further the first objective s.1A requires a timeshare operator to provide anyone who requests it with information about the accommodation. Failure to do so is a criminal offence. If the consumer purchases a timeshare this information is deemed to be a term of the contract. One of the common complaints of disenchanted timeshare owners is that they were subjected to high pressure selling techniques and did not realise what they were accepting. To combat this s.5 provides that a cooling-off period must be provided during which the consumer can choose to cancel the contract. Timeshare operators must give consumers

---

[9] See Insurance Companies Regulations 1981 (S.I. 1981 No.1654), regs 70, 71, Schs 10–12.
[10] See Insurance Companies Act 1982, ss.76, 77.
[11] *Timeshare* (OFT, 1990).
[12] Timeshare Regulations 1997 (SI 1997/1081), with effect from Apr. 29, 1997. Further amendments were made by Timeshare Act 1992 (Amendment) Regulations 2003 (SI 2003/1922), with effect from Sept. 1, 2003.
[13] [1994] O.J. L.280/83.

who have entered into a timeshare agreement a notice informing them or this right and the cooling-off period must be at least 14 days from the date of the contract.[14] Not only may consumers withdraw from the contract during the cooling-off period, the operator cannot enforce the agreement during that period. That means, for example, that the seller may not ask for or accept any money from the consumer during it.[15] The 14-day cooling-off period will be extended to three months and 10 days if the operator fails to include certain information which must be given under s.1A about the timeshare. The 1992 Act also covers "timeshare credit agreements" which are those financed by credit but which do not come within the cooling off provisions of the Consumer Credit Act 1974. Here the same notice of cancellation rights must be given.

ESTATE AGENCY

11–97 Estate agency has been the subject of much criticism over many years because of the sharp practices of a minority of those involved in it.[16] The Estate Agents Act 1979 controls certain aspects of the work of estate agents. Enforcement of the 1979 Act is under the overall supervision of the OFT, but district councils also have enforcement powers. The 1979 Act does not control entry into the profession: instead, it creates a system of negativing licensing. The OFT is given powers to ban persons from acting as estate agents if it finds that they are unfit to do so. The grounds which may render a person unfit are set out in s.3. They include convictions for fraud, dishonesty or violence; convictions for breach of the 1979 Act; failure to comply with other obligations under the 1979 Act; and discrimination.

11–98 In addition, ss.12 to 21 impose duties on estate agents. They must give certain information about their charges and when these are payable. There is a duty to declare any conflict of interest or personal interest in the transaction. Where deposits are taken from a purchaser, there are duties relating to keeping the money in a clients' account. Failure to observe the duty to provide the client with information about charges results in the contract being unenforceable without the approval of the sheriff.[17]

11–99 The only reported case on this provision is *Solicitors Estate Agency (Glasgow) Ltd v MacIver*[18] where a client refused to pay his estate agent's fees because an advertising discount obtained by the agent had not been disclosed. This breached both ss.18(2)(a) and (d) as a failure to give details of any payment which is not part of the agent's remuneration but forms part of the payment to him, and a failure to give details

---

[14] Timeshare Act 1992, s.2.

[15] *ibid.*, s.5B.

[16] See *Estate Agency: A report by the Director-General of Fair Trading* (OFT, Mar. 1990).

[17] Estate Agents Act 1979, s.18(6).

[18] 1990 S.C.L.R. 595.

of the method of calculating the advertising charges. The sheriff, before whom the client had argued only that there was a breach of s.18(2)(d), did not think it fair to refuse to enforce the payment but ordered the payment of approximately three-quarters of the fee. On appeal the sheriff principal stated that the deliberate policy of concealing the advertising discount would have justified refusing to enforce the contract but that the sheriff's decision was not such an erroneous exercise of his discretion as to merit being altered. However, as he found that two provisions of the section had been breached he considered that the degree of culpability was so high that it would not be just to enforce the contract at all.

PART 2 OF THE FAIR TRADING ACT 1973

Part 2 of the Fair Trading Act 1973 provided a procedure under which **11–100** unfair trade practices could be banned using the mechanism of the criminal law. It applied where the Director-General of Fair Trading found that there was a "consumer trade practice" which adversely affected the interests of consumers with respect to their economic interests or their interests with respect to health, safety or other matters. He could send to an independent committee, known as the Consumer Protection Advisory Committee, a dossier setting out the evidence of harm and his proposals for the banning of the practice in the form of a statutory instrument. If the committee agreed with the Director-General's proposals, or agreed to them with modifications, they would be forwarded to the Secretary of State who, if he thought fit, could make the necessary order. The thinking behind this procedure was that it would provide a speedier method of proscribing unfair practices than is possible using primary legislation. A number of references were made to the committee and several of these resulted in orders.

The orders made under this section are the Mail Order Transactions **11–101** (Information) Order 1976[19]; the Consumer Transactions (Restrictions on Statements) Order 1976[20]; the Consumer Transactions (Restrictions on Statements) (Amendment) Order 1978[21]; and the Business Advertisements (Disclosure) Order 1977.[22] Section 10 of the Enterprise Act 2002 repealed all of Pt 2 except ss.22 and 23 which are necessary while there are orders still in force.

ADMINISTRATIVE METHODS

Traditional methods of consumer protection relying on individual action **11–102** by consumers or the enforcement of criminal statutes do not always

---

[19] SI 1976/1812 (repealed, by Consumer Protection (Distance Selling) Regulations 2000 (SI 2000/2334)).

[20] SI 1976/1813.

[21] SI 1978/127.

[22] SI 1977/1918.

work. Neither the criminal law nor the invocation of the civil law by individual consumers are sufficient deterrents to the unfair conduct of some traders. Relatively small fines lead some traders to ignore criminal sanctions and treat the occasions when they are convicted as minor inconveniences. Some are prone to refuse to honour their civil obligations to consumers knowing that the chances of an action being raised against them are remote. To deal with this situation this situation Pt 3 of the Fair Trading Act 1973 was introduced. It gave the Director-General of Fair Trading powers to deal with traders who persistently treated consumers unfairly. Traders could be required to give assurances that they would desist from unfair conduct and in extreme cases the Director-General could go to court to obtain an order to this effect.

11–103   In its first decade Pt 3 appeared to work well. A former Director-General of Fair Trading said that he had "no doubt about the effectiveness of Part 3 ... it is a valuable power which has demonstrated its worth over the years."[23] More recently it appears to have worked less well. A later Director-General noted: "Despite its laudable objective, the present law is inadequate and does not deal with those who continuously deceive consumers or take advantage of ignorance, inexperience, or trust".[24] A number of problems with the operation of Pt 3 had become obvious. The legislation required proof that a trader had "persisted" in a "course of conduct" and this had been interpreted to mean deliberate acts by a trader, which made it difficult to prove if the trader argued that it was the fault of a supplier or staff in a branch. The concept of unfairness was limited to breaches of the criminal or civil law and thus did not cover activities which, though not illegal, were grossly improper. A number of breaches were required so that action could not be taken on the basis of one action no matter how serious. The procedure was based on the assumption that traders would willingly co-operate with the Director-General so that no matter how persistent or blatant the misconduct he could not commence legal proceedings without first using his "best endeavours" to obtain a voluntary assurance as to the trader's future conduct. Some traders used this to delay the process often for considerable periods. The OFT was also hampered by the lack of investigatory powers.

11–104   In the face of these problems the OFT put forward proposals for reform in 1990[25] and in the White Paper, *Modern Markets: Confident Consumers* the Government indicated in 1999 its intention to carry out reform of this area.[26] This occurred in two stages: to implement the

---

[23] Sir Gordon Borrie, "Regulating Business — Law and Consumer Protection Agencies", Consumer Law Conference, Trinity College, Dublin (Mar. 23 and 24, 1984).

[24] *Consumer Affairs: The way forward* (OFT, 1998), para.4.10. See to similar effect the Better Regulation Task Force report, *Consumer Affairs* (Central Office of Information, 1998).

[25] *Trading Malpractices: A report by the Director-General of Fair Trading following consideration of proposals for a general duty to trade fairly* (OFT, July 1990).

[26] Cm. 4410 (1999), Ch.7.

Injunctions Directive,[27] the Stop Now Orders (E.C. Directive) Regulations 2001 were enacted.[28] The result was that for two years until Pt 8 of the Enterprise Act 2002 came into force, Pt 3 of the Fair Trading Act 1973 ran in parallel with the Stop Now Orders regime. With the coming into force of Pt 8 of the Enterprise Act 2002 both Pt 3 and the Stop Now Orders procedure have been replaced by a new, more coherent, system which is discussed below.

Enterprise Act, Part 8—Enforcement Orders

The enforcement order procedure set out in Pt 8[29] of the Enterprise Act **11–105** 2002[30] is designed to improve consumer protection by giving various enforcers strengthened powers to obtain court orders against traders who fail to comply with their legal obligations to consumers. It is important to note that it does not create new legal rights or obligations: it is a new enforcement tool. The concept is not new for, as we have seen, Pt 3 of the Fair Trading Act 1973 was designed to do something similar. It is nonetheless of great significance because it is designed to create a more consistent enforcement regime and it widens the range of organisations that can use these powers. It is particularly significant that local authorities can exercise these powers and this provides a considerable challenge to trading standards departments, who hitherto have largely been concerned with the enforcement of the criminal law, and their legal advisers in local authorities for whom consumer protection is a new area. They have a new and potentially powerful means of dealing with rogue traders.

Section 215 may be seen as the central provision of Pt 8 of the 2002 **11–106** Act. It provides that an enforcer may seek an enforcement order by applying to the Court of Session or the sheriff. This may be done where the enforcer thinks that someone "(a) has engaged or is engaging in conduct which constitutes a domestic or a Community infringement, or (b) is likely to engage in conduct which constitutes a Community infringement". This raises many questions such as: what is the nature of an enforcement order; what are domestic and Community infringements; and who are "enforcers"?

Enforcement orders can be obtained to prevent both domestic and **11–107** Community infringements. A domestic infringement is, to quote s.211(1):

"an act or omission which—

　　(a) is done or made by a person in the course of a business,

---

[27] Dir. 98/27.
[28] SI 2001/1422, which came into force on June 1, 2001.
[29] In force June 20, 2003.
[30] Hereinafter "the 2002 Act".

    (b) falls within subsection (2), and
    (c) harms the collective interests of consumers in the United Kingdom."

11–108   The definition has several elements. The first involves the definition of "business" which includes a professional practice, any other undertaking carried on for gain or reward and any undertaking in the course of which goods or services are supplied otherwise than free of charge.[31] The meaning of "consumer" for the purpose of a domestic infringement is slightly different from that in relation to Community infringements. For this purpose a consumer is one to whom:

> "goods are or are sought to be supplied to the individual (whether by way of sale or otherwise) in the course of a business carried on by the person supplying or seeking to supply them, or . . . services are or are sought to be supplied to the individual in the course of a business carried on by the person supplying or seeking to supply them."[32]

11–109   In addition, the individual must receive or seek to receive the goods or services otherwise than in the course of a business carried on by him. There is, however, an interesting extension to the range of consumers for this purpose. It also includes those who "receive the goods or services with a view to carrying on a business but not in the course of a business carried on by him".[33] This is designed to catch those who operate fraudulent homeworking schemes and vanity publishers.

11–110   To be a domestic infringement the act or omission must be one which falls within one of the paragraphs of s.211(2). It sets out a number of kinds of conduct which the Secretary of State can specify in more detail in a statutory instrument. These are very wide ranging including breaches of civil and criminal law both statutory or common law. The current statutory order is the Enterprise Act 2002 (Part 8 Domestic Infringements) Order 2003.[34] It lists a large number of statutes including the familiar consumer protection statutes such as the Sale of Goods Act 1979, the Consumer Protection Act 1987 and the Trade Descriptions Act 1968; but also lists under the heading "Rules of Law" "[a]n act done or omission made in breach of contract for the supply of goods or services to a consumer" and "[a]n act done or omission made in breach of a duty of care owed to a consumer under the law of tort or delict of negligence".[35] The result of this is that a very wide range of conduct can be subject to the controls on domestic infringements. To take statutory

---

[31] 2002 Act, s.210(8).
[32] *ibid., s.*210(3)
[33] *ibid.,* s.210(4).
[34] SI 2003/1593, in force June 20, 2003,
[35] *ibid.,* Sch.1, Pt III, para.1.

examples, breaches of ss.1 or 14 of the Trade Descriptions Act 1968 could found applications for domestic infringements. In the field of civil law failure to observe the obligations in s.14 of the Sale of Goods Act 1979 to provide goods of satisfactory quality could also amount to domestic infringements. As pointed out above,[36] it is not only statute that provides examples of possible domestic infringements. Breaches of the common law obligation to carry out work with reasonable skill and care could also amount to domestic infringements.

As s.211(4) makes clear, the legal obligation breached does not have **11–111** to be one which applies specifically for consumers. For example, the list of statutes includes sections of the Charities Act 1992 which are not specifically consumer protection provisions, and Scots common law on contractual misrepresentation which is a part of the general law not exclusively for the protection of consumers. The legislation does not have to contain any sanction for the benefit of consumers. It is not necessary for convictions to have been obtained where criminal offences are concerned or for legal proceedings to have been taken in civil cases. Particularly in the former case, an application will be strengthened if there are convictions though the absence of civil actions by individual consumers will be of less moment as it is well known that there are many factors which deter all but the most determined consumers from resorting to the courts. The fact that a consumer has waived his or her contractual rights does not prevent reliance being placed on the breach. An example given by the DTI is where a consumer decides to keep goods despite the fact that they were not supplied in the condition required by the contract.

The third element of the definition of domestic infringement is the **11–112** meaning of "the collective interests of consumers". What is meant by this will be discussed later as it is also relevant to Community infringements.[37]

The other kind of infringement that can justify an enforcement order **11–113** is a Community infringement. This part of the legislation implements the Injunctions Directive.[38] The DTI's consultation paper on implementation of the Directive explained its purpose succinctly:

> "The purpose of the Directive is to permit consumer protection bodies to apply to the courts or competent administrative authorities both in their own and in other Member States for orders to stop traders infringing the legislation implementing ... specific consumer protection directives where these infringements harm the

---

[36] See p.272.
[37] See para.11–118.
[38] Directive of the European Parliament and Council on injunctions for the protection of consumer interests, Dir. 98/27; [1998] O.J. L166/51.

collective interests of consumers. It is not intended as a means of seeking redress for individual consumers."[39]

11–114 Section 212 defines a Community infringement. Like a domestic infringement, it is an act or omission which harms the collective interests of consumers. That harm must flow from a contravention of one of the directives listed in Sch.13 to the 2002 Act as given effect to by the laws of an EEA state. It can also result from the contravention of aspects of these laws which go beyond the requirements of the directive. This results from the fact that many directives are what are called "minimum directives". They provide that a state must ensure that its law reaches a certain minimum level but do not prevent states providing a higher level of protection. The Directive on Certain Aspects of the Sale of Goods and Associated Guarantees was of this kind which was important in the UK as it meant that it was possible to retain our existing level of protection which was, in most respects, better than that mandated by the directive. Schedule 13 lists nine directives all parts of which are included, and a further two of which parts contain provisions which can be the subject of Community infringements. The legislation implementing these directives has been listed in an order made by the Secretary of State for Trade and Industry.[40]

11–115 The breach of legislation which may lead to domestic or Community enforcement orders is listed in statutory orders. For the most part legislation appears in one or other order. However, in two cases it has been thought necessary to included legislation in both. These are the Consumer Credit Act 1974 and the Control of Misleading Advertisements Regulations 1988.[41] This has been done because it is not possible to draw a clear distinction between some of the provisions of the Consumer Credit Act 1974 that implement the Consumer Credit Directive[42] and others that are outside the scope of the Directive. The same difficulty explains the appearance of advertising regulations in both lists. To ensure that there are no omissions which might led to gaps in the ability to enforce these pieces of legislation using Pt 8 of the 2002 Act they appear in both lists. As a result enforcement orders based on either domestic or Community infringements are possible in these cases.

11–116 An example of a Community infringement could be misleading advertisements by a trader. This is because one of the directives listed in the Injunctions Directive[43] is the Misleading Advertising Directive[44]

---

[39] *Injunctions Directive: Implementation in the UK* (DTI, 2000).
[40] Enterprise Act 2002 (Part 8 Community Infringements Specified UK Laws) Order 2003 (SI 2003/1374).
[41] SI 1988/915.
[42] Dir. 87/102.
[43] Dir. 98/27.
[44] Dir. 84/450.

which was implemented in the UK by the Control of Misleading Advertisements Regulations 1988.[45] Similarly, breaches of the Consumer Protection (Cancellation of Contracts Concluded away from Business Premises) Regulations 1987[46] which implement the Doorstep Selling Directive[47] could be the basis of a Community infringement.[48]

In the context of Community infringements "consumer" has a **11–117** slightly different meaning from that in for domestic infringements. Section 210(6) says that it means a person who is a consumer for the purpose of the Injunctions Directive[49] and the listed directive concerned. The reference to the Injunctions Directive is something of a red herring as it contains no formal definition of "consumer" and the only guidance it gives is a reference to a consumer as an individual which is one element of the definition of "consumer" common to the listed directives. There are slightly different definitions of "consumer" in the directives. Most define consumer as "any natural person who . . . is acting for purposes which are outside his trade, business or profession". The Consumer Sales Directive[50] speaks of a consumer as "any natural person who, in the contracts covered by this Directive, is acting for purposes which are not related to his trade, business or profession". The Package Holiday Directive[51] does not use the term "consumer" but speaks of "any person" and the Timeshare Directive[52] states that "'purchaser' shall mean any natural person . . . acting in transactions covered by this Directive, for purposes which may be regarded as being outwith his professional capacity".

As noted above, common to both types of infringement is the **11–118** necessity to demonstrate that the "collective interests of consumers" have been harmed. There is no definition of what this phrase means in the 2002 Act but as Pt 8, at least in part, implements the Injunctions Directive[53] from which the phrase is taken it is legitimate to seek help there. Recital 2 does not take matters much further but at least it explains that these interests "do not include the cumulation of interests of individuals who have been harmed by an infringement". This emphasises the fact that enforcement orders are not designed to provide redress in individual cases even where a number of individuals have suffered loss. In other words, it is not intended to be a kind of class action on the American model. What it is intended to do is to provide a

---

[45] SI 1988/915.
[46] SI 1987/958.
[47] Dir. 85/577.
[48] For discussion of Control of Misleading Advertisement Regulations, see Ch.3; and doorstep selling provisions, see paras 11–115 *et seq.*
[49] Dir. 98/27.
[50] Dir. 99/44.
[51] Dir. 90/314.
[52] Dir. 94/47.
[53] *op. cit.*, n.49.

mechanism to alter the behaviour of traders which is, or is likely, to harm consumers as a group. It is not to be used against an inadvertent breach of the law criminal or civil rather it is intended to discipline those whose conduct is likely to harm all consumers with whom they come in contact.

11–119   In the Explanatory Memorandum to the 2002 Act the DTI observes:

> "For both Community and domestic infringements, the Department does not consider that harming the collective interests of consumers means that a large number of consumers must already have been harmed. The Department believes it simply means that a continuation or repetition of an act or omission specified as a Community or domestic infringement could harm the collective interests of consumers, since the interests of future customers of the trader are actually or will potentially be affected."[54]

11–120   It goes on to point out that the fact that the product or service was of interest to only a small minority of consumers would not prevent the test of harm to the collective interests of consumers being met. It gives the example of expensive luxury goods.

11–121   It should be noted that, unlike the former Pt 3 procedure under the Fair Trading Act 1973, there is no requirement to prove persistence. In practice this will often be the case because Pt 8 of the 2002 Act is not designed to sanction isolated breaches of the law. It will often be impossible to show that there is harm to the collective interests of consumers unless there has been a course of conduct that has been persisted in. This, however, will not always be the case and it will be possible to base an application for an enforcement order on one incident. For example, this might be the case where one complaint to a trading standards department reveals that a credit company is using forms which do not comply with the Consumer Credit Act 1974. This one incident would reveal a breach of the law which could be said to harm the interests of consumers in general. Similarly, where a company offering goods over the internet had a website which showed that it did not comply with the Consumer Protection (Distance Selling) Regulations 2000[55] this would seem to be enough to demonstrate that there was a Community infringement.

11–122   While the Injunctions Directive and the 2002 Act do not give any examples of interests that are to be protected one can infer what these are from the list of directives attached to the Injunctions Directive.[56] These are directives designed to protect the safety, health and economic interests of consumers. Health and safety are clearly covered by the

---

[54] para.486. Available at *http://www.legislation.hmso.gov.uk.*
[55] SI 2000/2334.
[56] Dir. 98/27.

Product Liability Directive[57] and the Directive on the Community Code relating to medicinal products for human use.[58] The others are largely designed to protect the economic interests of consumers. The Television Advertising Directive[59] appears to extend the concept of collective interests with its references to ensuring that advertising does not offend human dignity and religious beliefs or involve discrimination. The list of domestic legislation set out in the Order amplifying s.211(2) can be said to protect consumers' economic interests as well as their interests in health and safety.[60]

There are three types of enforcer: general, designated and Commu- **11–123** nity. The general enforcers are the OTT, local weights and measures authorities in Great Britain (which means district councils in Scotland), and the Department of Enterprise, Trade and Investment in Northern Ireland. It is general enforcers who have the widest powers as s.215(2) provides that they can apply for enforcement orders in relation to both domestic and Community infringements. A designated enforcer is one which has been designated by the Secretary of State. This can only occur if she thinks that it has "as one of its purposes the protection of the collective interests of consumers". A public body may only be designated if it is independent. Guidance on designation and the current list of designated public bodies is contained in the Enterprise Act 2002 (Part 8 Designated Enforcers: Criteria for Designation, Designation of Public Bodies as Designated Enforcers and Transitional Provisions) Order 2003.[61] Those who have been designated so far are the Civil Aviation Authority, Directors-General of Electricity Supply and Gas for Northern Ireland, Director-General of Telecommunications, Director-General of Water Services, Gas and Electricity Markets Authority, Information Commissioner and Rail Regulator. It is also possible for a person or body which is not a public body to be designated but so far this has not happened. These designated enforcers can only make applications for enforcement orders with respect to those infringements for which they have been designated. As it happens, all the current designated enforcers have been designated to deal with all types of infringements but it is quite possible that others may be given only limited rights.

The result of this is that all these enforcers are able to deal with both **11–124** types of infringement. This means that in addition to taking action in the courts of the UK they may also take action in other EEA States. In practice, it is much more likely that only the OFT will take action abroad and indeed, it has already done so. In early 2004 the OFT took action in the Belgian courts to stop a mail order company sending what

---

[57] Dir. 85/374.
[58] Dir. 2001/83.
[59] Dir. 89/552.
[60] SI 2003/1593.
[61] SI 2003/1399.

the OFT considers to be misleading mailings to UK consumers, contrary to the 1984 Misleading Advertising Directive.[62]

11–125   The third type of enforcer is a Community enforcer which is a qualified entity for the purposes of the Injunctions Directive.[63] This means that it is a body listed in the *Official Journal of the European Communities*, but is not a general or a designated enforcer; thus, it will apply only to enforcers from other EEA states. Community enforcers can apply for enforcement orders only in relation to Community infringements and the court to which they apply "may examine whether the purpose of the enforcer justifies its making the application".[64]

11–126   While, ultimately, an enforcer can apply to a court to obtain an enforcement order the legislation is designed to try to ensure that this may not be necessary. Section 214 provides that before making a court application the enforcer must show that appropriate consultation has been engaged in with the trader and the OFT though this can dispensed with if the OFT thinks that an application should be made without delay. The purpose of this consultation is two-fold. In the case of consultation with the trader the purpose is to seek to resolve the problem with going to court. This might well lead to the matter being resolved by the trader giving the sort of voluntary undertaking envisaged in s.219. Under the Pt 3 procedure under the Fair Trading Act 1973 the Director-General of Fair Trading had a duty to consult traders which was one of the problem areas in that scheme. This has been avoided in this procedure by providing that the consultation period need only last 14 days, or seven days in the case of an interim enforcement order. The point of requiring consultation with the OFT is to assist the OFT's coordinating role. Section 216 provides that the OFT can direct that only it should make the application or direct which enforcer should make the application. This would avoid multiple applications relating to the same trader.

11–127   In its guidance on Pt 8 the OFT has stated:

> "[I]t will follow the principle that action under Part 8 should be taken by the most appropriate body and will encourage others to do the same. This means that, in nearly all cases, where local or sectoral action is required to prevent what is a local or sectoral problem, the relevant local or sectoral enforcer will take the action. Where the coordination procedure reveals that a number of enforcers are contemplating action against a single business, the OFT may direct which enforcer should bring the proceedings or that only the OFT may do so. This will avoid the possibility of

---

[62] Dir. 1988/915; OFT press release (April 6, 2004).

[63] Dir. 98/27.

[64] 2002 Act, s.215(6).

simultaneous multiple actions against a business failing to comply with the relevant legislation."[65]

If it is not possible to resolve the issue informally, s.217 governs the **11–128** powers of a court to make an enforcement order. There is a slight difference between the requirements for making an order based on a domestic and one based on a Community infringement. To make the former it must be shown that the trader has "has engaged or is engaging in conduct which constitutes the infringement"[66] whereas in the case of a Community infringement the order can also be granted if the court finds that the trader "is likely to engage in conduct which constitutes the infringement".[67] The legislation was drafted in this way because the Government took the view that this was necessary to comply with the Injunctions Directive.[68]

In deciding whether to make an order a court will take into account **11–129** whether the trader has given an undertaking or has failed to comply with an undertaking. Instead of making an order the court may accept an undertaking. Both the order and the undertaking can include a requirement that the trader publish a statement about the terms of the order or undertaking or a corrective statement if these are thought necessary for the purpose of eliminating any continuing effects of the infringement.[69] This could be particularly useful where the infringement has taken the form of misleading advertising. In an interesting departure from normal practice s.217(12) provides that an enforcement order made in one part of the Unit UK applies in all other parts. Normally, interdicts or injunctions apply only in the part of the UK in which they are obtained.

In addition to the person against whom the order is made or an **11–130** undertaking obtained, which will often be a limited company, someone who consented to or connived at the conduct may also have action taken against them as accessories.[70] Orders against companies can also apply to other companies in the same group.[71] In all these cases failure to obey a court order or undertaking will be contempt of court. This means that a trader will face fines or even imprisonment as occurred in some cases under the old Pt 3 procedure under the Fair Trading Act 1973.

The former procedure under the Fair Trading Act 1973 was criticised **11–131** for not having any provisions enabling the OFT to obtain information. This has been rectified in Pt 8 of the 2002 Act, where s.224 provides powers for the OFT to require a person to provide information. This can

---

[65] *Enforcement of Consumer Protection Legislation* (OFT, Mar. 2003), para.3.76.
[66] 2002 Act, s.215(1)(a).
[67] *ibid.*, s.215(1)(b).
[68] Dir. 98/27.
[69] 2002 Act, s.217(9).
[70] *ibid.*, s.222.
[71] *ibid.*, s.223.

be to enable the OFT to exercise or consider whether to exercise its functions under Pt 8 or to enable a Community enforcer or a designated enforcer other than one which is a public body to do so. Other general enforcers and designated enforcers who are public bodies are given similar powers in s.225.

SELF-REGULATION

11–132 In Ch.1 reference has already been made to the role of the OFT in encouraging sectors of trade and industry to develop codes of conduct. In addition, some other codes have been developed outwith this scheme by other sectors.[72] A major function of such codes is to raise standards in trade and industry and bring benefits to consumers, which might not easily be secured by legislation. It is difficult to know how successful such codes have been in this respect. Research carried out for the OFT has suggested that codes do result in a reduction in undesirable trading practices, such as the use of exclusion clauses.[73] However, the achievements of these codes have been limited, as the OFT itself recognised.[74]

11–133 While it is arguable that codes may have some success it is widely recognised that they do have limitations as well as advantages.[75] Codes are more flexible than statutes in that they can be altered more easily; those who know the problems of the sector intimately can design them; and they shift the cost of regulation from the state to the private sector. It is also argued that members of a trade association are more likely to comply with rules in a code whose drafting they have been able to influence. On the other hand, they can only affect those who adhere to them through membership of the relevant trade association, and it may well be that the sort of trader who most requires to improve the standards of his or her business is not likely to be a member of a trade association. Even among members of a trade association it may be difficult to attain high levels of compliance; and it is not always the case that trade associations devote much effort to ensuring compliance with their codes. Enforcement also depends on a willingness to discipline members from time-to-time, and to publicise this. There is also the potentially anti-competitive effect of codes in that where they are most widespread in their coverage they may inhibit consumer choice.

---

[72] See, *e.g. British Code of Advertising Practice, Sales Promotion and Direct Marketing.*

[73] Pickering and Cousins, *The Economic Implications of Codes of Practice* (UMIST, 1980).

[74] *Raising Standards of Consumer Care: Progressing beyond codes of practice* (OFT, 1998).

[75] For a discussion of the advantages and disadvantages as well as self-regulation in a consumer context, see *Models of Self-regulation: An overview of models in business and the professions* (NCC, 1999).

Despite the limited achievements of the codes sponsored by the OFT **11–134** there has recently been increased debate about the use of codes to improve standards in the interests of consumers. The National Consumer Council's paper *Models of Self-Regulation*[76] has already been referred to. The Better Regulation Task Force is studying the issue and has issued an interim report.[77] In the consumer White Paper,[78] the Government indicated that it saw codes of practice approved by the OFT as an important method of raising the standards of service that consumers can expect from business. This was reflected in the Enterprise Act 2002 which gives the OFT power to approve consumer codes of conduct.[79] It goes further than the earlier power contained in the Fair Trading Act 1973 in that the OFT must draw up criteria for approving codes and also provides for a symbol to show that a code is approved by the OFT.

The OFT issued a consultation paper in February 2001 on its new **11–135** approach and in July 2001 the responses to it.[80] The new approach involves a two stage approach to the approval of codes. In the first stage code sponsors, such as trade associations, will develop codes complying with the core criteria drawn up by the OFT. If the OFT is convinced that the code meets the core criteria, and are likely to be of practical benefit to consumers and good traders, it will confirm that the code has passed the first stage.[81] Among these core criteria are the ability to demonstrate that the code sponsor has a significant influence on the sector; that the code will be mandatory on its members; and that there are independent disciplinary procedures. Sponsors must be able to demonstrate that they have the resources to operate the code and that there will be consultation with consumer organisations in drawing it up, operating and monitoring it. An important aspect of codes is to be complaint handling and the provision of low-cost dispute resolution. The code should also address problems of high pressure selling, the fairness of contract terms and the problems of vulnerable consumers.

Initially, the OFT identified seven priority sectors from which it **11–136** encouraged applications by code sponsors. These were used cars, car repair and servicing, credit, funerals, travel, estate agents and direct marketing. Increased resources have now permitted applications from outside the original sectors to be considered. Five code sponsors have successfully completed stage one and are working towards OFT approval of their codes of practice. They are the Ombudsman for Estate

---

[76] *Models of Self-regulation: An overview of models in business and the professions* (NCC, 1999).

[77] Self-regulation: Interim Report, October 1999.

[78] DTI, *Modern Markets: Confident Consumers*, Cm. 4410 (1999).

[79] s.8(2).

[80] *Consumer Codes of Practice: The OFT's response to the consultation* (OFT 344, July 2001).

[81] The detailed criteria are now set out in *Consumer Codes Approval Scheme: Core criteria and guidance* (OFT 390, Mar. 2004).

Agents Company Ltd (OEA), Vehicle Builders and Repairers Association Ltd (VBRA), Direct Selling Association (DSA), Association of British Travel Agents (ABTA), Retail Motor Industry Federation (RMIF) and Scottish Motor Trader Association (SMTA). These codes will now move to stage two of the approval process. The code sponsors will now be invited to provide the OFT with evidence that these processes are working to achieve OFT approval. If they can demonstrate that their code is effective in promoting consumer interests it will be approved and receive an OFT logo and official promotion.

REFORM—A DUTY TO TRADE FAIRLY?

11–137   While self-regulation and the controls on trade practices discussed above have their merits, it is still the case that there will be practices that will slip through the net and cause harm to consumers. There will always be traders who will finds ways to circumvent the rules against specific unfair practices. In the timeshare field this is evident with some traders devising schemes that do not fall within the rules in the Timeshare Act 1992. To deal with this problem the OFT produced new proposals in 1990.[82] This was the culmination of a long process begun when the idea of a statutory duty to trade fairly was floated by the OFT's report on Home Improvements in 1982.[83] More detailed proposals were set out in 1986.[84] These advocated the creation of a broad statutory duty to trade fairly which would reinforce the existing civil and criminal law. The statutory duty would be supported by codes of practice, which would set out the practices, which would be regarded as acceptable or unacceptable. Further consultation resulted in more limited proposals which rejected as too ambitious the earlier attempt to combine raising trading standards with improvements in redress procedures. It is essentially these proposals in the 1990 report which the OFT recommended to ministers. They combined reform of Pt 3 of the Fair Trading Act 1973, which has happened, and the creation of a duty not to trade unfairly.

11–138   Earlier editions of this book discussed the idea of a general duty to trade fairly in some detail. Such discussion has been abbreviated in this edition, partly because it is clear that in its purest form this is not going to happen, but also because considerable progress towards the goal has been made. While it is true that there is not at present a duty to trade fairly, the combined effect of a number of pieces of legislation together with Pt 8 of the 2002 Act come close to that point. This chapter has discussed a number of practices which are forbidden. The Consumer Credit Act 1974, in addition to restricting certain practices, comes close,

---

[82] *Trading Malpractices: A report by the Director-General of Fair Trading following consideration of proposals for a general duty to trade fairly* (OFT, July 1990).
[83] *Home Improvements* (OFT, 1982).
[84] *A General Duty to Trade Fairly* (OFT, Aug. 1986).

through the licensing provisions, to imposing a duty to trade fairly on the credit industry. Section 10 of the Consumer Protection Act 1987 imposes a general duty to supply safe goods. The Unfair Contract Terms Act 1977 prevents the use of certain terms in contracts and applies a standard of fairness and reasonableness to others. This has been taken further in the regulations implementing the Unfair Contract Terms Directive.[85] Clearly we are inching closer to having a general duty to trade fairly. This may be hastened by a proposal of the European Commission, made on June 18, 2003, for a directive on unfair commercial practices.[86] The directive is a cornerstone of the European Commission's consumer policy strategy and is intended to be a radical reform of the current EU legislative framework for the protection of consumers' economic interests. It does not provide for a general duty to trade fairly but a general prohibition on unfair commercial practices. The process of negotiating this directive is continuing.

---

[85] Dir. 93/13.

[86] Directive of the European Parliament and of the Council concerning unfair business-to-consumer commercial practices in the internal market, COM (2003) 356 final *http:// europa.eu.int/comm/consumers/cons_int/safe_shop/fair_bus_pract/directive_prop_en. pdf.*

CHAPTER 12

CONSUMER REDRESS AND ENFORCEMENT[1]

INTRODUCTION

12–01 As the earlier chapters have shown, there is now an impressive body of law protecting the consumer as well as various organisations, notably local authority trading standards and environmental health departments, who enforce it and provide advice to consumers. However, in many cases it is up to individual consumers to take action to assert their rights.

12–02 It is a commonplace of debate on consumer protection that settling disputes between consumers and traders is a major problem. Much discussion has centred on this issue. The Scottish Consumer Council (SCC), like its parent body the National Consumer Council (NCC), has devoted considerable resources to it. The OFT has also been in the van of efforts to deal with the issue in a number of ways. In 1991 it devoted a major conference to the topic of redress, the results of which are set out in *Consumer Redress Mechanisms*[2] and in its recent strategy document[3] it confirmed its continuing commitment to improving access to redress. As one would expect, the consumer White Paper devotes a chapter to redress and stresses the importance of an integrated system of information and redress.[4] The problem is not confined to Scotland or the UK, as the Florence Access to Justice Project amply demonstrated.[5] At European level it has featured prominently in all the consumer protection initiatives of the EU and was given further impetus with the publication of a Green Paper.[6] It was a major item at the EC's Tampere Summit in October 1999.

---

[1] Some of the material in this chapter, especially that on small claims and ADR, first appeared in R.E. Mackay and R. Moody, *Guide to Alternative Dispute Resolution* (W Green, Edinburgh, 1995). I am grateful to the editors for permission to use it here.

[2] *Consumer Redress Mechanisms: A report by the Director-General of Fair Trading into systems for resolving consumer complaints* (OFT, 1991).

[3] *Consumer Affairs: The way forward* OFT 241 (1998), para.5.11.

[4] *Modern Markets: Confident Consumers*, Cm. 4410 (1999), Ch.6.

[5] See M. Cappelletti and J. Weisner, *Access to Justice*, Vol. 11, Bk 1, Pt 4.

[6] Commission of the European Communities, *Access of Consumers to Justice and the Settlement of Consumer Disputes in the Single Market*, COM (93) 576 final. In the recent Commission Consumer Policy Action Plan 1999–2001 (1999/C 206/01) the Commission notes: "Access to justice for consumers in pursuing their complaints is still imperfect" and promises to take steps to improve enforcement mechanisms.

To set the scene for what follows it will be useful to indicate the scale **12–03** of consumer complaints about goods and services. The best source of information on this is derived from the statistics of consumer complaints published by the OFT and the annual consumer dissatisfaction surveys that it has published. These surveys show a consistently high level of complaints. Around 40 per cent of the adult population of the UK felt that they had some cause for complaint and 76 per cent took some action. Those complaining about goods were much more likely to succeed, 74 per cent being successful as against 34 per cent of those complaining about services. Within categories success was much more likely if the complaint related to a low value item such as food, drink or clothing rather than higher value products such as household appliances or cars.

Although the surveys show that approximately three out of four **12–04** consumers took some action about their complaint, few went beyond a complaint to the supplier. Fewer than one in a thousand of all consumers, or under one-quarter of a per cent of those with complaints, resorted to any kind of redress mechanism.[7] This pattern was also found in Genn and Paterson's more recent study.[8] A complaint to the supplier of the goods or service is the appropriate first step and in many cases this will resolve the problem with, or without, the assistance of some other agency. Should it not be possible to reach a settlement what courses are open to the consumer? This is what we investigate below.

COURT PROCEEDINGS

The traditional answer is to point to the courts. In Scotland the **12–05** appropriate court for most consumer disputes is the sheriff court. There are three main procedures, which may have to be used to resolve a dispute. The ordinary cause will be the appropriate one where the value of the claim is over £1,500. This is a relatively complex procedure which, in practice, requires professional assistance. If the claim is for between £751 and £1,500 the summary cause procedure may be used. This was introduced in 1975 in an attempt to provide a simpler and quicker procedure. While it is certainly simpler than the ordinary cause procedure it has lengthy and complicated rules and does little to provide realistic access to justice for consumers though the most recent revision of the rules has much improved the drafting. To try to create a more user-friendly procedure a small claim procedure was introduced into the sheriff court in 1988.

---

[7] See Consumer Redress Mechanisms: A report by the Director-General of Fair Trading into systems for resolving consumer complaints (OFT, 1991); see also Ch.3.
[8] H. Genn and A.A. Paterson, *Paths to Justice in Scotland: What people in Scotland think and do about going to law* (Hart Publishing, Oxford, 2001).

12–06   The legislative basis for the small claims procedure is to be found in
s.35 of the Sheriff Courts (Scotland) Act 1971 as amended by s.18 of the
Law Reform (Miscellaneous Provisions) (Scotland) Act 1985. The
definition of a small claim is to be found in the Small Claims (Scotland)
Order 1988.[9] It is wide enough to cover most consumer claims (though
it also covers many other types of case) where the amount claimed does
not exceed £750. The detailed rules of the procedure are set out in the
Act of Sederunt (Small Claim Rules) 2002.[10]

12–07   The Scottish Executive announced in 2000 that the financial limits of
the sheriff court procedures would shortly be altered and the Executive
have twice initiated the legislative process to achieve this but on both
occasions withdrew its proposals. The plan was that the small claims
limit would be raised to £1,500 and the summary cause limit to £5,000.
At the same time personal injury claims will no longer competent as
small claims. This failure to increase the limit, which has remained the
same since 1988, is deplorable and compares poorly with England and
Wales where the limit is £5,000 and Northern Ireland where it is £2,000.
In answer to a parliamentary question on April 29, 2004, the Deputy
Justice Minister confirmed that the Executive "continues to support an
increase" and added that "[w]e hope to do that at the earliest opportunity".[11]

12–08   A small claim is begun by filling in a form, known as a summons,
setting out the names and addresses of the person making the claim and
the person sued, as well as a brief account of what is being claimed. This
form, together with the appropriate fee, is lodged with the sheriff clerk
who, where the pursuer is an individual,[12] will arrange for it to be served
on the defender. Where the defender intends to dispute the claim this is
done by completing and returning the appropriate part of the summons.

12–09   In a disputed case under the new rules the next stage is called the
'Hearing' and a deliberate attempt has been made to try to resolve most
cases at this stage. One of the major criticisms of the original small
claim procedure was that preliminary hearings (as this stage was then
termed) were not always being conducted as intended or, indeed, as
directed by the rules. The Scottish Office research report found that
while all sheriffs interviewed noted the defence not all of them went on
to discover the issues in dispute as the then rules required.[13] It is not
surprising that the same research project revealed that few disputed
cases were resolved at that stage, although the rules encouraged the

---

[9] SI 1988/1999.
[10] SSI 2002/133.
[11] Scottish Parliament, OfficialReport (Apr. 29, 2004).
[12] This privilege applies to anyone who is not a partnership or company so could be
availed of by a one-man business.
[13] *Small Claims in the Sheriff Court in Scotland* (Scottish Office, Central Research Unit
Papers, 1991), p.79.

sheriff to effect a settlement at that point. The new rules expand on the guidance in the original rules in a way which leaves no room for doubt about the purpose of the Hearing. Rule 9.2 is entitled "Purpose of the Hearing" and directs the sheriff to:

"(a) ascertain the factual basis of the claim and any defence, and the legal basis on which the claim and defence are proceeding: and
(b) seek to negotiate and secure settlement of the claim between the parties."[14]

This clearly indicates a more interventionist role for sheriffs than many have been prepared to contemplate in the past. Particularly where lay litigants are involved it will require a more inquisitorial attitude on the part of the sheriff. **12–10**

Where the case is not resolved at the Hearing a hearing at which evidence is given will be held. Like the Hearing this is held in public "as informally as the circumstances of the claim permit."[15] To make it more realistic to expect the parties to present their own cases the legislation dispenses with the rules relating to the admissibility or corroboration of evidence.[16] For those who do not wish to present their own cases advocates or solicitors are not the only alternatives as lay representatives are permitted. In practice, relatives, citizens advice bureaux staff and trading standards officers have acted in this capacity. **12–11**

A major barrier to going to court is expense, or the fear of it, in a system where the losing party will normally have to meet the expenses of the winner. Small claims procedure resolves this problem by providing that in disputed cases involving less than £200 no expenses of any kind are recoverable by the successful party; and that above this figure an award of expenses is limited to £75. If the new financial limits are introduced these figures are also likely to change. **12–12**

The Scottish small claims procedure has the potential to be a genuinely radical approach to resolving consumer (and other) disputes. The research into its first year of operation showed some positive features. It deals speedily with cases in a way that bears favourable comparison with its English equivalent and trade arbitration schemes; and, as was to be expected, advisers were unanimous in acknowledging the fairness of sheriffs. Court staff were also found to be very helpful to litigants, and the explanatory literature was well received. The new rules should improve the operation of the system with its clearer guidance about informality and early resolution of cases. The rules have been more clearly drafted and a glossary added that should make it easier for **12–13**

---

[14] r.9.2(2).
[15] r.9.2.
[16] See Sheriff Courts (Scotland) Act 1971, s.35; and Civil Evidence (Scotland) Act 1988, ss.1, 2.

the lay person to use them. The guidance material available from sheriff clerk's offices has also been improved.

12–14   As has been pointed out more than once,[17] much depends on the approach of the sheriff whose role is central to the operation of the process. Here the limitations of the procedure in practice have been exposed. The research into its operation revealed a variety of approaches in different courts. Variation, while it cannot be entirely eliminated, is inimical to the development of confidence in the system by consumers and, perhaps more importantly, those who frequently provide them with advice. Too often, hearings are held in an atmosphere which does. not encourage individuals to represent themselves. Commonly, they take place before a sheriff in traditional court dress in a normal court room where a number of solicitors are waiting to deal with other business. Full hearings tend to be held in less busy surroundings but, again, traditional court rooms are normally used instead of other rooms such as jury rooms. However, there are examples of good practice, such as the "consumer court", as it is commonly termed, in Glasgow which deals with cases involving unrepresented parties.

12–15   Insufficient attention seems to have been given to the particular needs of persons bringing small claims on their own. Simple things such as good signposting within court buildings is essential for people who will, in all probability, be making their first and possibly only visit to a court. There is, as the Director-General of Fair Trading has pointed out, scope for improved timetabling of cases to prevent litigants spending long periods waiting for their cases to begin; and for experiments with evening or weekend hearings.[18] This is one of a number of issues which is under review by the Lord Advocate at the moment.

LEGAL AID

12–16 In theory the availability of legal aid should have overcome the problems of lack of access to the courts. There are two forms of assistance in civil matters. Under the Legal Aid (Scotland) Act 1986 it is possible to get advice and assistance from a solicitor on any matter of Scots law and to assert rights in any way short of going to court. In addition, there is a legal aid scheme which funds litigation in the civil courts. In both cases these services are means tested and their availability has diminished dramatically in the past few years as a result of the government's policy of reducing public expenditure. It is estimated that the proportion of the population eligible for legal aid in Britain fell from 79 per cent in 1979 to 47 per cent in 1990. Further restrictions on

---

[17] See, *e.g. Consumer Redress Mechanisms* (OFT, 1991), p.47; and Ervine, "The New Small Claims Procedure", 1989 S.L.T. 65.

[18] *Consumer Redress Mechanisms* (OFT, 1991), p.50, n.8.

eligibility applied in 1993 will have reduced this proportion still further.[19]

Speculative Actions

On public policy grounds it is illegal for solicitors, though not for **12–17** others,[20] to pursue a case on the basis that they will be remunerated by a share of any sum recovered. This is often referred to as the contingent fee system and is widely used in the United States. However, the speculative action has a long and honourable history in the Scottish legal system. This is the name given to the practice of solicitors taking on a case on the understanding that they will receive no fee for their services unless they are successful. The Law Reform (Miscellaneous Provisions) (Scotland) Act 1990 provides a variation of this action. Where a lawyer takes a case on a speculative basis they can now do so under an agreement with the client that they will receive, if successful, up to twice the normal party and party level of expenses. In the event of failure the solicitor is not entitled to a fee but may recover outlays from the client who is also liable for the other side's legal expenses. An experienced practitioner has suggested that these new provisions are not likely to prove attractive to lawyers as expenses on a party-and-party basis do not normally properly remunerate them.[21]

ALTERNATIVE DISPUTE RESOLUTION

Given the difficulties experienced by consumers in using the courts to **12–18** resolve disputes, it is not surprising that other avenues have been explored. These are now often known collectively as alternative dispute resolution (or ADR). There is no definitive or agreed definition of ADR but one that might be used is that it is any means of providing a resolution of a dispute between two or more parties which does not involve traditional court procedures.[22] In this sense the small claims procedure referred to above is a form of ADR. In addition, there have been a number of interesting developments which are discussed below involving conciliation, mediation, arbitration and ombudsmen schemes.

---

[19] For further detail on the provision of legal aid and advice, see R. M. White and I. D. Willock, *The Scottish Legal System* (3rd. ed., Butterworths, 2003), pp.364–372.

[20] *Quantum Claims Compensation Specialists Ltd v Powell*, 1998 S.C. 316; 1998 S.L.T. 228; 1998 S.C.C.R. 173

[21] See Semple, "Fees in Speculative Actions" (1994) 39 J.L.S.S. 57.

[22] W. C. H. Ervine, *Settling Consumer Disputes: A review of alternative dispute resolution* (NCC, 1993), pp.2, 3. See also Ervine, "ADR in Consumer Disputes" in *Alternative Dispute Resolution in Scotland*, S. Moody and R.E. MacKay (eds) (W. Green & Son, 1995).

The consumer credit White Paper[23] has advocated the use of ADR and one of the central features of the OFT's new approach to codes of conduct is the inclusion of ADR mechanisms. A further indication of the increasing importance attached to ADR in consumer matters was the commissioning by the DTI of a study into the availability of ADR for consumer disputes.[24] The EC has adopted Recommendation 98/257 on the out-of-court settlement of consumer disputes. This sets out the principles, which should be respected by ADR schemes, such as independence, transparency, efficiency and the respect of the law.

MEDIATION

12–19 Mediation or conciliation of consumer disputes commonly takes place under the provisions of codes of conduct governing a particular trade sector. Many of these codes were drawn up by trade associations in consultation with the OFT when the Director-General of Fair Trading had a duty to encourage the creation of such codes. Approval has now been withdrawn from these codes and a new procedure discussed in Ch.11 is in place to produce more effective codes. It is believed that several of the codes are still in operation and that their conciliation schemes operate. The NCC has pointed out that little is known about how conciliation operates in practice and that consumers tended to perceive conciliation as biased towards the trader.[25] The Association of British Travel Agents (ABTA) has long operated one of the more heavily used dispute resolution schemes and this has a conciliation stage. In 2002 it handled 17,500 complaints of which about 12,000 were settled using conciliation.[26] The new Scottish Motor Trade Association code, which has just passed stage 1 of the OFT's procedure for approval, contains dispute resolution procedures which include conciliation.

12–20 In addition to the sector specific schemes there is an interesting development in Scotland. This is an experimental consumer mediation project in Edinburgh. Consumer Advice Scotland launched a pilot mediation project in February 1995 which was not limited to consumer cases. Mediation is undertaken by qualified mediators nominated by the Centre for Dispute Resolution (CEDR) and is free to both parties.[27]

---

[23] DTI, *Fair, Clear and Competitive: The consumer credit market in the 21st century*, Cm. 6040 (2003), Ch. 3.

[24] M. Doyle, K. Ritters and S. Brooker, *Seeking Resolution: The availability and usage of consumer-to-business alternative dispute resolution in the United Kingdom*, DTI, 2004.

[25] *Out of Court: A consumer view of three low-cost trade arbitration schemes* (NCC, 1991).

[26] *op. cit.*, n.25, p.69.

[27] On the provision of Mediation in the civil sphere in Scotland, see Mays and Clark, *Alternative Dispute Resolution in Scotland* (Scottish Office, Central Research Unit, 1996).

ARBITRATION

Arbitration as a method of private dispute resolution has a long history **12–21** and is widely used in commercial disputes. Its advantages are that disputes can be decided by an adjudicator who is an expert in the subject-matter of the dispute and that they are held in private. Speed and cheapness are not necessarily characteristics of arbitration.[28] In Scotland, common law provides the framework, though there is now statutory intervention.[29] For reasons of cost arbitration, until relatively recently, has not been a realistic option for consumers.

Most consumer arbitrations take place as a result of arbitration **12–22** schemes contained in codes of practice originally drawn up by trade associations in consultation with the OFT. Arbitration under codes is only one part of the process of complaint handling. As noted above OFT approval for these codes has been withdrawn and new codes are being devised. One of the core criteria for approval of these codes by the OFT is the presence of effective complaints handling which must include a low-cost independent dispute handling. It is expected that this will often take the form of arbitration on a documents only basis using the services of arbitrators appointed by the Chartered Institute of Arbitrators. This is the case with the first code to pass the OFT's stage 1 procedure, the Scottish Motor Trade code.[30] The ABTA code which was not one of those created with OFT backing is one of the most used handling about 1,400 cases in 2002.[31]

Originally, the Consumer Arbitration Agreements Act 1988 sought to **12–23** ensure that arbitration was a genuine alternative to the courts in cases involving consumers and that they were not forced to submit to arbitration. That Act has now been repealed and replaced by provisions in the Arbitration Act 1996, ss.89 to 91. These extend the Unfair Terms in Consumer Contracts Regulations 1999[32] to arbitration agreements. Section 91 provides that for the purposes of the Regulations such agreements are deemed to be unfair where the amount claimed is up to £5,000.[33]

The former OFT approved arbitration schemes required the consumer **12–24** to pay a registration fee, usually of the order of £40, though it was refunded where the consumer was successful. The arbiter under most schemes was appointed by the Chartered Institute of Arbitrators. To

---

[28] Indeed, some types of arbitration may be more expensive than using the courts as the parties have to meet not only the costs of their lawyers but also the costs of the arbitrator and the venue.

[29] See Articles of Regulation 1695 of the Parliament of Scotland, Arbitration (Scotland) Act 1894 and Administration of Justice (Scotland) Act 1972, s.3.

[30] Available at http://www.smta.co.uk/public/codeofpractice.asp.

[31] *op. cit.*, n.25, p.48.

[32] SI 1999/2083.

[33] Unfair Arbitration Agreements (Specified Amount) Order 1999 (SI 1999/2167).

reduce costs, arbitrations are almost invariably on a documents only basis. Each side provides the arbiter with its written submissions and relevant documents. Normally, the parties have no direct contact with the arbiter except in the case of the Glass and Glazing Federation's scheme where site visits are quite common. It seems likely that this pattern will continue to be the case under new codes drawn up to obtain OFT approval and is certainly the case with the SMTA code which has got to stage 1.

12–25   In addition to the schemes approved by the OFT there are a number of other low cost schemes. Virgin Trains, British Telecom and the National Association of Funeral Directors have such schemes as have the Royal Institution of Chartered Surveyors and the Finance and Leasing Association. The settling of cross-border disputes could be particularly difficult using the traditional court procedures so the creation of the Chartered Institute of Arbitrators EEJ-Net Scheme is, potentially, very valuable. It is open to any consumer in the EU and is designed to deal with claims for general compensation arising from alleged breaches of contract or negligence. Fees range from £23.50 for claims up to £1,000, to £293.75 for claims above £50,000. Awards are enforceable in the 130 countries which are signatories of the New York Convention. Contrary to the usual situation in arbitration, the award is not binding on the consumer who can reject it and pursue a claim in the courts. All these schemes have in common that the client should take up a complaint in the first instance with the company concerned. It is only if this proves ineffective and conciliation does not resolve the problem that arbitration may be resorted to.

12–26   Not a great deal is known about the operation of these various arbitration schemes. Only with the publication of the NCC's study, *Out of Court*,[34] has empirical evidence about any of them become widely available. This study looked at the three most heavily used schemes, those of the Association of British Travel Agents (ABTA), the Glass and Glazing Federation (GGF) and British Telecom (BT). Unfortunately, the schemes do not keep statistics on a regional basis so it has not proved possible to produce figures relating to Scotland. In the course of the study the researchers learnt that many of the schemes operating under codes of practice are hardly ever used. At the date of the study the funeral scheme had never been used and the photography scheme only once. The main reason for this is probably consumer ignorance of their existence which is related to under-resourcing of the schemes.[35] The number of arbitrations under the ABTA scheme rose from 87 in 1977, to 1,312 in 1993. In these cases consumers in the last three years have

---

[34] *Out of Court: A consumer view of three low-cost trade arbitration schemes* (NCC, 1991).
[35] See *Consumer Redress Mechanisms* (OFT, 1991), pp.31, 32.

been successful in over 80 per cent of cases.[36] In the case of the GGF scheme the number of arbitrations rose from 12 in 1982, to 47 in 1989, with consumers being successful, at least to some extent, in about 75 per cent of cases on average.[37] The BT scheme dealt with 83 arbitrations in 1987, and this rose to 125 in 1989.[38]

Of the three schemes studied in detail claims in the BT scheme were **12–27** lowest on average at £222.28, whereas ABTA claims averaged £648.64, and GGF claims £1,691.82. The main criticisms of the ABTA scheme were that it took too long and that awards were low. The GGF scheme was also criticised for slowness and for difficulty in enforcing awards in some cases. The BT scheme was criticised for the fact that the arbiters had to rely on technical evidence from BT itself.

OMBUDSMEN

One of the most interesting additions to the range of redress mecha- **12–28** nisms available to consumers in the UK over the past generation has been the ombudsman. The concept has been borrowed from the public sector which in its turn had adapted an institution that originated in Scandinavia. A Parliamentary Commissioner for Administration, more commonly referred to as "the Ombudsman", was first appointed in 1967 to investigate allegations by individuals of maladministration by central government. This was followed by the creation of a Health Services Ombudsman in 1973 and local government ombudsmen, or Commissioners for Local Administration, to give them their official title, in 1974.

In response to increasing number of consumer complaints, first the **12–29** insurance industry and then the banks and building societies created ombudsmen as did the former Personal Investment Authority which was the self-regulatory organisation for retail investment. Following the creation of the Financial Services Authority (FSA) by the Financial Services and Markets Act 2000 the financial ombudsmen have been amalgamated in the Financial Ombudsman Service. In the private sector there is an ombudsman for corporate estate agents and, between 1994 and 2002, there was a Funeral Ombudsman. The Pensions Ombudsman was created by the Social Security Act 1990 and differs from the other ombudsmen in that investigations can be carried out into maladministration in both the private and the public sectors. All these ombudsmen have jurisdiction throughout the UK. The one specifically Scottish ombudsman is the Legal Services Ombudsman created by the Law Reform (Miscellaneous Provisions) (Scotland) Act 1990 to carry on,

---

[36] The figures for cases are taken from *Out of Court*, App.1, Table 2.1. for the years to 1989, and supplemented by information from ABTA for the years 1991, 1992 and 1993. The amounts awarded in arbitration during the NCC study were 46% of those claimed.

[37] *ibid.*, Table 2.5.

[38] *ibid.*, Table 2.6.

with slightly extended jurisdiction, the functions of the Lay Observer. So common have ombudsmen become that they have set up an association, the British and Irish Ombudsman Association (BIOS), one of whose functions is to try enable the public to distinguish between independent ombudsmen and schemes using the title but not operated by an independent person.

12–30   The ombudsmen in the financial services sector proved very popular and this continues to be the case with the new Financial Ombudsman Service (FOS). In the year to March 2003 it dealt with 62,170 cases, a 44 per cent increase on the previous year.[39] It is thought to be the largest ombudsman scheme in the world, with more than 400 staff, 10,000 member firms within its jurisdiction and a budget of approximately £20 millions. The FOS is operated by a company, FOS Ltd, set up by the FSA though it is operationally independent of it. The independence of its ombudsmen is assured by the fact that they are appointed by FOS Ltd not the FSA.

12–31   Like its private sector predecessors, there is no fee to use FOS the danger of frivolous complaints being dealt with by the power to make awards against claimants in favour of FOS where they have acted unreasonably, improperly or have been responsible for unreasonable delay.[40] The running costs of FOS are provided by a levy on firms subject to its jurisdiction and fees paid by firms involved in complaints. The ombudsman can require parties to provide it with information and member firms are required by the FSA to co-operate with him or her. Awards are binding on firms but not on complainants who may elect to pursue alternative means of redress. This is one way in which the ombudsman differs from arbitration. Another is that he or she can base judgments on what is fair, just and reasonable in the circumstances rather than on purely legal considerations. A shortcoming of arbitration schemes is sometimes said to be that their findings are not published and thus it is difficult to know how they are applying the law and whether a pattern of complaints is building up against particular firms. While the FOS scheme does not publicise the names of parties it can consider whether the conduct complained of merits regulatory action and refer the matter to the FSA.

12–32   The Scottish Legal Services Ombudsman operates in a different way from the Financial Ombudsman Service. Her task is not to receive complaints directly from aggrieved clients of solicitors and advocates but to review the way in which the professional bodies, the Law Society of Scotland and the Faculty of Advocates deal with complaints. Where the handling of a complaint is referred to her she cannot alter the decision merely make recommendations. The Annual Report of the Scottish Legal Services Ombudsman for 2002 to 2003 notes that complaints within her remit have risen steeply for two successive years,

[39] FOS, Annual Review, 2002–03.
[40] Financial Services and Markets Act 2000, s.234(4).

from 104 in 2000–01 to 245 in 2002–03. 206 complaints (a 30 per cent increase compared with last year) were made after the Law Society of Scotland and Faculty of Advocates had made a decision on a complaint about a practitioner, nine cases from the ombudsman in England and Wales and 39 complaints were about the way the Law Society of Scotland and Faculty of Advocates were currently handling a complaint about a practitioner. In almost one-half of the 87 opinions on complaints about the way the Law Society had handled a full complaint investigation the ombudsman was not satisfied that there had been an adequate investigation, and in 1 in 5 of the 98 opinions on complaints where the Law Society had refused to look into a complaint she concluded that the Law Society had failed to recognise a complaint which it is required by law to investigate. The Law Society was recommended to pay a total of £15,275 in compensation to complainants for inconvenience, distress and loss caused by poorly handled investigations, and that it reimburse a total of £895 to cover the complainants' costs in making a complaint to the ombudsman. There were 35 complaints about advocates on 13 of which the ombudsman had completed an opinion. In two-thirds of these cases she was satisfied that they had been properly dealt with. She recommended that the Faculty of Advocates pay a total of £850 as compensation for inconvenience caused by delay in 4 complaints, and reimburse a total of £75 to cover complainants' costs in making a complaint to the ombudsman.

Law Society of Scotland Complaints Procedure

As the Law Society's mechanisms do not easily fit into other categories **12–33** these are discussed here. Aggrieved clients can complain to the Law Society where their complaint will be dealt with initially by the staff of the Client Relations and Complaints Office which receives about 1,000 complaints each year. Where these relate to professional negligence they cannot be dealt with, but the complainant can be put in touch with a "troubleshooter" who is one of a panel of solicitors prepared to handle such actions. Complaints, which are competent, can, if relatively minor, be dealt with by the staff, and in this way a proportion of complaints are resolved by a form of conciliation. If not they are passed to the Complaints Committee composed mainly of solicitors but also comprising two lay representatives. One member is appointed reporting officer and investigates the complaint making a report to the committee containing a recommendation. If the complaint is upheld the committee has various sanctions including reprimand and, since the amendment of the Solicitors (Scotland) Act 1980 in 1990, the power to award compensation of up to £1,000.[41]

---

[41] For the background to the system, see Christie, "Complaints Against Solicitors" (1994) J.L.S.S. 43.

OTHER METHODS OF OBTAINING REDRESS

12–34 Most methods of obtaining redress place the onus on the consumer to take action. There are various reasons why consumers may not do so. They may not be aware of their rights; and, if they are, they may be inhibited by the cost of litigation or fears about going to the alien environment of a court. In addition, if the loss is small, it may not be thought worthwhile to seek redress although it is realised that the individual consumer is but one of a large number who has been the victim of a legal wrong. Professor Cappelletti in his major study of these problems has argued:

> "It is necessary to abandon the individualistic, essentially laissez-faire, 19th century concept of litigation, a concept which awards the right to sue, if at all, solely to the subject personally aggrieved in his own narrowly-defined individual rights for example, to the owner of a neighbouring property in a case of pollution or of a zoning violation. The new social, collective, 'diffuse' rights and interests can be protected only by new social, collective, 'diffuse' remedies and procedures. Indeed, the quest for these new remedies and procedures is, in my judgment, the most fascinating feature in the modem evolution of judicial law."[42]

12–35 Scots law has not gone far in the direction of meeting these concerns but there have been a number of steps and these are discussed below.

12–36 Where a consumer suffers loss which also results in a criminal conviction Pt 4 of the Criminal Justice (Scotland) Act 1980 introduced a procedure designed to remove the need for separate civil proceedings. The criminal court may make a compensation order directing the offender to pay compensation to the victim. If made by a judge, other than a stipendiary magistrate in the district court, these are limited to level 4 on the standard scale, currently £2,500, and to £5,000 in summary proceedings if made by a sheriff or stipendiary magistrate.[43] In solemn proceedings there is no limit on the amount that may be awarded. Orders should take precedence over fines[44] but may not be made in respect of death or of injury, loss or damage due to an accident arising out of the presence of a motorvehicle on a road, except damage treated as caused by the convicted person's acts.[45]

12–37 Like the equivalent English scheme, the procedure is designed to apply to fairly clear cases where no great amount is at stake and the compensation can be assessed easily and quickly. An obvious example

---

[42] M. Cappelleti and B. Garth (eds), *Access to Justice*, Vol.111, pp.519, 520.
[43] See Criminal Procedure (Scotland) Act 1975, s.289B (amended by Criminal Justice Act 1991, s.17(2)).
[44] Criminal Justice (Scotland) Act 1980, ss.61, 62.
[45] *ibid.*, s.58(2), (3).

in a consumer context where orders have been made is following a conviction under the Trade Descriptions Act 1968 for "clocking", *i.e.* turning back the odometer of a car. A weakness of the procedure, apart from an apparent unwillingness of some sheriffs to apply it in what seem to be appropriate circumstances, lies in the fact that there is no formal procedure for invoking it. The victim has no standing to make an application and much depends on the procurator fiscal raising the matter and having some evidence on which the sheriff can base a compensation order.

In earlier chapters we have already seen a number of examples of a **12–38** government official having power to take action for the benefit of consumers as a whole. The enforcement order procedure under Pt 8 of the Enterprise Act, designed to allow the OFT and other regulators to curb illegal conduct, is an example. The OFT also has powers to seek an interdict to stop misleading advertisements under the Control of Misleading Advertisements Regulations 1988[46] and may also seek an interdict where he considers that a contract term is unfair,[47] a power which has been extended to other bodies.[48] The consumer credit White Paper has also recognised the importance of this kind of action in making private law rights effective in its proposals for reforming unjust credit transactions. There it proposes that named third parties could bring a group-claim against a trader engaged in rogue trading practices.[49]

Beyond these examples there are few other methods by which one or **12–39** a small number of persons may take action to benefit a larger class, or the public at large. An action by one individual may, incidentally, benefit a large number of other people as where one person who is affected by a nuisance obtains an interdict to put an end to it and thereby improves matters for all those living in the vicinity.[50] Scots law does have the *actio popularis* and the possibility of action by the Lord Advocate or a local authority in certain circumstances, but these seem to have fallen into disuse.[51]

Where a number of individuals are affected by the same wrong it is **12–40** possible to deal more efficiently with litigation by the use of a test case or, if several actions have been raised, these may be heard at the same time or may even be formally conjoined. Beyond the special circumstances of unincorporated societies, Scots civil procedure does not

---

[46] SI 1988/915, reg.5.
[47] Unfair Terms in Consumer Contracts Regulations 1999 (SI 1999/2083), reg.10. See Ch.10.
[48] See Ch.10.
[49] DTI, *Fair, Clear and Competitive: The consumer credit market in the 21st century*, Cm. 6040 (2003), para.3.41.
[50] An example is *Webster v Lord Advocate*, 1985 S.L.T. 361.
[51] See *Class Action in the Scottish Court* (SCC, 1982), Ch.2.

permit a representative action such as is available in limited circumstances in England and Wales. In the United States and some Commonwealth countries a special procedure, known as a class action, exists permitting one or more people to raise an action on behalf of a larger number who have been affected by the same wrong. A widely quoted example from California, *Daar v Yellow Cab Co.*,[52] involved one pursuer taking action for the benefit of all those who had been overcharged by a taxi company. In the Canadian case of *Naken v General Motors of Canada Ltd*[53] four plaintiffs sued on behalf of all those who had purchased new 1971 or 1972 Firenzas claiming $1,000 for each as damages for misrepresentations contained in advertising.

12–41   In 1982 the SCC produced a report of a working party which it set up recommending the introduction of class actions into the Scottish legal system.[54] Following some high profile disasters such as the Lockerbie bombing and the Piper Alpha disaster which produced multiple claims the issue was referred to the Scottish Law Commission which published a report advocating the introduction of class actions.[55] A class action is a court procedure which enables a number of individuals with similar complaints against the same defender to seek a judicial remedy in one action instead of each raising separate actions. It is important to note that it is a legal procedure only: it does not give claimants any new substantive rights. There are many situations where such a procedure might be appropriate. In the so-called mass disaster cases where many people are killed or injured as a result of, for example, a rail accident at least some of the legal issues could be dealt with by such a procedure. It might also be of use in 'creeping' disasters, of which claims for damages in respect of allegedly defective drugs such as tranquillisers are examples. In these cases there is no connection between the victims except that they have all suffered from the same drug though at different times and, possibly, in different ways. Claims falling within these two categories will often arise in consumer situations but it is also usual to refer to a third category more specifically as 'consumer claims'. These are cases where a large number of consumers of goods or services claim relatively small amounts of money which, individually, it might not be economic to recover through litigation. Examples could be found in cases where a number of holidaymakers are misled by the same error in a package holiday brochure or many people purchase the same shoddy product.

12–42   The class action is a subset of the group or multi-party action. The other kind of group action may be termed the 'public interest action'.

---

[52] 433 P. 2d. 732 (1967).

[53] [1983] 144 D.L.R. (3d.) 385.

[54] See *Class Action in the Scottish Court* (SCC, 1982). The council have recently returned to this subject see, Ervine, *A Class of Their Own: Why Scotland needs a class actions procedure* (SCC, 2003).

[55] *Multi-Party Actions* (Scot. Law Com. No.154, 1996).

The public interest action is one where a public official takes action for the benefit of the public at large or a section of it; or one brought by an organisation such as a consumer protection or environmental organisation on behalf of its members and the public. The SCC Class Actions report,[56] in addition to advocating the introduction of a class actions procedure, envisaged further reforms which would develop group actions. Ironically, while no progress has yet been made on class actions considerable progress has been made in relation to the other type of group action.

The overriding reason for advocating the introduction of class actions **12–43** is that it is essential in the interests of upholding the rule of law. It is unacceptable that consumers or others should be given rights which they cannot effectively enjoy. Such a situation is a reproach to a legal system. The importance of a remedy has been recognised in the introduction of small claims procedures and other methods of improving access to justice. The class action is but one more way of doing so. There is also the deterrent argument in favour of the class action. To quote an Australian judge, "Why should a defendant secure benefits by unlawful conduct, relying on the inadequacy of the legal system and the timidity and lack of organisation of those wronged?"[57]

Not infrequently, there are situations where many individuals lose **12–44** small amounts as the result of unlawful actions by traders but few find it worthwhile to take action. The result is that the wrongdoer makes a windfall profit. An example of this kind of situation was the Hoover flights saga in the early 1990s when the company failed to honour an offer in a marketing promotion to provide free flights. Many thousands of consumers appear to have been disappointed but few seem to have resorted to the small claim courts. That few of those disappointed in the Hoover case took their cases to court is not surprising. The amounts were not large and many may not have thought it worthwhile to do so. One may also speculate that fear and ignorance of the workings of the legal system may also have played a part. Research on small claims both in Scotland and England demonstrates that many potential litigants are reluctant to embark even on the simplified procedures offered by the small claims courts.

Where larger sums are at stake, as there will usually be in the mass **12–45** disaster and creeping disaster cases, there are other factors to be taken into account. In these cases the claims may involve considerable difficulty. In many product liability cases, especially those involving drugs, the evidence required is elaborate and controversial. Much research is required and expert evidence will be needed to assess the viability of the claims. These claims can also involve considerable legal complexity and areas of law with which few lawyers are familiar. For

---

[56] *Multi-Party Actions* (Scot. Law Com. No.154, 1996).
[57] Kirby J. (then chairman of the Australian Law Reform Commission), "Class Actions: A panacea or disaster?", 1978 *The Australian Director* 25 at 33.

cases to be litigated separately is inefficient where similar issues arise in many aspects of the case. It makes much more sense for claimants to band together. Common issues can be explored on behalf of a group of potential claimants and the cost of doing so can be spread over the whole group. In this way the unequal struggle between the individual victim and the well-resourced corporation can be made fairer. Dealing with similar disputes against the same defender in one litigation also prevents inconsistency. If individual cases are dealt with in different courts there is the possibility that different judges will arrive at different conclusions.

12–46   It is not only victims who benefit from the more efficient handling of litigation by means of group procedures. Defendants can benefit also through fighting only one action rather than a series of actions. Not only may there be a saving in litigation costs for companies in such situations but also other savings in less loss of management time to the unproductive business of dealing with litigation. The courts too may benefit. The Ontario Law Reform Commission[58] noted that one benefit that is commonly attributed to class actions is judicial economy in that they may benefit both the parties and the courts by diminishing the total amount of litigation and thus reduce the total cost of settling disputes arising from mass wrongs.

12–47   Having recommended that class actions should be included in the Scottish legal system the SCC Class Actions report[59] concluded with a perceptive chapter looking further ahead. Further steps were envisaged, though it was not thought appropriate to recommend these steps at the time because they went well beyond procedural reform and required reform of substantive law. Ironically, two of the steps envisaged have been adopted by government, one with conspicuous success. The first step beyond class actions was labelled the 'external pursuer class action' or 'public interest class action'. The main type of class action recommended by the report is sometimes referred to as an 'internal pursuer class action' because one or more people take action on behalf of themselves and others who have suffered harm. In the external pursuer action a group or association would be granted standing to sue on behalf of consumers for damages suffered by them. A tentative step in this direction has recently been taken with an interesting change to the Competition Act 1998 made by the Enterprise Act 2002. This permits bodies approved by the Secretary of State to bring claims for damages before the Competition Appeal Tribunal on behalf of consumers of goods and services. How successful this will be remains to be seen. These claims will be particularly difficult and expensive and there is little incentive for organisations to become involved, particularly as the normal legal expenses rules will apply and will probably leave them out of pocket even if the action is successful. To make this kind of action

---

[58] *Report on Class Actions*, Ontario Law Reform Commission, 1982.
[59] *op. cit.*, n.53.

more attractive probably needs some financial incentive such as the treble damages actions available in American anti-trust law or, at least, some enhancement of the legal expenses normally awarded to a successful party.

The second recommended step beyond the traditional class action **12–48** was to allow consumer groups to seek remedies by way of interdict or declarator. It was argued that this was a particularly appropriate method as consumers face suppliers on unequal terms. The report noted that the powers of the Director-General of Fair Trading to take action under Pt 3 of the Fair Trading Act 1973 against traders who persistently treat consumer unfairly provided a model. This suggestion has proved to be extraordinarily prescient. The Pt 3 model has not proved as effective as had once been hoped, but has been replaced by the Enforcement Order procedure under Pt 8 of the Enterprise Act 2002. This permits the OFT and various other organisations to take action on behalf of consumers against infringements of a wide range of laws. The Enforcement Order procedure is similar to other more specific procedures under the Control of Misleading Advertisements Regulations 1984[60] and the Unfair Terms in Consumer Contracts Regulations 1999.[61] The latter is an excellent example of the value of the public interest class action. The regulations supplement the traditional means of redress through individual litigation by giving the OFT and a number of other organisations, including the Consumers' Association, power to require traders to remove unfair terms from their contracts. This has the great benefit not only of making the new legislation effective but also of operating on the principle that prevention is better than cure. These regulations have been very successful in dealing with almost 7,000 cases, with one exception, without having to take court action. Two spectacular examples of the benefits of the regulations are contained in a recent report by the Comptroller and Auditor General which shows the agreement of a mortgage company to remove unfair penalties from their loan agreements has saved consumers £65.2 million and amendments to mobile telephone contracts are estimated to be saving consumers between £60 and £80 million each year.

As Cranston has pointed out: "Class actions are not a universal **12–49** panacea for consumers".[62] Indeed, it must be remembered that redress procedures are only one aspect of consumer protection. It must be seen as part of an overall strategy involving the enforcement work of the OFT and trading standards departments. Just as important is the provision of advice and information for consumers. Without this they may never learn of their rights or be able to avail themselves of the redress procedures that exist. The importance of an integrated network

---

[60] SI 1988/915.
[61] SI 1999/2083.
[62] R. Cranston, *Consumers and the Law*, Weidenfeld and Nicolson (2nd ed., 1984), p.98.

of advice agencies has been emphasised by the SCC.[63] This was recognised in the 1999 consumer White Paper and after research was carried out Consumer Direct, a new national telephone and online consumer advice and information service is being launched. One of the first areas to benefit is Scotland where the scheme was launched in July 2004. Its aim is to provide consumers with the knowledge, tools and confidence to resolve their consumer problems themselves. It is operated in partnership with local authorities, trading standards and other Consumer Support Network members. It is the first point of call for consumers, delivering first tier advice on a range of consumer matters, and where further help is required it will be a gateway to other complementary services.

---

[63] See *Let the People Know: A report on local advice services in Scotland* (SCC, 1977); and *Following Our Advice: A review of advice services in Scotland* (SCC, 1988).

INDEX

ST